LINCOLN'S HERNDON

Lincoln's Herndon
A Biography

BY

DAVID HERBERT DONALD

New introduction by the author

A DA CAPO PAPERBACK

Library of Congress Cataloging in Publication Data

Donald, David Herbert, 1920–
    Lincoln's Herndon / by David Herbert Donald; new introduction by the
author.
    p.   cm. — (A Da Capo paperback)
    Reprint. Originally published: New York: Knopf, 1948.
    Includes bibliographical references.
    ISBN 0-306-80353-4
    1. Herndon, William Henry, 1818–1891 — Friends and associates. 2. Lincoln,
Abraham, 1809–1865 — Friends and associates. 3. Biographers — United States —
Biography. I. Title.
E457.4.H558D66   1989
973.7′092′2 — dc19   88-34290
[B]   #18909603   CIP

Published by Da Capo Press, Inc.
A Subsidiary of Plenum Publishing Corporation
233 Spring Street, New York, N.Y. 10013

TO

The Randalls

Introduction to the Da Capo Edition

I LIKE TO think that William H. Herndon would be pleased by the frequency with which his name has appeared in recent issues of the *New York Review of Books*, where Gore Vidal, Richard Nelson Current, and other experts have learnedly debated the character of Abraham Lincoln.[1] A contentious man, confident of his own importance, Herndon would doubtless think it only right that his defender, Mr. Vidal, had the last word in the controversy, but he would take pleasure in noting that all the other contributors also acknowledged that—for better or worse—our picture of Lincoln is one that largely derives from Herndon's recollections and the sources that he collected.

Herndon might, I fear, be a little less enthusiastic about the republication of this book, which was originally issued in 1948, for he did not take kindly to criticism. There would be justice to some reservations he might have. I am sure my suggestion that the agitation of people like Herndon helped "make a needless war an irrepressible conflict"[2] would have angered him as a morally insensitive view of the conflict between slavery and freedom. As I look back, I think that my argument on this point—and it appears in several scattered passages in the first half of the book—had less to do with my understanding of the 1850s than with my concerns in the late 1940s. While writing Herndon's biography, I, like so many others, desperately feared that the Cold War between the United States and the Soviet Union might erupt into a shooting war. Despite my obscurity as a neophyte historian and a beginning instructor at Columbia University, I was trying to urge that peace was not merely possible but necessary for continued human existence.

[1] Gore Vidal and C. Vann Woodward, "Gore Vidal's 'Lincoln'? An Exchange," *New York Review of Books*, April 28, 1988, pp. 56-58; Harold Holzer, Richard N. Current, and Gore Vidal, "Vidal's 'Lincoln': An Exchange," *ibid.*, August 18, 1988, pp. 66-69.
[2] p. 102.

Introduction to the Da Capo Edition

A larger, and legitimate, reservation might be that this biography of a reformer was written by one who failed to understand the temperament of reformers. Again, I plead guilty to the charge. Though I have spent much of my life studying the history of agitators, I have never grown to like them, or even particularly to sympathize with them. There is something about the reformist temperament, with its zealotry, its absolute certainty of goals and its indifference to means, that I have never found congenial. It is easier for me to understand a pragmatist like Lincoln than an ideologue like Charles Sumner.

Finally, legitimate objection could be raised to the failure of this biography to comprehend and to sympathize with the problems of an alcoholic like Herndon. Writing this book as a very young man, who grew up in the totally "dry" state of Mississippi, I then tended to think of alcoholism as evidence of moral depravity, rather than of disease, and I fear my intolerance may show in these pages.

Despite these limitations, *Lincoln's Herndon* has held up surprisingly well as a biography. Over the years, readers have detected very few errors in my book, and these have been silently corrected in the present edition. My interpretation of Herndon and of his biography of Lincoln has been sufficiently persuasive that in the forty years since this book was first published nobody else has attempted to write another life of Herndon. Indeed, there has not been a great deal of additional scholarship devoted to him. The only considerable body of Herndon's papers that has turned up since 1948 is a group of his letters to Wendell Phillips. Recently edited and published by Irving Bartlett, they add texture to our understanding of his relationship to Northeastern abolitionists,[3] but they do not require any significant changes in the story I have told. The only other substantial publication relating to Herndon is an admirable article by Gary Lee Erickson, which includes valuable information on Herndon's finances during the final years at Chinkapin Hill and suggests that he was more highly esteemed by his rural neighbors than I have indicated.[4]

If I were rewriting *Lincoln's Herndon* today, I should, of course, take these new findings into account, yet I am reasonably well satisfied

[3]Irving Bartlett, *Wendell & Ann Phillips: The Community of Reform, 1840-1880* (New York: W. W. Norton & Company, 1979), pp. 152-163.

[4]Gary Lee Erickson, "The Last Years of William Henry Herndon," *Journal of the Illinois State Historical Society* 67 (February 1974): 101-119.

Introduction to the Da Capo Edition

with the book as it stands. Herndon's life of Lincoln, which Horace White called "not only the best of all the biographies of Lincoln that have been written but . . . in my judgment the best American biography that has ever been written," remains a fundamental source for all subsequent Lincoln scholarship. I am, therefore, happy if my analysis of the origins and composition of that work continues to provide, as Carl Sandburg said in his generous introduction to the original edition of this study, "a detailed account of how one of the most strangely made of all biographies came to be written across years of weaving it piece by piece — of how when at last it found a publisher it met tribulations and miseries enough to sink any ordinary book and leave it lost and forgotten — of how the book survives and there have been twenty-five different editions, issues, and printings." Even more am I pleased that my biography presents the fullest, and I hope truest, portrait of a man that Sandburg called "the paradoxical, hifalutin, abrupt, whimsical, corn-on-the-cob, owlish, temperamental, convivial, forlorn, transcendental, lonely, reverent, eloquent Bill Herndon."

— DAVID HERBERT DONALD
Lincoln, Massachusetts
October, 1988

Acknowledgments

THIS BOOK was begun at the suggestion of Professor J. G. Randall. Whatever merit it has is due in large part to his expert guidance and friendly assistance. To my great profit both he and Mrs. Randall have critically examined every page of the manuscript. I like to consider the Randalls the "mental godparents" of this biography.

Reading over the entire manuscript, Mr. Carl Sandburg has generously given me the benefit of his vast understanding of both the letter and the spirit of Lincoln subjects.

Other Lincoln experts have saved me many a misstep. On Dr. Paul M. Angle I have repeatedly drawn for authoritative information concerning Lincoln's Springfield years. Dr. W. E. Baringer has given wise and witty advice on Lincoln's political career. Over a period of years Miss Margaret A. Flint of the Illinois State Historical Library has repeatedly proved indispensable, with the correct answer to any question on Illinois history. Besides lending valuable material from his own researches on Lincoln biography, Dr. Benjamin P. Thomas very kindly read all but four chapters of my book in manuscript. Like virtually every other writer in the Lincoln field, I have drawn on Mr. Frederick Hill Meserve's notable collection for illustrations.

My indebtedness to Miss Marion D. Bonzi of the Abraham Lincoln Association is profound. Expertly and meticulously she has read the book both in manuscript and in proof. Her passion for accuracy has saved me from a score of errors.

The blessed librarians everywhere have the gratitude of a troubled and troublesome researcher. Very heavy is my obligation to Mr. Jay Monaghan and his splendid staff at the Illinois State Historical Library, who patiently answered, during more months than I care to count, my every inquiry. From Dr. Louis A. Warren and the Lincoln National Life Foundation at Fort Wayne I have received not nuggets but veins of information. Dr. St. George L. Sioussat, Dr. C. P. Powell, and Dr. Elizabeth McPherson have my gratitude for assistance during many weeks of research in the Manuscripts Division of the Library of Congress.

Again and again I have turned to experts for aid on difficult subjects. Miss Norma Cuthbert of the Henry E. Huntington Library, Dr. W. Neil Franklin of the National Archives, Dr. R. Gerald McMurtry of

Acknowledgments

Lincoln Memorial University, Dr. Joseph Fort Newton of Philadelphia, Miss Margaret C. Norton of the Illinois State Archives, Dr. Robert Price of Otterbein College, and Dr. Milo M. Quaife of the Detroit Public Library are those to whom I have most frequently appealed for assistance.

It has been my great good fortune to use manuscript material in private collections; this debt is acknowledged in my footnotes. I want to thank again some of those who have given invaluable assistance in this regard: Mr. Oliver R. Barrett, Mr. C. Norton Owen, and Mr. Alfred W. Stern of Chicago; Mr. Thomas I. Starr of Detroit; Mrs. Edna Orendorff Macpherson and Mrs. Bertie Trainer of Springfield; and Mr. W. H. Townsend of Lexington, Kentucky.

This is in no sense an authorized biography, but it is pleasant to record that I have had the kindest assistance from friends and relatives of Herndon. That dear lady, Mrs. Mollie Herndon Ralston, the daughter of William H. Herndon, has told me much of the father she so loved. Mr. James S. Miles of Petersburg, a nephew, has enlivened my investigations by his remarkable store of anecdote and reminiscence; my obligation to him is great. A granddaughter of Herndon, Mrs. Earl Bice of Springfield, kindly permitted me to copy records from the Herndon family Bibles. The crayon drawing of Mrs. Herndon reproduced in these pages was unearthed by Miss Beulah Wood of Springfield. Dr. John G. Herndon of Haverford College has generously shared with me his exhaustive knowledge of Herndon genealogy. Far away in Santa Fe, Miss Amelia E. White carefully searched the papers of her father, Horace White, and provided copies of many important Herndon letters. For a transcript of the very significant diary of her father I am greatly indebted to Miss Mary H. Weik.

This book was begun at the University of Illinois. Most of it was written there. To the librarians and other officials of that great institution I owe much. Especial thanks go to Professors P. V. B. Jones, A. H. Lybyer, J. W. Swain, and F. W. Znaniecki, who read the manuscript in an early stage.

To the Social Science Research Council I am indebted for a year of research and travel which helped greatly in understanding Herndon's intellectual climate.

I owe a particular debt of gratitude to Mrs. Helen Hart Metz of Elmwood, Illinois, who generously undertook the heavy task of index making — work requiring both her expert knowledge and her tireless patience.

With so much assistance I should have produced a perfect book. I have not, of course, and for all errors I alone am responsible.

CONTENTS

xiii

ILLUSTRATIONS

LINCOLN'S HERNDON

CHAPTER *i*

Son of the Indian Queen

I

GEORGE ALFRED TOWNSEND knew everybody. As the columnist "Gath," he went everywhere, met everyone, saw everything, and told it all and more to his newspaper audience. He thrilled American readers with poignant tales of Civil War daring and heroism; he reported the dramatic, the unique, the personal. Human interest was Townsend's business. It was inevitable after the assassination of President Abraham Lincoln that "Gath" should make an expedition to Springfield, Illinois — a pilgrimage for profit. He, the first of a long generation, would tell his public all about the *real* Lincoln.

In the Illinois capital everybody said that there was one man he must see. Billy Herndon, they told Townsend, had been the late President's law partner for twenty years and could tell more tales about "Old Abe" than any ten other men. Eagerly the reporter sought out the Herndon law office on the west side of Springfield's public square. Stooping to avoid the freshly painted Herndon & Zane shingle that creaked over the entrance, he climbed the dusty stairway and hesitated before the half-open door. "Gath" was used to judging men. At a glance he took in the solitary figure reading there: muddy brogans propped against the table; yellow breeches, turned up twice at the bottom; chapped fingers stiffly caressing a meerschaum; tobacco-stained teeth; an unruly thatch of graying hair. Could this farmer, wind-hardened and grizzle-bearded, know anything about a President?

But when introductions were made, "Gath's" first impression proved wrong. Townsend was startled to find a poet and a dreamer, a man of books and of memories. Half closing one eye for accuracy in conversation and pointing a bony forefinger at his interviewer, Herndon began: "Friend! I'll answer you." And off he started, reliving the years

3

of his past — his childhood, his political career, his law practice, his partnership with Lincoln.[1]

There was much that Herndon could tell. His memory was crowded to overflowing, like a rag bag. Here were the bright red patches of a victorious law suit, the blue scraps of philosophical discussions in the office, the flaming orange bits of a speech on the hustings. Here too were soiled edgings and rough wool tatters not so pleasant to remember. Endlessly, without apparent order he evoked memories of the past and laid them before his hearer. And when they were all spread out together, there was the pattern of a man, contradictory and confusing, as beautiful and as ugly as life itself.

Billy Herndon remembered so many things. There had been that glorious spring day in 1832 when he and the other Springfield lads had scrambled upon their horses for a ride down the Sangamon. Springfield was excited, for it had news that Captain Vincent Bogue's "splendid upper cabin steamer, TALISMAN" was chugging its way up the river.[2] Down to meet it went every able-bodied man and youth of the community. It was a fabulous sight for the prairies of Illinois, a steamboat, with pounding boilers and a fuzzy cat's tail of smoke. So narrow was the Sangamon near Springfield that men armed with long-handled axes had to cut back the overhanging branches from either side of the stream. But the boat puffed and wheezed its slow way forward under the skilled piloting of a six-foot giant variously called Abe, Abram, or Abraham Lincoln. It was Billy Herndon's first sight of a future President.[3]

That night when the boat was safely secured in the river a few miles north of Springfield, the whole company adjourned to the village for refreshments. There were banquets and dances and speeches. Airily optimistic, Springfield's 762 inhabitants saw for their city a future in terms of bustling docks and caravansaries and factories. In rhymed effusions "small beer poets" welcomed a great day coming. For more substantial inspiration men looked to the taverns of the village and con-

[1] "Gath," in New York *Tribune,* February 15, 1867. For details as to Herndon's personal appearance I have been greatly assisted by Herndon's nephew, Mr. James S. Miles, Sr., of Petersburg, Illinois.

[2] Harry E. Pratt, "Lincoln Pilots the Talisman," *Abraham Lincoln Quar.,* II, 319–329.

[3] William H. Herndon and Jesse W. Weik, *Herndon's Lincoln: The True Story of a Great Life* (Chicago: Belford, Clarke & Company, [1889]), I, 87. Hereafter cited as *Herndon's Lincoln;* all subsequent references, unless otherwise expressly indicated, are to the original three-volume edition. Herndon's memory of this occasion was by no means so precise as his statement would indicate. See below, p. 349.

gregated at the "Indian Queen," where Billy Herndon helped his father pour the drinks.[4]

This frank, warm-hearted landlord,[5] Archer Gray Herndon, was no mere bartender; he was a power in state politics. In every campaign he was called on to speak for the Democratic cause. A hostile observer might remark his "uplifted hands, the veins in . . . [his] neck distended, — like a bull frog in the dog days, almost to bursting — . . . fingers extended like grappling irons, as if to seize upon and strangle some approaching foe," [6] but his was rough eloquence to sway frontier folk. In a few years he would enter the state senate as one of Sangamon's "Long Nine" — so-called because they averaged six feet in height — who logrolled the bill through to make Springfield capital of Illinois. Bluff, boisterous, and bibulous, Archer Herndon had made a name for himself in Illinois.

The saga of the Herndons was the story of young America, the tale of boundless optimism, of grim determination, of triumph over impossible odds. There had been Herndons in Virginia since 1674, proud, respected folk, who married into the families of colonial governors and held up their heads in the best of society.[7] After the Revolution the family had drifted westward. Archer Herndon had been born in Culpeper County, Virginia, in 1795. When he was a lad of four his family had crossed into Kentucky and the youth grew up on the frontier. It was a hard life, full of risks and deprivations, but years afterward he recalled only the gaiety and color of pioneer society: "We horse raced it — cock fought it. We played cards — game called all fours — ie seven up — We fox hunted it in the morning — fished — sang songs going to corn shucking — . . . ." [8] When the war of 1812 broke out, this high-spirited youth volunteered for a year's service in the militia.

[4] The Herndon tavern-hotel was also known as the "Herndon House." Harvey Lee Ross, *The Early Pioneers . . . of Illinois*, 123.

[5] *Illinois State Journal*, January 4, 1867.

[6] *Sangamo Journal*, June 19, 1840.

[7] For information on the Herndon ancestry I am deeply indebted to Dr. John Goodwin Herndon of Haverford College. Dr. Herndon's *The Herndon Family of Virginia: Volume I. The First Three Generations* is an authoritative work. See also John W. Herndon, "A Genealogy of the Herndon Family," *Virginia Mag. of Hist. and Biog.*, IX, 318–322 (continued in succeeding issues); Myrtle M. Lewis, "Herndon and Allied Families," *Americana*, XXXI, 639–648; and John Goodwin Herndon, "Six Herndon Immigrants to Colonial America," *William and Mary College Quar. Hist. Mag.*, XXIII (2 ser.), 331–335.

[8] Interview of W. H. Herndon with A. G. Herndon, undated [but 1865], Herndon-Weik Coll. A portion of the Herndon-Weik Collection has been published in *The Hidden Lincoln: From the Letters and Papers of William H. Herndon*, edited by Emanuel Hertz. The original manuscript collection, now in the Library of Congress, is cited exclusively in the following pages.

Upon his return to Green County, Kentucky, he married an attractive widow, Rebecca Day Johnson, a strong-minded woman, descendant of a strong-minded family. Her Virginia-born father detested slavery and voluntarily set all his Negroes free. Selling his lands, he carried his family over the Cumberlands and began a new life in the wilderness.[9] Pioneering, it was said, was hell on mules and women, yet Rebecca, like her husband, remembered only its pleasures: singing "Bonny Doon" or "songs against the Yankees"; visiting and sociables; night gatherings where the girls picked seeds out of the cotton and spun it into rough thread.[10] She was a little superior to the common run, well enough educated to serve as a schoolmarm and priding herself on her descent from a prominent family.

II

On a bleak October day in 1818 a lonesome nine-year-old boy in an Indiana clearing watched his father lower the coffin of Nancy Hanks Lincoln into the grave. On the third day of December a twenty-first star was added to the American flag for the new frontier state called Illinois. Ten days later there was rejoicing in the family of well-to-do Robert S. Todd of Lexington, Kentucky, at the birth of a beautiful girl child, christened Mary. And on Christmas Day, in backwoodsy Green County, eighty miles away, Archer Herndon's first son was born.[11] Fate had her wits about her to concatenate these stray links into a curious chain.

Archer named his eldest child William Henry Herndon — which inevitably became Billy. In later years Billy Herndon liked to think affectionately of Kentucky as his "Child home," but he had little chance to acquire a Kentucky accent. In 1820 Archer Herndon sold his property, packed his belongings, and father, mother and two-year-old child, accompanied by Rebecca Herndon's parents, set out to seek greener pastures. Illinois was the great country of the future, and Archer Herndon headed for Madison County, along the Mississippi. Here surely he could make a home. Those were hard years for poor folk, and the Herndons were too proud to beg for help. With one ox to draw a plow that he fashioned from the fork of a tree, Archer Herndon scratched the top of the soil and planted corn. They stayed in southern Illinois just long enough for one crop to be made and for a second child to be

[9] Caroline H. Dall, "Pioneering," *Atlantic Mo.*, XIX, 404.
[10] Interview of W. H. Herndon with Rebecca Herndon, September 28, 1866, Herndon-Weik Coll.
[11] Date given in Rebecca Herndon's Bible, now owned by Mrs. Earl Bice, Springfield, who generously permitted me to copy these records.

born, the lame, irascible Elliott. Then, restless as ever, Archer learned of the Sangamon country in central Illinois, a land of rich bottoms and black soil. And off again they went.[12]

They lived a few years on the Sangamon, at what is known as German Prairie. It was rough country, thinly settled, and there was still lurking danger from the Indians. Once when Billy was five years old his father had to carry corn to the gristmill. By late afternoon he had not returned, and Mrs. Herndon, left alone with two small children, began to worry. Toward dusk a band of redskins approached the Herndon cabin.

"Where is your man?" demanded the foremost, doubtless hoping for firewater.

"In the woodland," Rebecca lied gallantly.

"Go after him," ordered the Indian.

When she turned toward the cabin to get her baby, the Indian feared a trick. In an instant he drew out her comb, lifted her long hair, and made a quick warning gesture with his scalping knife. Billy screamed when he saw the flicker of the steel. Shoving him through some loose boards in the rear of the cabin, his mother whispered that he was to run into the forest. Then she hid her baby under her shawl and left in pretended search for her husband. Clutching her two children, Rebecca hurried to her nearest neighbors — a mile and a half away — where she could spend the night in safety. The incident made a deep impression on Billy Herndon. "I saw the savage lift my mother's long hair and threaten to scalp her," he recalled with a shudder, even after four decades. "I was but five years old, yet I shall never forget that." [13]

A few years in the Sangamon bottom were quite enough, and in 1823 Archer Herndon "made a small board cart, into which he threw the chickens, the little pigs, and the young children," and moved to Springfield — and a most unlikely place it was when Archer and Rebecca Herndon chose the village for their home. "The marks of bears' claws were deep in the trees right round us," Billy Herndon remembered; he himself killed over a hundred snakes within three quarters of a mile of his father's house.[14] In 1825 Archer opened the "Indian Queen," the first tavern-hotel of any pretension in Springfield, and he did a good business. For a time he operated a general store, selling —

[12] *Illinois State Register*, January 4, 1867; interview of W. H. Herndon with Rebecca Herndon, September 28, 1866, Herndon-Weik Coll.; J. C. Power, *History of the Early Settlers of Sangamon County, Illinois*, 372–373.

[13] Dall, "Pioneering," *Atlantic Mo.*, XIX, 405–406; *History of Sangamon County, Illinois* (1881), 455–456 [pages misnumbered 355 and 356].

[14] Dall, "Pioneering," *Atlantic Mo.*, XIX, 406.

among a wide assortment of other objects — sugar, pasteboard, muslin, butter, coffee, and calico to his neighbors.[15] He lost money at merchandising, but by judicious loans and heavy land speculations Archer soon was able to retire to his farm, where he raised fine cattle, listing his occupation for the inquisitive census taker as "None." Before his death his property was conservatively appraised at $60,000.[16]

Meanwhile Billy Herndon was growing up. He was a child of the frontier, a man's man. He had the earthy flavor of the prairies; he knew the talk of racing and cockfights and horses and women; he liked ribald anecdotes and practical jokes. His was a horselaugh, not a titter. He was the cock of the walk among the youths of the town, not alone because of his father's prosperous financial condition. Billy had daring. During the winter Springfield gallants liked to take their belles sleighing. To annoy them, the younger boys would catch on behind and steal rides, but of them all only Billy Herndon could hang on for a whole trip.[17]

But there was more to this youth than the boy on the streets or hanger-on at the tavern. When Grandfather Day recounted tales of his hardships during the American Revolution, little Billy "used to fire up & . . . [his] eyes run over with tears at the recitle [sic] of American wrongs."[18] Proud of his oldest son's fondness for books, Archer Herndon sent him to the village school, where each parent paid for the schooling of his own children, and Billy studied "Reading — writing — arithmetic — geography — grammar — and some of the higher branches." Later, still helping his father in the store during the evenings, he attended a privately owned high school for two or three years.[19]

III

Though Archer Herndon had had no formal education, he and Rebecca were ambitious for their children. There were two other boys,[20] but Billy was the favorite. Nothing was too good for him. When

[15] Account of Mrs. Salome Enos with A. G. Herndon, receipted January 12, 1835, P. P. Enos MSS.; *Sangamo Journal,* October 5, 1833.

[16] Illinois census returns, 1850 and 1860 (MS., National Archives).

[17] Zimri Enos, "Description of Springfield," Ill. State Hist. Soc., *Trans., 1909,* 206.

[18] Interview of W. H. Herndon with Rebecca Herndon, September 28, 1866, Herndon-Weik Coll.

[19] Undated MS. fragment in the writing of Weik, probably an interview with Herndon, *ibid.;* "Herndon's Biography," undated, *ibid.*

[20] Elliott Bohannon Herndon, born August 1, 1820, and Archer Gray Herndon, Jr., born November 29, 1825. A fourth son, Nathaniel, died in childhood. Rebecca Herndon's Bible, in possession of Mrs. Earl Bice, Springfield.

Son of the Indian Queen

Springfield's schools were outgrown, his parents decided to send him to Jacksonville, where since 1829 a group of devout Yale graduates had been building Illinois College, a New Haven in the West.

In the fall of 1836 Herndon entered the preparatory department of the college. A classmate, whose recollections may have been confused after the passing of many years, recalled that Billy arrived in Jacksonville unexpectedly. With his love for practical jokes, he had accepted compensation from both political parties to carry ballots to an outlying precinct in Sangamon County and then had doused one set in a creek, leaving those opposed to his political persuasion without an opportunity to vote. Billy found it advisable to leave Springfield without waiting to pack his trunk.[21]

For the modern college student, with three or four hours of class a day, Illinois College would seem more like a penitentiary than an educational institution. The faculty of five men agreed that the sixty-four students should never have a chance to find out whether idle hands really were the devil's workshop. The college ordinances have a grim tone.

> Morning prayers [read the rules adopted in 1837] shall be attended half an hour after the ringing of the second bell for breakfast, and evening prayers at 6 in the summer and at 5 in the winter Term. Study hours shall commence immediately after morning prayers and continue until 12 o'clock in the forenoon, and at 2 in the afternoon, and continue until evening prayers, and, in the evening, during the winter Term, at 7 and continue till 9.

It was hardly surprising that one of Herndon's schoolmates, after detailing his day's routine in a letter home, lamented: ". . . my whole time is taken up."[22]

Most of the upperclassmen at Illinois College were serious-minded young men, many destined for the ministry. So ambitious were they that on one occasion the student body petitioned "that the hour of morning prayers be changed from 5 o'clock to ½ past 4 . . . so as that, after two hours labor subsequent to breakfast, they might have an ½ hour to themselves between labor & study hours." The petition was denied because their teachers did not wish to get up so early.[23] The faculty, however, was heavily overworked. In one semester the "Prof. of Math. and Nat. Philosophy" was supposed to impart instruction in

[21] Ross, *Early Pioneers*, 123–124.

[22] *Laws of Illinois College in Jacksonville* . . . (1837), 12; Samuel Willard to Mrs. Julius A. Willard, December 10, 1836, Willard MSS.

[23] "Records of the Proceedings of the Faculty, Illinois College, 1833 [to 1842]" (MS., Illinois College Library), entry for January 12, 1833.

algebra, plane and spherical trigonometry, mensuration, navigation, surveying, pneumatics, electricity, magnetism, optics, and astronomy. But apparently not even so exacting a round of classwork could keep boys from being boys, for there were college laws to prohibit visiting in other students' rooms, to threaten the users of intoxicating liquor, and to forbid shooting firecrackers in the dormitory.

Since admittance to the freshman class required passing examinations in geography, arithmetic, Latin, and Greek, Herndon enrolled in the high school department, where Reuben Gaylord, A.B., Yale, presided over classes in "Arithmetic and the Languages, preparatory for admission to the Freshman class." Billy could never read either Latin or Greek; he had more important things to do. A lively youth of eighteen, he made friends quickly and engaged in practical pranks which kept him constantly in trouble with the authorities.[24]

Still, he learned much. There was the inspiring personal contact with great teachers, Edward Beecher, Julian M. Sturtevant, and Jonathan B. Turner, in whose judgment and integrity he had unlimited confidence.[25] He caught a fleeting glimpse of vast ranges of knowledge to be explored, and from the college library, where he was permitted to borrow either one large volume or two small books each week, he acquired an insatiable appetite for reading. The professors' liberal religious views, assailed by the fundamentalists as unorthodox, proved especially attractive to a young mind disgusted with the ranting of camp-meeting orators. In a desultory way Billy began reading philosophy, studying by himself, a little reluctant to ask his teachers for help lest they think his questions silly.[26] As he looked back on his year of college many decades later, Herndon remembered the whole time there as a perpetual romance.

At Illinois College Herndon became involved in the agitation over Negro slavery. Billy had been born in the slave state Kentucky. His grandfather ·Herndon had owned slaves. Rebecca Herndon's father had freed his Negroes because he hated the peculiar institution. One of the motives driving the Herndon family in their exodus from Kentucky had been Archer Herndon's vow: "My labor shall never be degraded by competition with slave labor." [27] But all this had been

---

24 Ross, *Early Pioneers*, 123–124; "Records of the Proceedings of the Faculty, Illinois College, 1833 [to 1842]," entry for July 20, 1837.

25 Herndon to J. M. Sturtevant, March 29, 1864, MS., Illinois College Library.

26 Herndon to Theodore Parker, February 1857, Herndon-Parker MSS. Most of the letters in the Herndon-Parker MSS. have been printed in the pioneer study of Dr. Joseph Fort Newton, *Lincoln and Herndon*. The original manuscripts, now in the University of Iowa Library, are cited in the present work.

27 Herndon to Parker, February 16, 1856, Herndon-Parker MSS. In later years Herndon wrote of his "father being a pro-slavery man." Herndon to James H. Wil-

rather remote. At Illinois College slavery was a live issue. Jacksonville was a border town, where Southern currents of immigration from Kentucky, Virginia, and Tennessee mixed with the Northern tides from New York, Massachusetts, and Connecticut. Many from the South looked back with nostalgia to the plantation-slavery system of their origin, while some Northerners — though only a minority — were convinced that slavery was a moral cancer.

All the prominent members of the Illinois College faculty were originally from New England, and all became converts to abolitionism. At first they had felt that education and the slow processes of time would eradicate the peculiar institution, while demands for immediate abolition might aggravate Southern antagonism. In 1836–37, however, most were persuaded that direct action was necessary, not only to eliminate slavery in the South but to prevent its malignant growth into the free North. Stubborn, self-righteous Elijah P. Lovejoy, a Presbyterian minister from Maine, had voiced antislavery views in his St. Louis newspaper. Repeatedly threatened by mob violence, Lovejoy crossed the river to Alton, Illinois, where he began publishing the *Observer,* at first largely eschewing discussion of abolition but eventually damning slaveholders to a Calvinistic hell. Alton residents, mostly from the South and looking to Southern cities for their markets, were alarmed. Angry at what they considered a breach of the editor's pledge not to ride his antislavery hobbyhorse, the citizens took the law in their hands, again and again threw his printing presses into the river, and finally killed Lovejoy and some of his followers.

The news of Lovejoy's death on November 7, 1837, traveled quickly. Abolitionists canonized him as a martyr to the holy cause, and "the Alton catastrophe did more to increase their numbers and inflame their feelings, than their warfare upon slavery itself." [28] Jacksonville, with its turbulent mixture of Yankee and Southern settlers, was particularly upset. President Edward Beecher of Illinois College had been in Alton the week of Lovejoy's death and had vigorously and uncompromisingly championed his right to publish abolitionist views in the face of universal opposition. Others among the Illinois College faculty were also in full sympathy with Lovejoy. When the news of the editor's

---

son, August 28, 1889, copy, Herndon-Weik Coll. This meant that in the 1850's Archer Herndon supported the Democratic party, which William H. Herndon had come to think of as the slavery party. From this confusion has grown the mistaken belief that Archer took an active part on the proslavery side in the contest of 1822–23, when there were plans to make slavery legal in Illinois (Newton, *Lincoln and Herndon,* 3). There are no contemporary records to indicate that Archer really favored slavery, though like most of his contemporaries he scorned and despised abolitionists.

[28] Albert J. Beveridge, *Abraham Lincoln, 1809–1858,* I, 226.

death reached Jacksonville, an indignation meeting was held on the campus at which "faculty and students were loud and unrestrained in their denunciation of the crime."[29]

Many years later the story was told of Herndon's part in this mass meeting. Since the people of Jacksonville who attended were mostly Southern, the memorial exercises seemed likely to end in a row. "At this critical moment the young student, Herndon, made his way towards the front and took the platform. The student body caught the excitement, and seeing Herndon speaking privately with President Beecher, on the platform, they raised the college yell, and shouts for 'Herndon,' 'Herndon' — 'The son of a Democrat. Let us hear what this "son of a gun" can say!' Beecher . . . in his perplexity told young Herndon to speak if he chose." And, the tale continues, Herndon did speak, winning the attention of an adverse audience even while denouncing the Lovejoy murder, and at the end of his extemporaneous address he "was picked up by his college mates and borne off the campus on the shoulders of his fellow-students" in a blaze of glory.[30]

As a sequel to this affair, it was said, Archer Herndon, hearing of his son's antislavery pronouncements and fearing that he would become "a damned abolitionist pup," promptly withdrew William from the college and forced him to come home. Back in Springfield, Billy's soul was still permeated with the "rank poison" of abolitionism, and Archer in raging fury literally disinherited him. From that day Herndon had to leave home "bereft of all ties there save his mother," who had sympathized with him. The favorite son had become an outcast.[31]

This story has grown with age. The account of Herndon's participation in the Lovejoy protest meeting was first published by Henry Bascom Rankin, a notoriously inaccurate writer. Not a witness to the events he described, Rankin apparently based his narrative on memories of conversations with Herndon, but his *Personal Recollections of Abraham Lincoln* did not appear until 1916 — seventy-nine years after Lovejoy's death. At least three other authors have used the story,[32] but so far as can be ascertained, the Rankin reminiscences were their only source.

Careful searching of strictly contemporary records leads one to ques-

---

[29] *Herndon's Lincoln,* I, 187.

[30] Rankin, *Personal Recollections of Abraham Lincoln,* 115–116.

[31] Frank J. Heinl, "Congregationalism in Jacksonville and Early Illinois," Ill. State Hist. Soc., *Jour.,* XXVII, 451–452; *Herndon's Lincoln,* I, 188; interview of Weik with Hardin Masters, March 7, 1925, Herndon-Weik Coll.; Rankin, *Personal Recollections,* 117.

[32] Heinl, in Ill. State Hist. Soc., *Jour.,* XXVII, 451–452; Rammelkamp, *Illinois College: A Centennial History, 1829–1929,* 110–111; introduction to Paul M. Angle's ed. of *Herndon's Lincoln,* xiv.

tion whether Herndon was even at Jacksonville in November 1837; the Illinois College faculty minutes for September 14 of that year carry the ominous resolution: "That Herndon be informed he cannot study here next term [which was to begin in November] unless he study so as to pass a satisfactory examination in Arithmetic." The difficulty was that in November the preparatory department was to be discontinued, and Herndon was unable to meet the college entrance requirements. There is no record that Billy passed his examination or that he was admitted to the college at the start of the new term. Certainly his name does not appear in the 1837–38 catalogue. The indications are strong that his "college" career ended not with a bang but a whimper.

Even if one could accept Herndon's later positive statement that Lovejoy's death occurred while he was attending college,[33] it is hard to credit the dramatic story of his antislavery oration and of the resulting removal from school by an irate parent. No contemporary report identifies Herndon with the Lovejoy commemoration in Jacksonville. During his lifetime none of Herndon's friends or schoolmates ever mentioned Billy's presence on such an occasion, nor did Herndon himself ever refer in writing to his supposed antislavery speech.[34]

Herndon did not attend the college more than one year — that is all that can be proved. At this date one can only speculate about causes. Perhaps Archer Herndon, hard hit by the depression, could not afford the expensive luxury of supporting a son in college. It is possible that the father, who had publicly sworn eternal hostility to abolitionists,[35] did hastily yank his favorite son from the hotbed of antislavery — or perhaps Billy, having flunked out of school, was safely in Springfield before Lovejoy was murdered.

Back at home Billy faced that trying emotional strain which occurs when father and son both think strongly and differently on fundamentals. Archer Herndon was a Democrat and a Southerner. For those who hoped to emancipate the slaves or to enfranchise the free Negroes, he had unbounded contempt. Never a strict party man in the sense of obeying the Springfield regency, he remained throughout his life "identified with the True Jacksonian Democracy" and characteristically lumped together all those he disliked as "Abolition federal silk stocking ruffle shirt Whigs."[36]

[33] *Herndon's Lincoln*, I, 187.

[34] Herndon himself said simply that his father believed "the college was too strongly permeated with the virus of Abolitionism," and forced his withdrawal. *Ibid.*, I, 187. See also undated interview of Weik with Herndon, Memorandum Book II, Weik MSS.

[35] *Sangamo Journal*, June 12, 1840.

[36] Isaac Cook to Jacob Thompson, April 30, 1858, Records of Interior Department, National Archives; *Illinois State Register*, June 19, 1840.

Equally self-willed, his oldest son had acquired a new set of values in Jacksonville. If Billy Herndon was converted to the cause of abolition, the results did not become apparent for many years, for it was not until 1856 that he was prominently identified as an antislavery man; yet as soon as he returned to Springfield he showed his independence of mind by joining the Whig party so detested by his father. Naturally there was friction in the family, and Billy left home to sleep in the room above Joshua Fry Speed's store. It seems that the stories of Herndon's exacerbated relations with his parents have been exaggerated. There may have been a temporary misunderstanding when the son returned from college, but it was certainly not of long duration. In the years to come father and son endorsed each other's bonds, Billy served his father as attorney, and before Archer Herndon died he turned over to his eldest son a large farm. As Billy put it: "There is no earthly reason why I should hate my father, brother or friend, because we cannot agree in opinion of measures or principles, and there is no reason why either should feel embittered towards me." [37]

IV

Young Herndon did have a few bad years after his return to Springfield. Finally he got a job as clerk in Joshua Fry Speed's store and slept in the big room upstairs with Speed, Charles R. Hurst, a fellow clerk, and Abraham Lincoln, who had come to Springfield to practice law. [38] Speed paid his clerk seven hundred dollars a year — which "was considered good pay then" [39] — and Billy supplemented his income by making small loans, sometimes at a usurious rate of interest. [40] But times were very hard, and as late as 1842 Herndon confessed gloomily that "poverty is staring us all in the face." [41]

Working hours were long, but when there were no customers Billy could wander back to the cracker barrel and listen to Lincoln and Speed and the other young blades of Springfield — James H. Matheny, Noah Rickard, Evan Butler, Milton Hay, and Newton Francis — argue and tell tales. The boys formed a "society for the encouragement of debate and literary efforts" in Springfield, and many a night they gath-

[37] W. H. Herndon, *Letters on Temperance*, 23.

[38] Herndon to John E. Remsburg, September 10, 1887. I have been allowed to copy this important Herndon manuscript through the courtesy of its owner, Mr. Alfred W. Stern of Chicago.

[39] *Herndon's Lincoln*, I, 188.

[40] James P. Langford *v.* W. H. Herndon, July 1841 term, Christian Co. Cir. Court. The legal documents are in the Herndon-Weik Coll.

[41] Herndon to Massachusetts Historical Society, March 29, 1842, MS., Mass. Hist. Soc.

ered around the potbellied stove to hear Speed's latest effusion about his Kentucky belle or to roar at Lincoln's ribald stories.[42]

Herndon was not the man to sit his life out on a cracker barrel. Besides, he was in love. Unlike the aristocratic Edwardses, Todds, and Stuarts, the Maxcys made no pretense to lofty birth or exaggerated elegance. They were good middle-class people, respectable, honest, industrious. James Maxcy, father of the clan, was born in Virginia, but since 1834 he had lived in Springfield. He had been elected first marshal of the town, and so well did he perform his duties that he was reelected to some city office each year for twenty-six successive terms.[43] The youngest Maxcy daughter was Billy Herndon's junior by four years, a shy, retiring girl, as quietly beautiful as a daisy. Herndon fell in love, proposed marriage, and was accepted. They were wed on March 26, 1840.[44]

Mary Maxcy Herndon remains a shadowy figure. Her memory still lives among older residents of Springfield, faint as the perfume of lavender, the pale fragrance of a life bounded by home, husband, and children. It was a deep love that united these two; for Herndon his married life was an eternal stream of happiness.[45] Mary Herndon did much for her husband. She read books for him and gave wifely advice; most of all she was a tactful, soothing influence on his ebullient personality. Their first child was born in 1841, a son whom they named Nathaniel. From that time the family increased rapidly, until there were six children in the Herndon home on the corner of First and Jefferson streets.[46]

It was a happy home, for Herndon was devoted to his family. Never was he too busy to answer questions and help solve childish difficulties. Every Sunday he would hire a carriage and take the children out on the country roads to teach them botany, geology, and ornithology. Nothing escaped his eye; his nephew asserted he "never saw a botany book that knew more about plants" than did Herndon.[47] Picking a wild flower, he would show its parts to the children and marvel at its perfection. "Remember," he would admonish, "a great Power made all this." A great teaser, Billy was always playing practical jokes on his children. When he came home from town, he would ask his daughter:

---

[42] *Herndon's Lincoln*, I, 188–189.
[43] Power, *History of the Early Settlers*, 484–485.
[44] Records of Marriages, Sangamon Co., 1835–1849, 105.
[45] Herndon to Weik, November 29, 1890, Herndon-Weik Coll.
[46] Herndon's children by his first marriage were: Nathaniel J., born in 1841; Annie M., 1843; Beverly P., 1845; Lizzie R., 1849; Le[i]gh W., 1852; and Mary, 1856. W. H. Herndon's family Bible, owned by Mrs. Earl Bice, Springfield.
[47] Statement of Mr. James S. Miles, Sr., to me, November 15, 1944.

"Who was that dirty-faced little boy I saw kissing you through the fence?" And as the child made indignant denials, he would catch her up in his arms and roar with laughter. A kind parent was Herndon, yet not an overindulgent one. The children had to know their place. He loved to have Mollie and Lizzie and Annie romping in his flower garden — but if they picked a rose, remembers his daughter, "believe me he'd know it." And when Nat interrupted his father's speech at a Republican rally by shouting "Hurrah for the Democrats!" the razor strap was put into use that night.[48]

[48] W. E. Barton, *The Paternity of Abraham Lincoln*, 365; Mrs. Mollie Herndon Ralston's statement to me, August 16, 1944.

CHAPTER *ii*

A Laborious, Studious Young Man

I

SPRINGFIELD was a place to spur a man's ambition. Here gathered the greatest men the Sucker State could offer — governors, legislators, lawyers, judges. A man got ideas. Herndon was not the kind to spend his life behind a counter doling out plowshares and vinegar. Besides, with a wife and a growing family he "had to push & hustle along." [1]

The lawyer ruled the roost in Illinois. There were land titles and charters and statutes to be drafted — and contested — the frontier was litigious. It was natural that Herndon should turn to the law as a profession, for he could study Blackstone and Chitty while he clerked in the store or at nights. There was no need for a college degree, since passing the bar examination meant generally an informal conversation with one of the older advocates in the community.

About 1841 Herndon determined to become an attorney. He looked for assistance to his former roommate in Speed's store, Abraham Lincoln, who had become one of the most prominent of Springfield's numerous lawyers. From pioneer beginnings in Kentucky and Indiana he had developed into a New Salem pilot-storekeeper-postmaster-surveyor-politician. All alone he had read law and in 1837 had moved to Springfield to become John Todd Stuart's partner. After a few years the association was dissolved, and Lincoln joined with Stephen T. Logan to found what rapidly became the most active legal firm in the Illinois capital.

He was a likeable fellow, this Lincoln, full of dry wit and side-splitting anecdote, yet patient, kindly, and understanding. When he first saw Lincoln piloting the *Talisman* Herndon had liked the man. They had come closer together in later years when Lincoln and Archer Herndon had campaigned for the legislature at the same time. But

[1] "Big Me," Herndon's autobiography, Herndon-Weik Coll.

17

most of all Herndon had learned to know and love the gaunt six-footer during those years they had roomed together above Speed's store. To Billy, Lincoln was a friend whose advice was well worth taking. Lincoln, genuinely attached to the younger man, suggested that he read law in the Logan & Lincoln office. The senior partner, Stephen T. Logan, was dour and Scotch, he was not lovable, but this "little dried and shrivelled up man," "cold — ungenerous — snappy — irritable, fighting like a game fowl," [2] knew his profession. Lincoln, on the other hand, was genial, easygoing, and tolerant, popular with juries. From these two masters Herndon could learn much.

For about three years [3] Herndon read law at night or in odd moments, studied case after case, and listened attentively to court sessions. Since he had a wife to support, he "had to act vigorously & energetically." Every time Mary Herndon had to buy thirteen yards of domestic or a pair of children's shoes it might lead to a financial crisis in the family.[4] Billy was, he recollected later, "studious — too much so for . . . [his] own health — studied from 12 to 14 hours a day." [5] Soon he had a working knowledge of legal procedure and could draw up the necessary papers for cases Logan and Lincoln were handling.[6]

Finally, on November 27, 1844, Herndon was given a certificate of good moral character by the Sangamon County Circuit Court, and on December 9 was admitted to the bar.[7] It was about this time that Lincoln, his coattails flapping behind him, came dashing up the office stairs. "Billy," he asked breathlessly, "do you want to enter into partnership with me in the law business"? Herndon was flustered but he managed to stammer: "Mr. Lincoln this is something unexpected by me — it is an undeserved honor; and yet I say I will gladly & thankfully accept the kind and generous offer." Lincoln by-passed the speechmaking by remarking easily: "Billy, I can trust you, if you can

[2] "Lincoln as Lawyer Politician & Statesman," undated Herndon monograph, Herndon-Weik Coll.

[3] "Big Me," Herndon autobiography, *ibid.* It is difficult to determine exactly how long Herndon read law in the Logan & Lincoln office. In his later years Herndon wrote: "I studied law with Logan & Lincoln — two great lawyers — in 1842–3." Herndon to John W. Keys, April 14, 1886, MS., Hist. Soc. of Penn. But by this time his memory was faulty.

[4] Items from Herndon's account with Robert Irwin & Co., photostat, Abraham Lincoln Assoc.

[5] "Big Me," Herndon autobiography, Herndon-Weik Coll.

[6] In Sackett *v.* Miller, begun in 1843, the declaration for Logan & Lincoln appears to be in Herndon's handwriting. Files, July 1845 term, Sangamon Co. Cir. Court.

[7] Roll of Attorneys, Office of Clerk of Supreme Court, Springfield; Pratt, *Lincoln, 1840–1846*, 257.

trust me," and, sensing the younger man's almost hysterical gratitude, said nothing more until the partnership papers were drawn up.[8]

In later years considerable confusion arose over the exact date when the Lincoln & Herndon partnership began. It has been a widely accepted tradition that the Logan-Lincoln association was dissolved on September 20, 1843, and that the Lincoln & Herndon firm was formed on that same day, but there appears to be no factual basis for this story. To be sure, in his later years Herndon declared the partnership dated from 1843, but it is easy to understand how an error could be made by an aging man whose memory was at times very shaky. The most reliable evidence points toward a later year for the formation of the partnership. The Logan & Lincoln business card continued to appear in Springfield newspapers until early in 1845, while it was not until much later — 1847 — that the professional announcements listed Lincoln & Herndon. Certainly Logan and Lincoln were acting regularly as partners in suits commenced during 1844.[9] In his earlier correspondence Herndon always referred to the firm of Lincoln & Herndon as having been formed in 1844, and this is confirmed by Lincoln's statement that Herndon had been his partner "from the autumn of 1844." [10] Though Herndon was not admitted to the bar until December of that year, the partnership was very likely begun a few weeks before his license was granted.[11]

II

For years Lincoln specialists have speculated why Lincoln chose Herndon for his new partner. Association with Logan had done much for Abraham Lincoln. He had learned much of both law and practice; he had an established reputation; he was a competent and a popular advocate. If partnership with Logan proved unsatisfactory — whether because of financial difficulties, because of latent political rivalries be-

---

[8] Since there are no contemporary accounts of this conversation, it is, of course, impossible to reproduce exactly the words of the speakers. Herndon to Caroline H. Dall, December 30, 1866, Dall MSS.; *Herndon's Lincoln,* II, 266.

[9] Logan & Lincoln were counsel for the plaintiff in John Rhea *v.* James Rhea's Heirs, for which papers were filed April 29, 1844. Files, Sangamon Co. Cir. Court. By July 1845, however, a suit was brought in the name of "Stephen T. Logan and Abraham Lincoln, late doing business under the style and firm name of Logan and Lincoln." W. H. Townsend, *Lincoln the Litigant,* 19.

[10] Herndon to Charles Henry Hart, February 12 and 17, 1870, Hart MSS.; Angle, ed., *New Letters and Papers of Lincoln,* 117.

[11] Angle, "Where Lincoln Practiced Law," Lincoln Centennial Assoc., *Papers, 1927,* 29–30.

tween the two, or because Logan wanted to take his son as a partner — surely Lincoln could have had his pick of Illinois lawyers for his new associate. Why did he not choose someone older and better known — John Todd Stuart, for example, or Orville H. Browning? Why pick young and inexperienced Herndon?

Many solutions have been hazarded: Lincoln took Herndon for a partner at Joshua F. Speed's urging; because Lincoln was outraged at the way Archer Herndon was treating his oldest son; because Lincoln owed a political debt to Archer Herndon; because Billy Herndon came from such an influential family; because Herndon was poor and needed help; because Herndon could furnish money needed for the firm.[12] To read motives into a man's mind after the passing of a century is a doubtful business. Perhaps Herndon's answer is the best one. When asked "what the motives were that actuated Lincoln in taking me into partnership," he replied frankly: "I don't know and no one else does."[13]

It is probably incorrect to think that Lincoln picked his partner out of pity for his straitened circumstances. Ambitious politically and hampered by debts incurred during his New Salem period, Lincoln was in no position to play the philanthropist. As a matter of fact, Herndon was doubtless right in recalling: "I, according to the best of my recollection, was at that time, in 1844, the monied man of the firm."[14] Nor is it likely that Lincoln would have selected a partner merely because friends urged it or because he liked Herndon's father. Lincoln knew himself, he knew his previous partners, and he knew Herndon. He had observed this young man for years, first as an acquaintance, then as a roommate, and as a law student. Herndon was a promising young man. With his intimate knowledge of his partner's character Lincoln could write in July 1848: "You have been a laborious, studious young man. You are far better informed on almost all subjects than I have been. You cannot fail in any laudable object, unless you allow your mind to be improperly directed."[15]

Lincoln's previous partners, John Todd Stuart and Stephen T. Logan, had both been older than he and better equipped with legal and worldly wisdom. He had learned much from them, but he had always

---

[12] For these conjectures, in the order quoted, see: Interview of Clinton L. Conkling with John W. Bunn, December 13, 1917, C. L. Conkling MSS.; Ross, *Early Pioneers*, 124 ff.; T. G. Onstot, *Pioneers of Menard and Mason Counties*, 56; *Illinois State Journal*, September 1 and 24, 1883.

[13] Herndon to Weik, February 24, 1887, Herndon-Weik Coll.

[14] *Illinois State Journal*, September 24, 1883.

[15] John G. Nicolay and John Hay, *Complete Works of Abraham Lincoln*, II, 57–58. Hereafter cited as *Works*.

been the junior partner of the firm, having the tedious duty of keeping files and records. Now he was starting out for himself and took Herndon in, supposing that Billy "had system & would keep things in order" even though he might "not make much of a lawyer." [16] Another advantage of having the young man in the office was that Herndon, unlike both Stuart and Logan, did not have political ambitions. Lincoln "had learned that a law office could not be run when all the members wanted to be Congressmen." [17]

Still, politics must have been a factor in making Lincoln's decision. His trouble was that he was married. The Whig party in central Illinois was split into two distinct factions. On the one hand were the eminently respectable Stuarts, Todds, and Edwardses, few in number but rich in family traditions of political leadership. But the numerical strength of the Whig party came from the "shrewd, wild boys about town." [18] This younger generation of Whigs, "self made men — men who had power," scorned the older leadership and wanted a hand in shaping party policy. [19] Lincoln intended to work through the Whig party. He had to have the support of both factions. For many years his hardscrabble beginnings had identified him with the young Whig element, but in 1842 Lincoln had married the elegant Mary Todd, and it was whispered that he too had become the representative of "pride, wealth, and aristocratic family distinction." [20] Though Lincoln went out of his way to assure friends that marriage into the exclusive Todd-Edwards clan had not changed him, insurgents in Springfield began to desert him in favor of Edward D. Baker, whom they supported in the congressional race of 1844.

Billy Herndon had dabbled in every campaign since he was old enough to vote. Early he had affiliated himself with the Whig party and had frequently spoken for Lincoln. Without political ambition for himself, he carried much weight with the young Whigs, who knew that he was sincere and that he stood with them against conservative leadership. [21] It was partly shrewd politics, therefore, that Lincoln exhibited in selecting a new partner. He was giving assurance to the young men that he had not deserted them.

[16] Statement of Henry Clay Whitney, undated, photostat, Hertz Coll.
[17] Onstot, *Pioneers*, 56.
[18] Nicolay and Hay, eds., *Works*, II, 50.
[19] "Lincoln & Mary Todd," undated Herndon monograph, Herndon-Weik Coll.
[20] Nicolay and Hay, eds., *Works*, I, 262.
[21] "Lincoln & Mary Todd," undated Herndon monograph, Herndon-Weik Coll.

III

Whatever the reasons for its formation, the partnership was a success. From its first appearance in 1847 until long after Lincoln's election to the presidency, Springfield newspapers carried the professional card: [22]

Abraham Lincoln.   Wm. H. Herndon.
LINCOLN & HERNDON, Counsellors and Attorneys at law, will practice in the courts of law and Chancery in this State.

For an office Lincoln and Herndon rented a room in the new Tinsley Building on the south side of Springfield's public square. It was a wretchedly bare spot in the first year of the partnership. "The furniture, somewhat dilapidated, consisted of one small desk and a table, a sofa or lounge with a raised head at one end, and a half-dozen plain wooden chairs. The floor was never scrubbed. . . . Over the desk . . . was the office bookcase holding a set of Blackstone, Kent's Commentaries, Chitty's Pleadings, and a few other books." [23] Though Lincoln was indifferent to his physical surroundings, Herndon soon took the lead in securing adequate office equipment, buying desks, a table, and books at a cost of $168.65, half of which was charged to his partner.[24] When Lincoln returned from Congress in 1849, the office was moved to the northwest corner of the public square, where it remained until Lincoln left Springfield.

At the outset it was not an equal partnership. Older by nine years in time and a generation in discretion, Lincoln naturally handled most of the cases, wrote the important papers, and pleaded the suits in court. Herndon, still the student and the learner, performed routine jobs; he answered inquiries as to Lincoln's whereabouts or "'toated books' & 'hunted up authorities'" for the senior partner's use.[25] It has become a tradition that Lincoln and Herndon so trusted each other that they never kept accounts but divided fees equally as they went along. As a matter of fact, there were books kept — after a fashion — and this was part of Herndon's work. During the first years of the association Billy kept careful track of the money he spent for office furnishings and even listed such items as "postage from the time you

[22] *Illinois Journal,* December 30, 1847.
[23] Statement of Gibson W. Harris, who studied in the law office, in Weik, *The Real Lincoln: A Portrait,* 106–107.
[24] Statement of Herndon to Lincoln, August 1, 1846. I have examined this valuable manuscript item through the kindness of its owner, Mrs. Edna Orendorff Macpherson, Springfield.
[25] Herndon to Henry Enoch Dummer, April 11, 1847, Dummer MSS.; Herndon to Lamon, March 6, 1870, Lamon MSS.

went to Alton to the present & cash loaned wife $1.37" in a detailed statement of his account with Lincoln. For the law practice itself a daybook was kept, listing the cases the partners argued and the fees charged.[26] As the men grew into their partnership, they came to depend less and less on even such loose accounting methods.

Business began slowly for the new firm. Not until March 1845 was their first case in the Sangamon County Circuit Court heard,[27] and the partners' initial suit in neighboring Menard County was called for the May term of the same year.[28] Lincoln's name soon drew clients, and before long the partners had as much business as they could well manage. During the first twelve months of the partnership the firm had only fourteen cases in the circuit court at Springfield; the following year more than twice as many were handled. As early as November 1845 Lincoln and Herndon were running legal affairs for firms as far distant as Peoria, while the following spring Herndon attended to five Lincoln & Herndon cases before the Christian County Circuit Court.[29]

The Lincoln & Herndon daybook for 1847 lists over one hundred cases handled before Lincoln left for Washington in October. In three instances a fee of fifty dollars was charged, and one appearance before the Illinois Supreme Court brought one hundred dollars. But these were exceptions. Pleading ordinary suits before the justice of the peace brought five dollars, while ten to twenty-five dollars was the usual fee for work in the circuit courts.[30] Lincoln's services were frequently solicited to aid other lawyers during these first few years, and in addition he handled many cases by himself. Herndon, still a novice, had few cases alone and rarely appeared with anyone but his partner. But he was learning, and soon he thought himself a better lawyer and speaker than Lincoln. And, added a contemporary: "In some views he was." [31]

IV

Just as the firm was getting established, Lincoln was elected to the House of Representatives. Herndon had vocally championed his part-

---

[26] Statement of Herndon to Lincoln, August 1, 1846, collection of Mrs. Edna Orendorff Macpherson; "Day Book of Lincoln & Herndon, 1847," MS., Ill. State Hist. Lib.

[27] Thomas M. Hope *v.* Isaac W. Beebe *et al.*, filed March 3, 1845. Judge's Docket, 1845–1849, Sangamon Co. Cir. Court.

[28] The praecipe in the case of the People *v.* James Dorman was filed May 10, 1845. Lincoln file, Menard Co. Cir. Court.

[29] Herndon to Powell and Bryan, November 15, 1845, MS. in collection of Mr. Wayne C. Townley, Bloomington; Pratt, *Lincoln, 1840–1846*, 336.

[30] "Day Book of Lincoln & Herndon, 1847," Ill. State Hist. Lib.

[31] A. Bergen, "Abraham Lincoln as a Lawyer," Am. Bar. Assoc., *Jour.*, XII, 392.

ner's nomination by the Whigs and in May 1846 had served as secretary of the district convention which selected the candidate.[32] The Democratic nominee, the venerable Methodist circuit-rider, Peter Cartwright, was defeated, and Lincoln became the sole Whig representative from Illinois. When the Lincolns left Springfield in October 1847 for a stay in Kentucky before going to Washington, Herndon took over as the active member of the legal firm and as Lincoln's political ears in the Illinois capital.

It was no small order for a young man. Many of the clients who had depended on the experience of the older partner now turned to other lawyers for advice. Some writers have asserted that Herndon was able to maintain only a nominal practice while Lincoln was in Congress and have noted that during his partner's absence Herndon had only two cases in the Illinois Supreme Court, which involved the small sums of $21 and $4.10 and costs.[33]

A fresh study of the evidence reveals this conception to be incorrect. It is true that Herndon had few cases in the Supreme Court while Lincoln was away, because in 1848 he began serving as deputy clerk to the court and was no longer free to plead frequently before that bench.[34] By delving into the manuscript records of central Illinois courts and by referring to the Lincoln & Herndon fee book it can be demonstrated that Herndon was able to keep a fair amount of business while Lincoln was in Washington. The partners' daybook for 1847 lists one hundred and twenty-five cases handled by Lincoln and Herndon together and over sixty "attended to since Lincoln went to Congress." The notations show that Herndon appeared in the Sangamon, Menard, Logan, and Christian County Circuit Courts, and that he was able to command fees as high as those Lincoln had charged.

There was never any question of dissolving the partnership in 1847. As soon as Lincoln reached Washington he began mailing Herndon the *Congressional Globe,* urging Billy to "be careful to preserve all the numbers, so that *we* can have a complete file of it." [35] From the law office Herndon wrote of suits commenced, judgments won, and sums collected. From Mrs. Spriggs's boarding house in Washington Lincoln rejoiced in the payment of a fee in a bank case; he did not, he said, "expect to hear another as good a piece of news from Springfield"

[32] *Sangamo Journal,* May 7, 1846.

[33] Frederick T. Hill, *Lincoln the Lawyer,* 161; John T. Richards, *Abraham Lincoln, the Lawyer-Statesman,* 73–74.

[34] Herndon to Weik, July 10, 1888; "Notes on Lincoln — Judges & Law[y]ers at The Supreme Court Room," Herndon-Weik Coll.

[35] Lincoln to Herndon, Washington, December 12, 1847, MS., Ill. State Hist. Lib. Italics supplied.

while he was away. Would Herndon apply Lincoln's share against his "national debt" (as he humorously called the obligations incurred during his New Salem days) and against his obligations to Springfield tradesmen? In another case, pestered by an importunate client with "cursed, unreadable, and ungodly handwriting," Lincoln turned over the tedious litigation to Herndon for settlement.[36]

V

To Lincoln in Washington, Herndon was more than a law partner. He was a sort of political barometer, and the senior partner was to suffer when he failed to heed Billy's storm warning. Herndon knew Illinois Whig opinion. In view of his later repeated declarations that he was an abolitionist *"sometime before . . . [he] was born,"* [37] it is rather amusing to note Herndon's rigid Whig orthodoxy. Prior to 1849 voting in Illinois was done orally, and each citizen's choice of candidates was marked opposite his name. The Springfield poll books reveal that Herndon's record as a regular party man would be hard to equal. Virtually every election, even for school commissioners and justices of the peace, showed him present and backing the straight Whig ticket. If he had antislavery views at this time, they were held rigidly within the bounds of conservative Whiggery. In 1840 and 1844 James Gillespie Birney ran for President on the Liberty party ticket, but Herndon's vote went to the regular Whig nominees — Harrison and Clay, neither of whom could be described as an abolitionist.[38] Even more significant in showing that Herndon in these early years was notably lacking in real emancipationist tendencies was his vote on the adoption of the Illinois constitution of 1848. Deferring to widespread anti-Negro sentiment, the constitutional convention permitted voters to decide separately on an article "to effectually prevent the owners of slaves from bringing them into this state, for the purpose of setting them free." [39] Herndon joined Southern-born Democrats in voting to adopt the article.[40]

A paragon of Whig regularity and a speaker powerfully influential with the younger elements of the party, Herndon was in an excellent position to give Lincoln "back home" advice, and his partner soon needed it. At first everything had gone well. Lincoln had written of

[36] Lincoln to Herndon, December 13, 1847, MS., Mass. Hist. Soc.; Nicolay and Hay, eds., *Works*, I, 350–351.
[37] Herndon to Lamon, March 1, 1870, Lamon MSS.
[38] Springfield Poll Books, Ill. State Archives.
[39] Article XIV of the Illinois constitution. See also 33 Ill. 390–398.
[40] Springfield Poll Book, election of March 6, 1848, Ill. State Archives.

the organizing of the House of Representatives and had referred to his own speechmaking plans in a typical Lincolnism: "As you are all so anxious for me to distinguish myself, I have concluded to do so, before long." [41] When Lincoln did make an address, Illinois reaction was favorable, and Herndon dashed off a letter to say that there were many who believed his partner should be re-elected. Lincoln replied that "if it should so happen that nobody else wishes to be elected, I could not refuse the people the right of sending me again." [42]

The contingency did not arise. On December 22, 1847, Lincoln introduced into the House a series of resolutions which seemed for a time to end his political career; he made the nearly fatal mistake of continuing politics-as-usual during war time. For many years footloose American pioneers had been crossing the southwestern border into the Mexican province of Texas. In 1836 they cast off Mexican suzerainty, after a bitter war achieved independence, and asked to join the United States. Over Mexican protest, Congress in 1845 annexed the Texan republic. Texans claimed their territory extended to the Rio Grande, while Mexicans, still denying the independence of the Lone Star republic, placed the boundary at the Nueces or farther north. When American troops were sent into the disputed region they met Mexican opposition and hostilities followed. Claiming that American blood had been shed on American soil, President James K. Polk sent a war message to Congress.

Except in certain parts of New England, where it was looked upon as a plot to extend slavery, the Mexican War at first met with enthusiastic approval. The West, always imperialistic, had eagerly offered company after company of volunteers, and the Illinois Whig John J. Hardin met a hero's death at the battle of Buena Vista. When Lincoln ran for Congress in 1846 the war had not been an issue, but he had given no indication that he opposed it. After arriving in Washington and talking with party leaders, he changed his tune. The official Whig position was that this was a Democratic war: the Democrats had started it, and now let them take the blame for it. Without denying supplies to the American forces or endeavoring to block acquisition of Mexican lands, they tried to fix on the Democratic President the odium of beginning an unjust war of aggression.

As a part of this campaign Lincoln late in December 1847 introduced his famous "spot" resolutions, demanding "a full knowledge of all the facts which go to establish whether the particular spot on which the blood of our citizens was so shed was or was not at that

[41] Lincoln to Herndon, December 13, 1847, MS., Mass. Hist. Soc.
[42] Nicolay and Hay, eds., *Works*, I, 326.

time our own soil." A few days later he supported his resolutions by a speech denouncing President Polk as "a bewildered, confounded, and miserably perplexed man," with "something about his conscience more painful than all his mental perplexity." [43] And to top it all off, Lincoln voted for the Ashmun resolutions declaring that the war had been "unnecessarily and unconstitutionally begun by the President of the United States."

Reaction in Illinois was immediate and unfavorable. He became known as "Spotty Lincoln," a Congressman who failed to back up the fighting forces. Herndon heard all the rumors in Springfield and immediately began writing his partner dire warnings. No longer was there any talk of renomination; the question was whether Lincoln could be prevented from ruining himself and his party. Lincoln should not, Herndon thought, have voted for the Ashmun resolutions. Not only was his vote a political blunder, but Billy felt that there could be a good case established for President Polk's actions in ordering American troops into the disputed territory.[44]

Lincoln replied with the indignation of a man unsure of his own thinking. What did Herndon think he should have done when the Ashmun resolutions came up? Would Herndon "have voted what . . . [he] felt and knew to be a lie?" Would he have "gone out of the House — skulked the vote?" ". . . I will stake my life," Lincoln subtly flattered his partner, "that if you had been in my place you would have voted just as I did." He was not, the Congressman explained at length, denying supplies to American soldiers; he was merely joining with other Whig leaders in refusing to justify the war. All the important party leaders — "little, slim, pale-faced, consumptive" Alexander H. Stephens of Georgia, for example, who made "the very best speech of an hour's length I ever heard" — were with Lincoln in denouncing the administration. As for Herndon's argument that the President had the power to repel a contemplated invasion, Lincoln answered firmly but in a spirit of kindness that his partner was confused. Not even the Democrats would give such authority to the Chief Executive. By giving unreined license to the commander-in-chief Herndon was overruling the wishes of the fathers of the Constitution and was placing "our President where kings have always stood." [45]

[43] *Ibid.*, 319, 345.
[44] *Herndon's Lincoln*, II, 280.
[45] Nicolay and Hay, eds., *Works*, I, 351–354; II, 1–3.

VI

Lincoln's logic may have been correct, but Herndon knew Illinois politics. Lincoln became a marked man politically; his "spot resolutions" were to haunt him as late as 1860. Not only did his antiwar stand blight his own political prospects, but it was a major handicap to Logan, proposed by the Springfield junto as his successor. A disturbing rumor reached Herndon that Richard Yates or some other Morgan County Whig would not back the selection of the Springfield ring but might enter the race against Logan. Distressed to "hear that the good whigs of Old Morgan intended or even harbored the idea of flinching from any good whig candidate," Herndon wrote Yates a warning letter. Confessing that he himself had "no very decided predilections" for Logan, Herndon thought it only fair that Morgan County should "firmly knit" with the Sangamon Whigs in this election. He added tactfully: "Judge Logan . . . wishes to go but one term and Lincoln not wishing to run at all, I think it would be the better policy of the people of Morgan to help us for this term and after this is over I think the field will be clear to all men who have any idea of running for that seat." His letter was "not prompted by improper motives," Herndon assured Yates, but was "written for the best interests of the Whigs of our mutual counties."[46]

Though Morgan County did finally "stick up" for Logan, party morale was badly shattered and not even the approaching presidential election could bring Illinois Whigs together. At the Philadelphia convention of 1848 the Whigs ignored their perennial standard-bearer, Henry Clay, and nominated a military hero, Zachary Taylor. It was hard to get excited about "Old Rough and Ready," and Herndon and Illinois were not enthusiastic about the election. Again and again Lincoln urged: "Cannot something be done, even in Illinois?" Could not the "shrewd, wild boys about town" be organized in a Rough and Ready Club? "Let every one play the part he can play best, — some speak, some sing, and all 'holler.'" They should hold meetings in the evenings, and the club would be "an interesting pastime, and improving to the intellectual faculties of all engaged." Besides, it would help to elect "Old Zach." "Don't fail to do this," Lincoln admonished.[47]

Lincoln was nettled by Herndon's apparent indifference,[48] and he

[46] Herndon to Yates, April 6, 1848, photostat, collection of Mr. Thomas I. Starr.
[47] Emanuel Hertz, *Abraham Lincoln: A New Portrait*, I, 30; Nicolay and Hay, eds., *Works*, II, 49–50.
[48] Herndon to Hart, November 23, 1866, Hart MSS.

probably thought his letters directed the organizing of the Taylor campaign in Illinois. As a matter of fact, Herndon had helped to form a Taylor Club at Springfield three days before Lincoln's letter urged such a program.[49] He was also a member of the Whig state central committee, appointed the day after Lincoln wrote his hortatory message and, of course, several days before it could have reached Springfield. Days before he received his partner's urgent epistle Herndon attended a mass ratification meeting at Springfield, where he helped compose resolutions praising Taylor as "a patriot worthy of the best days of the Republic," characterized by "inflexible honesty, sound judgment, upright intentions, strong active talents."

But Herndon's heart was not in the cause. He was still confused and irritated by the unpopular Whig position on the Mexican War,[50] but even more important was his resentment over the local political situation. The older Whig politicians, it seemed to Herndon — men like Logan, Stuart, and perhaps Lincoln himself — "old fogies," all of them, glared with "eyes *bloodshot* with political power" upon the younger, democratic element of the party,[51] and dispensed nominations only to obedient pets like James C. Conkling, who would "bark when Logan rubs his ears." Herndon was bitter about "the arbitrary dictation of a self-constituted dynasty whose sole object is the spoils of office, and who make it a rule to put their foot upon the neck of all who presume to come into competition with them." [52] He wrote a pointed letter to his partner, reflecting "severely on the stubbornness and bad judgment of the old fossils in the party, who were constantly holding the young men back." [53]

Lincoln's reply was sharp but not peevish. Herndon's disaffection, he declared, was exceedingly painful to him. As "one of the old men" himself,[54] there was nothing that could afford him more satisfaction than to learn that Herndon and "others of my young friends at home are doing battle in the contest, and endearing themselves to the people, and taking a stand far above any I have ever been able to reach in their admiration." "The way for a young man to rise," he pointed

---

[49] *Illinois Journal,* June 29, 1848, reporting the organization of a Taylor Club on June 19. Lincoln's letter suggesting the formation of such a group was dated June 22.

[50] Nicolay and Hay, eds., *Works,* II, 50–52.

[51] Herndon to Richard Yates, July 23, 1852, Reavis MSS.

[52] *Illinois State Register,* June 30, 1848.

[53] *Herndon's Lincoln,* II, 285.

[54] Lincoln at this time was not quite forty years of age. When Herndon was forty-two he thought of himself as "young and untried." Herndon to Caroline H. Dall, February 28, 1860, Dall MSS.

out, "is to improve himself every way he can, never suspecting that anybody wishes to hinder him." Herndon had such fine qualities that Lincoln wished to save him from a fatal error.[55]

Outwardly Herndon was convinced. Lincoln apologized for his "serious, long-faced letter" of admonition and expressed unalloyed pleasure when Herndon came back to the fold.[56] In spite of Democratic efforts to exploit his dissatisfaction, Billy continued active in the Whig organization, addressed Taylor clubs all over Sangamon County, and joined in a denunciation of Lewis Cass, Taylor's Democratic opponent, as "a candidate courtly . . . in his manners . . . but monarchical in his disposition." As a reward for his exertions he was appointed "Assistant Elector" for central Illinois, and the Whig newspapers had no doubt he would render "Old Zach" good service.[57] But his campaigning was halfhearted, and he frankly admitted that he was entitled to no credit for the respectable showing made by Sangamon Whigs.[58] When election day came, for the first time since he was eligible to vote, Herndon did not go to the polls. He was sick of politics.

VII

When his congressional term drew to a close, Lincoln found that he had lost much of his popularity by his antiwar declarations and honorably offered to withdraw from the law partnership. Herndon urged him to remain, and the firm of Lincoln & Herndon gradually increased its business in the central Illinois courts.[59]

His partner's election, the unsatisfactory term in Congress, and the rival bickerings among Springfield Whigs produced in Herndon an aversion to public life. Seeing Illinois Whig leaders "fight & bite each other like dogs in a ring," Herndon decided he did not want office of any kind, either political or legal. Never, he swore, would he be an aspirant for office and have "envy to shrivel up . . . [his] soul." [60] Herndon was still interested in politics, and in coming years he was to be elected to city offices and to serve prominently in the Republican party. But where his candidacy might mean personal difficulties or party schism he would gracefully withdraw from a contest unworthy

---

[55] Nicolay and Hay, eds., *Works*, II, 56–58.
[56] Angle, ed., *New Letters and Papers*, 46–47.
[57] *Illinois Journal*, July 6 and 27, August 16, 1848.
[58] Herndon to Richard Yates, July 23, 1852, Reavis MSS.
[59] *Herndon's Lincoln*, II, 307.
[60] Herndon to Weik, January 15, 1886, Herndon-Weik Coll.; Herndon to Richard Yates, July 23, 1852, Reavis MSS.; Herndon to John Alexander McClernand, December 8, 1859, McClernand MSS.

of his strife.[61] The future would see Herndon battle sincerely and at times fanatically for causes he thought just, but he never quite escaped the conviction that "Three fourths of the political world — those who lead especially — are corrupt-fish — dollar-power seekers — mud hunters — scoundrels." [62]

Herndon was not greatly perturbed by the agitation of the slavery question at the end of the Mexican War. After long strife over the proposed Wilmot Proviso, which would have prohibited slavery in all territories acquired by the peace treaty, Congress finally adopted a series of compromise measures in 1850, giving the South an effective fugitive slave law in return for the admission of California as a free state and other concessions to Northern antislavery sentiment. Unlike the abolitionist extremists who denounced any concession to the South, Herndon joined fellow Whigs in urging the "speedy adjustment of the questions touching the subject of slavery," and in stoutly supporting the compromise proposals.[63]

By 1852 Herndon was beginning to overcome his apathy and was thrilled by the nomination of General Winfield Scott as the Whig candidate for the presidency. "The whig fire, the Scott fire," he exulted, was spreading an "exhilerating [*sic*] glow over the whole political body." Illinois must free herself from the political "sin" of Democracy, throw out the "jackalls" and elect Whig candidates. It was his hope to organize the "self sacrificing" young men of Sangamon in this crusade for right; "on no portion of Gods footstool" would the Whigs fight so hard and zealously.[64] His was a belated flowering of party spirit, for Democratic Franklin Pierce swept Illinois and achieved election. In another four years the Whig party was dead.

[61] In 1852 Herndon was suggested for prosecuting attorney for the Springfield district. When another Whig entered the race, Herndon withdrew, commending his opponent as "a young man of talent, integrity and industry." *Illinois Journal,* October 1, 1852.

[62] Herndon to Lyman Trumbull, January 27, 1861, Trumbull MSS.

[63] *Illinois Journal,* August 2, 1850.

[64] Herndon to Richard Yates, July 23, 1852, Reavis MSS.

CHAPTER *iii*

Lincoln & Herndon

I

WITH brisk, short steps Herndon walked four blocks east, passed by his father's house, waved to his mother on the front porch, and turned south to the law office. This was his invariable routine, and he arranged his schedule so as to unlock the office promptly at eight o'clock. The young men studying law in the office arrived shortly afterwards, and about nine o'clock the senior partner would appear with a cheerful "Billy — how is your bones philosophy this morning?" Lincoln & Herndon was open for business.[1]

There was a regularity and sameness about the law practice. Every day Herndon looked at the Lincoln & Herndon sign swinging on its rusty hinges over the street on the west side of the square. Every day he climbed the narrow stairs, crossed the dark hallway, unlocked the door, and drew back the curtain from its glass pane. The law office was always the same. Its unscrubbed windows looked out over the monotony of a trafficless alley. There were two worktables arranged in the shape of a lopsided "T" — one very long, its pine surface "numerously indented with a jack-knife," the other beige-covered and much shorter. A secretary with bulging drawers and overflowing pigeonholes, several heavily burdened bookcases, four or five cane-bottomed chairs, and a long, rickety sofa propped against the wall completed the office furnishings. The very disorder of the place — the scattered papers, the assortment of gold pens, the splattered earthenware inkwell — were symbols of long use and established security.[2] Proudly Herndon looked at the bookshelves furnished, at his instance, with needed reference books. Happily he counted his volumes of

---

[1] *Herndon's Lincoln*, III, 430; Herndon to Weik, July 25, 1890, Herndon-Weik Coll.

[2] Herndon to Weik, July 10, 1888, *ibid.;* H. C. Whitney, *Life on the Circuit with Lincoln* (Angle ed.), 404; W. H. Townsend, "Lincoln's Law Books," Amer. Bar Assoc., *Jour.*, XV, 126.

Illinois Statutes and the gold lettered Illinois Reports. He loved to finger the bindings of his Chitty, Redfield, Kent, and Blackstone.[3] The office was dingy and dirty, for the somewhat casual efforts of the law students and of the occasional charwoman never made much impression on the dust, but it was a place where work could be done.

There was a kind of systematic lack of system about this firm. Lincoln was absent on the circuit much of the time and had early entrusted the management of the office to Herndon, who was supposed to attend to such records and files as the partners kept. But Herndon was not an orderly person, and it is doubtful whether anyone could have kept Lincoln's desk neat. As a result the partners were constantly searching for letters which were somehow misplaced and for papers which simply vanished. Lincoln frequently stuck important notes in his stovepipe hat, and Herndon might take letters home from the office; in either case correspondence could be held up for months.[4] And there were times when the partners had to confess frankly that documents sent them were "lost or destroyed and cannot be found after search among the papers of Lincoln & Herndon." [5]

Records were of the most desultory sort, and after the first years of the partnership apparently not even a daybook or list of cases was kept. It was not customary to take notes of conversations with clients, and at least once Herndon forgot the amount of damages for which he was supposed to sue.[6] Nor was bookkeeping more systematic. After the first year or so Lincoln and Herndon kept no accounts against themselves, simply dividing equally the fees paid to them. Lincoln made a practice of setting aside one-half of the money he received, marking it "Case of Roe vs. Doe. — Herndon's half," while Herndon would bring in fees collected on the circuit in a small gunny sack and would count out the gold pieces in equal shares. As Lincoln told Henry C. Whitney: "Billy and I never had the scratch of a pen between us; we *jest* divide as we go along." [7]

There was, however, one aspect of office management in which

---

[3] For books not in the office the partners used the library of the Supreme Court. On Herndon's law library see Herndon to John Keys, June 8, 1886, MS., Hist. Soc. of Penn.; *Catalogue of Articles Owned and Used by Abraham Lincoln* (1887); Townsend, "Lincoln's Law Books," Amer. Bar Assoc., *Jour.*, XV, 125–126.

[4] G. A. Tracy, ed., *Uncollected Letters of Abraham Lincoln*, 42; Nicolay and Hay, eds., *Works*, V, 90.

[5] Affidavit in Herndon's writing, September 28, 1857, in the collection of Mr. C. N. Owen.

[6] Herndon to the clerk of the Christian Co. Cir. Court, May 22, 1849, in the case of Killbourn *v.* Baker, Herndon-Weik Coll.

[7] *Herndon's Lincoln*, II, 333; statement of Mrs. Mollie Herndon Ralston to me, August 16, 1944; Whitney, *Life on the Circuit*, 405.

Herndon was proficient, the supervision of students reading law in the office. He had the final word on their selection and after Lincoln became prominent politically had to reject many applicants, sometimes referring them to a less crowded firm.[8] When a young man was accepted, Lincoln would greet him with a hearty "Glad to see you, young man," but it was Herndon who supervised his studies and prodded him on to a mastery of Blackstone. According to one who read law in the office for a short time, Herndon "had the rare gift of control[l]ing and stimulating with energy the best there was in the young men who came to him as students."[9]

Such was the office on the west side of the square. It was a center of political activity, of gossip and friendly banter, and of discussion of such remote problems as the merits of Walt Whitman's poetry, but after all it was a law office. The law was its principal business. To this room came clients of all sorts: a widow claiming dower; a policeman who had "gently laid his hands" on a drunkard in arresting him; two Negro maids who attempted to poison their mistress; victims of slander; holders of unpaid notes; wrongfully treated wives. The firm acted before the justice of the peace and in the Supreme Court of Illinois; it handled "ten cent" cases and major railroad suits.

II

There is no definitive study of Lincoln's law career. For the most part his biographers have said a few words about the musty office, have noted the distinctive features of life on the circuit in the old Eighth Judicial District, and have concluded with an account of three or four cases of dramatic interest.[10] Such a cursory treatment may easily be explained on a number of grounds. The terminology of the law itself is a sufficient barrier for most investigators. Distinctions have to be made between simple trespass and trespass on the case, covenant-broken and assumpsit, replevin and ejectment. Even those obvious distinctions between traverses and demurrers, between mandamus and *quo warranto,* between real property and chattels can hardly be made in other than the formal legal language which is itself inexplicable to

[8] Angle, ed., *New Letters and Papers,* 183; Charles S. Zane, "Lincoln as I Knew Him," Ill. State Hist. Soc., Jour., XIV, 75.

[9] Newton, *Lincoln and Herndon,* 249–250; Rankin, *Intimate Character Sketches of Abraham Lincoln,* 272–273.

[10] The two older studies of Lincoln the lawyer are really very little better: Richards, *Abraham Lincoln, The Lawyer-Statesman* and Hill, *Lincoln the Lawyer.* Albert A. Woldman, *Lawyer Lincoln,* is more comprehensive. There are some excellent monographs by Paul M. Angle, Harry E. Pratt, and Benjamin P. Thomas, cited below.

the layman. A sage observer of these difficulties has wisely remarked: "Perhaps no good historian was ever a good lawyer: whether any good lawyer could be a good historian might be equally doubted." [11]

But not all the difficulty lies in the lack of training and experience on the part of the investigator. An exhaustive study of Lincoln's law practice would require a complete examination of all the legal papers in fifteen circuit courts and in nearly as many county courts and probate offices, in the United States federal courts at Springfield and Chicago, and in the Illinois Supreme Court. This is, it may be surmised, no simple task, for the records of any one of these courts include files of original pleadings, together with demurrers, rejoinders, and exhibits; the judge's docket; the record of the court itself; and the execution and judgment dockets.

In many cases these records are incomplete. Fire completely destroyed all the court records for the Lincoln period in two of the county circuit courts, and most of those for the federal district court. Many volumes of dockets are missing from courthouses, with no explanation of their absence. In some counties the records were kept badly, while in nearly every court the approaching end of a session with its rush of business meant that all records were of the most fragmentary sort.[12]

Another difficulty is the destruction or removal of legal papers by vandals or collectors. Today almost no documents in Lincoln's handwriting are to be found in the files of any court of the old Eighth District. An examination of the resources of the leading Lincoln libraries reveals the reason. To a considerable extent this was Herndon's work. After his partner's death he made the rounds of the central Illinois courts, assiduously removing from the files for use in his projected biography all documents pertaining to Lincoln. Many of these were lost; others were given away or later sold; the remainder, considerably battered by years of inadequate care, are now housed in the Library of Congress. While Herndon's "borrowing" cannot be passed over lightly, it should be pointed out in his defense that he took the papers with the consent of the clerks, that such practices were usual in his day, and that he probably preserved many documents from later destruction through vandalism or lack of care.

But even assuming that all the records could be gathered and read and that the records were complete in all cases, it would still be extremely difficult to present a study of Lincoln as a lawyer. Obviously

[11] Henry Adams, *History of the United States* . . . , III, 45.
[12] Angle, "Abraham Lincoln: Circuit Lawyer," Lincoln Centennial Assoc., *Papers, 1928*, 19–41. The Abraham Lincoln Association in Springfield has a notable collection of photostats of Lincoln legal papers, gleaned from courthouses all over central Illinois.

no general reader is interested in a list of separate, unrelated cases; three or four major trials have some human interest, but for the most part legal proceedings are of the dry-as-dust sort, involving a disputed title to the northwest quarter of the southwest quarter of section thirty-three, township seventeen, range sixteen, or an action to secure payment of an overdue note for $100.15.

The real question is: How successful were Lincoln and Herndon as lawyers? The answer is not a simple one. How can success in the law be measured? Perhaps it might appear that the lawyer who makes the most money is the most successful, but those Illinois attorneys who did accumulate wealth — Jesse W. Fell, for example — did so through real estate speculation rather than by the pursuit of their profession. As Judge David Davis wrote Lincoln: "The practice of law in Illinois . . . promises you but poor remuneration for the Labor." [13] Neither Lincoln nor Herndon "had much an ambition for . . . wealth — but more for the *Know* ie the knowledge of things," [14] and their achievement cannot be measured in pecuniary terms. Nor is the number of cases tried an absolute index of an attorney's success. If it could be known precisely how many suits each lawyer in Illinois brought to court during each year of the 1850's, that would not be the last word on their relative standing in the profession. Some lawyers, especially beginners, concentrate on petty cases, because they can get no others; better lawyers may pick and choose.

Moreover, it is frequently difficult if not impossible to tell who won a case. Many actions are settled by agreement, out of court. A defeat on a specific question may be a victory on a general principle. When a lawyer sues for $500 damages, it is impossible to know whether he will consider a verdict for $300 a defeat or a victory. Besides, the more successful the lawyer, the more likely he is to attract difficult cases, where his chances for victory are at best slight. Where defeat is certain from the start, an adverse decision is not necessarily a failure. [15]

III

These difficulties are made almost insuperable by the nature of the Lincoln & Herndon partnership. To some it has seemed that there was no real division of labor in the firm, that the association amounted to two lawyers practicing in the same office, having different cases and

---

[13] David Davis to Lincoln, February 21, 1849, Robert Todd Lincoln Coll.

[14] "Herndon's Biography," undated MS. fragment, Herndon-Weik Coll.

[15] Angle, "Abraham Lincoln: Circuit Lawyer," Lincoln Centennial Assoc., *Papers, 1928*, 37–38.

different clients. To a certain extent this view is justified. Both Herndon and Lincoln performed all the duties of a lawyer: each interviewed clients, wrote the necessary legal papers, and attended to cases in courts; each appeared alone in many cases and in conjunction with other lawyers in Springfield or elsewhere. Both went out on the circuit and both practiced in all the courts accessible — county, state, and federal. About the only restriction either observed was not to appear in a case opposite his partner.

Yet certain lines of distinction can be drawn between the work the two men performed. As noted above, Herndon was entrusted with the management of the office. Though he did some out of town practice, Billy minded affairs in Springfield while Lincoln was on the circuit beating the bushes for business. When the men worked together in a case, it was usually Herndon who did the research and "book work" while his partner had the dealings with clients and the courts. Both these statements need careful qualification, but they represent the best conclusions that available data warrant.[16]

Herndon's own statement that Lincoln did less office work than any other lawyer in Illinois [17] is refuted by the hundreds of legal documents in Lincoln's own handwriting that have been preserved. There is, however, considerable evidence that Herndon did most of the legal research and briefing for the partnership. Lincoln was not, it is generally admitted, well versed in legal technicalities and precedents; he argued usually from the logic of the facts and the principles of justice involved. Herndon, on the other hand, had real skill in the search for authorities and citations to bolster his pleadings. In the remarkable Lincoln collection of Mr. Oliver R. Barrett in Chicago there is a large notebook filled with Herndon's careful memoranda of briefs and authorities for cases handled by Lincoln & Herndon during the eleven years following 1849. The reverse side of the notebook is a sort of law index, written entirely by Herndon, and giving the principal precedents on such topics as Corrupt Motives, Physical or Moral Nuisances, Trusts, and Specific Performances. These citations, made with painstaking care, prove that Herndon had examined, among many others, the Illinois, Arkansas, Missouri, New York and Kentucky reports, together with the standard law commentaries and digests, and that he had a thorough mastery of their contents.[18]

[16] I have been greatly aided in my study of the legal partnership by the expert advice of Mr. Oliver R. Barrett of Chicago, who first brought this basic division of labor to my attention.

[17] *Herndon's Lincoln*, II, 312–313.

[18] In many cases Lincoln presented Herndon's authorities to the court without any alterations — e.g., Webster *v.* French, 11 Ill. 254. I have examined this ex-

There is little evidence to show that during his partnership with Herndon Lincoln ever performed the drudgery of digging up legal precedents.[19] It is not a slur on Lincoln to note that his court work was based on the solid foundations furnished by his partner; almost every lawyer today has similar service rendered him by his assistants. When due allowances are made for his Southern prejudices, acidulous Albert T. Bledsoe, who practiced law in Springfield during the forties, seems to have remembered the situation fairly well. Lincoln, he wrote, "did his reading, as some men do their religion, by *proxy*, by his Good-Man-Friday, William H. Herndon, who, with creditable zeal and industry, would collect all sorts of cases and authorities for him. From these he would make his selections, and prepare his arguments, to the great disgust often no doubt, of Mr. Herndon, who saw so much of the material collected by him thrown aside as useless." [20]

I V

There was an easy informality about the Springfield law office. A client was welcomed by one of the partners with a few moments of conversation about the weather and crops, or Lincoln might be reminded of a story he had heard "down in Egypt" (southern Illinois). Usually the senior partner interviewed the client, heard his tale of trouble, and gave advice. If adjudication appeared desirable, he would frequently write out the declaration [21] in the client's presence, so that he should not make errors through defective memory. Even in a complicated case Lincoln had a gift for expressing the essential facts in a clear and concise fashion. The pleading, together with a praecipe, or formal notice that summonses were to be issued, was filed with the clerk of the appropriate court, and another cause was listed on the judge's docket for the next term.

This was the basic pattern for handling the many clients who came

tremely significant notebook through the kindness of Mr. Barrett. In the Herndon-Weik Collection there is a small book, known as the "Campaign Notebook," which was apparently used first by Herndon as a similar, though much smaller, index to legal precedents and authorities.

[19] In many of his pleadings Lincoln cited authorities and precedents (see Lewis *v.* Moffett, Herndon-Weik Coll.), but in almost every case he seems to have been writing from notes, probably prepared by Herndon.

[20] Albert Taylor Bledsoe, *"The Life of Abraham Lincoln* . . . By Ward H. Lamon . . . ," *Southern Review*, XIII, 332. Bledsoe later moved to Mississippi and became an ardent Southern nationalist.

[21] The declaration is the pleading which asserts that a certain state of facts exists and that in view of those facts the plaintiff is entitled by law to the redress from the defendant which his action claims. It is assumed for clarity that the Lincoln & Herndon client was a plaintiff.

into the office during a year. Each case, of course, was unique, but there was a certain sameness about them all. The run-of-the-mill business was tedious and monotonous, involving no very large principle and rewarding with no very large fee. Lawyers have to deal with people in trouble, and as a rule their business is with fundamental human emotions of a baser sort — greed, avarice, and hate. As Herndon wrote: "A law office is a dry place for incident of a pleasing kind. If you love the stories of murder — rape — fraud &c. a law office is a good place. . . ." [22]

A glance at the files of the Sangamon County Circuit Court for February 1860, the last year Lincoln was active in the law, reveals the sort of cases in which the partners ordinarily were engaged. One plaintiff sued for the payment of $1379.60 due from the sale of property; another petitioned a perpetual injunction to prevent renters from stripping his land of timber; yet another protested that his tenants had used up corn stored on the rented land. One Short claimed that he had been unable to bring his payments on a promissory note into Springfield because of the illness of his child; Harmon petitioned for the recalculation of a decree already granted him by the court; Mershom defended his failure to pay a promissory note by contending that the account of his obligations was incorrect. There were two cases for the foreclosure of lands listed as security for overdue notes and one suit for divorce brought by a husband who claimed his wife had committed adultery.

And so it went. Obviously it was not ordinarily an exciting life. The partners were concerned with "petty controversies or acrimonious disputes between neighbors about trifles . . . in attempting to decipher who was the owner of a litter of pigs, or which party was to blame for the loss of a flock of sheep, by foot rot; or whether some irascible spirit was justified in avowing that his enemy had committed perjury." [23] The law practice was a business, not a crusade for justice; it was hard work; it had to do with the sordid elements of human nature; never the same, it was nevertheless monotonous.

V

On the east side of the square in Springfield stood the white, Doric columned county courthouse. Above the county offices was the barn-like circuit court room, which occupied nearly the whole second floor. At one end of the room stood the bench, and immediately in front

[22] Herndon to Weik, February 18, 1887, Herndon-Weik Coll.
[23] Whitney, *Life on the Circuit*, 62–63.

there was a large semicircular table where lawyers stood when addressing the court. In the winter the room was heated by a square wood-burning stove, placed for safety in a box of sand, which also served as a receptable for quids of tobacco. Here lawyers and clients gathered before the court opened, joking and exchanging news.

Circuit court was held in Springfield two or three times a year, and the calendar was always crowded. The Sangamon bar in the fifties was the best in the state. For many years the court was presided over by rotund, jovial David Davis, whose informality was equalled only by his sense of justice. Before him appeared the best advocates Springfield could offer: Stephen T. Logan, whose unruly hair and disheveled clothing belied an orderly mind crammed with legal lore; suave, bland John Todd Stuart and his monumentally respectable partner, Benjamin S. Edwards; Elliott B. Herndon, always to his brother "an odd genius" [24] but in court a master of incisive irony; John Rosette, Republican agitator par excellence; and James C. Conkling, pompous pillar of society. Springfield was full of good lawyers. "History," to Herndon's way of thinking, "contained no names shining with brighter lustre than attached to the names . . . of early members of the [Sangamon] County Bar." [25]

By the fifties Lincoln & Herndon was regarded as one of the leading firms in the Illinois capital. Both partners appeared frequently in court, but their legal tactics were not at all the same. With Lincoln the emphasis was on casual, friendly questioning of the witnesses, free from technical matters of law. He would good-naturedly concede nine points out of ten to the opposing counsel, until it seemed he had given his case away. But on the tenth point he would insist, and it was the nub of the action. In presenting the arguments to the jury Lincoln excelled. With the utmost care he would go over the ground covered by the testimony until it seemed to his partner that he was driving his tacks with a sledge hammer. When the jury looked bored or lost, he would summarize a point in a well-told anecdote, phrased in simple, earthy terms. Herndon thought that though his partner "knew nothing of the laws of evidence — of pleading or of practice, and did not care about them: he had a keen sense of justice . . . throwing aside forms — methods and rules of all law." [26] For lucidity of statement and patient explanation to a jury Lincoln had no equal in Springfield.

Herndon's approach was entirely different. He read, thought, wrote

24 Herndon to Weik, October 4, 1888, Herndon-Weik Coll.
25 *Illinois State Journal,* February 22, 1876.
26 "Lincoln as Lawyer Politician & Statesman," undated Herndon monograph, Herndon-Weik Coll.

HERNDON ABOUT 1870

This is the earliest known picture of Herndon, who was camera-shy. On May 23, 1870, he wrote Ward Hill Lamon: "I never had a photog taken — dont know how it would look." A drawing based on the above likeness appeared in Lamon's *Life of Abraham Lincoln* in 1872.

MY PARTNER & FRIEND, LINCOLN

This recently discovered photograph, made probably in 1860, shows the Lincoln Herndon knew and loved. "He is a good man," Herndon wrote Charles Sumner on June 20, 1856; "he loves man — the rights of man . . . Lincoln is for human freedom."

rapidly. He dashed off legal papers in nervous spurts of energy, with much splattering of ink. Though his clients were usually perfectly satisfied with his services, he at times acted impetuously, before making a careful examination of his facts and arguments.[27] He questioned witnesses briefly and humorlessly; he spoke rapidly and positively; he made short, impassioned gestures; when he became heated he might explode into profanity. He was a man under tension.

There was a kind of wild determination in the way Herndon managed a case in court. He never conceded an issue but battled fiercely over each minor point. Far more than Lincoln he was likely to use every technical legal trick in his bag, even when it could only delay certain defeat. Herndon was a popular man with the juries. Partly this was due to his affectation of kinship with the common man, which went over well in agricultural Sangamon County. He was startlingly informal in court; he occasionally swore; he was intentionally careless in his dress when he appeared in court. He would "often allow his trouser legs to rest in the top of one boot," and on a famous occasion, growing heated in his argument, he pulled off his coat and, flinging it aside on the floor, proceeded to address the jury in his shirt sleeves.[28] He was eloquent, too, in his own way, emphasizing an emotional appeal in "strong energetic & massive language."[29] To his nephew Herndon confided: "When you get tears on the jury, you win your case."[30]

Herndon considered that he was "*possibly* as popular a man as Lincoln, and *possibly* as good a lawyer."[31] In his later years he became careless and was regarded as "a good offhand lawyer, [who] . . . as a rule did not spend much time in the preparation of his cases," but even his enemies had to admit that he "was of good repute — not strong as a lawyer but truthful."[32] Any effort to compare Lincoln and Herndon as lawyers breaks down because of their entirely different approaches to legal proceedings. Each was effective in his own fashion, and fortunately each complemented the other.

[27] Newton, *Lincoln and Herndon,* 252–253.
[28] Interview of Weik with John C. Lanphier, March 8, 1925, Herndon-Weik Coll.
[29] Herndon to Parker, May 13, 1854, Herndon-Parker MSS.
[30] Statement of James S. Miles, Sr., to me, November 14, 1944.
[31] *Illinois State Journal,* September 24, 1883.
[32] Newton, *Lincoln and Herndon,* 252; interview of Weik with John C. Lanphier, March 8, 1925, Herndon-Weik Coll.

VI

On one matter the partners were in perfect agreement — both disliked to be left out of any important litigation. They kept a keen watch on affairs and when a major suit was pending became fidgety lest Lincoln & Herndon have no part in it. The decade following 1850 was a period of rapid railroad expansion in Illinois, and courts were full of suits concerning right-of-way, stockholders' control over companies, and obligations of carriers to passengers. Railroad practice was the most remunerative branch of the law, and a railroad attorney corresponded to the present-day corporation lawyer.

One of the largest issues brought before Illinois courts in the 1850's was the question of a county's right to tax the lands of the Illinois Central Railroad which lay within its limits, and the decision involved millions of dollars — indeed, the very existence of the railroad itself. Lincoln was consulted by Champaign County officials as to legal procedure but no steps were then taken to assess the company's lands. In September 1853 he learned that adjoining McLean County had determined to tax the company's property and that an effort would be made to bring a suit as a test case before the Illinois Supreme Court. The railroad now offered to engage Lincoln, but he felt "somewhat trammelled" by his previous negotiations with Champaign officials. He informed the clerk of that county that his services could still be retained, but he added quite frankly: "The question . . . is the largest law question that can now be got up in the State, and therefore in justice to myself, I can not afford, if I can help it, to miss a fee altogether." Neither county employed Lincoln, however, and he promptly wrote the railroad officials: "I am now free to make an engagement for the road, and . . . you may 'count me in.'" [33] It proved to be a very profitable association, as Lincoln and Herndon eventually received five thousand dollars for their services in the case.

Herndon had a similar problem with the little Tonica & Petersburg Railroad, which had secured subscriptions to its stock by promising every landowner along the projected route that a depot would be located just adjacent to his property. Once the pledges were secured, the company forgot its promises and farmers found themselves little nearer a rail stop than before. Indignant Menard and Mason County citizens refused to pay their subscriptions, and the company went to court to collect the sums pledged. Herndon was engaged by his friend Richard Yates, an official of the railroad, to bring one of these suits to

[33] Tracy, *Uncollected Letters*, 47; Nicolay and Hay, *Works*, II, 179–180. On the preliminaries of the Illinois Central case see Beveridge, *Lincoln*, I, 584–588.

trial. Herndon drew up his papers carefully and predicted a judgment for the company. "This is to be a test case," he informed Yates, "& will be fought from the 'but' up." "I have been asked by several persons to defend in those Cases . . . springing out of the R. R Co affairs," he added, "and have not yet consented to act for the defence." But in view of the circumstances "Would it not be prudent in your Co. to make a permanent Engagement with some one — say pay them $500., a little more or less, Commencing from this date?"[34]

The railroad did not immediately retain the "some one" Herndon had in mind, and he grew nervous over the good fees he was missing. In two weeks he again wrote Yates that the farmers and townspeople of Athens, Illinois, had offered him five hundred dollars *to tear up the County subscription to your Road.*" "I have always studied your side of the Case, and would rather take your view; because I am so Educated — have always studied your side," he pointedly told his friend, "but am put up on the other side well enough to defeat you." This time there was no mistaking his meaning; Yates's secretary briefed the letter as: "W H Herndon Wants retainer or will take other side and defeat you."[35] The threat was effective, for Herndon was employed by the Tonica & Petersburg, brought several suits in favor of the railroad, and — as an anticlimax — lost both of the company's cases which he argued in the Supreme Court.

VII

Springfield furnished the nucleus of the Lincoln & Herndon practice. The number of cases argued by a lawyer does not, of course, really reflect the professional standing of the advocate, and in any case such statistics cannot be complete for the Illinois courts, since the records as a general rule omit the names of defendants' attorneys. In 1850 the Lincoln-Herndon firm was just getting reestablished after the senior member's return from Washington, but even so early the partners were handling one out of every five cases tried in the Sangamon County Circuit Court — a practice exceeded only by that of the redoubtable S. T. Logan. Five years later Lincoln and Herndon led the Springfield bar in the number of cases argued and appeared in every fourth case on the court docket.[36]

[34] Herndon to Yates, October 6, 1857, photostat, collection of Mr. Thomas I. Starr.

[35] Herndon to Yates, October 20, 1857, *ibid.*

[36] At the March 1850 term of the Sangamon County Circuit Court 177 cases were listed. S. T. Logan appeared in 46; Lincoln & Herndon in 35. In March 1855, of 351 cases docketed, Lincoln & Herndon argued 92; their nearest rivals, Stuart

The Lincoln & Herndon practice was a fluctuating one. During the fifties the partners' interest in politics worked to their financial detriment, for correspondence was often neglected and practice slumped while Lincoln and Herndon were "dabbling in politics, and of course neglecting business." [37] Based on admittedly incomplete data, the following table gives some idea of the yearly variations in the firm's business in the Sangamon County Circuit Court: [38]

1850	—	Lincoln and Herndon were connected with	18%	of	all	cases.
1851	—	" " " " " "	17%	"	"	"
1852	—	" " " " " "	18%	"	"	"
1853	—	" " " " " "	34%	"	"	"
1854	—	" " " " " "	30%	"	"	"
1855	—	" " " " " "	25%	"	"	"
1856	—	" " " " " "	20%	"	"	"
1858	—	" " " " " "	9%	"	"	"
1861	—	" " " " " "	8%	"	"	"

Examination of the court records reveals that most of Lincoln's and Herndon's work in the Sangamon County Circuit Court — and this constituted the major part of their practice — was performed under the firm name. The cases where either partner appeared alone or with another lawyer, while by no means exceptional, were not very numerous.[39]

VIII

Illinois was divided into a number of court districts, in each of which a circuit judge was elected. For many years David Davis presided over the courts of the Eighth Judicial District, which sprawled out over central and eastern Illinois and at times included fifteen large counties. He was required by law to make a semiannual pilgrimage around his circuit, holding court for a week or so in each county in his

---

& Edwards, had 63. Statistics compiled from Judge's Dockets of Sangamon Co. Cir. Court for these terms.

[37] Nicolay and Hay, eds., *Works*, II, 278.

[38] Statistics compiled from the Judge's Dockets of the Sangamon Co. Cir. Court for the years indicated. I have been unable to find dockets for the missing years. The percentage includes cases argued by the firm alone, by the firm in connection with other lawyers, by either partner alone, and by either partner in connection with another lawyer. Since the number of cases docketed increased sharply during the decade, the numerical decline in number of cases handled by Lincoln and Herndon was not so great as the table above might indicate.

[39] In 1853, for example, the Lincoln & Herndon firm alone was listed for 208 cases; Lincoln & Herndon appeared together along with other attorneys in 7 additional cases; Lincoln appeared alone or with another associate in 13 cases; Herndon appeared alone or with another lawyer in 23 cases.

district.[40] Since not even Sangamon County could offer a lawyer a regular, year-round business, it became the custom for a number of advocates to ride the circuit, traveling with the judge from courthouse to courthouse and pleading such cases as were offered them.

Unlike most of the Springfield lawyers, Lincoln traveled the whole Eighth Circuit with Judge Davis twice each year, even after Sangamon County itself was removed from that district. The day-by-day records of Lincoln's life reveal a regular spring and fall migration over the circuit, and sometimes he remained away from home two or three months. To the people on the circuit he became an institution; he was known to nearly every man in central Illinois. With an established reputation for integrity and ability, he could nearly always secure business in any county. Besides, it was good politics to be out among the people.

Herndon, on the other hand, generally stayed in Springfield. As circuit court in adjoining Menard County, in the First Judicial District, conflicted with sittings of Judge Davis's court, Lincoln could not attend, and after 1849 Herndon represented the firm at Petersburg. The judge's dockets for the Menard court reveal that after 1850 Herndon handled all cases there in his own name — not in that of Lincoln & Herndon. He built up a reputation as "a distinguished Lawyer," [41] and at almost every session of the Petersburg court appeared in more cases than any other out-of-town attorney. After 1856 Herndon's Menard practice declined, partly because he was increasingly absorbed in politics, partly because his affiliation with the distrusted Republican party offended Democratic Petersburg.

At times Herndon went with Lincoln to other county courts, but he was never one of the regular riders of the circuit like Lincoln, Ward Hill Lamon, Leonard Swett, and Henry C. Whitney. His own estimate that he was with Lincoln on the circuit one-fourth of the time seems a generous one.[42]

This circuit court life was something more than a business of making a living; it was a way of life. Every schoolboy is familiar with tales of Lincoln on the circuit: the trips in buggies or carryalls over muddy and all but impassable roads; the informality of court procedures; the ambulatory law offices "on the sunny side of a court house" or "under the shade of a convenient tree"; the free and easy congeniality of judge, lawyers, and witnesses in the tavern after court adjourned; the

[40] Thomas, "Lincoln and the Courts, 1854–1861," Abraham Lincoln Assoc., *Papers, 1933*, 47–103.
[41] C. Worthington to I. S. Merriam, March 2, 1860, Robert Todd Lincoln Coll.
[42] *Herndon's Lincoln*, II, 309.

judge's *"orgmathorial* [43] court" hilariously held to try any lawyer who committed a breach of decorum; and, above all, the storytelling that went on until far into the night.[44] As the years went by, the railroad took the place of the irregular stagecoach, and most of the lawyers would return to their homes over the week end. By 1860 a glamorous and distinctively American institution had generally disappeared.

It was not purely a matter of business that Herndon did not usually travel with his partner. The circuit life was a part of Lincoln, and he loved every minute of it. To Herndon, on the other hand, "to travel on the Circuit . . . was a soul's sore trial." Years later he recalled with distaste: "No human being would now endure what we used to on the Circuit. I have slept with 20 men in the same room — some on bed ropes — some on quilts — some on sheets — a straw or two under them; and oh — such victuals — Good God! Excuse me from a detail of our meals. I would not undertake for a considerable [?] sum of money to write out my experience at the bar *while on the Circuit.*" A serious, thoughtful man, he could never really lose himself in the storytelling and rollicking at the end of the court day. "Such amusements," he felt in 1883, "would not be tolerated now in any American Society. . . ." [45]

Yet there were times when even Herndon enjoyed circuit life. "After court adjourned," he remembered with pleasure, "we lawyers would take a ramble in the woods — over the prairies — or through the village — anywhere to kill time — take a game of 'old sledge' or euchre for the cigars — in short anything to while away time. On such tramps we would discuss politics — talk over our cases — talk about the laws of nature. . . ." He recalled sitting up "till 1 or 2 o'c in the night" listening to "story telling — joking — jesting" until "Our sides & back would ake." There was an informality about the circuit which, in retrospect at least, pleased him. And in his old age, Herndon regretfully dreamed of "the jolly times we always had — the good drinks we had, and the songs we sang." The lawyers on the circuit, he thought, had a "good, jolly and a glorious time," yet it was a "rough — semi barbarous" manner of living, after all.[46]

[43] It was a made-up word.

[44] The best and most familiar account of these days on the circuit is Whitney, *Life on the Circuit,* 61–68, 174–197.

[45] Herndon to Isaac Newton Arnold, October 24, 1883, Arnold MSS.

[46] Herndon to Mrs. Leonard Swett, February 22, 1890, Swett MSS.; Herndon to Weik, November 13, 1885, Herndon-Weik Coll.; Herndon to Lamon, December 1, 1885, Lamon MSS.

IX

In the higher federal and state courts the Lincoln & Herndon firm did a flourishing business also, though the share of the junior partner was rather sharply limited. From 1855 to 1860 the partners were employed in ninety-one cases in the United States Court for the Southern District of Illinois in Springfield,[47] but as virtually all the pleadings and even minor legal papers are in Lincoln's handwriting it seems safe to assume that the senior partner did practically all of the work before the federal judge.[48]

In the Illinois Supreme Court most of the business was transacted in the firm name, though it was usually Lincoln who appeared in court. Herndon's record did not compare with the phenomenal 243 cases in which Lincoln was interested,[49] but he made a respectable showing. From his first appearance in the Illinois Supreme Court through the January term of 1861 Herndon is listed in the printed reports as attorney in eighty-nine cases, in thirty-six of which he was not associated with Lincoln. During the same period thirty-four cases are reported in which Lincoln appeared alone or with a lawyer other than Herndon.[50] These eighty-nine cases represent a larger practice than the small average of six or seven cases a year might indicate, for any one case might be argued before several terms of the court. Herndon usually appeared without assistance from Lincoln in cases appealed from Menard County.

Herndon's share in the winning of cases before the Supreme Court was large, for it was here that his citation of precedents had the most effect. Sometimes neither the printed nor the manuscript reports list him in connection with cases for which he did the all-important legal research. This is true, for example, of the Illinois Central suit involving the counties' right to tax property worth millions of dollars; for his services Lincoln received a $5,000 fee, which was divided with Herndon.[51] In the notable Dalby suit, involving the major question of legal

---

[47] Pratt, *Personal Finances,* 57.

[48] Angle, "Lincoln in the United States Court 1855–1860," Lincoln Centennial Assoc., *Bulletin,* No. 8. See also Woldman, *Lawyer Lincoln,* 132.

[49] Pratt, "Lincoln's [Illinois] Supreme Court Cases," *Ill. Bar Jour.,* XXXII, 23–35.

[50] These printed *Illinois Reports* are far from complete, do not always give all of the attorneys in each case, and sometimes list them incorrectly. The figures given above, therefore, are to be considered as rough ratios, not as the final word on Lincoln's Supreme Court practice.

[51] Though "Mr. Lincoln was known alone in the case," Herndon wrote, "I was in it and recd my $2,500." Herndon to Weik, December 5, 1887, Herndon-Weik Coll.

responsibilities of railroads and their agents to the traveling public, Lincoln & Herndon appeared for the appellee, who had been forcibly ejected from a train because of his unwillingness to pay an excessive fare.[52] Lincoln made the argument in court, but he based his entire case on Herndon's elaborate legal research.[53] In the decision, which has been cited in at least ten subsequent cases of major importance and which has been termed "the most far-reaching case . . . [Lincoln] ever argued in the Illinois Supreme Court,"[54] the Court followed Lincoln's persuasion and Herndon's precedents. It was another example of the partners' successful cooperation.

In the usual dramatic presentation of Lincoln's law work, Herndon's share is frequently overlooked. He was not associated with Lincoln in the McCormick reaper case, the Rock Island bridge case, or the Chicago sand-bar case, and his name did not appear in the printed reports in the Illinois Central case. Yet a study of the manuscript records proves that Herndon's part was an important one. At times Herndon felt gloomily: ". . . I made out his best briefs in the largest law cases and . . . Lincoln would argue his case from those briefs and get the credit for them while I was the power behind them."[55]

Such a complaint, of course, was not fair, for it is the work of actually presenting the case that determines the decision; anyway, Lincoln divided his fees equally with his partner. But it is true that Herndon's share of the law work was generally routine drudgery, which he hated but which had to be done. The only real exception was that Herndon, unlike his partner, took an active part in the defense of fugitive slaves brought before the United States Commissioner in Springfield; this was work that he loved and which he felt was service to the cause of liberty.[56]

Partly because of the monotonous nature of his work, Herndon came to dislike the law. In 1852 he had written cheerfully of having his "path . . . *chipped* or blazed" towards acquiring "a little reputation as a Lawyer. This accomplished I am done."[57] By the end of the decade, however, he felt that court proceedings were "utterly disgusting." Listening to "a Counsellor, who is expatiating on the solidity of a special plea with an *'absque hoc,'* and who is twisting up his mind into

[52] 19 Ill. 353–376.

[53] Herndon's careful searching of legal records for this case is attested by the voluminous papers preserved in the Herndon-Weik Coll.

[54] Woldman, *Lawyer Lincoln,* 164.

[55] "Ingratitude of Lincoln," undated Herndon monograph, Herndon-Weik Coll.

[56] Herndon's fugitive slave cases are discussed in connection with his antislavery activities.

[57] Herndon to Yates, July 23, 1852, Reavis MSS.

knots, attempting to show the substantial and essential difference between such a traverse, whose specific qualities are a *certainty* to a *certain intent* in *every particular,* and one whose properties only require *certainty* to a *common intent* in *every particular,*" he complained that in legal matters "Reason & Justice will never decide." Despising the "heated foaming discussion" of jurists, he wrote: "*I hate the Law:* it cramps me: it seems to me priestly barbaric. I am here above the suspicion of not knowing somewhat of the History — Spirit & Principles of the Law, and my flings do not Come from disappointment. I say I hate the Law." [58]

[58] Herndon to Parker, April 27, 1858, and January 15, 1859, Herndon-Parker MSS.

CHAPTER *iv*

A Good Position in Society

I

Springfield Ills March 29th 1842

The Mass Historical Society
  Gentlemen

Unacquainted with you as I am [began Herndon modestly], think not that this proceeds from a desire upon my part to be known in your city and by you as a society. Your object has often been a source of useful knowledge to me, because I think it is one of the most useful branches of practical information that we have. It has been said that History is philosophy teaching by example to which I concur. In short the cause of this letter to you can soon be explained. We here have no such thing as your institution. I wish to put such a thing on [*sic*] motion and I believe it can easily be done. Then please send me a copy of by laws and constitution; if you have any printed. By these I may know the exact objects of your society and the reason I do not know the exact object is, because I have not seen a full and satisfactory account; though I suppose its object is the dissemination of *Historical* knowledge. Please send me some lectures delivered by Everett, Adams and Webster or Bancroft to your society, now and from time to time as best suits your convenience. If it is ever in my power I will return the favors a thousand times[.] I have but one more request to make, and if you cannot do it as a society, will some young Gentlemen do it. That is I wish if they can be procured, some lectures delivered before any mechanical, agricultural, manufacturing and commercial community. Send them now and hereafter when they can be got with convenience. We have nothing of this kind out here and if we ever hear of such lectures it is a slight notice or a short extract which only excites our curiosity without having the means to gratify it. Whilst I took the N. A. Review I often got some in the back sheets. I should like to take that periodical again, but poverty is staring us all in the face. If I can succeed I will correspond with any of you and let you know all the particulars.

Your Ob^d Serv

Wm. H. Herndon

P. S.   I have inquired of Mr. Thayer who is from your city; where the society is. He says he does not know whether it [is] in Boston or not. I will not pay the postage upon this for this reason. It may never arrive where you are. Let this then be sufficient excuse [1]

Thus runs the earliest known letter of Billy Herndon. In many ways it is typical of the man and of his career. Its gaucherie, its pompous phrasing, its pretensions to learning were to characterize everything that Herndon ever wrote. But in spite of elements of comedy, this is a pathetically human document; it is the testament of a seeker of truth.

Sometimes Herndon was desperately lonely in Springfield. The busy Illinois capital was concerned with courts and legislatures and governors. Its nineteen dry goods stores, one wholesale and six retail groceries, four public houses, four drug stores, one book store, two clothing stores,[2] were adequate for physical needs, but they did not help in the pursuit of wisdom. Like witty young John Hay, Herndon occasionally felt stranded "on the dreary wastes of Springfield — a city combining the meanness of the North with the barbarism of the South." [3]

It was not that Herndon was ashamed of Illinois — far from it. He thrilled with pride at the saga of the pioneers. He boasted of the intrepid souls who had braved the wilderness to carve a commonwealth out of the prairie. Had there ever been a people so generous, so bold, so true? "These men were great men in any sense and would have been great anywhere and under any circumstances . . . : they had great ambition and overflowed with manly spirit — health and strength: they came here to fight their way upward and they did so. . . ." "I think that by nature we were a great people," he wrote, identifying himself with the pioneers. "We were rude and rough — had no polish nor culture. Each man and woman was himself or herself. Individuality — distinct individuality was the rule. Each followed his inclinations and despised imitation. Lincoln was Lincoln — Grant Grant — Douglas was Douglas." [4]

Passionately he loved the rocks and streams of the Sangamon country. From his early boyhood he had rambled over the bottoms hunting.

[1] MS., Mass. Hist. Soc.

[2] John Mason Peck, *A Gazeteer of Illinois* (1837), 296.

[3] Tyler Dennett, *John Hay: From Poetry to Politics*, 32.

[4] "Lincoln as Lawyer Politician & Statesman," undated Herndon monograph, Herndon-Weik Coll.; Herndon to Truman H. Bartlett, July 8, 1887, Bartlett MSS.

Friends nicknamed him "Injin Bill" or "Turkey Bill," "for the reason, if he ever got after a deer or turkey he was always sure to capture it, if it took him two days." [5] It was not so much the hunting he cared for as the outdoors. "I love nature better than most men," he confessed. During the winter it seemed that he could not bear the confinement enforced by snow and ice; he longed for the days when "Spring . . . sent her electricity along the earth and made her smile in flower bushes," and for April, when nature invited "its lovers to '*Promenade all*' — dance a universal waltz." [6] In the middle of a letter on books and politics he would break off abruptly: "Let me turn . . . to something that my heart is full of — : namely — Spring has come, and the martin has returned — now twittering on the eves of our houses." [7]

When spring did come he could not bear the office. He had to see nature in the face, and off he would go on a long ramble through the Sangamon bottom. He had eyes for everything: the gooseberries in almost full leaf, the catbird fluttering along the ground, the lamb tongue, the Johnny-jump-up, and that universal flower, the bluebell. Up in an elm tree he saw the squirrels luxuriating. "A little fellow runs out as far as his limb & weight will let him; he cunningly puts out his paw and pulls the limb in and eats off the bud, and then lets the limb fly back again. . . . [O]ne, just now, got tired of his place; and so he wets his paw and stands quivering but one instant — leaps to and fastens his claws in an other limb, which waves in the wind with the shock. . . ." Farther on a fat and nimble bass played back and forth in Spring Creek; "he sees his shadow — supposes it is an other fish, for he seems to *woo* it — twists his tail, as if in love, and wants to hug his shadowy companion, yet it slips away from him." [8]

II

Solitary communion with nature could not satisfy Herndon's intellectual longing. During the course of a winter ramble along the Sangamon he would find "a large snag in the ice . . . , and the snow for some yards has been blown from the ice, leaving a clear path west of the snag, the wind having blown from the east." For yards he could "see the diverging paths of the wind, widening every inch from the tree . . . untill [*sic*] wholly lost by cross currents and its own failing power." Instantly his brain quivered with excitement. Here was a

[5] "Hunting Experience of R. W. Diller," *History of Sangamon County, Illinois* (1881), 181.

[6] Herndon to Parker, May 14, 1857, and April 7, 1858, Herndon-Parker MSS.

[7] Herndon to Caroline H. Dall, March 4, 1861, Dall MSS.

[8] Herndon to Parker, May 14, 1857, Herndon-Parker MSS.

curious phenomenon, one "worthy of study: the laws of winds — if they have any laws, can here be seen." And the snag in the ice led directly to a snag in Herndon's own thinking: Would this not also be an opportunity to study natural law in general? *"Is there any law in anything . . . ?"* he would query; *"Is not the idea of Law an abstraction?"* [9]

Feverishly he sought someone to talk to. In the second-story law office he and Lincoln and other Springfield wits would thresh over these abstract questions, but they usually found a high proportion of chaff. They talked of problems that have always haunted the minds of thinking men: What is the nature of the universe? Is there a natural law? What is the mind of man? Or they turned to ethical questions: Could there be an action "motiveless and disinterested — holy — pure, free from all selfishness"? [10]

Frequently they reverted to an incident that was one of Lincoln's favorites. As a small boy in Indiana, he had had to drive the horse at a gristmill. In a hurry, he had kept prodding the animal along, shouting: "Get up, you lazy old divil." Finally the mare kicked out and knocked the lad unconscious, just as he had yelled: "Get up, you — ." For hours young Abraham lay senseless, but when he did revive, he at once completed his admonition: " — old divil." In their bull sessions Lincoln and Herndon repeatedly puzzled over the questions: "why was not the whole expression uttered [when the lad regained consciousness]; & . . . why finish at all?" "We came to the conclusion," Herndon wrote, "I being somewhat of a psychologist as well as physiologist — he aiding me & I him — , that the mental energy — force had been flashd by the will on the nerves & thence on the muscles; and that that energy . . . had *fixed* the muscles in the exact shape . . . to utter those words — That the kick *shocked* him — *checked* momentarily the action of the muscles; and that so soon as that check was removed . . . by a returning flow of life . . . that the muscles fired off . . . acted automatically. . . ." [11]

But such homebred speculation failed to satisfy Herndon. He longed to have illumination from brighter lights than burned in Springfield. At Illinois College he had acquired an unmanageable appetite for books. A gullible law student thought that "in addition to all his professional reading, Mr. Herndon read every year more new books in history, pedagogy, medicine, theology, and general literature,

[9] Herndon to Parker, January 24, 1857, Herndon-Parker MSS.
[10] "Lincoln Individually," undated Herndon monograph, Herndon-Weik Coll.
[11] Herndon to Lamon, March 6, 1870, Lamon MSS. Compare Nicolay and Hay, eds., *Works*, VI, 28.

than all the teachers, doctors, and ministers in Springfield put together." [12] On his desk the *Westminster Review* lay beside the *Atlantic
Monthly*, and on his shelves were authors almost unknown in the Mississippi valley — Darwin, Kant, Spencer, Renan, Locke, Fichte, Buckle,
Froude. By his own account, Herndon's library cost four thousand
dollars,[13] and in those days when most families were proud to boast
of a Bible and a Shakespeare, Springfield regarded it as an incredible
extravagance. As late as 1866 a sophisticated Easterner was convinced
that Herndon's was one of the best private libraries in the West.[14]

III

"I am a southerner — born on southern soil — reared by southern parents," Herndon confided to a friend, "but I have always turned
New-Englandwards for my ideas — my sentiments — my education — ." [15] With poignant longing he yearned for Boston and *"the
world of matter and man."* [16] He could not praise highly enough the
great flowering of New England culture. Charles Sumner was to Herndon veritably "a man all over — inward & outward — from head to
foot"; Henry Ward Beecher, so "strong, vigorous, original — brave,"
was "a new rose fresh from the garden of the Almighty forces"; Wendell Phillips's oratory made Billy's nerves "snap & crackle"; and Ralph
Waldo Emerson was the real "genius of the spiritual and ideal." [17]

But to Herndon the noblest of them all was Theodore Parker. He
admired everything about the great Transcendentalist minister: his
enormous erudition, his religious liberalism, his boundless enthusiasms,
his limitless sympathy for the oppressed. Between the urbane and educated Parker and the backwoodsy Herndon there was indeed a vast
gulf, yet in his faith in natural law, his unquestioning acceptance of
the democratic dogma, and his courageous battles for the underprivileged, Parker was expressing ideals that the Illinoisan cherished.[18]
Billy purchased everything the Boston minister published; he was
"pulled" to Parker's writings. With childlike naïveté he wrote the

---

[12] Rankin, *Personal Recollections*, 119–120.
[13] Herndon to Weik, December 29, 1885; "Lincoln's Philosophy & Religion,"
undated Herndon monograph, Herndon-Weik Coll.
[14] Townsend, *The Real Abraham Lincoln*, 4–5.
[15] Herndon to E. L. Pierce, March 4, 1861, Herndon-Weik Coll.
[16] Herndon to Parker, April 28, 1856, Herndon-Parker MSS.
[17] Herndon to Parker, October 30, 1855, and February 16, 1856, *ibid.*; Herndon to William Lloyd Garrison, November 23, 1858, Garrison MSS.; Herndon to
Joseph Smith Fowler, February 18, 1886, collection of Mr. C. N. Owen of Chicago.
[18] The definitive biography of Parker is Henry Steele Commager's vivid *Theodore Parker*.

preacher: "May I say You are my Ideal — strong, direct, energetic & charitable." [19]

In this fashion began a correspondence that lasted till Parker's death. Herndon was happy to find in this new friend a confidant with whom he could discuss everything — philosophy, nature study, and law practice, religion, politics, and books. "I am troublesome I know," Herndon's letters would begin apologetically, "yet I am bothered, and want to free myself, if I can." And off he would be on his latest disquisition on the laws of the winds, on the "All-All," on "zo-ophyte & man," on the nature of law and special providence. [20] If Parker grew restive under the downpour of amateur philosophizing, he never gave a sign but wrote to Herndon as often as his crowded schedule would permit. Taking time off from his sermons, his lectures, the thousand letters he averaged in six months, "besides a variety of other work belonging to a Minister & Scholar," he apologized to his much valued friend Herndon for apparent neglect and praised Billy's brave manly words. [21] With infrequent letters he sent his sermons and published lectures, for which he would accept no money. In the intercourse Parker was not the loser, for Herndon furnished him real insight into behind-the-scenes developments in Western politics. And, as Billy wrote: "I do you and Emmerson [*sic*] or rather *Truth* some good here. I have made presents of your sermons . . . rather than not have them read." [22]

It was a peculiar friendship. Herndon and Parker met only twice, each time under unfortunate circumstances. After much prodding by Herndon, Parker came to Springfield in the fall of 1856 to lecture on "The Progressive Development of Mankind." It was the very worst time of the year, immediately prior to a presidential election, and Springfield people, tired out by constant campaign addresses, neglected to attend. Herndon himself was just back from a Republican speaking engagement and described himself as "worn down . . . — was not well — had neglected my person — my clothes — my home — office all — all." It had been his hope to have a long chat with Parker in order "to state . . . things as they exist west," but he was so embarrassed by his shabby clothing and so mortified by a misunderstanding as to financial arrangements for the lecture that his plans for enter-

---

[19] Herndon to Parker, May 13, 1854, Herndon-Parker MSS.

[20] Herndon to Parker, February 1857, *ibid.*

[21] Parker to Herndon, April 17, 1856, *ibid.* Apparently a good number of Parker's replies to Herndon have been lost.

[22] Herndon to Parker, June 11, 1854, *ibid.* Herndon gave Lincoln a complete set of Parker's writings. Jesse W. Fell to Lamon, September 26, 1870, J. S. Black MSS.

taining the visiting celebrity were *"cut . . . through."* Parker left for the East none too favorably impressed by Illinois or by Herndon.[23] Later, in 1858, Herndon visited Boston and received an equally inhospitable reception. The Herndon-Parker friendship, however, was able to stand the stress of personal incompatibility, and the two continued to exchange long letters. "The reason I write to him," Herndon confided to Parker's wife during a serious illness of the minister, "is this — He is about the only man living who can hold me steady. That is a decided compliment." [24]

Contact with Parker did much to stimulate Herndon's mental development. Always disposed to talk in glittering abstractions and fond of the largest words Webster could provide, Herndon considered himself something of a backwoods philosopher. His reading, his correspondence with Eastern thinkers, and above all his clairvoyant intuition qualified him, he felt, to tackle the most abstruse problem. He acquired the habit of talking in philosophical terminology about everyday affairs. Even in politics he was to apply his metaphysics. "Let us," he would counsel his friends, "philosophise intently — broadly — generously upon these various phenomena in Springfield — Washington — Boston &c." [25]

IV

In what might rather pretentiously be termed the philosophical system of William H. Herndon there was little if anything original. In the main stream of American thought, Billy was only a ripple. Nevertheless, his gropings after truth must not be dismissed too lightly. Abstract thought was rare on the frontier, and the wonder is not that Herndon philosophized so poorly but that he bothered at all.

Billy's most ambitious effort was presented in a twenty-page pamphlet entitled *Some Hints on the Mind,* originally a lecture — or as he put it, "a *Conversation* Stenographed"— read to "some few friends" in March 1864.[26] Though he had no share in having the lecture printed, Herndon was far from ashamed of his product. He was sure he had *"stumbled* upon a principle of the mind, if not its law." This remarkable new idea would for the first time "Compell all the mind's manifestations [to] bend — bow & *squat."* So stimulating was the pride of authorship that he thrust a copy upon Ralph Waldo Emerson, with a

23 Herndon to Parker, December 27, 1856, Herndon-Parker MSS.
24 Herndon to Mrs. Lydia Parker, March 30, 1857, *ibid.*
25 Herndon to Trumbull, March 2, 1857, Trumbull MSS.
26 Herndon to Hart, November 23, 1866, Hart MSS.

request that he have the pamphlet reviewed in the Eastern periodicals. Another copy went to Henry C. Carey, the Pennsylvania economist, whose works Billy had long admired. Herndon was very proud of his psychological conclusions. "In my Theory," he wrote, "I have no essences no substances — no quiddities — no entities, and such other 'tom foolereys.' The mind is a very very simple thing — the most simple thing in the universe. I try to be governed by Common sense, but may fail." [27]

In retrospect Herndon's thoughts seem neither so novel nor so important as he had imagined. For metaphysics Billy could spare no time. "Matter is, or nothing is," he ruled dogmatically, and was not disposed to argue the reality of the "hard, granitic and flinty" earth on which he lived. [28] Of far more importance was the question of how this world operated. In his answer Herndon was at one with all other Americans of that optimistic era: Natural law ruled the universe.

By natural law Herndon did not mean the intervention of a personal God. The frontier conviction that an omnipotent deity watched over every sparrow's fall carried no appeal for him. He was never swept away in the mass hysteria of the camp meeting and was never thrilled by the nasal oratory of the circuit rider, promising hell-fire and damnation to the unredeemed. The popular, sectarian religion of the frontier he recorded as "simply a feeling that will in the end die out, leaving the soul in the centre of darkness." [29] For himself, he was proud to be counted one of the *free thinkers or free thinking men*." "I was," he proudly boasted, "born a skeptic." [30]

Reacting against the Christian faith in an omnipotent deity, Herndon in his early years even doubted the existence of natural law as an objective reality; he was willing to see "method — order, & succession, or paths" in phenomena but not *Eternal Rule in Nature*, objective to the mind." If, he had concluded, rocks fell to the earth by gravitational pull, only the fact of the falling actually existed; the law was but "a generalization of and in the mind — . . . a subjective concept." [31]

But as he grew older, avoiding the issue of the independent existence of natural order, Herndon decided that "Law is a constant mode of operation — a rule by which things act and move, and have their

[27] Herndon to Julian M. Sturtevant, March 29, 1864, MS., Illinois College Library; Herndon to Joseph Gillespie, April 13, 1864, Gillespie Coll.; Herndon to Emerson, March 28, 1864, Emerson MSS.; Herndon to Henry C. Carey, April 4, 1864, E. C. Gardiner Coll.

[28] *Some Hints on the Mind,* 17.

[29] Herndon to Parker, April 17, 1858, Herndon-Parker MSS.

[30] Herndon, "Abraham Lincoln's Religion," *Index,* I, 5; Herndon to "Mr Foster" [the correct name was Joseph S. Fowler], August 15, 1889, MS., Lib. of Cong.

[31] Herndon to Parker, February 1857, Herndon-Parker MSS.

being." This included "all things which are created and exist," all matter and mind, with no exceptions.[32] The discovery of natural law, he declared, had been "a mighty declaration of the future independence of the human mind." "The idea of law," he predicted, "will in the end free our race from all errors and all superstitions." [33]

V

Truth, Herndon felt, could be achieved not alone from books, nor by the labored processes of logic. Indeed, to arrive at a natural law was more a matter of emotion than of reason. Doubtless Isaac Newton had been thinking about "the facts and their relations that surrounded matter"; doubtless he had observed "that the earth wheeled round on its own axis, the north pole grinding in crushed ice . . . day and night — year in and year out, bringing summer and fall, winter and spring." But it was not until he commenced trembling with the tremendous emotional experience of stumbling on the principles of attraction and repulsion that he was able to formulate the law of gravitation. Law dawned on him, intuitively, dim at first, but the emotion grew apace. Newton, added Herndon, must have been struck by too much emotion to make the necessary mathematical calculations to prove his theory.[34]

In the same fashion, thought this frontier Emerson, truth was accessible to all men; to reach it was a matter of "mud instinct" and "dog sagacity," of seeing "to the gizzard" of a question.[35] In this position Herndon was absolutely at one with the Transcendentalist thinkers of the East whom he admired so greatly. It was an axiom of the Transcendentalist faith that the questioning heart could "from the primitive Facts of Consciousness given by the power of instinctive intuition . . . deduce the true notion of God, of Justice and Futurity." [36] It was a noble belief in the innate goodness of the universe and in the perfectibility of human society that bound such men as Emerson, Thoreau, Parker, and Bronson Alcott together. In his small way Herndon was a disciple of these great masters.

Since law could be reached by any seeker, no matter what his training, it was only natural that Herndon, a true Emersonian individualist,

[32] *Some Hints on the Mind*, 4.
[33] "Laws. Lincolns Philosophy & Religion," undated Herndon monograph, Herndon-Weik Coll.
[34] *Some Hints on the Mind*, 13–14.
[35] Herndon to Parker, November 24, 1858, Herndon-Parker MSS.
[36] *Theodore Parker's Experience as a Minister*, 43–44.

should try to make his own explorations. And off he went stalking through the thick underbrush of metaphysics. If he was less successful at this type of hunting, it should be remembered that other brave souls have also been lost in the philosophical jungle. Law for matter, Herndon concluded, had been discovered for all time by Isaac Newton. Darwin and Spencer had done similar service for the biological and societal worlds in providing the theory of evolutionary development.[37] There remained only the field of psychology, the study of the mind, and here Herndon felt he could pioneer.

Since all things are regulated by natural law, Herndon concluded there must be some fundamental principle underlying the manifestations of the human brain. Discarding the accepted phrenological jargon of sensations and manifestations and faculties, he compared the brain to a train. To get a true science of the mind, he decided, one had to sit with the engineer of the locomotive, with the passengers in the cars, and with the spectators on the depot platform. This many-sided view would teach the most skeptical that the mind was not a bundle of faculties but "a unity — *a one*." [38] The functioning of the brain must be explained simply as "creative activity" playing on "the rude (first) Conscious perceptions *in* the mind, thereby *creating* thoughts — ideas — words — language — science — &c." In precisely the proportion that creative activity played on perceptions and that a man transformed his ideas into actual practice, he would rise "to his destiny — his highest being." This led, Billy asserted, to startling conclusions as to the nature of insanity and idiocy, which he would disclose in a succeeding lecture, but an eager posterity waited in vain for his never revealed secret.[39]

Once man realized that the natural law of the mind could be discovered and formulated Herndon felt sure the broad highroad of progress would be opened. There was literally no limit to man's future. That day would surely come when "man will be his own Providence and his own Rede[e]mer." [40] Under the banner of progress Herndon would greet the unseen with a cheer. "The Struggles of this age and

[37] It would be difficult to overemphasize the influence of Spencer on Herndon's thinking. Herndon carefully annotated and indexed his copy of Spencer's *The Principles of Psychology* (London, 1855) and evidently used it frequently. It is now owned by Mrs. Bertie Trainer of Springfield, Illinois.

[38] *Some Hints on the Mind,* 5, 9.

[39] Herndon to H. C. Carey, February 7 and March 23, 1865, E. C. Gardiner Coll.

[40] "Laws. Lincolns Philosophy & Religion," undated Herndon monograph, Herndon-Weik Coll.

succeeding ages for God & man — Religion — Humanity & *Liberty* with all their Complex and grand relations," he prayed, "may they triumph and Conquer forever, is my ardent wish and most fervent soul-prayer." [41]

VI

Herndon was not the man to endure an hour and see injustice done. He had no longing for the ivory tower. To those who urged the value of scientific detachment, he retorted: ". . . should I stand still like an Atheist and say this world is only a dancing concourse of atoms bound together by chance — the world is a farce, let it go? I cannot do so. I want a betterment of conditions and circumstances for all classes and all climes — here and everywhere." [42] He would run in every race and fight in every battle. Billy Herndon was a child of that universally optimistic age when everyone had the cure for the world's ills: all that one had to do was to read this book or hear that lecture, join this sect or form that colony, support this law or vote for that statesman, and the kingdom would surely come. It was the day of the crank, the crusader, and the crackpot. Elizabeth Cady Stanton and woman suffrage, William Lloyd Garrison and abolition, Neal Dow and temperance, John Humphrey Noyes and communal marriage, Dorothea Dix and eleemosynary reform, Charles Sumner and the peace crusade, Horace Mann and public schools, Albert Brisbane and Fourierism — all these and dozens of others were clamoring for support. Everybody had a cause. Everybody believed in immediate perfectibility through reform.[43] And in his own way, Herndon in Illinois carried on the great tradition.

He was so proud of his city and state that he fairly burst with civic spirit. He had a spoon in every kettle, a finger in every pie. If there was a railroad subscription, a school picnic, a handball club, a New England supper, a Thanksgiving ceremony, a Fourth of July festival in Sangamon County, Herndon was there — and usually talking. He had high ideals for his Athens on the prairies. As soon as he had returned from Illinois College one of his first moves had been to help found a Young Men's Lyceum in Springfield which "contained and commanded all the culture and talent of the place." This flourishing

[41] Facsimile of Herndon's inscription in Henry B. Rankin's autograph book, February 23, 1858, in Rankin, *Intimate Character Sketches*, facing p. 106. Appropriately enough this sentiment has been carved on Herndon's tombstone.

[42] *Letters on Temperance*, 7.

[43] The best study of the many reform movements in the prewar years is Alice Felt Tyler, *Freedom's Ferment: Phases of American Social History to 1860.*

institution was the scene of more than one "most wonderful lecture"; its members soberly believed that from their midst would "arise our future philosophers — our statesmen & our orators . . . a noble phalanx of pure disinterested patriots." [44]

Not content with his own excellent private library, Herndon was one of the most energetic members of the committee to organize the Springfield Library Association in 1856. The society was open to members who would subscribe at least five dollars in stock, and about a thousand dollars was pledged. When the stockholders first met, they elected officers, including Herndon as recording secretary, and according to the newspapers a better choice could hardly have been made.[45] The Library Association was to hold weekly meetings, at each of which members should present an oration, an original essay, and a formal debate. Though some might consider this fare dry, the constitution warned: "No smoking or refreshments, except water, allowed in the association room." [46]

VII

The Library Association sponsored lectures to stimulate Springfield and, incidentally, to fill its treasury. The Illinois capital had already heard some of the nation's choicest thinkers and entertainers. Ralph Waldo Emerson gave three lectures in the State House in 1853, and in what was termed "unquestionably the most delightful and popular lecture ever given to a Springfield audience," Bayard Taylor revealed the secrets of "The Arabs." [47] To Herndon's ecstatic joy, Henry Ward Beecher stopped in the Sucker city for a talk.[48] Shrill-voiced Horace Greeley of the New York *Tribune* appeared before a Springfield audience in 1856 and strongly hinted to Herndon that he would not object to a return engagement.[49] Springfield like the rest of "America in the mid-nineteenth century seemed willing to spend the evenings, and often many daytime hours as well, in listening to lectures on every

[44] *Herndon's Lincoln*, I, 189–190; Deniza Hay to J. A. Hay, December 16, 1837, MS., Ill. State Hist. Lib.; MS. of address delivered by James Cook Conkling to the lyceum, January 5, 1839, J. C. Conkling MSS.

[45] John Todd Stuart to Elizabeth Stuart, February 24, 1856, Stuart-Hay MSS.; *Illinois State Journal*, March 11, 1856.

[46] *Constitution, Regulations, and By-Laws of the Library Association of Springfield, Illinois* (1858).

[47] Angle, *"Here I Have Lived": A History of Lincoln's Springfield, 1821–1865*, 187.

[48] Herndon to Parker, October 30, 1855, Herndon-Parker MSS. Herndon thought, however, that Beecher "did not say all he felt."

[49] Greeley to Herndon, February 27, 1855, copy, Herndon-Weik Coll.; Greeley to Herndon, December 4, 1859, Greeley MSS.

variety of subject by almost any speaker who felt he had a message to impart." [50]

Attempting to capitalize on this fondness for public addresses, the Library Association planned a home-talent lecture course for 1857, and Herndon was asked to present the first lecture at Concert Hall. His subject was to be "The Analysis of the Beautiful," and the papers announced: "Those who are personally acquainted with Mr. Hr. know that he is capable of delivering a beautiful and eloquent address." This was not precisely true, for some of the friends who knew Herndon best considered this "a curious move" beyond his sphere. "*Wait & see*," he admonished them; "All I ask is good weather and a fair house; and then we shall see what we shall see — " [51] When December 5 came, the hall "was well filled with ladies and gentlemen" who frequently applauded the speaker. Exhibiting "deep study and refinement of thought," Herndon fired both philosophical barrels at his audience. He expounded the "relations of man to the external universe; the laws which govern matter; the correspondences of nature with mind, and the hidden sources whence spring our ideas of beauty." If, the reporter noted, "At times, perhaps, there appeared a mysticism and a trancendental [sic] obscurity in the treatment, . . . they were accompanied by a grandeur which only the more fixed and riveted the attention of the listener." [52]

There was considerable dissatisfaction with the plan of using Springfield talent; a visiting lecturer always had a world-girdling reputation. Still the Library Association was too timid to go after speakers very actively. "This is our rule," wrote Herndon concerning a proposed lecture of Wendell Phillips: "Let every or any lecturer come, we getting a crowd — preparing for him, and give us a '*Talk*' he paying for room and pocketing the whole funds." [53] Under such arrangements the quality of the visitors naturally fell off. By 1859 the lecture series could boast only of such minor luminaries as W. H. C. Hosmer, "the American Bard of Avon"; Mortimer "Doesticks" Thompson; and B. F. Taylor of the Chicago *Daily Journal*. So unsuccessful were the speakers that receipts for one evening's meeting totaled only two dollars.

By 1860 newspapers were sneering that "those . . . who consider the Association dead, are more than half right," but determined read-

[50] Tyler, *Freedom's Ferment*, 52.
[51] Herndon to Yates, December 29, 1857, photostat of MS. in collection of Thomas I. Starr. These words referred to a repetition of the address in Jacksonville on January 4, 1858, but doubtless they also applied to the Springfield première.
[52] *Illinois State Journal*, December 5, 1857.
[53] Herndon to "Mr. Wood," November 15, 1856, MS., Ill. State Hist. Lib.

ers with civic spirit would not easily give up. Blaming the failure on the "several indifferent lectures from *foreigners*," the library committee once again projected a course of twelve lectures "from talented *natives*," with admission at twenty-five cents and "ladies, accompanied by gentlemen, free." [54] The topics were certainly not exciting — eminently dull and respectable subjects like the Reverend J. H. Brown's discourse titled "Character as Bearing on Success in Life." Lincoln was scheduled to give his talk on "Discoveries and Inventions," and Billy was embarrassed for his partner when he rose before the audience. "I knew that Mr L was not fitted — qualified in any way to deliver a lecture to our people who were intelligent," he said; the speech was "a lifeless thing." [55]

Nor, if the newspapers can be trusted, was Herndon's own contribution well received. Though the *State Journal* had advertised his address with a masterly understatement that the treasury of the Library Association was not quite full, Billy drew an exceedingly small crowd for his "Sweep of Commerce" speech. His lecture, it was said, "was for the most part historic and could not fail to interest all, and when the lecturer indulged in anticipations of the future, or moralizing on the past, it was in the clear and comprehensive view of a man who has studied well his subject and shows himself capable both to please and interest." [56] But citizens of Springfield thought otherwise; they stayed away in droves. What made it so humiliating was that the night before, the notorious Lola Montez, mistress of the king of Bavaria, "a woman who has violated every known rule of life, mocked the sacredness of the marriage relation, and publicly sets at naught all that is beautiful and modest in womankind," had attracted no fewer than four hundred of Springfield's elite. Whether it was because, as one newspaper ambiguously phrased it, she was "almost clothed in male apparel" or, as another poetically reported, her voice was "as clear as a lighthouse beacon on a starry night," Lola had something that Billy could not offer. [57]

[54] *Illinois State Journal*, February 2, 7, and 21, 1860.

[55] *Ibid.*, April 28, 1860; Herndon to Weik, February 21, 1891, Herndon-Weik Coll. Lincoln had previously given this lecture at a number of the outlying communities.

[56] *Illinois State Journal*, March 19, 1860.

[57] Petersburg *Semi-Weekly Axis*, March 21, 1860; *Illinois State Journal*, March 15, 1860. Herndon repeated his lecture in Petersburg, where he drew a "large audience."

VIII

Not content with informing his neighbors, Herndon wanted to reform them. But there was a conflict between his crusading impulse and his political thinking. Like Lincoln,[58] Herndon was fundamentally a Jeffersonian democrat. It is true that in these prewar years both men were first Whigs and then Republicans, but after the forties it was difficult to determine who was wearing the mantle of Jefferson. Opposition to his father, attachment for Whig leaders in Illinois, and feeling on the slavery issue caused Herndon to abuse the Democratic party and to support conservative, centralizing political factions. In later years he was to be sorely ashamed of his choice.[59]

The federalist tendencies of the Whigs and Republicans did not represent Herndon's real position. "Governments," he declared, "are instituted among men for the purpose of promoting their general welfare, and to prevent wrong or injury to the rights of persons or property." This was not an unlimited gigantic implied power but a part of the constitutional contract that the people "should never inflict an injury on one single individual though the act promoted the welfare of the world." [60] Herndon was afraid of authority, of officeholders with vested interests in their jobs, of behind-the-scenes lobbyists. "I hate power . . . ," he said.[61]

Followed rigidly, such a political philosophy would seem to reduce the state to the bare minimum of suppressing crime and preserving the peace. But evil was stalking in the world — poverty, vice, disease. As a humane and feeling man Herndon could not but fight for a brave new world; ". . . the people in their wisdom," he conceded, "may prevent the wrong — legislate against the evil and promote the good, and the general welfare." He realized that towering opposition would confront any efforts to aid the oppressed. The American people were fat and easy — conservative. "Wealth gives us ease and power; office gives us influence; education makes us stubborn in our mode of thought." When the reformer appeared with his axe and rifle and Bible, demanding the adoption of his "shaggy, wild-eyed and bony" reforms, the conservatives and the hunkers howled like the wolf in the desert. But "We the reformers, see and know we are correct and right in reason and in humanity. We are abused, wronged, love our kith and kindred; we are scourged and weep; become strong and con-

[58] Randall, *Lincoln the President: Springfield to Gettysburg,* I, 23–25.
[59] Herndon, *Address on Free Trade vs. Protection* (1870), 19.
[60] Herndon, *Letters on Temperance,* 3.
[61] Herndon to Trumbull, February 19, 1858, Trumbull MSS.

quer." Right was with the reformer. "The State and people now demand [that] . . . good men and citizens . . . give up . . . privileges for the good of all; which is humanity." [62]

If it was a choice between being a contented moneybags or a wild-eyed crusader, Herndon felt he had no discretion. He burned with sympathy for the underprivileged. When reports trickled in of suffering in Ireland or Hungary, he was quick to speak for the oppressed. [63] Through reading and debate he became convinced that slavery was an evil, and his political activities after 1856 were centered about the problem of the Negro. In the crusade for woman's rights — which was at that time more for equal rights under the law than for suffrage — Herndon was on the liberal side. "For my life," he exclaimed, "I cannot see why there should be any distinction between men and women, when we speak of rights under government." [64] So eager was he to promote this cause that he took time from his professional duties to condense and summarize Illinois statutes on woman's legal position for Mrs. Caroline H. Dall, a minor Massachusetts crusader in the woman's movement.

In gratitude Mrs. Dall offered to mention Herndon in the preface of her book on woman's rights, but he modestly tried to decline. Perhaps, he declared, Mrs. Dall should "double me up and stick me in a note." "You and I are Strangers," he counseled, "and I am somewhat young and untried. I have never yet been put on the rack and so Cannot say what my soul would utter. I am untried. However, at present I occupy a good position in society . . . ; but I may fall, & so that would hurt you. *Be Careful.*" [65] Ignoring the warning, in the preface of her *Woman's Rights under the Law*, Mrs. Dall acknowledged her indebtedness to her Illinois friend for "books lent, and service proffered, with a generosity and graceful readiness cheering to remember."

IX

In another crusade Herndon was still more active — the cause of temperance. To those who know only of Billy's later habitual drunkenness it comes as a surprise to learn that for many years he was a sincere and devoted advocate of prohibition. It is easy to overestimate the importance of liquor in shaping Herndon's career. He grew up in an age when practically everybody drank. At almost every store a customer

[62] Herndon, *Letters on Temperance*, 3, 21–23.

[63] *Illinois Journal*, August 25, 1848; January 6, 1852.

[64] Herndon to Caroline H. Dall, quoted in Mrs. Dall's *Woman's Rights under the Law* (1862), 129.

[65] Herndon to Caroline H. Dall, February 28, 1860, Dall MSS.

who paid cash was entitled to a free swig of corn liquor from the community dipper. Billy was raised in a tavern-hotel. His father drank heavily. A "hail fellow well met and a little too generous and convivial," [66] the son staggered in his father's steps. Like many another drinker he soon found that liquor made dull conversation seem sparkling. "When I . . . wished to say something smart," Billy confessed, "I took a toddy as *exciter*. . . ." [67] That Herndon drank — and sometimes drank to excess — is undeniable. Yet before 1865 his habits were irregular rather than sottish, and at that not so irregular as those of some of his more distinguished contemporaries — Richard Yates, Ulysses S. Grant, or even Stephen A. Douglas, for instance.

Through his reading and through his wife's influence Herndon became convinced that drinking intoxicating liquor was wrong in principle and that it was ruinous both to the drinker and to his family. More as a matter of strengthening his own will than of convincing other people he joined the temperance movement. It was a lonely and losing battle that he fought, a struggle between a reasoning mind and a limitless appetite. In the years after the Civil War, desolated by the death of his partner, and impoverished by unwise investment, he let his appetite win. But in the prewar years he fought the good fight.

From the time he embraced the cause Herndon joined all the temperance organizations going. In the early forties he was a member of (or at least regularly attended the meetings of) the Washingtonians, reformed drunkards who sought to drag other sots from the gutters. [68] In the fifties Billy joined the Springfield Temple of Honor, a group pledged not to "make, buy, sell, or use as a beverage, any spirituous or malt liquors, wine, or cider, or any other alcoholic beverage." Herndon must have convinced his fellow members of his sincerity, for he was repeatedly elected to fill its offices and in 1855 was chosen president of the group. [69]

In spite of considerable success, temperance advocates over the country gradually came to despair of voluntary reformation of the drunkard. Where their earlier appeal had been a sweetly reasonable discourse on the sinfulness of drinking, now they produced a strident denunciation of the liquor manufacturer and retailer. "Remember," Herndon advised his comrades, "we do not attack a man's *right to drink*. . . . Remember we do attack the *right to sell*, and the whole

[66] Interview of Weik with Herndon, undated, Memorandum Book II, Weik MSS.

[67] Herndon to Weik, February 5, 1891, Herndon-Weik MSS.

[68] *Herndon's Lincoln*, II, 260–261.

[69] *Illinois Journal*, May 14, 1852; *Springfield City Directory, and Sangamon County Advertiser for 1855–6*, 55.

whisky traffic." [70] In 1851, after skillful lobbying by Neal Dow, the first state-wide prohibition law was adopted in Maine. The new "Maine Law" was imitated in Massachusetts, Vermont, Michigan, Rhode Island, and Connecticut before 1855, and temperance men everywhere began to advocate liquor control by legislative enactment.[71]

X

The year 1854 was the busiest of Billy's life. He had irons in a dozen fires. A growing law practice claimed much of his time. The renewal of the slavery controversy made for a reconsideration of his political orientation. It was the height of the temperance crusade. And to top it all off, in the spring elections, he was chosen mayor of Springfield. He had not sought the office, but when *"Many Democrats and Whigs"* publicly advertised that Herndon was their only choice, could he refuse to run? In spite of a last minute candidacy by one Presley A. Saunders, nonpartisan balloting gave Herndon a heavy majority.[72]

To be mayor of Springfield's 6,218 inhabitants was not a major responsibility. Billy was no stranger to the ways of city politics, for as city clerk and attorney he had during two terms attended city council meetings and drafted ordinances. He understood that his council sessions would ordinarily concern "Sales of Market Stalls," "G. L. Huntington & stable Nuisance," "4½ mills necessary for accruing expenses," "Notice to occupants on S.E. & N. S. Public Square to grade," "City scrip to be destroyed," "City pauper provided for," "Bridge on the Branch 8th St," and a hundred other petty items, trivial but necessary to the smooth functioning of a city government.[73]

But Herndon was not going to be just another mayor. There was a new spirit in the air. Citizens were tired of letting things jog along in the old way. It was no coincidence that in the same election citizens chose Herndon mayor and prohibited hogs from running loose in the square. People objected to the mud on the street — so deep that visiting Bayard Taylor was afraid he would lose his overshoes — to the horses hitched around the State House, to "the nuisance by the Post Office [where] . . . . the stench, if it does not knock one down, will

[70] Herndon, *Letters on Temperance*, 2.

[71] The best treatment of the prewar stages of the prohibition crusade is John Allen Krout, *The Origins of Prohibition*. On the Maine Law campaign in Illinois, with special reference to Lincoln's alleged share in the prohibition effort, see W. H. Townsend, *Lincoln and Liquor*, 63–89.

[72] *Illinois Journal*, March 9 and 17, April 5, 1854.

[73] All these and many other similar subjects were acted on by the city council at a single typical meeting on August 14, 1854. Springfield City Council Records (MS.), III, 445–448.

at least give him the staggers." They were ashamed of streets clogged with dog fennel in the summer. One local wit burst into rhyme on the subject:

> Let Romans boast their Coliseum —
> Greece of her sages dream;
> But when I sing of Springfield glory,
> Dog-Fennel be my theme.
>
> . . .
>
> O, City Council! for wise uses,
> Permit the plant to grow!
> It is a cloak for much street nuisance; —
> A cheap one too, you know.[74]

Still others wanted control of the local "doggeries" and the prohibition of the liquor traffic. The *State Journal* came out bluntly for changes: "a school house, a city hall, gas lights, plank streets, water works, fire engines." [75]

Billy was a reform mayor. Wasting no time on a formal inaugural, he proceeded at his first council meeting to outline the work he hoped to accomplish during his administration. The record of Herndon's twelve months as mayor shows that he kept his promise to do things. During that year there were no fewer than seventy-six meetings of the full city council, not to mention frequent sessions of the eight standing committees. Never had Springfield seen such a flurry of civic excitement. There should be no more horses hitched in front of the State House; the streets would be graded and plank walks laid; gas lighting was introduced; bonds were voted to help extend the Sangamon and North West Railroad Company to the state capital. The rickety market hall, a veritable eyesore, was ordered destroyed; lot owners were required to cut the dog fennel; and the owner of a smelly privy was ordered to remove it forthwith. A new city hall was rented for $250 a year; all men over twenty-one were required to work on the city roads or pay a tax substitute; and the police force was expanded by the simple expedient of making the mayor and council members *ex officio* city watchmen.

In long-range results the most important of Herndon's acts as mayor were his efforts to start a public school system. Billy fully understood the real need "that all the children in the city, the high and the low, the rich and the poor, may . . . receive a good, practical English edu-

---

[74] *Illinois Journal,* July 1 and 20, 1854.
[75] *Ibid.,* April 28, 1854. For a colorful picture of Springfield in the fifties see Angle, "*Here I Have Lived,*" 162–203.

cation."⁷⁶ It was a project in which he was especially interested, and he named himself chairman of the council's committee on education. Personally investigating the various sites suggested for the new public school buildings, Herndon supervised the expenditure of thousands of dollars to buy suitable lots in each of the city's four wards.⁷⁷ Though the schools did not begin operation until later, the Springfield educational system owed much to Billy's forceful advocacy.

XI

In spite of other solid and carefully planned measures Herndon's administration became famous — or notorious — in Springfield because of the imposition of city-wide prohibition. Probably it was known from the time he first became a candidate that Herndon was in favor of local prohibition; at any rate, the Temple of Honor was forced to deny that it had taken his part in the election.⁷⁸ Shortly after his inauguration, in response to a referendum, Herndon pushed through the council an ordinance forbidding the sale of any liquor, except for medicinal purposes, within a half mile of the city limits.⁷⁹

From the outset there was powerful opposition to the measure. Liquor interests were naturally outraged at the loss of their profits. Many another merchant feared, or professed to fear, that Springfield would lose business to communities where customers might buy alcohol. Irish immigrants joined for once with the Germans in denouncing this restraint on their personal habits. Though the cause was in a large measure nonpolitical, the Democratic *State Register* gave considerable support to the opponents of prohibition.

But behind Herndon and prohibition stood a strong muster of public opinion. Following Springfield's example by a matter of months, the state legislature adopted a Maine Law, to become effective when approved at a special election. During 1854 and 1855 the papers were flooded with editorials on the liquor question and with letters from earnest temperance workers. One saw whiskey-making as desecration of the Sabbath; another described intoxicating liquors as shooting a great "volley of hateful arrows around the fire-side"; still others wished to extend the fence of liquor control erected about Springfield "round the whole field" of Illinois. It was puerile and untrue that prohibition destroyed business, they said, and the city merchants, however

---

⁷⁶ *Illinois Journal,* April 11, 1855.
⁷⁷ *Ibid.,* June 14, 1854; Springfield City Council Records (MS.), III, 320–321.
⁷⁸ *Illinois Journal,* April 6, 1854.
⁷⁹ *Ibid.,* June 3, 1854. The popular vote was 468 for prohibition, 391 against. *Ibid.,* May 23, 1854.

much they might be opposed to it, surely would not violate the liquor law.

When there was a good fight, Herndon had to be in it. He was determined that his administration should stand or fall on the liquor issue; to enforce his ordinance he neglected some minor duties. As soon as the people had voted for prohibition, Herndon went in person to most of the "groceries" in Springfield and told their proprietors that "they *must* close their doors." "I told them kindly," he declared, "I intended to see the ordinances of the city executed — particularly the ordinance against the sale of intoxicating liquors. . . ." In a one-man campaign he gave "open public official notice of . . . [his] intention," and after that when he found any violation of the ordinance he turned the malefactors over to the police. These refreshingly novel procedures were, Herndon bragged in his valedictory as mayor, effective. "Women and children," he claimed, "can now walk through our streets, highways and alleys, at all hours, night or day, with scarce a fear of insult or harm. The peace, happiness and morals of this community have increased. . . . [U]pon the whole, great good and lasting results have followed. Not one half as much whiskey is drunk now as in former years." [80]

Herndon was not content to coerce citizens into obedience; he had to persuade them that prohibition was right in principle, right both for the city and for the state. When the *State Register*, that "slavite — whiskey, paper," [81] attacked the proposed state prohibition law as an unwarranted invasion of private rights and an illegal confiscation of property, Billy was glad of the excuse to get into the newspaper war. In a series of nine long letters appearing in the *Illinois Journal* through the early months of 1855 he attacked the *Register*, its editors, and the whiskey interests.[82] By quoting chapter and verse of legal authorities he proved that confiscation of property has been resorted to in American law enforcement and that a man's home is his castle only so long as his actions are innocent. So convincing was his argument that even the *Register* had to publish an editorial "admitting that we were wrong in our statement." [83]

Herndon's temperance letters were widely and extensively published in other Illinois newspapers, and in order to attain a wider cir-

[80] *Ibid.*, April 11, 1855.
[81] Herndon to Parker, April 12, 1855, Herndon-Parker MSS.
[82] Herndon's letters (usually signed °°°) appeared in the *Illinois Journal* between February 26 and March 20, 1855. Beveridge (*Lincoln*, II, 296n) suggests that Herndon also wrote a tenth letter, which appeared in the *Illinois Journal*, June 2, 1855. To me this appears unlikely.
[83] *Illinois State Register*, February 28, 1855.

culation were reprinted as a pamphlet. In his *Letters on Temperance* Herndon cited legal precedents; he gave statistics to reveal the fearful state of affairs operating against human life and the happiness and virtue of man so long as the "doggeries" should remain open; he played the emotional appeal against the fire that kindles insanity; he quoted the poor mother's wail to her child; he demonstrated that prohibition was one of the imperious laws of progress. What else could a man do?

Herndon's energetic administration made enemies. Some objected to the high taxes necessary to maintain improvements. Others deplored the necessity of having frequent council meetings. The city council, it was declared, had done as well as it could "without a *head.*" The mayor should draw his salary for administering the city government, not "for solely presiding, with the bombastic dignity of Dogberry, over the city fathers." Planning for a new election, some voters vowed: "We want no scheming busy bodies, who have . . . some personal end, or some peculiar hobby. . . ." The cry was for "a thorough practical business man for mayor — one who *can* understand his duty, and *will* perform it, one who will enforce *all* the ordinances of the city, and not select [one] . . . as a hobby, to the neglect of the city's general interests." [84] When his year expired, Herndon was not suggested for re-election.

In the long run the temperance crusade was defeated. When the state prohibition law was submitted to popular referendum, the Maine Law advocates were beaten. Not only was there state-wide defeat, but once Billy was out of office Springfield repealed its liquor ordinance. It seemed to Herndon that "human rights float in the bubbles of whiskey which swim upon the fire surface." Diverted by his interest in politics and the slavery question, Herndon himself started drinking again. "It is very hard," he concluded, "to overcome interest, appetite, habit & the low demagogue who rules the *synod* in the grocery." [85]

[84] *Illinois State Register,* March 15, 29, and 30, 1855.
[85] Herndon to Parker, October 30, 1855, Herndon-Parker MSS. The "grocery" was, of course, merely the ante-bellum version of the saloon.

CHAPTER v

Mr. Lincoln is All Right

I

THE MUSTY OFFICE on the west side of the square was a place where men talked. It might be the senior partner telling the latest story from down in Egypt or his junior expounding the theory of the "All-All" and the "zo-ophyte being." Or it might be a troubled client pouring out his tale of sorrow — one of the ever litigious Yoakum family or the inventor of a horological cradle which would automatically rock the baby to sleep. The law office was a place where something was usually happening. Herndon was nearly always there, and so was Lincoln when he was not on the circuit. There was a law student who doubled as janitor. Men liked to drop in, to chat and read the news and hear the latest joke.

But above all else they talked politics. Conversation in the Lincoln & Herndon office in the years following 1854 was filled with phrases almost meaningless today — squatter sovereignty, extension of slavery, abolitionism, nigger-driving Democracy; Kansas-Nebraska act, anti-Nebraskaites, pro-Lecompton. There were big names in the air, too — Buchanan and "poor Pierce," Trumbull and Toombs, Seward and Sumner. And men talked of Douglas.

Stephen Arnold Douglas was no stranger to these residents of Springfield. They could describe him in detail: his squat figure surmounted by a disproportionately huge head; his thick dark mane of hair; his dimpled cheeks and his pug nose; and — of course — his voice, rich, with an organ resonance. Born in Vermont, Douglas had come to be almost as much a part of Illinois as the prairies or the Sangamon. He was "little Dug" to Springfield — "the least man I have ever seen." It was hard to think of him as a United States senator, a presidential aspirant, and now the most prominent political figure in the nation. For Douglas in January 1854 introduced the Kansas-Nebraska bill, setting up territorial governments for the regions west

72

Mr. Lincoln is All Right

of Iowa and Missouri. To secure its adoption he had embodied in his territorial bill a provision explicitly repealing the old Missouri Compromise; the settlers of the plains would be free to determine their own domestic institutions — meaning slavery.[1]

It is not hard for a modern generation of historians to see that Douglas did not intend to introduce slavery into the West, that there was never any chance that the peculiar institution would flourish in the Great Plains, and that the principal motives behind the bill were such apparently extraneous factors as political rivalries in Missouri and the choice of a transcontinental rail route. It can also be pointed out that the problem of governing the territories was bound to arise; that it was impossible to secure Southern consent to the admission of additional free states under the Missouri Compromise; that even without Douglas there would certainly have been much the same kind of fight that actually developed.

But to his contemporaries, Douglas's actions were not easily justified. Clouded by personal animosities, old-time political prejudices, and the mumbo jumbo of slogans repeated till they became meaningless, thinking people convinced themselves that the Kansas-Nebraska measure was a deep-laid plot on the part of the South to extend slavery all over the nation and that Douglas, with an eye to his own presidential hopes, was a willing tool of the proslavery interests. To such men 1854 came as a test for their convictions. If the South had begun the fight for national domination, using Douglas as a tool, would Northerners submit — becoming Northern men with Southern principles — or would they resist this clear-cut case of proslavery aggression?

Such were the topics discussed in the Springfield law office in 1854. Recollecting from ten to forty years afterwards, Herndon felt that he had never hesitated; when the Kansas-Nebraska bill was passed he exclaimed: "Thank God for it, because it opens the whole question of freedom — human liberty." [2] His former abolitionist leanings, he said, were awakened. He instantly resolved that he would fight to the death against this cruel deed of the slave drivers. His partner, Mr. Lincoln, he recalled, was a more cautious man who was, perhaps, looking out for the main political chance; though naturally antislavery, he had to be managed carefully and urged to support the cause of justice and liberty. The Herndon story is, then, that he repeatedly prodded Lincoln, that he stood guard over his political fortunes, and that finally at

---

[1] For competent discussions of the complicated history of the Kansas-Nebraska act, see Randall, *Civil War and Reconstruction*, 128–135; Allan Nevins, *Ordeal of the Union*, II, 78–145; G. F. Milton, *The Eve of Conflict*, 144–154.

[2] Herndon to John E. Remsburg, August 9, 1890, copy in Weik MSS.

the opportune moment he brought forth Lincoln, an unwilling and "dodgey" Mr. Lincoln, to take the lead in the new Republican party. Though widely accepted by Lincoln biographers, the Herndon story seems to be mostly legend. When the repeal of the Missouri Compromise became known in Springfield, Lincoln and Herndon both pondered long before making any definite commitments. Both were opposed to the extension of slavery, and both were opposed to Douglas. But both were old-time Whigs and hesitated before making any final decision.[3] The political situation was so obscure that a man did not know how to choose.

There were many elements in Illinois opposed to Douglas, yet neither Lincoln nor Herndon could feel completely at home with any faction. The radical antislavery men, led by New England-bred Ichabod Codding and Owen Lovejoy, urged immediate extirpation of the peculiar institution, but in central Illinois "abolitionist" was "an odious epithet," applicable to scarcely a dozen men in Sangamon County.[4] With a deep love and appreciation for the South, where he had been born, Herndon at this time could not be an abolitionist; there were limits to his antislavery zeal.[5] Though "Personally . . . opposed to slavery — slavery aggression — despotism every where," he wrote, "I have no business to interfere with Southern Slaveholder's property. . . ." He did not "propose to wage war on them, but to let . . . the peculiar institution, alone where it is." "I love the South," he stated frankly, "and cannot help it: there is something open, manly, chivalrous to draw me." As late as 1856 he was afraid that section would be unjustly treated: "I will not act with any party which will not look comprehensively at the rights of all" and "do what is just to all and Each member of this Great Confederacy."[6]

Disagreeing with Douglas's policies, a significant fraction of the Illi-

[3] Lincoln's first public attack on the Nebraska measures, introduced in January 1854, did not come until late August. Angle, *Lincoln, 1854–1861,* x.

[4] *Illinois Journal,* October 19, 1854. It should be noted that the *Journal* usually reflected Lincoln's and Herndon's political views.

[5] This is, of course, a flat contradiction of Herndon's own statement made many years later: "At that time I was an ardent Abolitionist. . . ." *Herndon's Lincoln,* II, 362. It must be emphasized that this is a postwar recollection, that not one contemporary manuscript or newspaper in any way links Herndon with the abolitionist group before 1855–56. Horace White's *Abraham Lincoln in 1854* and Lamon's *Life of Abraham Lincoln,* the only accounts by contemporaries which support the Herndon thesis, were themselves written long after the event and were largely based on Herndon's own recollections. Had Herndon been an avowed abolitionist he could never have been elected mayor of Springfield in 1854.

[6] Herndon to Trumbull, December 20, 1855, February 15 and March 8, 1856, Trumbull MSS.; Herndon to Parker, February 13, 1855, and February 16, 1856, Herndon-Parker MSS.

nois Democrats split away from the regular party organization and under Lyman Trumbull, John A. Palmer, and Norman B. Judd became known as the Anti-Nebraska Democrats.[7] But as Whigs, it was difficult for either Lincoln or Herndon to unite with these; if party lines were to be crossed, declared the *Illinois Journal*, the insurgent Democrats would have to join the Whigs.

To complicate the situation there were side issues of major importance. The prohibition cause transcended party lines, making more difficult the conscientious voter's task. Then, too, there was the Know-Nothing issue. With the decay of the old Whig party, these "native Americans" began their campaign of racial intolerance and religious bigotry. Though their extreme positions were gradually abandoned, the Know-Nothings could carry no appeal for either Lincoln or Herndon; if slavery for the Negro was wrong, it was likewise "radically wrong to enslave the religious ideas and faiths of men." [8]

So it was that during the summer of 1854 both partners hesitated, both thoroughly disturbed yet fearing to do anything lest it be wrong. Because the state elections in the fall would determine the choice of United States senator, the canvass was one of major importance. For Douglas it was essential to secure the election of a legislature which would select as his colleague a supporter of popular sovereignty; should the anti-Nebraska forces win this major office it would amount to a repudiation of his whole program. Illinois became a sort of battleground in the summer and fall of 1854, with vigorous campaigning by both sides. Springfield attracted half a dozen of the nation's most prominent abolitionists that summer — Salmon P. Chase, Joshua R. Giddings, Cassius M. Clay, Ichabod Codding, and others — yet neither Herndon nor Lincoln spoke at any of these meetings.[9] It was not until Douglas came back from Washington and began to stump the state for his squatter sovereignty doctrine that Lincoln became active in the anti-Nebraska cause. And Herndon followed.

II

Herndon took an active part in the campaign against the Douglas supporters. Simeon Francis, editor of the whiggish *Illinois Journal* at Springfield, always welcomed a contribution, and both partners wrote

[7] A. C. Cole, *The Era of the Civil War, 1848–1870*, 101–152, gives a discussion of the involved political maneuvering of this period.

[8] Herndon to Lamon, March 1, 1870, Lamon MSS. This was Herndon's theory. In practice he cordially detested the Irish.

[9] Beveridge, *Lincoln*, II, 239. Lincoln was present when Clay spoke. W. H. Townsend, *Lincoln and His Wife's Home Town*, 254.

editorials for the paper, Herndon probably the more frequently.[10]
Herndon felt he "did all [he] . . . could for freedom — aided the
press — wrote late & early"; he "took pen in hand and aided . . . to
rouse the Country." In addition, he related, "I took to the stump —
kept it till it was over, and . . . spoke for Freedom as manful words
as my Constitution would let me." The condition of Illinois, he
thought, was one to give cause for optimism. Douglas could "no more
controll [sic] Illinois than a Hottentot chief," for men dared face each
other on the slavery issue and talk "without evasion or 'eye dropping.'"[11]

Lincoln spoke a number of times during the canvass in central Illinois, but his major address of the campaign was on October 4, during
the State Fair at Springfield, when he replied to Douglas's speech of
the previous day. He produced a careful, logical attack on Douglas's
position, reasoned yet burning with eloquence, a speech "wholly unlike any before made by him."[12] Herndon, who was present in the audience and took elaborate notes as Lincoln spoke, was disappointed
with the rather formal notice given his partner's effort in the Springfield papers and seized his pen to do justice to the occasion. In two
closely printed columns of the local *Journal* he dashed off his version
of the speech and of Douglas's answer; it was lush with adjectives and
rich in metaphor.[13] Lincoln's argument he proclaimed "the profound-
est . . . he has made in his whole life." He was eloquent; "he quivered with feeling and emotion." At the end of Lincoln's speech, Herndon daringly asserted, the feeling was universal that his logic was
"unanswerable; — that no human power could overthrow it or trample it
under foot." But for Douglas's rebuttal Herndon's scorn could hardly
be contained. He liberally berated the Little Giant with his choicest
assortment of lurid phrases: "haughty and imperative," "now flattering, now wild with excess of madness," "the grand master of human
passion," "evasive, deceptive, and full of declamation," "a scorched
monument of disgrace." Douglas, to Herndon, was "the greatest demagogue in America."[14]

It was announced that following Lincoln's speech there would be a
meeting of antislavery leaders to complete a state organization for the

[10] Rankin, *Personal Recollections*, 138; Beveridge, *Lincoln*, II, 238–239.
[11] Herndon to Parker, February 13, 1855, Herndon-Parker MSS.; Herndon to
Sumner, March 6, 1856, Sumner MSS.
[12] Beveridge, *Lincoln*, II, 244.
[13] Herndon to Horace White, December 4, 1890, Herndon-Weik Coll.; *Herndon's Lincoln*, II, 368.
[14] *Illinois Journal*, October 10, 1854.

Republican party, then composed almost exclusively of radical abolitionists. Lincoln's anti-Nebraska arguments raised some hope that he might be persuaded to appear at the gathering and perhaps to join the new party.[15] As Herndon told the story years later, he was a member of the abolitionist junto and heard of these plans in advance. Realizing that it would injure Lincoln's political career to be associated with violently distrusted abolitionists, while a direct refusal to speak would also be dangerous, he told Lincoln to hitch up his horse and quit the town immediately. Lincoln left for Pekin, in Tazewell County, and had no connection with the odious radical group, even though, without his consent, his name was put on the central executive committee.[16]

This account has been accepted by most Lincoln students, but it is open to grave suspicion. There is absolutely no evidence to link Herndon with the Republican radicals at this time. The newspaper reports of the abolitionist convention make no mention of Herndon.[17] There is little reason to believe that at this or any other time Lincoln placed the direction of his political career in another man's hands. Since, as Herndon himself remarked, "Lincoln was not a man who could be successfully threatened," [18] it was most uncharacteristic for him to be rushed or frightened into such a major decision.[19]

Nor, if Herndon's story is true, can one understand his own actions. It would have been most peculiar for a rabid abolitionist to betray party secrets and to warn another man from joining his clique. And if Herndon was the second most influential antislavery leader in Illinois [20] and desired to keep his partner away from dangerous contact with the Republican gathering, it is difficult to understand how Lincoln's name came to be placed on the state central committee. Such negative indications do not necessarily mean that the Herndon account is a falsehood, but it is out of character for both Lincoln and

---

[15] The meeting had for several weeks been scheduled for October 4, but when the leaders assembled, Douglas and Lincoln were occupying the State House, and the convention had to be postponed until the following day. Paul Selby in McLean Co. Hist. Soc., *Trans.*, III, 43–44. Herndon was in error in writing that the meeting was called under the inspiration of Lincoln's address. *Herndon's Lincoln*, II, 371.

[16] Herndon to Lamon, March 1, 1870, Lamon MSS.; Herndon to Weik, February 8, 1888, Herndon-Weik Coll.; *Herndon's Lincoln*, II, 371–372.

[17] The only detailed account of the meeting, written by Paul Selby, who was a member, does not refer to Herndon's attendance. McLean Co. Hist. Soc., *Trans.*, III, 43–47.

[18] *Herndon's Lincoln*, II, 283.

[19] Lincoln's own version of the incident makes no reference to Herndon's alleged share in making his decision. Nicolay and Hay, eds., *Works*, III, 224.

[20] Lamon, *Life of Abraham Lincoln*, 350.

Herndon, it is supported by no contemporary evidence, and it is on the surface improbable. It seems likely that delayed recollection distorted Herndon's remembrance of the episode.

All in all, the election of 1854 was an exciting contest, and if Herndon did not yet join the abolitionists in their denunciation of the South, he could go them one better in vituperation of Douglas. When the election returns were in, the anti-Nebraska coalition had a majority in the legislature. The new representatives appeared to Herndon "dignified, industrious & worthy." Illinois stood redeemed, he exulted; all he wished was that he could make the fight over every November of his life. Proud of his opposition to the Nebraska "outrage," he vowed: "I will never cease, I think, to pursue this course in behalf of human rights." [21]

It does not appear that Lincoln had seriously considered the possibility of his own selection to the United States Senate until the results of the election became known and it was recognized that the Democratic incumbent could be defeated. He then began an active campaign by letter to secure pledged support from the county anti-Nebraska delegations. Herndon's allegiance was divided, for his old Morgan County friend Richard Yates also privately hankered for the office and solicited Herndon's influence among the Sangamon representatives. Assuming a strict neutrality, Herndon wrote Yates: "As to you & Lincoln I owe neither of you a peculiar friendship one above the other, yet as individuals a peculiar friendship I do owe both. I stand for both and against neither. . . ." His main interest was not in the candidate but in the election; "A triumph over Douglass would be a great one for us boys — for Illinois & for the nation." [22]

In the actual balloting Lincoln emerged as the leading anti-Nebraska candidate for the Senate. Because of the obduracy of a handful of anti-Nebraska Democrats who would not vote for a Whig, Lincoln's election was blocked and New England-born Lyman Trumbull was selected on the tenth ballot. Herndon felt his partner's defeat keenly, and he never came to trust Norman B. Judd, the leader of the anti-Nebraska Democrats, whom he regarded as personally responsible for Lincoln's defeat. But neither Lincoln nor Herndon showed any resentment against Trumbull, the dark horse who won. The new senator was, Herndon reported to Parker, "a good man — no demagogue, & a . . . Great thorn, rough & poisonous, in the heart of Douglass." [23]

[21] Herndon to Sumner, February 15, 1855, and March 6, 1856, Sumner MSS.; Herndon to Parker, February 13, 1855, Herndon-Parker MSS.

[22] Herndon to Yates, December 14, 1854, photostat, collection of Thomas I. Starr.

[23] Herndon to Parker, February 13, 1855, Herndon-Parker MSS.

III

In spite of his partner's defeat, Herndon was greatly cheered by the outcome of the elections. As a rebuke to Douglas and as an evidence that the voters would oppose the expansion of slavery, it proved in the best manner possible that "The People are free." There were men in Illinois now who would brave Douglas's scowl; Herndon saw their determination in "the flash of the eye — the purpose of the lip & the closed fists," and in "a thousand other things that rest on looks, acts, deeds thoughts &c that speak." All these indications served to strengthen Herndon's own enthusiastic nature. Clinging fast to his demand that the South be maintained in her rights, he was "now prepared to advance to any Constitutional lengths." [24]

The year 1855 was a slack one politically. There were no important elections, and much of Herndon's time was consumed in performing his mayoral duties and in furthering the temperance cause. Both partners by dabbling in politics had neglected their law practice and had to buckle down to work. But the year was also a time for political planning. Typical of the off-the-record conferences held in the shabby office was a two-hour interview between Herndon and Zebina Eastman, editor of the rabidly abolitionist *Free West* and a pioneer Republican in Illinois.[25] The talk rambled from ships to sealing wax, and the two put their heads together over "Lincoln — slavery — the antislavery cause — the progress of it — hopes &c. &c." [26] Eastman had come to the office to learn whether Lincoln's views on the Negro were sound. In the absence of his partner, Herndon reassured the visitor. "Mr. Lincoln is all right," he whispered confidentially, and from that time the partners were spared the enfilading attacks from the radical antislavery newspapers which had injured them in the past.[27]

But more than anything else 1855 was a period for sober thought

[24] Herndon to Sumner, February 15, 1855, Sumner MSS.

[25] This incident is extremely difficult to date exactly. In various letters (cited below) Herndon wrote of the conversations as having occurred "in 1854 — probably in 1855, early" and "About the year '56." Eastman, on the other hand, remembered it as being after the elections in 1855. Since the *Free West* in January 1855 strongly opposed Lincoln because of his connection with the Whig "mummy of a party" (Cole, *Era of the Civil War*, 135), it is almost certain that Beveridge (*Lincoln*, II, 266) is in error in connecting this interview with the October 1854 meeting of the Republicans at Springfield.

[26] Herndon to Weik, September 24, 1890, Herndon-Weik Coll.; Herndon to Zebina Eastman, February 6, 1866, Eastman MSS.; Herndon to Caroline H. Dall, January 3, 1866, Dall MSS.

[27] Eastman to Herndon, January 2, 1866, Herndon-Weik Coll.; Zebina Eastman, "History of the Anti-Slavery Agitation, and the Growth of the Liberty and Republican Parties in the State of Illinois" (pamphlet in Eastman MSS.), 671.

and solemn reflection in political affairs. Both partners were forced by the necessities of the situation to become more and more radical on the slavery issue. Herndon's impressionable mind was stimulated by the letters which he now began to receive from Eastern abolitionist leaders. His friendship for Theodore Parker had begun the previous year on the placid plane of philosophy and literature, but it sent a chill up Herndon's spine when the Boston minister chanted his war cry against "Slavery, the most hideous snake which Southern regions breed . . . crawling North; fold on fold, and ring on ring, and coil on coil." Somehow Parker seemed always to appreciate his letters on the political situation in Illinois more than an elaborate dissertation on the laws of the winds. He was prompt to congratulate Herndon on any speech against slavery expansion, and Herndon purred delightedly at the slightest compliment.[28] With his infrequent personal notes Parker sent numerous speeches and sermons on the vexed question and Herndon absorbed them all. If Parker's letters were few, his influence in the antislavery direction was strong and compelling; Herndon found himself echoing not only the older man's ideas but his very words.

A similar correspondence with Charles Sumner began in 1855. Herndon was a reverent adorer of the pompous Massachusetts senator with his ornate oratory and his affectation of grandeur. He reveled in Sumner's "eloquent, chaste — classic" language [29] and tried to imitate him by sprinkling his speeches with quotations from the Bible and from English poets. "Candidly," he confessed, he liked Sumner's political views "because they are just." Part of his duty in the fight against the expansion of slavery, Herndon thought, was to correspond with friends, "encouraging them to action — to a rigid integrity to the Divinity within them," and it was partly from this cause that he wrote Sumner. But more important was the fact that "Sometimes I feel so vexed, that I am compelled to pour out my feelings to some one: there is no person in Washington to whom I can do this, more freely than yourself." [30] This friendship was not an entirely one-sided affair. When Herndon gave inside leads on the Illinois situation, Sumner was "charmed & encouraged," having "rarely read . . . home truth in fewer or better words." [31]

Herndon was also stirred by the exciting news that seeped in from Kansas. The complex Kansas situation has been so distorted that it is

[28] Herndon to Parker, April 28, 1856, Herndon-Parker MSS.
[29] Herndon to Parker, October 30, 1855, *ibid.*
[30] Herndon to Sumner, March 6, June 20, and May 20, 1856, Sumner MSS.
[31] Sumner to Herndon, March 27, 1856, Herndon-Weik Coll.

difficult even today to remember that most immigrants really went to Kansas and Nebraska for the purpose of building homes and farming, that the normal pursuits of life were carried on, and that the total loss of life by violence in the territory was something less than the number of casualties in American steamship disasters for one year. These were not the facts that received publicity back in the East. North and South imagined the other section was rushing in armed immigrants to seize the land by force. Northerners were particularly excited: the proslavery forces were pouring in "border ruffians" from Missouri to carry the territorial elections; federal officials were only rubber stamps for the slaveholding despotism; it was impossible for free-state men to secure justice or even the most basic rights; the slavery forces were commencing a career of robbery and violence that threatened the end of organized government; only recourse to arms could save the land for liberty.[32]

Eli Thayer's New England Emigrant Aid Company had been formed early in 1854 to help settlers who would vote to exclude slavery from the Kansas region. As excitement grew more intense, other similar groups were organized, and subscriptions were taken to send munitions to the free-soil forces in boxes labeled "Crockery," "Books," "Hardware," and "Bibles." The agitation was played for full value in the anti-administration newspapers such as Greeley's New York *Tribune*, which was widely read throughout the Middle West. Every tilt between the rival Topeka and Lecompton governments was made a world shaking struggle, and the burning of one small free-soil center became the "sack of Lawrence," a tale of unspeakable horrors.

Lincoln and Herndon were interested and alarmed by events in Kansas. The situation was, Lincoln wrote, precisely what he had expected from the Kansas-Nebraska act, "conceived in violence, . . . maintained in violence, and . . . executed in violence." [33] Naturally the more impetuous of the two, Herndon was swept off his feet by the Kansas "outrages." "[M]addened at the tyrannies and despotisms, and corruptions" in Kansas, a little group of radicals in Springfield banded together to oppose proslavery aggression. Precisely what to do or how to do it they did not know, but as a leader Herndon felt about ready to unfurl the standard of revolt. The junto was "energetic, vigilant, almost revolutionary," recommending "the employment of any

[32] Of course, most of these assertions were entirely false, but such was the feeling among many of the North who had not previously been greatly excited over the slavery issue. Randall, *Civil War and Reconstruction*, 135–138; J. C. Malin, *John Brown and the Legend of Fifty-Six*.

[33] Nicolay and Hay, eds., *Works*, II, 283.

means, however desperate, to promote and defend the cause of freedom" for the territory.[34]

Lincoln, as usual, intervened to calm his excitable partner. Appearing before this rabid little band, he made a moderating address, pointing out that "physical rebellions & bloody resistances" were both wrong and unconstitutional; any attempt to resist the law in Kansas would be criminal and wicked and would ruin the cause. The speech thoroughly squelched any ideas the Springfield radicals may have had of physical resistance to the proslavery government of Kansas and turned their interest into "other more effective channels" — namely, political action.[35]

Having appeased the group, Lincoln himself then made a contribution to the Kansas cause, with the restriction that his money be sent only when the conservative Judge Logan decided it was necessary for the defense of the people of the territory.[36] Herndon willingly matched the sum. It was, he knew, "the 'sweetest money' . . . man ever gave man . . . to defend the rights God gave him." [37]

[34] *Abraham Lincoln Quar.,* III, 189–190; *Herndon's Lincoln,* II, 379–380.
[35] *Abraham Lincoln Quar.,* III, 190–191.
[36] Logan never gave the word, and the money was never used. Nicolay and Hay, eds., *Works,* VI, 64.
[37] Herndon to Sumner, March 6, 1856, Sumner MSS.

CHAPTER *vi*

The Crown of My Life

I

DIVERTED from more incendiary policies, Herndon returned to politics. He perceived that central Illinois was to be "the battle ground for the slave power & for the Republicans," yet it was a "backward, timid & cowardly" section, and frightened politicians, uncertain of the people's feeling, deliberately kept their positions neutral. Herndon no longer had such hesitation. Intuitively he felt that the masses were ready and anxious to battle for what he considered justice and equity. "I hope," he asserted with his usual optimism, "to see them dynamic — vital — active, soon." To take advantage of this great ground swell, he and other anti-Nebraska leaders in the fall of 1855 commenced a systematic organization of Republicanism, desiring "to see it inaugurated into a vital, eternal, political power in the state, which shall cover us as nature wraps up her modest flower or gigantic mountain." [1]

All this verbiage meant simply that in order to follow up their victory over the Douglas supporters the anti-Nebraska factions had to set up party machinery and work together in an organized fashion. Early in 1856 at the instance of Paul Selby, editor of Jacksonville's *Morgan Journal,* a call was issued for a meeting of free-soil editors to consider an "arrangement for the organization of the anti-Nebraska forces in the state" during the coming presidential election. Still shying away from the name "Republican," a number of anti-Douglas editors met at Decatur on Washington's birthday. The sole non-editor at the convention was Abraham Lincoln. After issuing a statement of principles, the editors summoned a general anti-Nebraska convention to meet at Bloomington on May 29 and appointed a state central executive committee to make the necessary arrangements. Herndon was named the representative of the Sangamon region on the committee. [2]

[1] Herndon to Parker, October 30, 1855, Herndon-Parker MSS.
[2] Paul Selby, in McLean Co. Hist. Soc., *Trans.,* III, 37–38; *Illinois State Journal,* February 27, 1856.

He was flattered. It was, he asserted, the highest honor of his life, and he expressed his gratitude in a long open letter spreading over three closely packed columns of the *Illinois State Journal*. In this first public statement of principles he had made since the passage of the Kansas-Nebraska act, Herndon still carefully eschewed the title "Republican" and announced at the outset that he was "willing to give to the South all her rights under the Constitution." Nevertheless, he was opposed to the expansion of slavery and to the Kansas-Nebraska measure which, he wrote, "had its germination in selfish ambition . . . by Northern Senators, grasping for place." His main point was an elaborate argument against the "sole object of the bill" — the spread of slavery, a policy directly opposed to the teachings of the fathers of the nation. The bill was nothing less than "treason to the spirit of '76 . . . to the race of man." Claiming that Southern despots intended "to enslave all men, black and *white*," Herndon looked with darkest foreboding into a gloomy future unless the Missouri Compromise was restored. The duty was clear; "Illinois must wipe out this national disgrace." He would, therefore, accept the position proffered him by the editorial gathering and would promise to do his duty.[3]

Seeing this letter as an announcement of Herndon's "adhesion to black republicanism," the editor of the Democratic *State Register* was "pleased to know that he has found a resting place which he can publicly record as satisfactory to himself — he being the only party interested as to his location." [4]

Herndon took very seriously the duties imposed on him by the Decatur convention of editors and did his best to arouse anti-Nebraska sentiment. Editorials in the Springfield newspapers and a flourishing correspondence with other party leaders helped keep interest alive. Even so early in the season he at once took the stump for the anti-slavery cause and spoke all over central Illinois. One of his expeditions carried him to Atlanta, a hamlet in stalwartly conservative Logan County. With a characteristic lack of modesty Herndon told Theodore Parker of his efforts:

I . . . made a speech in Atlanta . . . — spoke for 2¼ hours to a large crowded house — say 700 or 800 — filled with men — women, God bless the women, and young men and pretty girls; and if I ever did a subject justice, in my poor way, I did it then and there. I took open, broad, deep antagonistic grounds against slavery every where

---

[3] *Illinois State Journal*, March 19, 1856. A long extract from this "spirited letter" was quoted approvingly by William Lloyd Garrison in *The Liberator*, XXVI, 70 (May 2, 1856).

[4] *Illinois State Register*, March 21, 1856.

in Gods habitable globle [*sic*]. I *really* expected to be hissed, but my words were warm, intense — hot from an impassioned nature. The crowd saw . . . my nervous excitement — my thrill, listened to me and really respected me — more, ten thousand times more, than a milk & cider *affair*. I never saw a more exultant crowd in my life.[5]

That Herndon's estimate of his performance was shared by at least one other person is attested by a letter which appeared in the *Illinois State Journal* shortly afterwards. Writing in the usual platitudinous pomposities of political nominations and mixing his metaphors in an amusing fashion, the correspondent proposed Herndon as anti-Nebraska candidate for governor in the fall elections, being "a true, firm and abiding statesman . . . a man that spurns to lick the hand of the political tricksters for the emoluments of office, but who . . . if selected . . . would not . . . prostitute himself into a political machine to be ground by others," in short, "a man that will in every requirement be a full and thorough exponent of the Anti-Nebraska party." [6] The suggestion met with some enthusiasm in Springfield, and the *Journal*, from which Herndon had been temporarily estranged because of its Know-Nothing proclivities, pronounced him "an earnest and eloquent defender of the constitutional rights of the north and an honest man . . . equal to any position to which the people may call him." Even the Democratic organ admitted that the anti-Nebraskaites could go farther and fare worse than by nominating Herndon, but it added: "It is a matter of little importance who [*sic*] they nominate; the result will be . . . the election of the democratic nominee." Herndon himself was tremendously pleased and sat down at once to write his idol Parker all about it. The suggestion was just a proof, he crowed, "that *Politicians* want boldness — want manliness." But he did not desire the office — "even could I get it" — and would "never consent to be a candidate for any thing," and the matter was allowed to drop.[7]

II

The most important of Herndon's duties as member of the state executive committee was the task of preparing for the general anti-Nebraska convention which the editors had summoned. The program of that gathering, he felt, should be "conservative . . . conciliatory — united, putting every man's individual opinions on other questions out

[5] Herndon to Parker, April 28, 1856, Herndon-Parker MSS.
[6] *Illinois State Journal*, April 21, 1856.
[7] *Ibid.*, April 22, 1856; *Illinois State Register*, April 22, 1856; Herndon to Parker, April 28, 1856, Herndon-Parker MSS.

of sight — , sinking them in the greater one of Slavery Extension." He understood that the leading Whigs such as Lincoln, Yates, and Browning would attend, and hoped that good Democrats would also be present. If the new party adopted a conciliatory platform, Herndon believed, it would stand a good chance for success.[8]

On May 10, 1856, there appeared in the Springfield *State Journal* a call for a local anti-Nebraska convention to select delegates to attend the state-wide gathering at Bloomington on May 29. Heading the list of signers were "A Lincoln" and "Wm H Herndon." [9] Years later Herndon gave an elaborate account of how Lincoln's name came to be signed to this document, which definitely committed him to the new party. "Believing the times were ripe for more advanced movements," Herndon wrote, "in the spring of 1856 I drew up a paper for the friends of freedom to sign, calling a county convention in Springfield to select delegates for the forthcoming Republican State convention in Bloomington. The paper was freely circulated and generously signed. Lincoln was absent at the time, and . . . I took the liberty to sign his name to the call." When indignant John Todd Stuart protested this unauthorized act affiliating Lincoln with the Republican party, Herndon assumed full responsibility for his action but wrote Lincoln, who telegraphed in reply: "All right; go ahead. Will meet you — radicals and all." [10]

This was Herndon's recollection more than thirty years after the event. Earlier he had been even less reticent concerning his part in drawing Lincoln into the Republican party. "I forged his name," he asserted, "but I knew what I was about"; "Whiggery & Know Nothingism tried to hold him, but they couldn't." To his crony Lamon he confided: "Mr. Lincoln was then backward — sorter dodgey — *sorter so & not so.* I was determined to make him take a stand, if he would not do it willingly. . . . I signed Mr Lincoln's name without authority . . . ." [11] After having been committed in this unauthorized fashion, Lincoln, so the story goes, from that hour experienced a great change of feeling and his whole soul seemed burning on the slavery question; Herndon had made up Lincoln's mind.[12]

Herndon's recital of this incident has seldom been seriously questioned. There are, however, a number of reasons for doubting the story. As has already been noted, the Bloomington convention and its

---

[8] Herndon to Trumbull, April 24, 1856, Trumbull MSS.
[9] *Illinois State Journal*, May 10, 1856.
[10] *Herndon's Lincoln*, II, 382–383.
[11] Dall, "Pioneering," *Atlantic Mo.*, XIX, 414n; Herndon to Eastman, February 6, 1866, Eastman MSS.; Herndon to Lamon, March 1, 1870, Lamon MSS.
[12] F. F. Browne, *Every-Day Life of Abraham Lincoln* (1st ed.), 260.

Springfield preliminaries were not isolated events but directly resulted from a call issued by the convention of anti-Nebraska editors at Decatur on February 22, 1856, at which Lincoln was a guiding spirit. It was this gathering which Paul M. Angle has termed "the real beginning of the Republican party in Illinois." [13] Lincoln's share in the proceedings was well known; for months he had been currying candidates to run on the anti-Nebraska ticket; he was prominently mentioned for governor on the new party's platform; and, as the Democratic *State Register* commented, he seemed "ready at the tap of the fusion drum, on all occasions."

Herndon's appointment to the general state executive committee by the Decatur editors could hardly have been made without Lincoln's knowledge and approval. After his selection Herndon was very active in the anti-Nebraska cause and was even suggested for governor on that ticket. His call for a Sangamon County anti-Nebraska meeting on May 10 was not, therefore, unexpected. It was precisely what the Decatur convention had intended him to do, and it was the logical culmination of his campaigning for the Republican cause during the three months interval between conventions. For at least four weeks of this period Lincoln was in Springfield, and it is impossible to imagine that that astute politician did not know of his partner's actions and plans. Lincoln had made the lead at Decatur; Herndon was now following suit.

There is a notable lack of contemporary evidence to bolster Herndon's statement as to Lincoln's backdoor entry into the Republican ranks. Neither of the Springfield newspapers expressed any surprise at Lincoln's signing the Republican call or hinted that he had not authorized the use of his name. At this period Herndon was writing frequent and verbose letters to his friend Theodore Parker, to whom he related the plans and dreams of the Illinois Republicans; they rejoiced together over every new convert to the cause. Yet in none of these letters, nor in his correspondence with Trumbull, Sumner, and other Republican leaders is there any mention of an unauthorized signature or of Lincoln's reluctance to support the new party. Quite the contrary. From Herndon's own contemporary letters it seems to have been Lincoln who was pushing the new enterprise. "I have never seen him so sanguine of success," Herndon wrote of his partner; "*he is warm.*" [14]

Herndon's story is not, of course, entirely false. Lincoln was at Pekin

[13] Angle, *Lincoln, 1854–1861*, 112.
[14] Herndon to Trumbull, May 20, 1856, Trumbull MSS. This letter should have been dated May 19. Pratt, *Concerning Mr. Lincoln*, 3–4.

the week the convention call was issued, and Herndon probably did sign for him. It is possible that he asked Lincoln for confirmation of his act. But there is no contemporary evidence that Herndon was un-authorized in signing the call, that he forged Lincoln's name, or that this action had a significant influence in determining Lincoln's polit-ical affiliation. Herndon's statements on these matters, made from ten to thirty years after the event, and differing significantly among them-selves, are unsupported by any shred of contemporary evidence. As an old man he was indulging in a human and perfectly understandable kind of self-glorification.

III

A few days before the Republican convention was scheduled to meet at Bloomington, an electrifying piece of news reached Spring-field. Charles Sumner, the arrogant Massachusetts solon, had made a much advertised address in the United States Senate on the "Crime Against Kansas." In spite of its perfumed quotations from the classics, the speech reeked of the sewer. Sumner went out of his way to de-nounce the South, and to attack the venerable senior senator from South Carolina, Andrew Pickens Butler, who, he said, had made his vows to "the harlot Slavery," "a mistress . . . who, . . . though pol-luted in the sight of the world, is chaste in his sight." [15] Filled with references to bowie knives and bullets, rifles and rapes, this ugly speech was destined to become one of the most effective Republican propaganda documents in the coming presidential campaign. In sedate little Springfield, far from either slavery or Kansas, Herndon read the address and jubilated that it was unanswerable, a grand effort "unsur-passed by any American production made in the United States Senate, 'lo, these many years.' " [16]

A hot-headed and irresponsible nephew of Senator Butler, Preston S. Brooks, a representative of South Carolina in the lower house of Congress, felt otherwise. His family and his state had been insulted; he conceived it his duty to vindicate their honor. On May 22 he en-tered the Senate room and brutally assaulted Sumner with a gutta-percha cane. The six-foot Massachusetts senator, trapped behind his desk and unable to resist, received some nasty wounds and had to be carried from the Capitol to receive a doctor's care. The incident sent a shiver down the national spine. Many in the South thought that Sum-ner was at last getting his just deserts, while to the North it seemed

---

[15] *The Works of Charles Sumner,* IV, 144.
[16] Herndon to Sumner, June 11, 1856, Sumner MSS.

that the slavocracy was attempting to crush out the right of free speech. To Herndon the assault on Sumner by "that fiend — bully, Mr. Brooks" was nothing less than an indignity done to all men. "The people are assaulted through you," he wrote to Sumner. "A feeling, wild & deep, is aroused here . . . which will not be easily put down or smothered out. It is plain to be seen why you were assaulted: they could not answer the charges and home thrusts of your logic and rhetoric." [17]

The effect of the whole affair was to make inflexible Herndon's determination to work with the new Republican party in the effort to control the expansion of slavery. Earlier he had pledged himself to the cause:

> I hope to live to see the day when I can make slavery feel my influence. That shall be *the one* object of my life. It and myself are enemies. I am feeble: it is strong, yet I am right and it is wrong. . . . Do not misunderstand me to say that I will live to see slavery abolished and that *I will do it.* I hope with others, to sow the elements, whose . . . power will do it after . . . my death.[18]

Now this pledge had become a holy vow; he intended, he swore, "to enlist for *the war.*" [19]

The first step was the organization of the numerous antislavery elements in Illinois into an effective party machine. This was to be the work of the Bloomington meeting, for which Herndon, with the other members of the state executive committee, issued the call. Naturally enough the Sangamon County anti-Nebraska convention selected Herndon and Lincoln as two of the delegates to the state gathering, but at the same time it adopted resolutions urging "no further . . . agitation of the question of slavery" except for the restoration of the Missouri Compromise.[20]

The Bloomington convention was a congeries of mutually suspicious anti-Nebraska factions. Everybody was there: unwhigged conservatives, disgruntled Democrats, Germans, disaffected Know-Nothings, temperance agitators, abolitionists — plus a good number who were neither more nor less than politicians. Roly-poly David Davis, assisted by Lincoln and Orville H. Browning, performed miracles of backstage management and prevented open feuding. By acclamation the convention condemned the Kansas-Nebraska act, called for a restoration of the Missouri Compromise, and mildly disapproved of nativism; a

[17] *Ibid.*
[18] Herndon to Parker, April 28, 1856, Herndon-Parker MSS.
[19] Herndon to Richard Yates, October 24, 1856, Yates MSS.
[20] *Illinois State Journal,* May 26, 1856; Angle, *"Here I Have Lived,"* 215.

slate of presidential electors was picked, including both Lincoln and Herndon; and "with nine long, loud, and hearty cheers" Col. William H. Bissell, hero of Buena Vista, now partially paralyzed, was nominated for governor.[21] Then there were calls for Lincoln, who made the concluding address of the session. He let himself go and with a passionate emotional appeal urged his hearers to subordinate all differences in the fight against the expansion of slavery — a masterly effort intended to fuse all the diverse anti-Nebraska factions into a working unit for the coming campaign. To Herndon it seemed that his partner stood seven feet tall that day.[22]

I V

The partners returned home with high hopes and lofty plans. They were met by a singularly cool Springfield, which wanted no truck with abolitionists. As Herndon remembered it later, about five days after the Bloomington meeting he and Lincoln got up a call for a Springfield rally to ratify the action of the anti-Nebraska convention. "We got out large posters," Herndon reminisced, "had bands of music employed to drum up a crowd &c. The court house was the place of meeting. As the hour drew near I lit up the Court [house] with many blazes & many lights — blowed horns and rang bells, &c." But when the time appointed came, "what do you think the number of the People was — ? How many? Three persons — namely John Pain [janitor of the building] — W H Herndon & A Lincoln." The ratification rally had turned into a rout.[23]

There are very strong reasons for questioning this story, written long after the event. It is impossible to imagine that a meeting so advertised, at which Lincoln was supposed to speak, would not have drawn at least a small audience. The Springfield newspapers reported a ratification rally held on June 10, at which, according to the anti-Nebraska organ, "The Court House was filled to overflowing with a very intelligent audience" and "Many were obliged to leave because they could not obtain seats, while a large number stood in the aisles for hours." Even the violently Democratic *State Register* admitted that "Pursuant to much drumming and drilling the black republican leaders . . . got together an assemblage of some two hundred persons at the court house." The meeting was admittedly a letdown after the

[21] McLean Co. Hist. Soc., *Trans.*, III, 155.
[22] *Herndon's Lincoln*, II, 384–385.
[23] Herndon to Lamon, March 1, 1870, Lamon MSS.; *Herndon's Lincoln*, II, 385–386.

emotional peak at Bloomington, but it was not the farce that Herndon made of it.[24]

The presidential campaign of 1856 proved to be one of the liveliest in American history. There were three major contenders. It had been known since February that Millard Fillmore would be the candidate of the American (Know-Nothing) party, but it was not until after the Democratic convention at Cincinnati adopted a popular sovereignty platform and nominated James Buchanan, that aging Pennsylvania bachelor whose noncommittal speeches and even more impressive silences had made him "available," that the issues of the approaching contest became clear. Herndon saw that the Democratic squatter sovereignty platform meant a hopeless division of that party on the territorial issue, and he rejoiced at the prospect of widening the breach. James Buchanan seemed to this Illinois Sucker the very archetype of the Northern man with Southern principles. Herndon's scorn was scorching. Buchanan was "a hunker — a federalist — a nigger-driver at heart." "If there be any species of animal existence . . . which I hate, I do despise just such a wet, cold lump of dough as Buckhannon [*sic*]. He is simply a supple, stolid, obedient, unresisting slave to the slave power: he is a tool and will be a blind one at that. . . . HE MUST BE BEAT." [25]

To pick the candidate to oppose Buchanan the Republicans held a national convention at Philadelphia early in June 1856. Adopting a platform condemning "those twin relics of barbarism — Polygamy and Slavery," the convention proceeded to select John C. Frémont, the dashing trailmarker of the West, as its candidate for the presidency. In the balloting for the vice presidential nomination Abraham Lincoln received strong minority support, though William L. Dayton of New Jersey received the honor.

The proceedings were not quite to Herndon's liking. As for Frémont, he supposed it was "the wisest Choice which could have possibly been made under all the Circumstances," though frankly he did not think so at first. It may be conjectured that he, like Lincoln, would have preferred a former Whig, perhaps Justice John McLean of Ohio. And Dayton was not Herndon's choice either. "[M]y partner & friend,

[24] *Illinois State Journal,* June 11, 1856; *Illinois State Register,* June 12, 1856. Beveridge (*Lincoln,* II, 384) suggests that there may have been two ratification meetings, the abortive one where three persons attended, and the one reported in the papers. A careful examination of the newspapers reveals neither any advertising nor any report of a meeting prior to June 10. Angle's comment on this point (Angle's ed. of *Herndon's Lincoln,* 315), rejecting the Herndon version, is undoubtedly correct.

[25] Herndon to Sumner, June 20, 1856, Sumner MSS.

Lincoln," he felt, "is a good man . . . : he loves man . . . and would die for his rights . . . — Lincoln is for human freedom." It was something of a blow when the compliment paid Lincoln in the balloting for the vice presidential nomination turned out to be nothing more than a gesture. Herndon did not intend to let these matters stand in the way of an active support of the Republican cause; he was willing to vote for any antislavery man "be he whig — Republican — Democrat or the Devil" — though to tell the truth he saw little difference between these last two. Somewhat wryly but nevertheless sincerely he informed Sumner that the Republican nominations were going over very well in Illinois.[26]

Regardless of his doubts in private correspondence, Herndon was ready to express himself vigorously in public for the Republican candidates. To Horace Greeley's New York *Tribune* he wrote a letter intended for publication, terming the nomination of Frémont and Dayton "quite popular . . . — the very best that could have been made." Characteristically exaggerating, he swore that the "prairie is on fire — the flames go with a leap and a bound, consuming the dry grass as they go. We think Illinois is safe . . . for Freedom, Free Speech and Freemont." [27] It was obvious to Illinoisans that this was untrue, for even the *Illinois State Journal* hesitated long before sponsoring Frémont's candidacy, and not a few complained that the Republican nominee had been "forced on the public by abolitionists." [28] The *State Register* promptly branded Herndon's letter as a roorback and taunted the author with "eloquently burn[ing] 'dry grass' . . . . by pen and ink process, on imaginary prairies." [29]

V

In spite of these inauspicious beginnings Herndon threw himself into the campaign with his usual zest. Ever since March he had been speaking for the anti-Nebraska cause, and now, as Republican elector for the sixth district, his services were more in demand than ever. As member of the state central committee he found himself burdened with administrative duties: clubs had to be formed, leaders trained, documents and campaign literature distributed, letters written, local canvasses made, rallies organized. He had no patience with the indifferent or the inactive. "Wake up and shake off that *timidity — sen-*

26 Herndon to Trumbull, July 12 and 29, 1856, Trumbull MSS.; Herndon to Sumner, June 20, 1856, Sumner MSS.
27 New York (daily) *Tribune*, July 8, 1856.
28 B. S. Edwards to Trumbull, July 24, 1856, Trumbull MSS.
29 *Illinois State Register*, July 12, 1856.

sitiveness or what not," he jacked up Richard Yates, whose republicanism seemed to be slipping; *"roll up your sleeves* & go into the fight like a tiger." "The Poets ought *to have said,"* he rather confusedly counseled his friend, "When you kiss a gal kiss her; but when in a fight then imitate the action of [a] Knightly hero." [30]

Even before the presidential nominations Herndon had collected two or three hundred dollars in the Springfield area and had purchased "Documents, speeches — books &c, and scattered them among our people." "I did this," he bragged proudly, "alone." Now that the lines were sharply drawn the Lincoln & Herndon office became the war office for the Republicans in central Illinois. In it were trained the active, vigorous young men who could be persuaded to join the party. Here, too, the party powwows were held, and to the partners the Republicans of the region reported.[31]

As a Frémont elector Billy was called to address anti-Nebraska rallies all over the state. Now for the first time he came into his own. He had an impressive sort of eloquence when he was sincerely roused, and his enthusiastic spirit was truly wrought up over the slavery extension issue. One of his auditors stated that he had heard Herndon many times before 1856 and frankly had heretofore classed him as a third-rate speaker; now, however, he was making "no common claptrap political speech" but a masterly effort characterized by facts, arguments and eloquence of the highest order.[32]

A part of Herndon's success lay in the fact that he had carefully studied the slavery issue and was an omnivorous reader of speeches and documents on the subject. The Richmond *Enquirer,* Fitzhugh's sociological defense of slavery, the Charleston *Mercury,* Bledsoe's *Liberty & Slavery,* Sumner's "Crime against Kansas" speech, reports of the congressional committees investigating Kansas, together with quotations from Thomas Jefferson and other founding fathers, furnished ammunition for his argument. Privately he was already convinced that there was an eternal antagonism between slavery and freedom, that "Freedom or slavery, reaching deep down into the white race, must perish quickly." [33] But impetuous as he was, Herndon throughout the campaign pitched his public arguments on a conservative note. He did not denounce slavery as such or deny the constitutional right of Southerners to hold slaves. The only question, he kept repeating, was "whether the fair plains of Kansas shall be preserved for freedom — or

[30] Herndon to Yates, September 11, 1856, photostat, collection of Thomas I. Starr.

[31] Herndon to Parker, December 27, 1856, Herndon-Parker MSS.

[32] "Viator," in *Illinois State Journal,* May 15, 1856.

[33] Herndon to Sumner, June 11, 1856, Sumner MSS.

cursed with slavery." [34] All other issues were irrelevant. If the North gave in on the question of extending slavery into Kansas, he said, it inevitably meant the spread of slavery over the whole country, to the white race as well as the black. His was an appeal directed toward the conservative Whigs of central Illinois.

It is extremely difficult to get any real idea of the success a speaker met in his rounds over the state. The Republican press played up every address and mass meeting as the outstanding event of the campaign and multiplied the crowds into inconceivable proportions. On the other hand, the Democratic newspapers felt it equally their business to sneer at the anti-Nebraska assemblies, to decry their orators, and to belittle their results. A perfect example of this problem is found in Herndon's address before a Republican rally at Jacksonville in June. According to the Republican *Morgan Journal,* Herndon began his speech in the county courthouse, but so large was the audience he was obliged to conclude it outside for the benefit of hundreds who could not crowd into the building. He tried to prove that the Democrats intended to make "*Slavery* national, and *Freedom* sectional." The argument, the reporter declared, was well taken and impregnably fortified; Herndon had proved that he would do good service as Republican elector. The orator had to stop in the middle of his speech (which had already lasted two and one-half hours) in order to catch a train, but after his departure nine lusty cheers were given for the Republican state ticket. [35]

It is almost impossible to recognize the same meeting from the account given in the ardently Democratic Jacksonville *Sentinel.* Reporting the attendance of a half-dozen of "the worshipers of the negro" and perhaps one hundred and fifty country people who happened to be in town to trade, the editor deemed the speech "mostly loose declamation of the slavery agitation stripe," "delivered in a stentorian voice and with the most animated gestures." Though Herndon "worked himself into a fury and nearly made the shingles on the old Court house jar from their places by his emphatic thumps, the speech seemed to fall cold upon the audience." So hostile was the reception, it was alleged, that Herndon finally gave up and "with a prolonged shriek for freedom sprung [*sic*] from the box in good leap-frog style" and ran away from the meeting. Nine cheers were proposed, but they "broke completely down about the fifth cheer, there being only some dozen

[34] Herndon's best, and most conservative, outline of the issues was an unsigned editorial in the *Illinois State Journal,* October 3, 1856.
[35] Jacksonville *Morgan Journal,* June 19, 1856.

voices joining in." The whole rally was "some considerable of a fizzle." [36]

Such reports, which are usually the only accounts of these meetings, were not meant to be accurate; they were intended to stir up partisan agitation and rivalry. It must be remembered when considering Herndon's activities during this canvass that all newspaper accounts were biased and intentionally inaccurate. In most cases it is impossible to reach the truth. The bewildered biographer simply pays his money and takes his choice.

All over the state Herndon stumped, in most cases apparently repeating the same speech. He addressed rallies at Decatur, Petersburg, Jacksonville, Middletown, Taylorville, Danville, Lincoln, Carlinville, Paris, Spring Creek, Springfield, Alton, Urbana, Athens — and at literally dozens of other towns. To Theodore Parker he confided that he "spoke on every stump and in every church & school house" in Sangamon County and "in almost every part of our wide extended state." [37]

There is no value in repeating the details of these appearances. In every case the Republican press acclaimed a smashing Frémont triumph, while the Democrats gloated over an absolute flop. By November Herndon guessed that he had spoken nearly a hundred times since the beginning of the canvass. This traveling over the state to address "tens and . . . ten thousands at once" was an exhausting life: railroad accommodations were primitive and stagecoaches were irregular; food was often bad and liquor too plentiful; the meetings were in the open air, so that the orator had to shout to reach the fringe of his crowd. An ordinary campaign address might last two or three hours, and a speaker was constantly bothered by heckling from the audience. But Herndon loved the excitement; "though I say it myself," he boasted, "I always spoke feelingly — earnestly — with force." Toward the end of the campaign, however, he was worn out and unwell. Nearly exhausted, he repeatedly complained of being "tired — throat sore — physically weak." [38]

VI

The role of political prophet is a hazardous one, and Herndon frankly avowed that he did not "speak from a tripod of inspiration." [39] Nevertheless, as Republican elector from the central Illinois region he

[36] Jacksonville *Sentinel,* June 20, 1856.
[37] Herndon to Parker, December 27, 1856, Herndon-Parker MSS.
[38] Herndon to Parker, December 27, 1856, *ibid.;* Herndon to Sumner, June 20, 1856, Sumner MSS.
[39] Herndon to Trumbull, March 4, 1857, Trumbull MSS.

was called on to make an estimate of the political situation. A former Whig himself, he could not understand why all his onetime associates did not follow him into the Republican camp; those who remained aloof must be both few and corrupt, a mere handful of men gaping for office. Since these were likely to join the Democrats, he thought that the Republicans should "indulge & rather assist" this minority in supporting Fillmore's candidacy.[40] With American (Know-Nothing) leaders at Springfield Herndon was on the best of terms and he even had access to the editorial columns of their newspaper, the *Conservative.* Freely the Democrats charged him with "intriguing with the friends of Mr. Fillmore." [41]

Herndon's delusion was shared by other Republican leaders until late in the campaign, when it suddenly became apparent that Fillmore was drawing votes not from Buchanan but from Frémont. By August the American forces in central Illinois were so strong as to split the anti-Nebraska vote "*right* in the *middle*," and a highly enthusiastic Fillmore mass meeting held in Springfield strikingly demonstrated that Lincoln, Herndon, and their friends had "met with a perfect rout in Sangamon." [42]

Belatedly the Republicans tried to right matters. Lincoln circulated a lithographed letter marked "confidential" to Whig acquaintances, advising that a vote for Fillmore in Illinois was really a ballot for Buchanan.[43] Herndon, too, tried to make this point by talking "in a kindly spirit — friendly feeling" with American leaders,[44] but he was not patterned for the role of peacemaker. In a more characteristic fashion he blazed out at John Todd Stuart, leader of the Fillmore forces, as "a very clever, honest sort of an old gentleman — who likes his ease." Stuart's real principles, Herndon asserted, were those of the Republicans, but he was simply too lazy to make the fight.[45] Such tactics were naturally resented; one need not wonder that Herndon could do nothing with the Fillmore men.[46]

In this desperate eleventh-hour fight against the American forces Billy resorted to an underhand expedient. Imposing on the friendship of the editor of the Springfield Fillmore newspaper, the *Conservative,* he had inserted in that journal an extract from the Richmond *En-*

[40] Herndon to Trumbull, May 20 and July 12, 1856, *ibid.*
[41] *Illinois State Register,* July 12, 1856.
[42] Richard Yates to Trumbull, August 3, 1856, Trumbull MSS.; *Illinois State Register,* October 11, 1856.
[43] Nicolay and Hay, eds., *Works,* II, 297–298.
[44] Herndon to Trumbull, August 4, 1856, Trumbull MSS.
[45] Editorial, unsigned but undoubtedly written by Herndon, *Illinois State Journal,* October 3, 1856.
[46] Edward L. Rankin to Richard Yates, October 7, 1856, Yates MSS.

quirer "endorsing slavery, and arguing that from principle the enslavement of either whites or blacks was justifiable and right." The article was displayed prominently in the August 28 issue of the paper, and it furnished effective ammunition for Republican orators to prove that "the leading Fil[l]more men . . . were bribed by the Buchanan corruption fund" and were really proslavery men.[47]

Toward the end of the campaign Herndon was nearly distracted. He was needed to speak at half a dozen places at once. Though exhausted he was "willing to work — toil — labor — encourage at any and all places and throughout every moment of time." He realized that the contest would be close and that central Illinois was not going to support the Republican candidates. "Sangamon," he mourned, "is very wrong. It is going to stay so & it cannot be helped." Though he was as hopeful and buoyant as ever, he clearly expected defeat. "The future," he wrote, keeping his chin high, "is however in my view." [48]

This time his prediction was right. When the ballots were counted in November it was found that Fillmore had diverted enough votes to give Buchanan the state's electoral vote.[49] But the new Republican party had made a strong showing. Frémont swept the northern half of the state with a heavy majority. "Our County has gone to the Devil to hunt Fremont," the Democratic election clerk from Henry County lamented. Douglas's friend, W. A. Richardson, was defeated by Bissell, who became the first Republican governor of Illinois. If the election was no anti-Nebraska triumph, at least it showed progress. "We Fremont men," Herndon rejoiced, "feel as if victory perched on our banner." The state election was "a burning — blasting censure to Douglass & Richardson." He chuckled: ". . . hell . . . will get two sweet morsels when they go. . . ." [50] After the votes were all in Herndon was tired but elated; crusading was a business he liked. "I shall ever hold the year 1856," he vowed, "the crown of my life." [51]

[47] *Herndon's Lincoln*, II, 369–370; Herndon to Weik, February 21, 1891, Herndon-Weik Coll. In reprinting the article, the *Conservative* ran an editorial denouncing the *Enquirer's* sentiments — but this was conveniently overlooked when Republican orators quoted the article.

[48] Herndon to Richard Yates, October 24, 1856, Yates MSS.

[49] The totals were: Buchanan electors, 105,528; Frémont electors, 96,278; Fillmore electors, 37,531. It is amusing to note that in this the only general election in which Herndon was ever a candidate, he received a few more votes (three) than did Lincoln. MS. election returns, Ill. State Archives.

[50] Herndon to Parker, November 12, 1856, Herndon-Parker MSS.

[51] Herndon to Sumner, February 11, 1857, Sumner MSS.

CHAPTER *vii*

Republican School Master

I

Five dollars a day was a lot of money, and with a wife and six children Herndon needed it. The family always had to have things: 1 pr Scissors, 1 Strip Flouncing, 1 pr Misses Shoes, 1 plush Cap, 1 pr Boys Boots, 8 yds Curtain Calico, 1 Silk Hkf 1.25, 1 Scrubbing Brush, 6 lb Best Coffee, Sad Irons.[1] Since income from the law was irregular and undependable, Herndon solicited from newly elected Governor Bissell an appointment as one of the three Illinois bank commissioners. Though strongly recommended by Lincoln, Trumbull, and Yates, Herndon thought his chances for office not very good; "this is the reason — I will never fawn — never will obtrude — Cannot dance attendance upon power; nor imperiously Exact what I want." Probably "some poor miserable creeper — adulator" would be the successful one in the race.[2]

Herndon was delighted when the governor sent his nomination to the senate, where it was quickly confirmed. "I will not disgrace the friends that assisted me," he pledged.[3] The new office paid five dollars for each day the commissioners worked,[4] it gave a certain position in society, and it furnished some political influence. Herndon was an ambitious young man, and this appointment was perhaps the first rung on the ladder of success. "I do not always intend to be where I am," he cryptically noted. "I do not want to say more. I think I know what Energy can do. Let this suffice for the present. . . ."[5]

[1] Items selected at random from Herndon's account. Jacob Bunn & Co. Journal [ledger] (Business Records Library, Univ. of Ill.).

[2] Herndon to Yates, November 24 and December 25, 1856, photostats in collection of Thomas I. Starr.

[3] Herndon to Yates, February 18, 1857, *ibid.*

[4] *Laws of Illinois, 1857*, 241. In 1857 Herndon earned $298.90 as bank commissioner; in 1858, $599.70; in 1859, $750.00; and in 1860–61, $2132.60. Illinois Warrant Ledgers (MS.), 1858–1862.

[5] Herndon to Yates, December 25, 1856, photostat in collection of Thomas I. Starr.

Republican School Master

To tell the truth, the bank commissioners did not have to do very much. The three men got together once in a while to determine whether the proper securities were deposited with the state auditor, and they would occasionally inspect some of the banks in the state to see that all was going well. Every year or so they would issue a report and make suggestions for the improvement of the state's financial system. It was not a sinecure by any means, but it was not very hard work either.

Herndon's appointment was made in February 1857, and he continued to hold this profitable position under Governor Yates during the Civil War years and probably under Governor Oglesby until the office was abolished in early 1865. These were years when the state's economic system was growing rapidly and was subject to the usual stresses of adolescence. There were two major panics — in 1857 and 1860–61 — and in both cases the Illinois banks "struggled nobly through the crisis." [6] This good fortune, however, was only in a negative sense due to Herndon. The commissioners did not do the wrong things, and the banks pulled through.

Herndon regarded his appointment a signal honor, and it made a considerable difference in his orientation. Prior to 1857 he had been an amateur in politics with no personal interest at stake. Now he was under heavy responsibility to keep the Republican machine lubricated and functioning smoothly. Owing his appointment in some measure to the influence of Lyman Trumbull, Herndon felt it his duty to keep the senator informed as to politics in Illinois. "I always intend to tell you the facts," he promised Trumbull; ". . . I should hate myself should I depart knowingly from this rule."

He soon had plenty of "facts" to tell his superior. The new legislature which assembled in the spring of 1857 was a disgrace. The Democrats in control proved themselves "viciously and idiotically mean, bordering upon . . . insanity; and would whirl men and constitutions to h—, if they could." It was absolutely true, he gossiped, that the Democratic legislators were drunk more than half the time. Sending up "their wild, silly, drunken guffaws" in the very capitol itself, they made "the *cheek* of a gentleman burn with shame." The chief sin of the legislators seems to have been an attempt to enact an apportionment law which would favor the Democrats in the approaching senatorial election. Herndon was a tolerant man, he said, but this was simply the limit of human endurance. Making "no foolish hot outbursting threats," he incoherently warned: ". . . if the nigger-drivers do not cease to drive men . . . and measures over the graves of man —

[6] *Reports Made to the General Assembly of Illinois, 1859*, I, 193.

faiths and constitutions, . . . if they expect submission to the infernal behests of their Satanic power, . . . they will be met — well, I know not where; but only fear." [7]

Slowly and hesitantly Herndon was coming to believe in an inevitable conflict between the sections on the slavery question. Theodore Parker had posed this issue in 1856, but Herndon did not then take it too seriously. He "*dreamed* that this question would wear [?] off and get more dim, and less terrible . . . somewhat like a mirage . . . slipping along over the sandy desert," but that was when prospects looked bright for Republican success. Now both state and nation were in the hands of the enemy, and the "firey logic of sweeping events" made it dazzlingly clear to Herndon that this intolerable situation could not long endure. [8]

II

Then in March 1857 Herndon's mind was made up. The Supreme Court of the United States in an interminable and inextricably involved series of opinions produced what was known as the Dred Scott decision. With nine separate opinions in the case, it was hard at first to know just what the Court had decided concerning the slave Scott who had claimed freedom because of temporary residence in free territory. But when the excess verbiage was cleared away it seemed that the highest tribunal had pronounced on two major issues: (1) a Negro could not be a citizen of the United States; (2) the Missouri Compromise was not and never had been constitutional. The case rapidly acquired notoriety far out of proportion to its real significance. After all, Scott was almost immediately freed by his owners, the question of citizenship was not a live issue in any Northern state, and the Missouri Compromise had already been repealed three years before.

But in the North the skillful propaganda of such Republican journalists as Horace Greeley spread an entirely different conception of the Dred Scott case. Calmer voices were shouted down and it was everywhere repeated that the Dred Scott decision was a thing of major importance, a triumph of the slavocracy in the national government. The Court was acting in "a conspiracy . . . of the most treasonable character" to hand over the whole nation "into the hands of the Slave oligarchy." Citizens had nightmares of Negro "coffle-gangs on their way through Illinois or Indiana to Kansas or Minnesota," with Chi-

[7] Herndon to Trumbull, February 17 and March 2, 1857, Trumbull MSS.
[8] Herndon to Parker, March 10, 1857, Herndon-Parker MSS.

cago becoming a slave market. "Freedom and white men are no longer safe," it was blatantly proclaimed.[9]

Central Illinois was particularly hard hit by the decision. Herndon caught the reaction graphically: "Did you ever see an ox knocked down in a butchers stall — So the People are hit right in the face; and did you ever see that ox rise and run reeling — wild — bleeding — bellowing, mad, furious and destructive — so gather up the People their quivering spasmodic energy."[10] For himself Herndon was convinced that the decision "whips out State rights — crushes justice — defies right . . . drives back this hoping, burning age . . . into barbarism."[11] It was the pronouncement of a "despotocratic Court"; never again would he quote the decisions of Chief Justice Taney in his legal work. The Dred Scott case was but an opening wedge by which the South intended to extend universal slavery over white and black into the Northern states.

Where did it lead? What could a man do? Like hundreds of thousands of excited Northerners, Herndon saw an inescapable conclusion: the South was dragging the nation into civil war. With painful frankness, Herndon exposed his mental processes to Theodore Parker:

> I have tremblingly, throbbingly, and as rationally and as cautiously, as I could, turned and returned, split and divided — analyzed and compounded this question — the slave question — ; and I see no way open but cowardice in the North — a "back down" in the south or — open, bloody, civil war. *It is horrible.* You will excuse my timidity . . . as you are aware that almost all my relations live in the South — that that is my . . . child-home. If, however, the worst comes I hope to act the part of a man — not cruelly, but firmly in humanity.

"I want peace, but not at the dear & degrading price of Cowardice & pusillanimity." The course of events was beyond human control, and "God . . . even if he *desires* . . . cannot turn away the catastrophy [*sic*]." Looking out over the dim gulf of the future, Herndon could only shudder and cry, " 'Horror' — 'Horror.' "[12]

In retrospect one is tempted to ask: Why all the excitement? Why all the noise and fireworks? Had anyone been injured? Why wreck the

[9] New York *Evening Post,* Chicago *Tribune,* and *Illinois State Journal,* quoted in Beveridge, *Lincoln,* II, 488–489.

[10] Herndon to Parker, March 30, 1857, Herndon-Parker MSS. Actually Herndon was exaggerating the amount of attention paid to the decision, in the newspapers at least. Beveridge, *Lincoln,* II, 497–498.

[11] Herndon to Parker, March 10, 1857, Herndon-Parker MSS.

[12] Herndon to Parker, March 30 and September 8, 1857, *ibid.;* Herndon to E. B. Washburne, February 10, 1858, Washburne MSS.

Union because a repealed statute was declared unconstitutional? Was anybody really serious in thinking that Illinois might be made a slave state? Why go about hearing ancestral voices prophesying war? Surely everything fundamental and sane in American society demanded peace. There was work for Americans to do. Out on the prairies houses were rising, and farm lands were rich with wheat and corn. In the East the pulse beat of the future could be felt. The city was growing, the huge metropolis, with tower climbing on tower and factories pointing dirty fingers at the sky. The future was pregnant with illimitable promise. There was a great day coming. All that was needed was to work together, to cooperate, to leave aside petty bickering. That was the American way.

Instead, of course, there came stupid, suicidal war. Ambition and avarice, blundering and bungling, politics and discordant personalities all worked together with the idiotic inanity of fate to make a needless war an irrepressible conflict. It is not hard to feel sympathy for the real leaders of the abolitionist crusade. One can only respect William Lloyd Garrison, swept away by the remorseless soundness of his logic: slavery was an evil; evil must be extirpated; therefore, slavery must be abolished. But it is the political leaders, the champions of little causes, who are so difficult to understand. They were not fighting slavery in the abstract; these St. Georges battled only dwarf dragons. Douglas would shortly dissolve the great national Democratic party over the future of two slaves in Kansas; Lincoln would let a nation rise in arms to prevent the extension of slavery to regions where nature had already prohibited it; Herndon would willingly sit down to the bloody feast of civil war in order to forestall a hypothetical attempt on the part of an imaginary Southern despotism to extend slavery into Illinois.

In retrospect Herndon's stand seems hard to justify, yet the utter sincerity of his beliefs is not to be questioned. It is his logic that is vulnerable. From any objective standpoint, the handful of Negroes in Kansas would appear to pose no world-shaking problem. From a historical point of view, the notion of a supposed project to nationalize the peculiar institution is groundless. Yet these were the issues for which Herndon was willing to split the nation, to "*Cut through the Constitution.*" [13]

The explanation is, of course, that man does not live by logic alone. Herndon's mind was a curious jumble of inherited proclivities and acquired dislikes, of selfishness and altruism, of impulse and reason and rationalization. When he reached into this grab bag in a time of crisis,

[13] Herndon to Parker, February 20, 1858, Herndon-Parker MSS.

102

the odds were against his acting at the dictates of pure reason alone. The tragedy was that Herndon himself was fundamentally decent. All his better instincts shuddered at the thought of sectional strife. He loved the South; he surrounded it with that golden aura that clings to one's "child-home"; he respected its traditions of chivalry and culture. But he was so impulsive, so impressionable, so easily influenced. He liked to think of himself as a sophisticated observer, a keen analyst of men and events, "hard to fool, friend, by man." If he considered himself a student of human nature, even more did he fancy the role of philosopher, a backwoods Thoreau, with an infallible instinct for truth, a clairvoyant intuition which permitted him to "see to the gizzard" of the most difficult question. He was "a kind of peoples boy," he believed; "I am with them, and when they do not know it, I am pillowing my chin on my hand, looking right into their souls." Lesser men might struggle to this high point of vision over the treacherous crags of logic, but Herndon leaped there with one bound. His "dog sagacity," his "mud instinct," told him what to do, and he did it.[14]

This was the way that Herndon thought about his own mental processes. What actually happened in his brain was considerably different. Herndon's main failing was an undue respect for the printed page. He read omnivorously — and believed everything he read. But having once studied a book he tended to think of its views as his own, arrived at by intuition and, therefore, unalterably true and valid. Did Wendell Phillips make a speech denouncing the Constitution? Herndon read it and — until he got another book — was absolutely certain that "the only way to cut the knot" was to *Cut through the Constitution.* Did Theodore Parker denounce "Everett, Winthrop, Choate, & the like"? Herndon promptly concluded that Choate, Everett, and Winthrop were "Poor fools." With an unusually retentive memory he would echo, often unconsciously, the sentiments of the last author he had been reading, even as to words and shades of meaning; it was a case of impressing "the hard steel upon a softer plate." [15]

The antislavery agitation had an unfortunate effect on Herndon's personality. He lost something of that exuberance and versatility that had made him a worthy example of the *Aufklärung* in the Middle West. Now all his emotions were squeezed through one wine press and the juice was bitter. In his calmer moments Herndon himself realized what was happening. "My *colored brethren* here," he wrote in joshing style

---

[14] Herndon to Parker, April 8 and December 19, 1857, September 20 and November 24, 1858, Herndon-Parker MSS.

[15] Herndon to Parker, April 23, 1855, and February 20, 1858; Parker to Herndon, December 31, 1857, *ibid.*

to a Democratic friend, "say — 'why — Good *Lord-a-massy* Billy — de Nigger am the great object of the American Globe . . . — dey am always de talk — Can't legislate for mail bags: but that the nigger am in the threads. . . .'" [16] But for the most part Herndon had the intolerance of a man whose knowledge comes entirely from books. He knew all about slavery — about the number of Negroes, and slave insurrections, and the value of Southern crops. He could give a disquisition on European forms of servitude and denounce the Inquisition and the Bastille. He could detail the legislative history of the Missouri Compromise and the Kansas-Nebraska bill. But did he really know slavery? He left Kentucky an infant, and, except for one hasty visit in 1858, probably never returned to a slave state. Lincoln was bound by birth and marriage to the Southern tradition; Douglas had firsthand knowledge of slavery in actual practice; Herndon knew it only from books. It was a thing to be pointed at — from a distance — to be censured, to be feared. It never occurred to him that slavery was something more than organized oppression, that the plantation was a way of life.

Serious and sardonic, Herndon lacked the genial tolerance of Lincoln. He was obsessed by the notion of a mission to be performed. And, like Joshua R. Giddings, he was sure "that the truth was *all on one side*' — his own — and it followed that whoso disagreed with him must be at least unprincipled, and probably downright villainous." [17] For this moral crusade he stripped himself of all extraneous interests. Temperance? He was still for it, but it should not be discussed just now. Springfield could stay drunk until the slaves in Kansas were freed.[18] Woman's rights? Public schools? Civic improvements? They would have to wait. With terrifying single-mindedness and utter sincerity of purpose Herndon was to devote the next three years to the stirring up of antislavery sentiment. He had deliberately chosen to sow the wind.

III

The summer of 1857 was terrifically hot, and men neglected business to sprawl under the shade of the State House in the public square. It was much too warm to get excited over politics. Since the city elections in the spring, at which the Republicans were defeated, even routine party work was neglected, and Herndon was forced to admit that

---

[16] Herndon to J. A. McClernand, December 8, 1859, McClernand MSS.

[17] Robert Phillips Ludlum, "Joshua Giddings, Radical," *Miss. Valley Hist. Rev.*, XXIII, 56.

[18] Herndon to Parker, April 8, 1857, Herndon-Parker MSS.

in spite of some speaking by Lincoln there was "a lull in the political horizon generally." [19] To woo radical elements unattracted by the sedate *Illinois State Journal*, party leaders agreed to support a new paper for the state capital, the Springfield *Republican*. It was what Mrs. Lincoln justly termed "another worthless little paper," [20] but Herndon found its editorial columns congenial for the type of anti-Democratic abuse with which he hoped to stir up enthusiasm for the Republican cause.

In June Douglas returned to build fences and to explain how the Democrats ought to react to the Dred Scott case. Speaking in Springfield, he declared that, while the decision was law, there was no cause to believe that slavery could exist in any territory without local legislative protection; since slave owners would fear to take their property into a region where police protection was not assured them, the decision, so far as Kansas was concerned, was of no special importance. Herndon, along with other Republican leaders, was in the audience, and the *State Register* sarcastically hoped that the speech had done him good. [21]

It did not. He returned home and dashed off a series of scathing articles attacking Douglas and his speech in a most virulent manner. For several days his editorials appeared in the *Republican*, which had little other matter to print, and Herndon boasted that they were "said to be good — high toned." [22] The Little Giant, he wrote, "is not the Douglas of 1850 or 1854. He is conscious of . . . the power of the people outraged . . . ; and so he . . . is somewhat cut; he is full of seeming humility; his long whip fore-finger did not crack so commandingly as was its wont." "[P]inched, cramped, shriveled up," his "squat form is low and his voice harsh." Poor man! "Poor tool of Southern despots!" Did he really hope to allay the uprising bubbles in the seething national cauldron? He and the "boastful iron-chain democracy" had received orders from the South "to 'file in and obey,'" and they had fallen in line. [23] "O — what a scoundrel" was Douglas! [24]

Having become "a kind of Republican school master" for central Illinois, [25] Herndon was naturally involved in all the political maneuver-

[19] Herndon's letter in New York (daily) *Tribune*, July 6, 1857.

[20] Nicolay and Hay, eds., *Works*, II, 314.

[21] Henry A. Converse, "The House of the House Divided." Ill. State Hist. Soc., *Trans.*, 1924, 161.

[22] Herndon to Parker, June 17 and 22, 1857, Herndon-Parker MSS.

[23] Springfield *Republican*, June 15, 1857, quoted in Newton, *Lincoln and Herndon*, 118; unsigned editorial, unquestionably by Herndon, Springfield *Republican*, July 6, 1857.

[24] Herndon to Parker, July 4, 1857, Herndon-Parker MSS.

[25] Herndon to Parker, September 8, 1857, *ibid*.

ings in that part of the state. When a crucial election had to be carried, he was willing to "COLONIZE — some four or five districts, and begin now . . . with money — and the end Justifies the means in this instance. . . ."[26] Frequently he was called in for conferences with party leaders in Chicago to make plans and set up committees. Politics was getting to be his business.

But he was not too busy to drop everything when he heard the trumpet of justice calling. Late in July Springfield was shocked to learn that a Negro in Logan County, a few miles north, had been arrested as a fugitive slave and was to be haled before the United States Commissioner at the state capital. Some anxious fears were aroused over this first fugitive slave case to be tried in central Illinois. In the East when the Negro Anthony Burns was returned to slavery Theodore Parker and Wendell Phillips had incited a riot, the jail was stormed, one man was killed and others wounded, and Boston was in tumult as federal troops returned the slave to the waiting ship in the harbor. The only previous case in Illinois had been an attempt to seize a Negro hiding in Chicago. There too the populace had been vastly perturbed, and the federal authorities were unsuccessful in attempting to return the slave. What would happen now in Springfield?

It may have been the weather or it may have been the "superiority of the moral condition of Springfield,"[27] but though there was much interest there was little excitement in the state capital. The Negro was, of course, poor, and Herndon "freely — quickly as well as freely" volunteered his legal services for the defense,[28] securing also the assistance of John E. Rosette, a better Republican than he was a lawyer. For the slave's owner appeared Herndon's brother, the crabbed and crippled Elliott. Perhaps Billy Herndon had dreamed of making an excoriating attack on the institution of slavery, of flaying the fugitive slave law, of roasting the United States Commissioner; his friend Theodore Parker had done all these things in Boston, and Herndon had enthusiastically pronounced the effort "good . . . didactic, but powerful."[29]

Springfield was to see no explosion. When the case came up, it concerned not the basic rights of humanity but such prosaic points as the sufficiency of the claimant's power of attorney and the right of the Negro to produce counsel in court. In this last matter Herndon felt especially aggrieved. ". . . I came near having my own dear rights

[26] O. M. Hatch to Trumbull, July 13, 1857, Trumbull MSS. This letter was written after Hatch had a talk with Herndon.
[27] *Illinois State Register*, August 2, 1857.
[28] Herndon to Parker, August 4, 1857, Herndon-Parker MSS.
[29] Herndon to Parker, February 16, 1856, *ibid*.

stricken down," he complained, "by my own brother. I fought till I got my own rights. It was contended that I *had no right to appear in Court* for the negro. I repelled this in language strong & manly, if *I* may say so." But all his efforts were of no use when ten dollar gold pieces were "gingling [*sic*] in the ears of the hell-gopher Commissioner," and the Negro was returned to his Kentucky owner.[30]

Springfield was stirred up over the case for days. The Democratic *State Register* was so happy that the episode had passed over without public disturbance that it mildly complimented "Col. Herndon" for his display of "those powers of eloquence for which he is distinguished." [31] But most people thought Herndon's stand outrageously wrong and a bad example to young lawyers in the city. Only the radical *Republican* praised Herndon's "unwearied efforts in behalf of justice and Freedom." [32]

I V

Meanwhile the United States was again having Kansas trouble. It was a rash that broke out before each election in the East. The whole situation was an impossible complex of politics, personalities, and principles, and there were those who deliberately chose to make the muddle more obscure. The affair was full of errors, but he was sardonic indeed who could see it as a comedy. At long last, in 1857, Kansas was ready to draw up a constitution in preparation for entrance into the federal union. Now popular sovereignty was to be put to a test, for Kansas could choose whether it desired slavery. As a preliminary step a registration of voters in the territory was conducted by federal officials. Distrusted as tools of a slavocracy, the registrars were refused permission to enter certain of the antislavery counties. When the time for election of the constitutional convention approached, it was ruled that only registered voters should participate. The free-soil elements were utterly outraged; the whole business, they swore angrily, was a trick on the part of the slave drivers. At the advice of Eastern Republican leaders, it was determined that no antislavery votes should be cast in the election. The election took place, free-soil voters abstained, and most of the members chosen for the convention came from the Southern element of the population. In writing a constitution for Kansas the proslavery convention determined not to submit the whole

[30] Herndon to Parker, August 4, 1857, *ibid.* For full reports on the case see *Illinois State Register,* August 1, 1857.

[31] *Illinois State Register,* August 1, 1857.

[32] Herndon to Parker, September 8, 1857, enclosing undated clipping from Springfield *Republican,* Herndon-Parker MSS.

document to the people for acceptance or rejection but to allow voting only on that clause relating to the establishment of slavery in the state. Kansans would have the constitution willy-nilly, but could vote on the "Constitution with Slavery" or the "Constitution with no Slavery." In this way, regardless of the action of the voters, the property rights vested in the few slaves already in the region would be safeguarded.

The document was sent East so that Congress could approve it and admit Kansas as a state. Naturally the Republicans would fight this Lecompton constitution, but they objected to everything that was ever done in Kansas, and tired old James Buchanan determined to disregard their thunderings. The constitution was not exactly what he had wanted, for he would have preferred that the whole document be submitted to the people; but it had been written by a perfectly legal convention, and if popular sovereignty meant anything, it was that the people of a territory could determine their own course. If Kansans did not want to vote on their whole constitution, the President felt, it was their business. And with a desperate appeal not to loose again the baying hounds of sectional strife, he submitted the Lecompton constitution to Congress.

In Congress the leader of the opposition was not one of the "Black Republican" guard; it was none other than the father of popular sovereignty himself, the senior senator from Illinois, Stephen A. Douglas. His had been a hard decision to make. There were personal factors in his choice, of course; he did not like Buchanan, and he had been slighted in the handing out of federal patronage. Besides, he was shortly coming up for re-election and Illinois opinion was virtually unanimous in opposing Lecompton. But there was more to his stand. Popular sovereignty meant that the whole people of a territory should decide on their domestic institutions, while this Lecompton constitution was admittedly the work of a minority of the inhabitants of Kansas. Was the principle which Douglas considered a fundamental rule of democratic procedure to be sacrificed because of expediency and mere technical legality? After solemn deliberation the Little Giant announced he would fight the Lecompton constitution and would endeavor to have the whole document submitted to the people of Kansas. From that day the great national Democratic party was split, and from that moment the road to war was all downhill.

Republican leaders naturally rejoiced when Douglas rose to denounce the President from the Senate floor. This "Mad-dog . . . grown fat by devouring our sheep" now was *"biting our enemies,"* opined Theodore Parker; "'Dog eat *Wolf*,' say I."[33] Here was a recruit as powerful as Seward, Sumner, or Chase. True, he had formerly been a foe, but he was a brave man. The best thing to do would be to "Forget the past and sustain the *righteous*."[34] To the Douglas house on Minnesota Row came the leaders of the Republican party for consultation and advice in the battle against Buchanan. Bald, benignant Horace Greeley, beneath whose shiny pate whirled a multitude of intrigues, hustled to Washington to interview the new convert and dashed back to New York convinced that Douglas was already a Republican in all but name. Other Republican politicos were there too, prompting and prodding. Reporters observed that Douglas was receiving an unusual number of guests — Massachusetts senator Henry Wilson, "the Natick cobbler," for example, and New York's William H. Seward. Republicans everywhere rejoiced over Douglas's defection. And if the Little Giant was going to fight the Republican battle in Congress, did not decency as well as common sense demand that Republicans support him in his race for re-election to the Senate?

V

Back in Illinois, Springfield Republicans were pleased too, at first. Why should they not also say to Douglas: "Seize 'em — bite 'em Kill 'em Choke 'em"? Why should they complain if their enemies were divided? Illinois Democrats were certainly confused enough by Douglas's bold maneuver. Some, like Herndon's father and brothers, sided with the President, and many more supported the senator. It was obviously the duty of every Republican to "create the split wanted" among the opposing party, "to make it wider and deeper — hotter and more impassible . . . between the worshipers of Buck & Dug." The position of the Republicans was considerably improved. No longer were the Douglas men so positive that Herndon was "*crazy*" or "ought to be sent to an asylum" for his earlier opposition to Buchanan; some of them even sidled apologetically into the office and borrowed speeches of Seward and Sumner. To top it all, Douglas began sending public documents to the Lincoln & Herndon office. Astounded, the junior member was now sure that "The world does move I verily believe."[35]

[33] Parker to Herndon, December 31, 1857, *ibid.*
[34] Herndon to Lincoln, Boston, March 24, 1858, Herndon-Weik Coll., quoting Horace Greeley.
[35] Herndon to Parker, December 26, 1857, January 8 and February 24, 1858, Herndon-Parker MSS.; Herndon to Trumbull, February 19, 1858, Trumbull MSS.

So far the Illinois Republican leaders could agree with their Eastern contemporaries. And in spite of themselves they were impressed by the magnificent fight Douglas was putting up against the administration. Even Herndon confessed with admiration: "Douglas is more of a man than I took him to be: he has got some nerve at least." Deep down in his heart Billy had always hidden a secret respect for the man, "a kind of undeveloped feeling," and he too was happy to welcome this valuable ally.[36]

He was certain, though, that Douglas was not honest in any particular and that the only principle upon which he acted was an insatiable lust for political power. "I can read him about as well as he knows himself," Herndon told his correspondents, and he said he could deduce Douglas's motives by clairvoyant insight.[37] Did any man think that Douglas cared a hoot about the principle of popular sovereignty? Nonsense. He was only "a *policy educated Devil*," who realized that the Buchanan hatchet men were out for his scalp anyway.[38] By his dramatic attack on the Lecompton bill Douglas would hope to win united Northern support, for by 1860 the free states would dominate the electoral college. The North was "the real *place* of power," and "where Power is *there is the political buzzards*." Douglas's course was charted out by the law of his ambition, and he would inevitably move to join the Republican party. There might be "some perturbations — some obscurations," but unless he was "a fool — an ass — a mad orb blazing unchained towards h—," he was destined to "gyrate and wheel and blaze and shine" in the antislavery galaxy. Meanwhile, Herndon felt, Douglas was certainly helping the Republicans along.[39]

With high hopes Illinois Republicans began planning for the elections of 1858, which would determine the choice of United States senator to succeed Douglas. Herndon was in constant correspondence with all the party leaders — Senator Trumbull, Representative E. B. Washburne, editor Joseph Medill of the Chicago *Tribune,* and a dozen others. There were mailing lists to be made up, and he had to see to the collection of a "'pony' purse" to buy campaign documents. In January 1858 he attended private Republican meetings at which it was agreed that the party must support as Douglas's opponent "a man — good & true — generous & noble, hating Slavery, loving man," a bill which only Abraham Lincoln could fill. Herndon did his best to per-

[36] Herndon to Trumbull, December 16, 1857, and April 24, 1858, Trumbull MSS.
[37] Herndon to Parker, September 20, 1858, Herndon-Parker MSS.
[38] Herndon to Sumner, January 28, 1858, Sumner MSS.
[39] Herndon to Trumbull, December 25, 1857, Trumbull MSS.; Herndon to Parker, December 26, 1857, Herndon-Parker MSS.

suade Eastern friends that his partner was the equal of either Douglas or Trumbull — "if not their superior"; this was, he knew, "saying a good deal, yet it is true." [40]

So well was the battle shaping up that Billy could afford the luxury of "a kind of dim — distant sympathy for those poor deluded fools" in the Democratic party. As for Douglas, the "paths of a simple *politician* are narrow — straight & slippery: below is the gulf, deep yawning." He had tripped, and now, "the Devil will get him: he is lost & gone." "Poor Dug!" [41]

[40] Herndon to Trumbull, January 15 and February 27, 1858, Trumbull MSS.; Herndon to Sumner, January 28, 1858, Sumner MSS.

[41] Herndon to Trumbull, February 27, 1858, Trumbull MSS.

CHAPTER *viii*

Lincoln's Man Friday

I

For years Herndon had nursed a desire to go East, to visit the historic sights and to see the great intellectual leaders of his time. It would be a grand event for a Sucker, a man whose horizon had been limited to Kentucky and Illinois, to *"come East & see the world of matter and man."* [1] In 1858, for the first time in his life, he could spare time for the trip. As was usual with state officials, he traveled on a railroad pass, but anyway he had plenty of money then; [2] and early in March he bundled up and started on the way to Washington, New York, Boston, and points east.

There has been much misunderstanding about this trip of Herndon's. Democrats in Illinois speculated that his excursion was connected with the struggle then raging in Congress over the adoption of the Lecompton constitution. It was widely believed that "the Republicans do not wish the defeat of the Kansas constitution," because all the credit would redound to Douglas; if the Lecompton measure were defeated, Democrats feared, "the Republicans will turn all . . . [Douglas's] good intentions to their own benefit." [3] It was erroneously rumored that Lincoln and the editor of the *Illinois State Journal,* had entrusted Billy with "the necessary instructions to the Illinois black republican members" of Congress as to how to act on Lecompton. [4]

Herndon's own account of the incident, [5] though it has been frequently repeated, is equally distorted. Early in 1858 Illinois Republicans, he recollected, were preparing for the coming senatorial campaign with Lincoln as their chosen leader, but they waited until Horace

[1] Herndon to Parker, April 28, 1856, Herndon-Parker MSS.
[2] Herndon to Weik, December 23, 1885, Herndon-Weik Coll.
[3] Joel A. Matteson to Stephen A. Douglas, March 5, 1858, Douglas MSS.
[4] *Illinois State Register,* March 6, 1858.
[5] Herndon's long delayed reminiscence of his trip East may be found in *Herndon's Lincoln,* II, 390–396.

Greeley's tremendously influential New York *Tribune* should open the ball by giving the signal. Instead, Greeley and other Eastern Republicans were seriously thinking that Illinois should support Douglas for his Lecompton stand, no signal came, and the party in Illinois "slumbered as with a chill — a *bivouac* of death upon an iceberg." [6] Lincoln, Herndon said, was "dejected — melancholic," and told his partner that "Greel[e]y is not doing me, an old republican and a tried Antislavery man, right: he is taking up Douglas — an untrue and an untried man. . . . I wish that some one could put a flea in Greel[e]y's ear — see Trumbull — Sumner, Wilson — Seward — Parker — Garrison — Phil[l]ips & others, and try and turn the currents in the right directions." The impetuous Herndon "*inferred*" that Lincoln wanted him to go, immediately packed his valise, and set out on a one-man crusade to enlighten the East. He talked to Republican leaders everywhere, and from that time "things began more and more to work for Lincoln's success." Again Herndon had saved the day.[7]

It is not hard to see how this story could rise and how Herndon could convince himself that it was true. Certainly Greeley and other Republican leaders had thought of dickering with Douglas, even though the negotiations never went very far. Lincoln himself was afraid of the "constant eulogising, and admiring, and magnifying" of Douglas in the columns of the New York *Tribune* and feared it portended "sacrificing us here in Illinois." [8] But the rest of the story has a counterfeit ring. It was never the practice of the Republican party in Illinois to wait a signal from a New York paper to open their campaign. Nor is there any evidence that Herndon and his friends were particularly distressed by Greeley's course early in the year. On the contrary, they were sure that "Douglas is dead . . . — knows he is lost," and were, therefore, quite enthusiastic.[9] There is no word in any of Herndon's letters in early 1858 to indicate that he feared a selling out of the Illinois Republicans or that his trip was caused by dread of such a potentiality.

To Theodore Parker, from whom he kept no secrets, Herndon confided his real purposes for going East. He fully expected to be Republican elector in Illinois again in 1860, and in order to make more effec-

[6] Herndon to Parker, September 25, 1858, Herndon-Parker MSS.

[7] Herndon to Weik, December 23, 1885, Herndon-Weik Coll. In this same letter Herndon confessed: "It is now 30 years since I went . . . ; and I may have forgotten much of what was said — when — where &c. &c. . . . I may err in some things."

[8] Tracy, *Uncollected Letters*, 83–84.

[9] Statement of N. B. Judd quoted approvingly in Herndon to Parker, February 20, 1858, Herndon-Parker MSS.; Herndon to Trumbull, February 27, 1858, Trumbull MSS.

tive speeches he "wanted to see the places of Revolutionary memory, and the three living *institutions* of Boston — Garrison, Parker & Phil-[l]ips" so as to be able to "talk knowingly" about them. En route he was going to stop in Washington to "see in Douglas' face: . . . to look *him* in the eye." Herndon had, he told Parker, been with the Little Giant "in all conditions & *states*," and because of that "peculiar *tie* which binds men together, who have drank 'bouts' together" could "read him about as well as he knows himself." "[I]f I could look Douglas *in the eye*," he was confident, "I could tell what was going on." Parker, rather shocked, agreed noncommittally that there might be a sort of "Freemasonry in *drinking*." [10]

II

With these objectives Herndon set out on his travels. The bustle and the brilliance of the national capital were confusing to this son of the prairies; he felt like "a stranger and a wanderer in the lands of proud haughty men." "To tell you the truth," he was forced to confess, "I did not like Washington." [11] Senator Trumbull cordially welcomed this Illinois friend and passed on to him an amazing piece of news: among certain Republican leaders there was "a DISPOSITION to sell out Illinois" and support Douglas's bid for renomination. Herndon was both "astonished . . . and thunder struck," for this put an entirely new light on the whole political situation. [12] Where he had formerly justified Greeley "*in full*, as to . . . Compliments of Douglas," he now began to fear that the New York *Tribune's* "puffs" might mean that Douglas would be "elevated over the heads of long and well tried Republicans — men who have toiled and battled for us a quarter of a century." [13] Alarmed, he felt that something had to be done; his pleasure jaunt began to have political implications.

In Washington Senator Seward, the outstanding national leader of the Republican party, and Henry Wilson, Massachusetts cobbler turned solon, confirmed Trumbull's startling news, but Herndon missed the chance to sound Charles Sumner, who was then in New York. Douglas was ill, but when Herndon presented his card he was shown up to the senator's room, where he had his chance to look him in the eye. They sat puffing cigars and discussing all manner of things

[10] Herndon to Parker, March 4, May 29, and September 20, 1858; Parker to Herndon, September 23, 1858, Herndon-Parker MSS.
[11] Herndon to Trumbull, April 7, 1858, Trumbull MSS.
[12] Herndon to Parker, September 20 and November 24, 1858, Herndon-Parker MSS.
[13] Herndon to Greeley, April 8, 1858, Greeley MSS.

— from Southern filibustering expeditions to the credibility of Horace Greeley. Douglas remarked that he had achieved his purpose, that he was not in the way of Lincoln or his party, and that he did not intend to provoke conflict. It was an inconclusive sort of interview, and for the first time it occurred to Herndon that the senator might also be an expert at reading eyes. At the end Douglas said warmly: "Give Mr. Lincoln my regards . . . when you return, and tell him I have crossed the river and burned my boat" — and Herndon wondered what he really meant.[14]

From Washington Herndon hurried to New York to straighten out Horace Greeley. The erratic New York editor talked bitterly against Illinois Republican papers for not supporting Douglas in his present course and said they were fools; quite evidently, thought Herndon, he wanted Douglas sustained and sent back to the Senate.[15] After considerable argument Herndon left the *Tribune* office convinced that he had converted the editor to the Lincoln cause; Greeley, apparently unaware that Herndon was Lincoln's partner, was sure that Illinois would henceforth support Douglas.

After New York, Boston. What a wonderful place it was, this grand city, this "world of granite — a city of *places* and *squares*"! And there was so much to see: "men — manners — intellect — power — Nature, material & spiritual . . . — machinery — the arts & sciences." Herndon was so excited that he studied while he ran and almost reflected while he slept.[16] As he had imagined, Massachusetts was "the brain of this social, religious & political organism."[17]

For ten days Herndon "footed it alone over Boston's rocky streets — *green* and unnoticed."[18] He had letters of introduction to the bobbin-boy-governor, N. P. Banks, but Massachusetts political managers gave him scant attention. Who, they asked, was this nobody? Worst of all Theodore Parker snubbed him. For months Herndon had been storing up wise remarks and profound observations to tell the Massachusetts minister; he would straighten him out on so many matters and reveal so much that could not be said in letters. When he visited the great man in his library Herndon released this "*gasseous gush*" of philosophical politics. With acute self-consciousness he realized that he was becoming "too social — too talkative," but he was so embarrassed he

[14] *Herndon's Lincoln*, II, 393–394; Herndon to Parker, June 1, 1858, Herndon-Parker MSS.
[15] Herndon to Lincoln, Boston, March 24, 1858, Herndon-Weik Coll.; Herndon to Trumbull, April 12, 1858, Trumbull MSS.
[16] Herndon to Parker, April 7, 1858, Herndon-Parker MSS.
[17] Herndon to Sumner, February 11, 1857, Sumner MSS.
[18] Herndon to E. L. Pierce, March 4, 1861, copy in Herndon-Weik Coll.

could not stop. Used to giving Delphic pronouncements himself, Parker had no time to waste on this babbling oracle and cut Herndon off short. "*You* chained me," Herndon grieved.[19]

It was no wonder that Herndon became homesick and found these Yankees "repulsive"; they were all so "cold and incommunicable," so busy with their own affairs. The women were a little more polite, and he found them "spontaneously good — generous and true," but as "a poor ignorant sucker" with a gift for "intuitive *seeing* of human character" Herndon pronounced anathema on the men. Miserably he felt he had been a proud reigning ass for ever hoping to know and like them.[20]

Only one man in Boston had time for the Illinois visitor. The "nation's great outlaw," William Lloyd Garrison, whom Herndon had pictured as "shrivelled — cold — selfish — haughty," welcomed him cordially into the *Liberator* office, where they had a short conversation. So happy was Herndon to find a friend that he at once pronounced Garrison to be "warm — generous — approachable, and Communicative" and vowed he would go back to Illinois and tell that "wild and generous people" the truth about this man.[21]

Called home suddenly on business, Herndon returned by way of Niagara Falls, where he was "overwhelmed at the Beautiful — the Grand and Sublime." It was a fitting conclusion for his expedition, which, "bating a little for disappointments," was "one of delight — amusement — pleasure and profit." Nature, at any rate, had "*grandeured* upon close *jointed* acquaintance," and Herndon returned with "a fresh — vigorous confidence in . . . the eternal and absolute love of God for all His creatures"; now he could "breathe freely & rest Easily — a kind of new man."[22]

III

Back in Illinois Herndon raced about excitedly, revealing to his Republican friends the deep-laid plot on the part of Eastern leaders to ditch Lincoln and support Douglas. Emergency conferences were called in Chicago and Springfield, and Herndon reported his news. Should Illinois Republicans adopt the Little Giant after all? Hard-

[19] Herndon to Parker, May 29, 1858, Herndon-Parker MSS. Later Herndon gave a rather improbable account of a long discussion he and Parker had. *Abraham Lincoln Quar.*, III, 196–197.

[20] Herndon to Lincoln, Boston, March 24, 1858, Herndon-Weik Coll.; Herndon to Parker, April 7, 1858, Herndon-Parker MSS.

[21] Herndon to Garrison, May 29, 1858, Garrison MSS.; Herndon to Parker, April 7, 1858, Herndon-Parker MSS.

[22] *Abraham Lincoln Quar.*, I, 405; Herndon to Parker, April 7, 1858, Herndon-Parker MSS.

headed, sharp-tongued Jesse K. Dubois gave answer for them all: "God Forbid *Are our friends crazy.*" [23] If the Republicans should support Douglas, they warned, the people would be outraged and "would drag us from power and grind us to powder." Besides, "Douglas' abuse of us as Whigs — as Republicans — as men in society, and as individuals, has been so slanderous — dirty — low — long, and *continuous,* that we cannot soon forgive and *can never forget.*" [24]

To Herndon was deputed the job of writing to Greeley, urging a change in his course. It was a blunt, curt letter. "We want to be our own masters," he warned, "and if any *politician* wants our respect — confidence or support now or hereafter let him stand aloof and let us alone." To Sumner Herndon spoke with equal frankness: "We do not want to be *huckstered off* in the political alleys or on corrupt corners by pimps of legislation *without our consent.*" If the Republicans adopted Douglas, Herndon vowed that he, for one, would leave the party. [25]

It was with a great deal of relief, therefore, that he chronicled the convention held by the Douglas Democrats at Springfield in late April. On the same day a minor fraction of bolters, supporting the Buchanan administration, met, and Herndon pronounced them both "eminently cut-throat bodies." With rejoicing Republicans watched these "Plunder[er]s of the People now at bloody war with each other over the spoils" and gloatingly predicted war to the knife. When the Douglas supporters adopted a platform reaffirming popular sovereignty, Herndon knew that any compromise between Douglas and the Republicans was now forever excluded. Illinois Republicans would fight a divided Democracy with a good chance of winning. "[A]*ll looks right,*" Herndon cheered. [26]

During the early part of May, Illinois Republicans held county conventions, nominated candidates for the state legislature, and pointed to Abraham Lincoln as their choice for United States senator. The Republican state convention, Herndon predicted, was going to be composed of "many good men and true"; the senatorial race would be "hot — energetic — deadly"; and the Democracy would certainly go "gurgling down beneath the red waves of slaughter." Lincoln was the

---

[23] Dubois to Trumbull, April 8, 1858, Trumbull MSS.
[24] Herndon to Greeley, April 8, 1858, Greeley MSS.; Herndon to Washburne, April 10, 1858, Washburne MSS.
[25] Herndon to Greeley, April 8, 1858, Greeley MSS.; Herndon to Sumner, April 10 and 24, 1858, Sumner MSS.
[26] Herndon to Sumner, April 24, 1858, Sumner MSS.; Herndon to Trumbull, April 24, 1858, Trumbull MSS.; Herndon to Parker, April 27, 1858, Herndon-Parker MSS.

Republican champion, and Herndon pledged: "I will do all I can to hold the leaders hands up." [27]

Lincoln, assured in advance of the senatorial nomination, had for weeks been thinking about a speech of acceptance. Mulling over the familiar theme of sectional conflict on the slavery issue, he scribbled down his thoughts on scraps of paper and corners of envelopes and stored them in his plug hat. Shortly before the convention he laboriously wrote out the words that he would speak, weighing carefully each phrase. Then one night he and Herndon returned to the law office, and Lincoln prepared to read the speech aloud to his one-man audience. Inquisitive Jesse Dubois came wandering in as he commenced and wondered what was going on. "It's none of your d − d business," Lincoln replied tartly, and the visitor left in a huff.[28] Then slowly and deliberately the senior partner began reading:

> If we could first know *where* we are, and *whither* we are tending, we could better judge *what* to do, and *how* to do it.
>
> We are now far into the *fifth* year, since a policy was initiated, with the *avowed* object, and *confident* promise, of putting an end to slavery agitation.
>
> Under the operation of that policy, that agitation has not only, *not ceased*, but has *constantly augmented*.
>
> In my opinion, it *will* not cease, until a *crisis* shall have been reached, and passed −
>
> "A house divided against itself cannot stand." [29]

At the end Lincoln asked for Herndon's criticism. In later years, Herndon remembered, with remarkable hindsight, that he had advised: "It is true, but is it wise or politic to say so?" [30] As a matter of fact, he probably said nothing of the kind but urged his partner to make the speech as written. It was, he wrote in a contemporary letter, "compact − nervous − eloquent: . . . the best Executive Expression of the ideas of . . . Republicanism . . . that I have seen." The only defect was that the speech was perhaps a little too conservative, but after all "Prudence is written all o'er the political world, and we cannot help it." [31]

A day or two before the Republican convention Lincoln called together some friends in the State House to hear the speech and to re-

[27] Herndon to Garrison, May 29, 1858, Garrison MSS.; Herndon to Parker, June 1, 1858, Herndon-Parker MSS.

[28] Herndon to Weik, October 29, 1885, Herndon-Weik Coll. It is possible that Dubois came in while Lincoln was writing the speech, rather than reading it. *Herndon's Lincoln*, II, 397.

[29] Roy P. Basler, ed., *Abraham Lincoln: His Speeches and Writings*, 372.

[30] *Herndon's Lincoln*, II, 398.

[31] Herndon to Parker, July 8, 1858, Herndon-Parker MSS.

ceive their advice. There were some ten or twenty persons present in all, mostly conservatives like Dubois, James C. Conkling, and James H. Matheny, men who would shy away from anything approaching abolitionism. Herndon was also there. To this little set Lincoln read his speech. They listened, and one auditor after another shook his head. This business of phrase-making was dangerous, much too radical; it was "a d — d fool utterance." When Lincoln had finished, each man solemnly warned that "the whole Spirit was too far in advance of the times." Herndon was the last man to be called on, and he sprang up impatiently. "By — God," he swore, "deliver it just as it reads. . . . The speech is true — wise & politic; and will succeed — now as in the future. Nay it will aid you — if it will not make you President of the United States." Lincoln sat silent for a moment, and after thanking his listeners, declared that his decision was inflexible; he would make the house-divided speech.[32]

The Republicans gathered on June 16 for "the best & largest convention ever held in our state." It was a grand affair, Herndon reported. With wild cheers Lincoln was put forward as the Republican choice to succeed Douglas. Then at night Lincoln mounted the platform to address the crowd. Thrilled, Herndon listened again to that ominous theme: "A house divided against itself cannot stand." Even while hoping that "Stump orators will take higher and more lofty grounds," he rejoiced over his partner's success.[33]

IV

Most of the writing about the Illinois campaign of 1858 — and there is a mountain of tedious literature on the subject — misses the point of the contest. The tale of seven earth-shaking debates between mighty protagonists of conflicting principles may be good fiction, but it is not history. Actually, the situation was vastly complicated.

(1) The name of neither Lincoln nor Douglas appeared on the ballots placed before the people in 1858. The voter chose one of a number

[32] This is one of those incidents which seem almost too good to be true, but there are three witnesses — Herndon, William Jayne, and John Armstrong — who confirm the essential story as here given. William Jayne, *Personal Reminiscences of . . . Abraham Lincoln*, 39–40; undated interview of Herndon with John Armstrong, Lamon MSS.; Herndon to Weik, October 29, 1885, Herndon-Weik Coll. Many years later Herndon recalled his words as "Lincoln, deliver that speech as read and it will make you President," but as Paul M. Angle has pointed out, Herndon's foresight was probably not so remarkable (Angle's ed. of *Herndon's Lincoln*, 326–327). The version above is based on an 1870 interview with John Armstrong, whose recollection antedates those of Herndon and Jayne by nearly twenty years.
[33] Herndon to Trumbull, June 24, 1858, Trumbull MSS.; Herndon to Parker, July 8, 1858, Herndon-Parker MSS.

of candidates for the state legislature who were generally pledged to either the Democratic or the Republican senatorial candidate. In the balloting local issues, personal differences, and irrelevant county politics were likely to be at least as influential as a speech by one of the major candidates.

(2) The seven set debates formed only a small fraction of the activities of the senatorial candidates. Lincoln and Douglas traveled widely over the state, addressed crowds, greeted friends, and encouraged local leaders. Their formal forensics were but interruptions in the regular campaign schedule.

(3) The canvass by no means began and ended with Lincoln and Douglas. There were literally dozens of other speakers stumping the state: imported orators, visiting dignitaries, state leaders, county candidates, party workers. While it was a matter of considerable satisfaction to friends when Lincoln acquitted himself creditably in an encounter with Douglas, realists like Herndon understood very well that "Those men who will go 20 miles through heat & dust to hear speeches are [already] Democratic or Republican but those who will not go 20 rods to hear speeches are neither one way or the other. . . ." [34] It was these indifferent voters, not the cheering throngs at a joint debate, who would determine the election.

(4) Illinois political opinion ran through the spectrum from ardent abolitionist to Southern sympathizer. From firsthand knowledge of the factors which made his state "a peculiar one politically," Herndon made an acute analysis of the problem. First of all, Illinois was divided geographically: the northern group of counties, settled largely by Easterners, was "all for Freedom," while more backward Egypt (southern Illinois) was "pro-slavery and *ignorant* 'up to the hub.'" Between lay the belt of central counties, of doubtful political allegiance, and it was here that the great battle was to be fought and won. Cutting across these divisions were several shades of party politics. There were Republicans, sure to go for Lincoln; Americans (Know-Nothings), largely conservative Whigs, who would hesitate long before deciding; anti-Lecompton Democrats, ardently for Douglas; and National Democrats, supporters of Buchanan. "Quite a muss." [35] Lincoln would win if the Republicans could carry the central counties, if he could woo the Know-Nothing vote, and if he could keep alive the feud in the Democratic party.

To promoting these ends Herndon devoted himself. Realizing that "*the* places where good can be done" were the school houses and vil-

[34] Herndon to Parker, October 3, 1858, Herndon-Parker MSS.
[35] Herndon to Parker, August 31, 1858, *ibid.*

lage churches too insignificant to attract the political "big bugs," he set himself to canvassing the smaller villages in the Sangamon region: Taylorville, Mechanicsburg, Pleasant Plains, Lincoln, Petersburg, Berlin, Williamsville. And if he drew "no great crowds at these cross-roads places," he still managed to make himself heard. For the problem of the lazy or indifferent voter he had an answer — to "*go to them,* and erect a '*Stump,*' or goods-box, right at their door" so that they had to listen. And, he said, he converted many.[36]

A popular speaker, Herndon was in constant demand. "Tell Bill Herndon," S. C. Parks urged Lincoln, "that our Rep. Club meets next saturday night & the boys want him to come up . . . & make them a rousing speech." "If you can prevail on friend Herndon to speak at Tremont on the 14th inst.," begged another, "please let me know immediately, and I will get out handbills." "I wrote to Bill Herndon," David Davis informed Lincoln, "to go to Pekin [Illinois]. . . . If there was any *fighting* to do there, he can lend a hand." [37]

In rural Menard County, where he had practiced law for years, Herndon built up a personal following of impressive proportions. One enthusiastic Petersburg advocate, carried away by Herndon's oratory during the senatorial canvass, proposed Billy for Congress.

> I would like to suggest [he wrote to Lincoln] that if they start the name of Wm. H. Herndon Menard will do something very handsome — there are many Democrats here anxious to vote for "Bill" — & there is no other name half so potent here . . . We are all for Bill.[38]

Herndon's success was largely a tribute to the moderation of his argument, aimed, as in 1856, at the former Whig element, men who had supported Fillmore for President and were a little afraid of Republican radicalism. Everywhere he emphasized that the slavery principles of "Washington, Clay and Lincoln, were identically the same." It was Douglas and the Democracy who were in conflict with the teachings of the illustrious Clay, a name revered by every Whig. "In the name of all that is just and true," how could an American degrade himself by supporting "a man who ever glorified in vilifying, traducing and slandering that great champion"? "Will old line Whigs do this?" [39]

---

[36] Herndon to Parker, October 3, 1858, *ibid.*

[37] Parks to Lincoln, August 9, 1858; T. J. Pickett to Lincoln, August 3, 1858; Davis to Lincoln, August 25, 1858 — all in Robert Todd Lincoln Coll.

[38] Albert J. Brooks to Lincoln, December 16, 1858, *ibid.* Brooks referred to a special election to choose the successor to Democratic Congressman Thomas L. Harris, who died November 24, 1858. Herndon was not a candidate.

[39] *Illinois State Journal,* October 20, 1858.

Early in the struggle Herndon had answered his own question. He was positive: "The Fillmore boys are uniting with us fine — they knit close — close as shattered ice of a cool night on a mill pond, forming a solid sheet of ice over which the Republicans may march to victory."[40] As usual he was too optimistic. "Many of the Old Whigs — having no shepherd and in doubt where to go" were readily turning into Douglas's fold.[41] Though he cherished not "a single particle of personal unkindness or opposition" to Lincoln, John Jordan Crittenden, the leading Kentucky Whig and a man of vast influence among conservative Illinoisans, after long hesitation concluded that Douglas's "re-election was necessary as a rebuke to the Administration, and a vindication of the great cause of popular rights & public justice."[42] The *Illinois State Journal* tried to insinuate that Crittenden really "wanted *Douglas* crushed out," but Illinois conservatives knew better. "Thousands of whigs," Herndon sadly reported, joined Lincoln's opponents "just on the eve of the Election."[43]

Herndon had other things to do besides make speeches. For some months before the canvass opened he and Lincoln had been collecting newspaper slips and comments which Herndon pasted and indexed in pocket-sized notebooks so that the material would be ready for instant use on the stump.[44] While Lincoln was away from Springfield, Herndon sent him "liberal clippings bearing in any way on the questions of the hour," and, in response to letters or telegrams, forwarded books which the standard-bearer needed during the debates.[45]

Herndon served as a sort of alter ego for his partner. It was generally understood that Herndon had inside knowledge of all Lincoln's plans and policies. "Did not Lincoln leave word with . . . Bill Herndon where he w[oul]d be . . . ," questioned Judge David Davis, who had apparently lost track of the senatorial aspirant. Henry C. Whitney concluded a confidential letter detailing undercover political maneuvers:

[40] Herndon to Trumbull, June 24, 1858, Trumbull MSS.

[41] W. P. Boyd to Crittenden, Bloomington, Ill., July 17, 1858, Crittenden MSS.

[42] Crittenden to Lincoln, July 29, 1858, Robert Todd Lincoln Coll.

[43] Herndon to Crittenden, November 1, 1858, Crittenden MSS.; Herndon to Parker, November 8, 1858, Herndon-Parker MSS.

[44] Sometimes it is mistakenly asserted that these scrapbooks, now in the Library of Congress, were "compiled by Lincoln" (Hertz, *Hidden Lincoln*, 21). Actually every word of the writing, identification, and indexing is in Herndon's hand. There is no evidence at all that Lincoln ever referred to these little books, though he did frequently quote from clippings during the course of his debates. The two scrapbooks in the Herndon-Weik Collection were positively identified by Herndon as "political memoranda books which I used in the various political Canvasses from 1853 to 1866" (Herndon to Weik, November 15, 1886, Herndon-Weik Coll.).

[45] *Herndon's Lincoln*, II, 411.

". . . I desire that Mr Herndon read this & digest it if Lincoln is away from Home." When a direct statement might prove embarrassing to Lincoln, Herndon could sometimes serve as his partner's mouthpiece. C. H. Ray of the powerful Chicago *Press & Tribune* wanted to publish a campaign biography of the Republican senatorial candidate and asked Lincoln to supply the facts for such a sketch. "To save the imputation of having done so," he advised Lincoln, "you might give Herndon the points, and he would send them to us." [46]

There was also the seamy side of politics, for Lincoln did not always know what Herndon euphemistically termed "the details of how we get along." When there was dirty work to be done, it was not the kind of thing that suited Lincoln's tastes; "nor does it suit me," complained Herndon, "yet I am compelled to do it — do it because I cannot get rid of it." In the 1858 election the National (Buchanan) Democrats, a tiny faction, strong only in the post offices and other federal jobs, might draw the deciding number of votes from Douglas. Obviously it was to the Republican interest to keep the National Democratic organization alive in Illinois. There was no "contract . . . either express or implied, directly or indirectly," yet Lincoln and Colonel John Dougherty, leader of the Buchanan forces, had an illuminating conversation on the progress of the campaign, and Herndon too knew all about the plans of the anti-Douglas Democrats. Herndon's father and brother Elliott were leaders of the Buchanan forces in Illinois; "they make 'no bones' in telling me what they are going to do," he wrote Parker.[47]

V

At first the campaign went beautifully. The Democrats were hopelessly split; the former Whigs were being assimilated "oily and rapidly, making no friction"; every speech of Lincoln's was a whaler; "Poor Dug" was doomed. When Horace Greeley promised, "Now, Herndon, I am going to do all I reasonably can to elect Lincoln," it seemed that Eastern Republicans at last had seen the light.[48] Big-hearted, Herndon was willing to forgive, because "we are not malicious out here." [49]

Then came trouble. Perhaps Lincoln was a little too much of the Kentucky gentleman to drub Douglas properly. Maybe Trumbull had bet-

[46] David Davis to [O. M. Hatch], August 16, 1858; Whitney to Lincoln or Herndon, July 31, 1858; Ray, Medill & Co. (by C. H. Ray) to Lincoln [June 29, 1858] — all in Robert Todd Lincoln Coll.

[47] Herndon to Trumbull, June 24, 1858, Trumbull MSS.; Herndon to Parker, September 2, 1858, Herndon-Parker MSS.

[48] Herndon to Trumbull, June 24 and July 22, 1858, Trumbull MSS.

[49] Herndon to Greeley, July 20, 1858, Greeley MSS.

ter hurry home from Washington to help out. The worst of it all was that Greeley and his unpredictable *Tribune* seemed again undecided whether to support Lincoln; he was " 'sorter sorter' . . . this way & that." "Greel[e]y had better attend to NY," Herndon stormed, for he realized that the indeterminate course of the *Tribune* did Illinois Republicanism infinite harm.[50]

As the election drew close Herndon became increasingly willing to believe any canard about the New York editor. Rumor had it that there had been a meeting — "by *accident* or otherwise" — between Douglas, Greeley, Seward, and Thurlow Weed at Chicago in 1857, at which time the Easterners pledged themselves to support the Little Giant in his bid for re-election.[51] It made no difference that no one had actually seen the men in Chicago or that Greeley and Seward had for years been bitter enemies. Had not Trumbull warned Herndon of such a conspiracy when he was in Washington? It must be true. Those "*Yankee traders*" were "*already lowering the Republican flag*," and Herndon dashed off a long protest to several Republican newspapers in the East. When his squib was rejected, he, like many another disappointed author, concluded that there was a "firmly fixed — wide-spread and universal" conspiracy to silence him.[52]

Then came the last straw. A year earlier Herndon had not been at all averse to "colonizing" Republican voters in certain doubtful counties, but now he thought that Douglas was importing "Celtic gentlemen" to cast fraudulent votes in the middle counties. Herndon, who had always been antagonistic toward the Irish, became truly indignant. Words could not express his loathing for these "wandering roving robbing Irish," these "robbing — bloated — pock-marked Catholic Irish," these "Ishmaelitish Irish," who were flooding the state. They afforded a solid and terrible problem, "looking us right in the face, *with its thumb on its nose.*" "[T]*hat point is now reached*," Herndon rumbled ominously, "beyond which forbearance ceases to be a virtue. . . ." There was great and imminent danger of a general and terrible row over the Irish, and he was not at all sure but that the Republicans should rise and cut their throats.[53]

It looked as though Herndon might start the bloodshed himself. When an inebriated Irish Democrat disturbed a National Democratic

[50] Herndon to Trumbull, July 22, 1858, Trumbull MSS.; Herndon to Parker, August 23, September 11 and 25, and November 24, 1858, Herndon-Parker MSS.
[51] Herndon to Parker, September 20, 1858, *ibid.*
[52] Herndon to Parker, September 25, 1858, *ibid.*
[53] Tracy, *Uncollected Letters*, 94; Herndon to Parker, October 30 and November 8, 1858, Herndon-Parker MSS.; Springfield correspondent, undoubtedly Herndon, in Chicago *Press & Tribune*, October 2, 1858.

meeting in Springfield, Billy leaped from his seat, yelling "God damn the Irish, I want it distinctly understood that *we* [the Republicans] . . . are willing to have war with them," seized the noisy drunk, and unceremoniously chucked him downstairs. It was, of course, a grave political blunder, for Democrats were able to charge that "Lincoln's man Friday" had acted upon the instructions of his partner.[54]

By November Herndon was so excited that he did not know his own mind. Reports trickled in from committees and clubs, and he believed the last news he heard. One minute he was ecstatically certain that the election was safe because "all . . . *feels right in our bones*," while four days later his "brute forecast" warned that "*all is* NOT *safe*." His last hunch was right. When the votes were in, Lincoln had carried the state, but, because of an antiquated apportionment law, the Douglas men won more seats in the legislature and the Little Giant was certain of re-election. "We are beaten in Ills," Herndon had to write. Mostly to relieve his own mind, Herndon sat down to write Theodore Parker the causes of the defeat. First of all, he explained, the state was so split up that Lincoln had not been able to please all the political elements; he "tried to stand high & elevated, so he fell deep." Then "Greel[e]y never gave us one single solitary manly lift," while the Whigs followed Crittenden and supported Douglas. Into Illinois had been cast money, men, and speakers for the Democrats, and as a final injustice unregistered Irishmen overran the polls. It was no one of these factors but the combination of all that "*cleaned us out*."[55]

Still, everything was not lost. Republicans had carried many of the state offices. Douglas "got all classes to 'boil his pot,' with antagonistic material and forces," and there was bound to be an explosion. Democrats were more demoralized by victory than Republicans by defeat. Lincoln's supporters were now a "well drilled — 'Fritz' Organized — educated — Liberty-loving — God-fearing Republican party broad & wide awake" who would certainly win the next round. Those who doubted, Herndon crowed, should just "feel our nerves, and muscles, and bones."[56]

[54] *Illinois State Register*, September 2 and 3, 1858; Angle, *"Here I Have Lived,"* 231.

[55] Herndon to Parker, October 26 and 30, November 8, 1858, Herndon-Parker MSS.

[56] Herndon to Parker, November 8 and 24, 1858, *ibid.*

CHAPTER ix

Billy, You're Too Rampant[1]

I

On the day the Illinois legislature re-elected Stephen A. Douglas to the United States Senate, Lincoln moped in the law office. When friends dropped in to see him, he complained mournfully: "I expect everyone to desert me except Billy." [2] He knew that not even repeated defeat would deprive him of this one advocate. That was the thing about the Lincoln-Herndon association: they could count on each other. In spite of his tendency to mount his hobbyhorse and go galloping off in all directions, Herndon could be relied on to remain loyal to his partner. And for his part, Billy knew that in time of trouble he could depend on Lincoln. When Herndon and a couple of cronies celebrated so wildly one night that they broke the tavern windows, they turned to Lincoln to pay their fines, and that good man got out in the gray morning to collect the one hundred dollars needed to keep his partner from jail.[3]

After one such episode, friends asked Lincoln why he did not get another partner, someone safe and solid, like John Todd Stuart or Orville H. Browning. Lincoln turned sharply on his interviewers with the reply: "I know my own business, I reckon. I know Billy Herndon better than anybody, and . . . I intend to stick by him." [4] After all, Herndon was a good law partner, who had repeatedly demonstrated his usefulness in political management. In politics as in law, Lincoln & Herndon

---

[1] The major portion of this and the following chapters appeared in the *Abraham Lincoln Quarterly*, III, 375–407.

[2] Henry C. Whitney to Herndon, July 18, 1887, Herndon-Weik Coll.

[3] Interview of Weik with John W. Bunn, October 15, 1914, *ibid.*; interview of C. L. Conkling with John W. Bunn, November 1917, C. L. Conkling MSS.; Weik, *Real Lincoln*, 204–205.

[4] There are a number of versions of this incident, differing slightly in the words Lincoln is supposed to have used. *Herndon's Lincoln*, II, 266; Dall, "Pioneering," *Atlantic Mo.*, XIX, 413; undated interview of Weik with Herndon, Memorandum Book II, Weik MSS.

pulled as a team. With unconscious humor Billy summarized the situation by declaring that he did the reading for the partnership while Lincoln did the thinking.[5]

During long years of association the partners had learned to get along with each other. There was only a minimum of friction in the office, those unavoidable irritations that occur when two men live close together. Lincoln insisted on reading the daily papers aloud — unless Herndon hid them first — spilling himself out "easily over ¼ of the room" and driving Herndon from the office by the noise. Those who thought of Lincoln the wit and raconteur never knew the other side of the picture — the deadly monotony of hearing stories repeated over and over again, the work interrupted to hear what Herndon considered a rather pointless tale of Lincoln's youth, the tedium of hearing the mill of anecdote grind away for days without end.[6]

Most annoying of all to Herndon were the Lincoln children, for their father would frequently bring "Tad" and Willie to the office on Sunday mornings. Left to themselves while Lincoln worked on legal papers, the children, according to Herndon, "soon gutted the room — gutted the shelves of books — rifled the drawers and riddled boxes — battered the points of . . . [Herndon's] gold pens against the stoves — turned over the ink stands on the papers — scattered letters over the office and danced over them." Of course Billy was exaggerating, but he felt many a time that he "wanted to wring the necks of these brats and pitch them out of the windows." They really needed whaling, he thought, but out of respect for Lincoln he kept his mouth shut — no easy assignment for Herndon.[7]

And on the other side, while Lincoln was occasionally embarrassed by his partner's eccentricities and inebriate habits, he was more often "vexed and sometimes foolishly so" over Billy's tendency to go off into meaningless metaphysics and gaseous generalities.[8] Again and again the older man had to counsel: "Billy, don't shoot too high — aim lower and the common people will understand you." [9] But it took persuasion to make Herndon abandon his latest ten-dollar word.

If either man had counted up his grievances over the previous decade, he would have found justification for breaking the association. The point was that neither wanted to make such a reckoning. A partnership is a matter of not demanding the impossible, of making allow-

[5] Herndon to James H. Wilson, August 28, 1889, copy, Herndon-Weik Coll.
[6] Herndon to Weik, October 21 and November 17, 1885, *ibid.*
[7] Herndon to Weik, November 19, 1885, and January 8, 1886; "Lincoln's domestic Life," undated Herndon monograph, *ibid.*
[8] Herndon to Weik, January 9, 1886, *ibid.*
[9] *Herndon's Lincoln*, II, 325.

ances, of compromising, of taking second choices. No doubt Lincoln might have found a lawyer who would have been more of a wheel horse, but would the new man have been as loyal and unselfish as Billy? Besides, it was fun to have Herndon around. Lincoln was amused by the high seriousness of Herndon's purpose, by his feeling that life was real and earnest. He was even tickled by Billy's inability to see a joke. When Herndon came back from Niagara Falls, he expatiated at great length on the Beautiful, the Grand, and the Sublime. Having — for once — exhausted his vocabulary, he asked Lincoln what *he* had thought on seeing the falls. Quite solemnly Lincoln replied: "The thing that struck me . . . was, where in the world did all that water come from?" What made it so funny was that Herndon did not know it was a joke. Thirty years later he chronicled that remark as proof that Lincoln did not appreciate nature.[10]

But Herndon was more than the end man in a minstrel show. Lincoln could count on excitement when he was about. There was always a new book, a new speech, a new cause that demanded another crusade in behalf of righteousness. With a pile of books under his arm, Herndon would dash into the office, breathless and effervescing over his newest fad: woman's rights, a state university, a city library association, the poems of Walt Whitman, the publication of Wendell Phillips's speeches. Every new brain child was certain to be the Messiah, and he swaddled each babe in layer after layer of adjectives. Exhausting, perhaps, but always interesting. Lincoln would lean back in his chair and drawl: "Billy, you're too rampant and spontaneous."[11]

Herndon knew what he was talking about — or at least he had read books on the subject. In fact, he had read books on almost every subject. When there was a lull in business, Lincoln would sprawl out over the sofa and yawn: "Billy, tell us about the books." And off Herndon would go, a hound after whatever hare he was chasing for the moment. He introduced to Lincoln the odd little book of George Fitzhugh, *Sociology for the South*, which suggested that Northerners might benefit by the enslavement of their white laborers,[12] and both men used the specious argument in attacking the Democrats. Herndon brought to the office a speech of Theodore Parker's with those pregnant words: "Democracy is Direct Self-government, over all the people, for all the people, by all the people."[13] Lincoln marked the passage for future use. But when

[10] *Ibid.*, II, 297; *Abraham Lincoln Quar.*, I, 405.
[11] *Herndon's Lincoln*, II, 362–363.
[12] Harvey Wish, *George Fitzhugh, Propagandist of the Old South*, 155–156.
[13] Theodore Parker, *The Effect of Slavery on the American People. A Sermon Preached at the Music Hall, Boston, on Sunday, July 4, 1858*, 5. A copy of this pamphlet is preserved in the Herndon-Weik Collection.

THE DREARY WASTES OF SPRINGFIELD

This view of the north side of the public square reveals what John Hay called "the dreary wastes of Springfield — a city combining the meanness of the North with the barbarism of the South."

A LAW OFFICE IS A DRY PLACE

An unusually tidy view of the Lincoln & Herndon office. "A law office is a dry place for incident of a pleasing kind," Herndon complained. "If you love the stories of murder — rape — fraud &c. a law office is a good place. . . ."

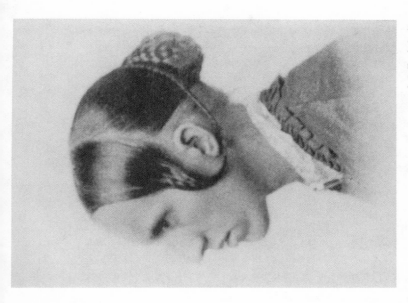

L. C. Handy Studios

MRS. CAROLINE DALL

Mrs. Dall wrote a long and flattering article about Herndon for the *Atlantic Monthly* in 1867. Herndon liked her even though she was "a Yankee," "a woman

Illinois State Historical Library

WARD HILL LAMON

Lamon, wrote Herndon, was "a great ass — an obstinate fool — suspicious, jealous and ungrateful — a very — very curious man."

Billy tried to talk about the latest "deep" book he had been reading — perhaps Kant or Buckle — Lincoln would wave it away as too indigestible for his mind.[14]

Herndon could never quite analyze his feelings for his partner, though he was to spend a good many thousands of words in trying. While the senior partner addressed him simply as "Billy" or, in letters, as "William," it was always "Mr. Lincoln" to Herndon, an older man, almost like a father or perhaps an uncle, a friendly, safe counselor. "[H]e was," Herndon explained, "the great big man of our firm and I was the little one. The little one looked *naturally* up to the big one. . . ." Lincoln had an unexplainable fascination for the younger man; "He moved me by a shrug of the shoulder . . . ," Herndon confessed.[15] It was not Lincoln's appearance that drew Herndon, for Billy with his erect five feet nine inches, his jet-black hair, his penchant for patent-leather shoes, kid gloves, and top hats, cut a much more distinguished figure than did his partner. Nor was it Lincoln's mind, for Herndon felt he could think circles around his slow-moving partner. When there was a discussion in the office, Herndon said, Lincoln was always about two steps behind, trying to "explain things . . . that needed no explanation"; "he used to bore me terribly by his methods — processes — manner &c. &c." [16] But the character of the senior partner inspired respect; Lincoln's heart was in the right place; he was as dependable as an alarm clock — nothing showy, but regular and faithful. Herndon had no stupid, dog-like devotion and he thought there were greater men than his partner, yet there was no one else he would ever trust so fully. Lincoln was his friend.

II

Again and again the question is asked: What, if any, influence did Herndon have on Lincoln? It is a subject on which there has been expended much sound and not a little fury. Lincoln experts tend to become violently pro- or anti-Herndon. On the one hand there is the school of writers, stemming directly from Herndon himself, who would characterize the junior partner as Lincoln's "political Mentor: [who] . . . had more to do with shaping his friend's great political career than any other ten men." [17] Some Lincoln specialists have become almost

[14] Weik, *Real Lincoln*, 8–9; *Herndon's Lincoln*, II, 363–364; Rankin, *Personal Recollections*, 123–124.

[15] Herndon to Joseph S. Fowler, November 3, 1888, Herndon Papers; *Abraham Lincoln Quar.*, I, 411.

[16] Herndon to Weik, January 1 and 9, 1886, Herndon-Weik Coll.

[17] Whitney, *Life on the Circuit*, 500.

rabid in their advocacy of Herndon's predominant influence: Billy was "the same to Lincoln, that John the Baptist was to Christ"; he was "the great instrument that enabled Mr Lincoln to enter the Presidency"; he was "the carburetor in the great man's career." [18] One devoted Herndon fan even projected a biography of his hero, to be titled "The Man Who Made Lincoln." [19]

The dissenting view stresses the undeniable fact that Herndon himself was the source of most of the stories of the Lincoln-Herndon intimacy. Whether actuated by intense malice toward his partner or merely carried away by his egotistic rhetoric, Herndon was, it is said, a cranky liar; in reality he exerted little if any influence over Lincoln.[20] An unusually calm observer concluded that Herndon "does not seem to have shaped appreciably the thinking of the older man on political issues," that "in spite of their intimacy . . . in the law office, they lived separate lives." [21]

Unfortunately this issue, like so many other fascinating bypaths, is one which the historian cannot pursue. How can one measure the results of mutual give-and-take of twenty years in the same office? And if, at times, the partners tended to think in similar terms, can it be said who gave and who took? It has been pointed out above that Herndon's claims of having guided Lincoln at critical moments — e.g., in avoiding the Republican convention at Springfield in 1854 and in joining that party in 1856 — are probably erroneous, but there could still have been a steady, day-by-day interaction. The trouble is that no man can set down even for himself the exact provenance of any one of his thoughts. An idea is likely to be the result of countless unmeasurable influences — emotion and logic and early habits of training and rationalization — all refracted through that particularly irregular prism, the human mind. The resulting spectrum will be cheerfully relinquished by the historian to the "psycho-biographer."

It is important, however, to understand Herndon's own idea as to the

[18] For these comments, in the order given, see Cyrus O. Poole to Herndon, January 16, 1886, Weik MSS.; Gilbert A. Tracy to Weik, July 13, 1917, Herndon-Weik Coll.; Albert J. Beveridge to Weik, June 1, 1925, photostat in Hertz Coll., Univ. of Ill.

[19] This was one Horace Saunders of Chicago, whose voluminous notes are deposited with the Abraham Lincoln Association, Springfield, Ill. For an elaboration of Saunders's views, see "Abraham Lincoln's Partner, Billy Herndon," [Chicago] *Lincoln Group Papers . . . , Second Series,* 145–158.

[20] Letter of Robert Todd Lincoln in [Anderson Auction Co.] *Library of the Late Major William H. Lambert of Philadelphia: Part I Lincolniana,* 45; Rankin, *Personal Recollections,* 90; Robert Todd Lincoln to H. M. Alden, November 27, 1895, MS., Mass. Hist. Soc.; Rankin, *Intimate Character Sketches,* 67.

[21] Allen Johnson in *Amer. Hist. Rev.,* XVI, 832.

influence he exerted over his partner, for this is a factor to be considered in any evaluation of his later writings about Lincoln. In his pre-1860 correspondence Herndon rarely mentioned Lincoln at all. Occasionally he reported that his partner had made a speech or — with painful frequency — that he had been defeated in an election, but one gets the impression that Herndon regarded Lincoln as a co-worker in the vineyard, not as the godlike figure that postwar reminiscence was to make of him.

In his published writings Herndon always maintained a discreet if rather provocative silence on the subject. "I was never conscious of having exerted any influence over him," he stated with what was apparently charming frankness.[22] This was, however, a pose. In his letters Herndon revealed his true belief. Lincoln, he said, had been his student, with whom he had "worked hard & . . . well"; it had been his policy "to *Educate* Lincoln up to *action*" and toward this end he "had many silent closet prayers" over the unregenerate senior partner. His share in making the Great Emancipator was, he felt, so great that modesty forbade him to write the true story; "I did much for Lincoln that the world will never know — don't intend to blow my own horn."[23]

III

One Lincoln biographer has regretted that Herndon told "so little about the wire-pullings which boosted his partner to the top" after 1858.[24] As a matter of fact, Herndon said little about Lincoln's nomination because he knew little. In earlier years his letters had been full of reports that "Mr. Lincoln wrote you on yesterday, and read it to me," or of attendance at "one or 2 private Republican meetings." Now, however, he could merely guess what was happening.[25] His membership in the Republican state executive committee was quietly allowed to lapse, and, though he had confidently expected the position, another man was chosen as presidental elector for central Illinois in 1860. The record shows that after 1859 Herndon was definitely out of the main political current in Illinois.

In these pre-election years the Republican party was making desperate efforts to attain respectability and to cast off the odium of sectionalism. The theme song was conservatism, caution, conciliation. It was

[22] *Herndon's Lincoln*, III, 479.
[23] Herndon to Zebina Eastman, February 6, 1866, Eastman MSS.; Herndon to Weik, December 29, 1885; Herndon's "A Statement — Memorandum," January 8, 1886, Herndon-Weik Coll.
[24] Baringer, *Lincoln's Rise to Power*, 164.
[25] Herndon to Trumbull, February 5, 1859, Trumbull MSS.

amusing to see rabid Republicans bravely mouthing words of brotherly love. Greeley openly declared that the team for 1860 should not be burdened by a radical leader; Seward rose in the Senate to proclaim that he had "never been more patient, and never loved the representatives of other sections more than now"; living down his house-divided theory, Lincoln reiterated his conservatism and pledged that the Republicans "had no purpose of entering into the slave States to disturb the institution of slavery." [26]

Herndon could not follow this about-face. For years he had been building up his distrust of the South. He thought in terms of slavocrats, iron-ball Democracy, and nigger-holding despotism. Now the sinners-come-to-doom talk was to be soft-pedaled and the Day of Judgment was indefinitely postponed. He could not go it. "I am ashamed that I am a Republican," he wrote, seeing his party leaders in Congress "grinding off the flesh from their knee Caps" in order to conciliate the South. Did the North have to lick the dust to prove it was cowardly? [27]

As the party turned conservative, men of Herndon's ultra views felt increasingly out of place. No longer was he the point of contact between Eastern party leaders and Illinois. Shrewder and more practical politicians like N. B. Judd and David Davis now acted as intermediaries. One by one Herndon's powerful friends in the East were dropping off. Theodore Parker had gone to Italy to die, and Charles Sumner was out of the country for his health. Desperately Herndon sought for new correspondents. Again and again he besieged William Lloyd Garrison with mail. While admitting Garrison's right to ignore his letters, Herndon vowed that he was "not to be kicked off by neglect or silence." [28] But an entirely one-sided correspondence, even for a man as articulate as Herndon, was not sufficient. To William H. Seward he wrote also, approving the irrepressible-conflict theory, and urging that he "seize some golden opportunity . . . to open, blossom lik[e], this flower of Rhetoric." [29] Seward answered in a formal note,[30] but though Herndon replied immediately urging an oration on the history of liberty over the last six thousand years,[31] the New Yorker let the correspondence drop.

[26] Greeley to Herndon, December 4, 1859, Greeley MSS.; Frederic Bancroft, *The Life of William H. Seward,* I, 515; Nicolay and Hay, eds., *Works,* V, 193–194.
[27] Herndon to Parker, December 15, 1859, Herndon-Parker MSS.; Herndon to Sumner, December 19, 1859, Sumner MSS.
[28] Herndon to Garrison, January 28, 1859, Garrison MSS.
[29] Herndon to William H. Seward, December 28, 1858, MS., N. Y. Hist. Soc.
[30] Seward to Herndon, December 31, 1858, copy, Herndon-Weik Coll.
[31] Herndon to Seward, January 17, 1859, MS., N. Y. Hist. Soc.

Billy, You're Too Rampant

There was still Horace Greeley, but after 1858 he could hardly be called a friend. At virtually the same time that Lincoln was urging that Republicans forget past differences and unite "in action upon a great principle in a cause on which we all agree," [32] Herndon was feuding with "horn eyed" Horace. The New York *Tribune* had not done the Illinois Republicans justice in 1858, and Herndon did not forget quickly. Through the columns of the widely read Chicago *Press & Tribune* a private letter from Greeley to Herndon was circulated to prove that the New York editor had been faithless during the Illinois senatorial race. Greeley replied that Herndon had misrepresented his letters, and the Chicago paper was forced to defend Herndon against charges of falsification.[33] It was, as Herndon said, a little quarrel,[34] but it created bitterness at the time when party leaders were emphasizing a united front.

Something like that was always happening. Herndon had been in politics so long that he had enemies. His record encouraged opposition. As mayor of Springfield his well-known crusade for prohibition united the liquor interests against him, while his own inebriate habits caused distrust among temperance advocates. On the nativist issue, also, Herndon embarrassed party leaders. When Massachusetts passed a law restricting the voting of naturalized citizens, he leaped into the battle with an eloquent plea for racial tolerance: ". . . my country is the world, and my love for man is as broad as the race, and as deep as humanity. As a matter of course I include native and foreign people, Protestant and Catholic, 'Jew and Gentile.' " [35] The Know-Nothings were, of course, wounded, while foreign-born voters, remembering Herndon's open hostility to the Irish, were not won.

For the Republican party it was a time for minced words and carefully chosen phrases, not for the "Huge burning characters" which Herndon "twirled between his teeth and spit out, scattering their scales of fire hither and thither, igniting the combustible material everywhere upon this continent." [36] In order to win the vital presidential election of 1860 the party had to attract all elements: "former anti-slavery

[32] Nicolay and Hay, eds., *Works*, V, 115.

[33] Chicago *Press & Tribune*, February 2 and 16, March 8, 1859; New York *Tribune* (semi-weekly ed.), February 18, March 4, 1859. See also Greeley to Schuyler Colfax, December 12, 1859, Greeley MSS.; Horace White to Lincoln, February 2, 1859, Robert Todd Lincoln Coll.

[34] Herndon to Trumbull, February 26, 1859, Trumbull MSS.

[35] Chicago *Press & Tribune*, May 21, 1859. Lincoln, too, looked with disfavor on the Massachusetts amendment.

[36] Petersburg *Semi-Weekly Axis*, April 7, 1860.

Whigs, erstwhile Old Line Whigs, die-hard Whigs, former Free-Soil Democrats, disgruntled organization Democrats, Know-Nothings, abolitionists, protective-tariff devotees, 'free land' reformers . . . , sponsors of a Pacific railroad, internal improvement champions, naturalized Germans, and others who for some reason hated Franklin Pierce, James Buchanan, or Stephen A. Douglas." [37] Men like Herndon who invited antagonism had to be shelved.

IV

In the fall of 1859 crazy John Brown with a handful of crack-brained disciples made a raid on the federal arsenal at Harpers Ferry, Virginia, with the notion of freeing vast numbers of slaves and establishing a haven for escaped Negroes. As a matter of course the party was captured and John Brown was hanged. Republican leaders went out of their way to repudiate Brown and to assure the South that they had no share in the plot. Lincoln, for example, specifically branded the Harpers Ferry raid as wrong and a violation of the law.[38]

But not Herndon. For him it was good and great John Brown, who would "live amidst the world's gods & heroes through all the infinite ages." When Wendell Phillips lauded Brown as "a Lord High Admiral of the Almighty" with a commission to sink the pirate ship, Virginia, Herndon applauded rapturously. It was a most glorious speech, "polished, chaste & . . . eloquent." [39] This was the sort of thing that Republican leaders were trying to guard against. Because of his business association with Lincoln, enemies could attribute Herndon's words to his partner, and there was no telling what Billy might say.

Early in 1860 a fugitive slave by the name of Edward Canter was arrested in Springfield. There could be no doubt that he was the property of the Missourian who claimed him. Herndon jumped into the case with aggressive sympathy, for this poor fellow was "in the clutches of *hounds*" and would be sent "to a southern Hell." [40] When every possible legal technicality was exhausted and it was positively demonstrated that the "smiling African" was indeed a fugitive, Herndon "rose and said that no *proof* had been offered of the existence of slavery in Missouri, and . . . the Commissioner had no right to *presume* from historical knowledge that Missouri was a slave State." Naturally his

---

[37] Reinhard H. Luthin, *The First Lincoln Campaign,* 21–22.
[38] Angle, ed., *New Letters and Papers,* 229.
[39] Herndon to Parker, December 15, 1859, Herndon-Parker MSS.
[40] Herndon to "Gentlemen," February 11, 1860, MS., Ill. State Hist. Lib.

plea was overruled.[41] The affair spoke well for Herndon's instincts of justice and humanity, but those were not exactly the qualities that were desirable in a Republican leader in 1860. What was wanted was a man who could be silent.

Out of step with the trends in the national party, Herndon was also lagging behind in state politics. Illinois leaders like Jesse W. Fell, David Davis, and N. B. Judd had been working ever since the Lincoln-Douglas campaign to promote a presidential boom for Lincoln, yet there is no evidence that Herndon joined or even favored the move. In the fall of 1858, after Lincoln's name had been prominently suggested for the place, Herndon felt that "We of the West have no Choice — we do not care who [the nominee] . . . is, so that he is a good Republican." [42] There has not been found a single letter in which Herndon urged or even especially supported Lincoln's nomination. It was not a question of disloyalty; it was merely that it was impossible to visualize his office mate as a serious contender for the presidency. The facts point to the conclusion that Herndon was no longer the recipient of Lincoln's political confidences. He had too often proved indiscreet.

More than once during these last years of the partnership Lincoln was annoyed by the political meddling of Herndon. If he was to appear as a presidential contender at the national convention, Lincoln had to secure united Illinois backing, but Illinois in 1860 was the scene of a vicious three-cornered battle for the Republican gubernatorial nomination. N. B. Judd of Chicago, Leonard Swett of Bloomington, and Richard Yates of Jacksonville were at each other's throats, yet Lincoln had to keep the friendship of all three. Herndon upset an uneasy equilibrium by charging that Judd as chairman of the Republican state committee was using the party treasury to promote his own political prospects. "I am advised that Herndon is . . . talking about misapplication of funds by me &c. &c.," Judd wrote Lincoln angrily. "This ought not to be and is not true — Cannot you set him right. . . ." [43] Before he received Judd's protest, Lincoln had already heard a rumor of Herndon's indiscretion.

> . . . I mentioned it to him [Lincoln reported to Judd]; he rather denied the charge, and I did not press him about the past, but got his solemn pledge to say nothing of the sort in the future. . . .
> I impressed upon him as well as I could, first, that such was untrue

[41] *Illinois State Journal*, February 10 and 13, 1860. The Negro's name was sometimes spelled "Cantor."
[42] Herndon to Parker, October 4, 1858, Herndon-Parker MSS.
[43] Judd to Lincoln, July 31, 1860, Robert Todd Lincoln Coll.

and unjust to you; and, second, that I would be held responsible for what he said.[44]

Sometimes even Lincoln found his partner a bit trying.

V

However one resolves the question of Herndon's earlier influence on Lincoln, one thing is certain: Billy was no President-maker. By his own statement Herndon was in Chicago during the time of the Convention (May 16–18, 1860) as one of the contingent which had Lincoln's interests in charge.[45] One suspects, however, that in this instance an old man's memory was playing him false. Certainly as late as May 14, when the real Lincoln managers, such as David Davis and Jesse K. Dubois, were on the scene, pulling wires and rolling logs, Herndon was still in Springfield.[46] No contemporary account has been found which mentions Herndon at Chicago or as one of the agitators in the Lincoln-for-President movement. With the exception of the belated memoirs of Henry C. Whitney (published in 1907) [47] even delayed reminiscences of the nomination have nothing to say about Herndon's activities. Reliable memoirs, such as those of Gustave Koerner, give elaborate details as to the work performed by David Davis, N. B. Judd, and Orville H. Browning but do not even refer to Herndon.[48] If Billy was in Chicago, it was in a humble capacity indeed.

Springfield welcomed the news of Lincoln's nomination with "a general firing of guns, shaking of hands, ringing of bells, hurras and shouts that set the whole town in an uproar." [49] It was a hullabaloo that would last until November. No one really thought that conservative John Bell and his Constitutional Union party, a last desperate effort to avoid sectionalism, had any chance to carry the Sucker state. Nor, when Southern elements of the Democratic party bolted the regular convention and selected John C. Breckinridge as their candidate was there much

---

[44] Nicolay and Hay, eds., *Works*, V, 290.

[45] *Herndon's Lincoln*, III, 461; Herndon to Weik, July 10, 1886, Herndon-Weik Coll.

[46] ". . . I wish *Herndon* was here. . . ." Mark W. Delahay to Lincoln, Chicago, May 14, 1860, Robert Todd Lincoln Coll.

[47] Whitney, *Lincoln the Citizen*, 289.

[48] T. J. McCormack, ed., *Memoirs of Gustave Koerner, 1809–1896*, II, 84–93. Immediately after the convention William Jayne of Springfield related how "Logan & Davis, Butler & Dubois, Judd, Cook & Palmer & Peck [and] Jack Grimshaw worked like turks for Lincoln's nomination," but did not refer to Herndon. Jayne to Trumbull, May 20, 1860, Trumbull MSS.

[49] *Illinois State Register*, May 19, 1860, quoted in Baringer, "Campaign Technique in Illinois — 1860," Ill. State Hist. Soc., *Trans., 1932*, 243.

excitement in Illinois, though federal officeholders like Herndon's brother Elliott had to be active in his support.[50] But when the Democratic convention at Baltimore selected Stephen A. Douglas to run as Lincoln's opponent, one could predict fire on the prairie. With two presidential contenders from within its borders, Illinois in 1860 was a boiling kettle of politics.

[50] Elliott B. Herndon was commissioned Attorney of the United States in and for the Southern District of Illinois on June 21, 1860.

CHAPTER X

The Election of a President
Makes No Change

I

IF Herndon was not one of the original Lincoln-for-President men, he was nevertheless enthusiastic when his partner was nominated. Illinois was "going almost unanimously & wildly for Lincoln." He saw "the sweep & roll of a grander civilization coming." "Hurrah for the West and God bless the human race." [1] It is perhaps well to discount Herndon's excitement a little. Ever since he had been able to vote, Herndon had assumed the standing-at-Armageddon attitude once in every four years; each presidential election was to him a battle against the forces of evil; and he always spread his adjectives thickly.

As a matter of course he took the stump for Lincoln. He may not have been an original Lincoln man, but Herndon was a Republican. Realizing that the central counties where the old Whig element had been strong would determine the election in Illinois, he refused invitations to address rallies in other parts of the state. Along with such local bigwigs as Shelby M. Cullom, William Jayne, James H. Matheny, and the brilliant Elmer E. Ellsworth, who was studying law in the Lincoln & Herndon office, he devoted "his energies to a thorough canvass of old Sangamon, speaking almost every night at schoolhouse and neighborhood meetings." [2] Though the open-air meetings required a terrific expenditure of energy, Herndon, half sick since spring, entered the lists and like other orators spoke almost every day on the "all absorbing issues of the present campaign." [3]

For the most part Herndon went on the byways of central Illinois. At Virginia, Illiopolis, Buffalo Hart Grove, Pleasant Plains, Berlin,

[1] Herndon to Sumner, June 20, 1860, Sumner MSS.
[2] Chicago *Press & Tribune*, August 30, 1860.
[3] Elmer E. Ellsworth to Carrie Spafford, October 20 [corrected in pencil to October 21], 1860, Ellsworth MSS.

Rochester, Richland, Laomi, and a dozen similar crossroads he spoke. He had one issue — the question of slavery in the territories — and except for a rather confused reference to the proposed homestead bill [4] he never left it. It was the same old story over and over again: the Founding Fathers, he said, had contemplated the extinction of slavery in the United States; conspiring slaveholders abetted by Pierce, Taney, Buchanan, and Douglas were seeking to extend the peculiar institution into the territories with the ultimate intent of enslaving even white laborers in the North; only by voting the Republican ballot could disaster be averted.

Herndon loved life on the stump. Lincoln, bound by his resolve not to "write or speak anything upon doctrinal points" during the campaign,[5] had to sit in Springfield all summer. The law office was hardly pretentious enough to house a presidential candidate, and after his nomination Lincoln used the governor's room in the State House for headquarters. There he read letters and welcomed countless visitors every hour from all sections. Herndon did not see how he endured it. "Good gracious, I would not have his place and be bored as he is." [6]

As in previous canvasses, the problem of the former Whigs was vexing Illinois Republican leaders. It was vitally necessary to secure this conservative support, yet with John Bell's Constitutional Union party in the field, Republicans were none too sure of their chances. For his part, Billy maintained his usual exuberant optimism. As in the two previous elections he knew for certain that "Almost all the old line whigs are with us *now*," and the rest were "yet on the fence, *leaning* Republicanwards." It was not that these were actuated by high motives; "Many men are now with us who see the sweep of our purse — our rule — our success, and our *Loaves & Fishes*." [7]

The real threat, as it developed, was not from Bell but in another direction. Under the leadership of Benjamin S. Edwards, a conservative Springfield lawyer, many Illinois Whigs determined to support Douglas in the hope of avoiding civil strife. The Little Giant's popular sovereignty, they said, was really only an application of Henry Clay's 1850 compromise principles on a national scale. In combating this heresy Herndon made his major speech of the 1860 campaign. On a hot Saturday evening in August Springfield's "Wigwam" on the corner

---

[4] He was quoted as saying: "Gentlemen I can say this much for Mr. Douglas, he is . . . a zealous and able supporter of the homestead measure. On this point the republicans have generally misrepresented him." — which may have been the truth, but was hardly good politics. *Illinois State Register,* October 30, 1860.

[5] Nicolay and Hay, eds., *Works,* VI, 48.

[6] Herndon to Trumbull, June 19, 1860, Trumbull MSS.

[7] *Ibid.*

of Sixth and Monroe was pretty well filled with "a mixed crowd of republicans, democrats, Union men, ladies, children and noisy urchins," numbering perhaps three thousand. The singing by the Republican glee club seemed for a time to be the leading attraction of the evening's performance, but finally Herndon appeared, stating that his speech was provoked by the political tergiversation of Edwards. He had evidently prepared very carefully, for he began, a hostile reporter noted, with "a great deal of prefatory thrash [*sic*] . . . about logical and legal conclusions and logical and legal deductions, all of which the speaker waded through, in a very floundering style." Herndon then proceeded to "a prosy disquisition on the old feudal system in Europe" and to a heated denunciation of the Inquisition. The *State Register* claimed that by this time most of his crowd was traveling in the land of dreams.[8]

The main portion of the address was a detailed demonstration that "Henry Clay's mantle has not fallen upon Mr. Edward's [*sic*] shoulders, nor upon the shoulders of any other man who follows in the crooked wake of the ambitious individual who . . . destroyed the Missouri Compromise." [9] Herndon concluded with a vehement indictment of the Little Giant:

> Had Mr. Douglas honestly carried out Henry Clay's *non-intervention* principles of 1850, in organizing Kansas and Nebraska . . . there had been no agitation in the land — . . . no bloody murders in Kansas — no massacres at Harper's Ferry . . . ; but peace would this day have been all over the land, and Justice sitting supreme. Let public indignation rest heavily upon his shoulders; . . . let public scorn "burn to ashes what it lights to death." Then I am content.[10]

Democrats charged that Herndon's reasoning was mere sophistry, denounced the effort as being "as strongly in favor of abolitionism as . . . John Brown," and claimed that the speech caused several honest Republicans to retire from the audience in disgust. The Republican press, on the other hand, announced that Herndon had knocked the Douglas cause into the middle of next week and wished that "every Whig in central Illinois had heard Mr. Herndon's speech." If every Whig did not, it was scarcely Billy's fault, for he made the same speech in virtually every hamlet in the Sangamon valley. It is doubtful just how great the effect of all this oratory was, but to judge

---

[8] *Illinois State Register*, August 27, 1860. The fact that the *Register* abused Herndon's speech at length would indicate that it was an able performance.

[9] *Illinois State Journal*, August 27, 1860.

[10] Several weeks later Herndon repeated this speech at Loami, and the quotation is from the *Journal's* detailed report on that occasion. *Ibid.*, October 4, 1860.

from "the commendation of the *Journal* and the squirming of the *Register*" some, at least, were paying attention.[11]

II

Against Herndon in 1860 was directed more vitriolic abuse than he had ever suffered in any previous canvass. All too often he was indiscreet and impolitic, and hostile newspapers could denounce "The Falsities and Fanaticism of Bill Herndon, the Law Partner and Confident of Mr. Lincoln" and could brand his radical statements, his "heresies and false dogmas," as "traceable to the law-office of Mr. Lincoln himself." It was alleged, with some reason, that Herndon placed himself "fully upon the Parker and Emerson theories of political economy" and that his speeches "abounded in all the extravagances of higher lawism and false philosophy." While the Republican party was striving to give proof of its conservatism, it was scarcely wise for Herndon to reiterate the theory of an irrepressible conflict between slavery and freedom and to ask "why all men are not gods enough to embark in the eternal conflict between right and wrong." [12]

Prepared for his speech, Sangamon Democrats were ready to heckle. At Spring Creek a farmer rose during Billy's oration to question whether the speaker would approve "several passages from the scripture," showing the inequality of races. Exasperated, Herndon incautiously replied: "Shut your mouth, and take your seat. If the Bible is your authority you can prove from [it] that God Almighty is a liar." Again, Herndon was showed a letter supposed to have been written by Henry Clay and was asked if he could approve it. He read it aloud, repeating after each sentence, "I endorse that." But the last three sentences seemed so strongly to support the Democratic position that Billy "got mad with everybody . . . and yelled out that 'I don't believe Henry Clay was ever the author of such sentiments.' This sudden repudiation of what he had just endorsed, again brought down the house with shouts of laughter." [13]

By hitting at Herndon's somewhat ridiculous affectation of dignity and sneering at him as Lincoln's "Dear William" or the "expectant attorney general of the U. S.," [14] Democrats repeatedly attempted to inflame his temper. When Herndon proposed a joint debate in Sangamon County with a Democratic champion, the Douglas men named

[11] *Illinois State Register*, August 27, 1860; *Illinois State Journal*, August 27, 1860; Chicago *Press & Tribune*, August 30, 1860.
[12] Petersburg *Semi-Weekly Axis*, April 7 and October 13, 1860.
[13] *Illinois State Register*, October 30, 1860.
[14] *Ibid.*

as his opponent one C. A. Keyes, a political nobody who would profit by the crowds Herndon might draw. The Republicans rejected this opponent as a man of "not heavy calibre enough for Mr. Lincoln's law partner," and the *State Register* was able to charge that Herndon had ignominiously backed down because of fright. Some Democrats even offered to furnish the best buggy and team in Crafton's stable free of charge so that Billy would be able to make the debates.[15]

Three days before the election the *State Register* featured a damaging accusation against Herndon and other Republicans in Sangamon. From black headlines readers learned of "Elegant Disclosures! Lincoln's Law Partner!! State Treasurer Butler! The Danite Alliance!!! Bribery and Fraud! 'Union of the Puritan and Blackleg!' The state paying for republican voter." The story, an exceedingly complicated affair, was basically that Herndon, State Treasurer William Butler, and other Republicans, with Lincoln's consent, were importing "corn huskers" to vote the Lincoln ticket. Through a mistake in identity — and through too many drinks — Herndon was said to have informed a Democrat "that corn huskers would be sent to every town, and that by (a little profanity) this county would be carried." As they progressed from one saloon to another Billy became more and more confidential and offered to give his interviewer a Lincoln & Herndon check to encourage the good work. All this, Democrats swore, was the work of "Mr. Herndon, Mr. Lincoln's law partner and confidential friend." [16]

It is impossible now to reach any conclusion as to the truth of these charges against Herndon. The Republican papers published statements and affidavits denying the whole account. Herndon himself swore that the *Register's* story was "*not a true or correct statement in substance or in form*" of his conversation. Other interested parties also issued denials.[17] Such stories were not uncommon in the partisan press of the time, and they were usually dropped promptly after election day. In view, however, of Herndon's known willingness to "colonize" voters in previous elections, and of his earlier dealings with "the details of how we get along," together with his unfortunate habit of drinking, it is impossible to dismiss the accusation completely. At any rate, the story served its purpose, for Douglas carried Sangamon County.

Lincoln's already excellent chance of election was greatly improved when those states which balloted in October gave their decision. Herndon was in Petersburg giving what a Democratic reporter called a

---

[15] *Ibid.*, October 16 and 30, 1860.
[16] *Ibid.*, November 3, 1860. The entire editorial was repeated on election day.
[17] *Illinois State Journal*, November 5 and 6, 1860.

"tirade of abuse upon southerners and southern institutions" when the news came in.[18] Lincoln had dashed off a hasty note to tell his partner that it was "entirely certain that Pennsylvania and Indiana have gone Republican very largely." Ohio too was safe.[19] Interrupting his speech, Herndon read the news to his audience. "The crowd yelled — screamed — threw up their hats — ran out of the doors — made bonfires — &c. &c," and thirty years later Herndon still remembered regretfully: "I never succeeded in finishing the speech." [20]

On election day, November 6, Herndon dropped by Lincoln's office in the State House and learned that the presidential candidate had scruples about voting for his own electors. Elbowing his way through the crowd, Herndon urged, "Lincoln you ought to go & vote," and insisted until Lincoln cut the list of presidential electors from the top of a Republican ballot and strode out to the polls. Swashbuckling Ward Lamon strutted on one side and Elmer Ellsworth walked on the other, while Herndon proudly brought up the rear. Republicans yelled and shouted as the little procession approached, and the crowd around the courthouse opened up a wide gap for Lincoln to enter. Escorted to the very ballot box, Lincoln cast his vote and returned to the office.[21] This was one of the last political services Herndon was ever to perform for his partner.

When the returns from the November elections came trickling in, it was at once apparent that Lincoln's election was likely. For the first time since Harrison, the Northwest might be represented in the White House. The Illinois capital went wild with excitement. Through the long evening crowds milled about the State House, where the latest returns were read out, and congregated at Watson's saloon, where the Republican ladies served bountiful refreshments. There were speeches and cheers and songs and more speeches. As the decisive vote of New York came over the wires, Republicans knew the election was won. Jesse Dubois ran with the news to the waiting mob, and they roared out the campaign jingle, "Ain't You Glad You Jined the Republicans?" Springfield had a President.[22]

[18] Petersburg *Semi-Weekly Axis,* October 13, 1860, copy in Herndon-Weik Coll.

[19] Nicolay and Hay, eds., *Works,* VI, 62.

[20] Herndon's note on copy of Lincoln's letter of October 10, 1860, Herndon-Weik Coll.; *Herndon's Lincoln,* III, 465.

[21] Herndon to Weik, November 14, 1885, Herndon-Weik Coll.

[22] Baringer, "Campaign Technique," Ill. State Hist. Soc., *Trans., 1932,* 275–276.

III

After the excitement was over and the bonfires were only ashes, thinking men in the country realized painfully that they knew almost nothing about this man they had chosen to head the nation. Who was Abraham Lincoln? A rail splitter. Debater against Douglas. Honest Abe. A homely, gaunt pioneer type. A former Whig. A Black Republican. The man who said: "A house divided against itself cannot stand." But was he a statesman? Could he run a country?

Some people had already made up their minds. In the Lower South Lincoln's election had been the signal for the first steps toward secession, and one by one seven commonwealths withdrew from the Union before the Republican President could be inaugurated. In the North, too, men were wondering what Lincoln's policy would be: What would he do ao ut slavery and secession and federal forts and property in the seceded areas? And there were quite as many who were concerned over the sharing of the loaves and fishes.

It was a time when the President Elect was carefully refraining from making any public statement lest he give offense and precipitate hostilities. The official Republican attitude was one of silence. Eager inquirers, failing to secure information from Lincoln himself, turned to his Springfield associates for hints as to the policy of the incoming administration. Some wrote to Herndon, little realizing how definitely out of touch he was with Republican policy making. There was not now or at any time an open break between Lincoln and Herndon. It was simply that the President Elect had to be guided by the best minds in the country, that he had to listen to cautious advice, that he had to talk only to the most discreet. Herndon could qualify under none of these heads. Swamped with mail and badgered by curious visitors and office-seeking dignitaries, Lincoln seldom came to the law office and, even if he had wished, he had no time for gossiping with his partner. Henry C. Whitney correctly stated that after 1860 Lincoln "took no advice, and sought no counsel from . . . Herndon." [23]

The estrangement, if it should be called that, can be measured in little things. In earlier years Herndon had as a matter of course read all the mail that came into the office; this was the "usual custom in the firm." Now when he tore open a letter to Lincoln inadvertently placed in his mail, Herndon hastily apologized by endorsing the envelope:

[23] Whitney, *Life on the Circuit*, 186.

The Election of a President Makes No Change

"Opened by mistake did not read." [24] A proud and sensitive man, Herndon was disgusted by the adulation heaped upon his partner by office seekers. With distaste he observed that "men & women rushed around . . . [Lincoln] — kissed his feet — rolled in the dust — begging notice . . . begged for a hair from the tail of his old horse: the very dogs and kittens pups & chicks running around Lincolns house assumed forms of beauty & power." Fearing to be classed among these beggars for office, Herndon went to the Lincoln home but once after the election — "and that on business." [25] For small things Billy could still be useful. When Lincoln retired to a secluded second-story warehouse in order to find a quiet place for writing his inaugural address, Herndon could send him the necessary reference books and keep away visitors. [26] But when it came to major matters of state, Billy was counted out.

People who did not realize Herndon's lack of influence turned to him for hints as to the Lincoln policies and plans. One canny Ohioan, desiring the appointment of Governor Salmon P. Chase to the cabinet, sought to promote that object by turning over his law business in the United States court at Springfield to Herndon. [27] Many others wrote Billy asking for an elucidation of Lincoln's views. Always willing to oblige, Herndon replied verbosely, but his statements were diametrically opposite to Lincoln's real position. While the President Elect was emphasizing that he had no intention "of harrassing [sic] the people either North or South" by interfering with slavery in the states, [28] Herndon was promising correspondents that "Mr. Lincoln will in thirty days after he is sworn in . . . order Gen. Scott to retake all Forts etc etc. The South will have a sweet time in Disunion — on paper." When basic questions of "justice — right — Liberty the government and constitution — Union — humanity" came up, his partner would oppose all compromise. Rather than make one move toward conciliating the South, Herndon said, Lincoln would prefer that "his soul might go back to God from the wings of the Capitol." [29]

[24] Herndon to John J. Crittenden, November 1, 1858, Crittenden MSS.; endorsement on envelope of N. Paschall to Lincoln, November 18, 1860, Robert Todd Lincoln Coll.
[25] Herndon to Lamon, March 1, 1870, Lamon MSS.
[26] *Herndon's Lincoln*, III, 478; Weik, *Real Lincoln*, 5; Rankin, *Intimate Character Sketches*, 147–148; Herndon to Weik, January 1, 1886, Herndon-Weik Coll.
[27] S. Stokely to Jesse W. Fell, December 21, 1860, Fell MSS.
[28] Nicolay and Hay, eds., *Works*, VI, 81.
[29] Herndon to Edward L. Pierce, February 18, 1861, copy, Herndon-Weik Coll.; Herndon's letter of December 21, 1860, quoted in Henry Wilson to Herndon, May 30, 1867, *ibid.*; Herndon to Samuel E. Sewall, February 1, 1861, copy, Garrison MSS.

Every thinking man in the nation desired peace. Lincoln was preparing his inaugural pledge: "In your hands, my dissatisfied fellow-countrymen, and not in mine, is the momentous issue of civil war. . . . You can have no conflict without being yourselves the aggressors."[30] The best minds in the country were working desperately to find some peaceful antidote for war hysteria. Plan after plan for adjustment of difficulties was suggested — the Crittenden compromise, a national convention, a convention of border states. But hotheads North and South wanted no peace. "Compromise — Compromise — !" stormed Herndon; "Why, I am sick at the very idea." The "Slavery question *must be met & met now.*" If this meant bloodshed, Herndon was ready for it. "Let this natural war — let this inevitable struggle proceed — go on, till slavery is *dead* — DEAD — DEAD." If the Republican party moved toward peace and conciliation, he for one would "help to tear it down, and erect a new party that shall never cower to any slave driver."[31] Lincoln did not seek this man's advice.

IV

As the day of departure for Washington approached, the President Elect again drew near the man who had shared so much of his life since 1844. Harassed beyond measure by appointment seekers and distressed by the perilous condition of the nation, perhaps Lincoln even regretted his election and sought to recover momentarily the carefree past in the musty atmosphere of the second-story law office. "I am sick of office-holding already," he told Herndon.[32] The passing of years may have lessened Lincoln's respect for his partner, but it did not dim his almost paternal affection. He took time out to talk with Herndon about a possible federal appointment but was probably relieved when Billy preferred to keep his state job as bank commissioner. He even made a special visit to the incoming Republican governor, Richard Yates, to urge Herndon's reappointment.

In the afternoon of his last day in Springfield, Lincoln revisited the office, and the partners talked briefly about legal matters and cases. Lincoln walked over and threw himself for a last time on the old office sofa. They sat silent for a moment — there are so many things that men do not say to each other. Presently Lincoln inquired: "Billy, . . . how long have we been together?"

[30] Nicolay and Hay, eds., *Works*, VI, 184–185.
[31] Herndon to Sumner, December 10, 1860, Sumner MSS.; Herndon to Trumbull, December 21, 1860, Trumbull MSS.; Herndon to Samuel E. Sewall, February 1, 1861, copy, Garrison MSS.
[32] *Herndon's Lincoln*, III, 484.

"Over sixteen years," was the answer.

"We've never had a cross word during all that time, have we?" Emphatically Herndon replied: "No, indeed we have not."

There was an awkward pause. "Billy," said Lincoln hesitantly, "there's one thing I have, for some time, wanted you to tell me. . . . I want you to tell me . . . how many times you have been drunk."

Flustered, Herndon tried to collect his wits. Lincoln said nothing more on the subject but went on to tell of various attempts to induce him to drop Billy as a partner. That was as close as he ever came to lecturing Herndon for drunkenness. Then he gathered up some books and papers, talked for a moment or so, and the two men walked downstairs together. At the bottom Lincoln glanced up at the battered law shingle. "Let it hang there undisturbed," he asked, lowering his voice. "Give our clients to understand that the election of a President makes no change in the firm of Lincoln and Herndon. If I live I'm coming back some time, and then we'll go right on practising law as if nothing had ever happened."

The two paused, silent. Then Lincoln reached out a bony hand. "Good-bye," he said fervently, and strode off down the street. Looking after that gaunt stooping figure, Herndon felt the cold ache of loneliness. The nation had gained a President. He had lost a partner.[33]

[33] *Ibid.*, III, 482–484; Weik, *Real Lincoln*, 301–302. Since this conversation was recalled years after the event, the precise words attributed to the speakers cannot be literally accurate.

CHAPTER *xi*

This Huge Rebellion

I

BEFORE I would buy the South by Compromises and Concessions," Herndon wrote Lyman Trumbull one week before the President Elect left Springfield, "I would die — rot & be forgotten willingly." This was no time for caving in. Had not the Republicans proclaimed an eternal antagonism between freedom and slavery? The Republican party represented liberty for the Negro and for the white man; if it yielded now when facing fundamental issues it must "Consider death as the Law." [1] Efforts to adjust sectional antagonism Herndon spurned as treachery to the eternal right. When Lincoln was in power he would assuredly be firm, for he was "true to Justice — to Right — to Liberty and Humanity." "I know Lincoln better than he knows himself," Herndon added owlishly. [2]

But on leaving Illinois, the President Elect did none of the things his partner had expected. Along his route to the capital he kept emphasizing the whipped-up nature of the crisis, the absence of vital issues between North and South. Herndon was disgusted. Either Lincoln was glossing over the seriousness of the crisis — "which was a crime under the Circumstances" — or he "never fully comprehended the situation." [3] Charitably Herndon accepted the latter explanation and hoped for better things. But even after the inaugural oath was taken, the President continued to ignore his partner's advice. General Winfield Scott was not ordered to retake the federal forts; the nation was not summoned to arms; Lincoln did not even castigate his Confederate enemies.

Then blundering, misunderstanding, and confusion did their work, and the Confederates fired on the Union troops stationed at Fort Sum-

[1] Herndon to Trumbull, February 9, 1861, Trumbull MSS.
[2] Herndon to E. L. Pierce, March 4, 1861, copy, Herndon-Weik Coll.
[3] Herndon to Weik, August 8, 1890, *ibid.*

ter in Charleston harbor. At long last the South had tapped the dinner gong and summoned "the wild, bony, quick, brave Peoples to a feast of Civil War." [4] Herndon heard the news of Sumter on Sunday morning, April 14, when he went to the post office. "I saw democrat & Republican shake hands on the Union," he recalled. "All party distinctions were wiped out. The people sprang up from mere politicians to patriots. You could see the jaws firmly set, while walking along and with fists double[d] up muttering wrath to those who ordered the bombardment of Fort Sumpter [*sic.*] . . . War — actual war — present war had come upon us." It was the war Herndon had been predicting for years, and he rejoiced that it had come. [5]

Now that fighting had begun, Herndon anticipated drastic measures. The whole nation would be called to arms; President Lincoln would "go out on the high & broad steps of the Capitol" and call the people to war. [6] Slavery was the root of the whole conflict, and slavery would be abolished. Jefferson Davis and his fellow experimenters in rebellion would be strung from the gallows. There would be no conservatism, no conciliation, no compromise.

Such expectations received little encouragement from the President. He refused to take extreme measures and he repudiated the drastic actions of his subordinates. For more than a year he did nothing to free the Negroes. Though by presidential proclamation the "rebel" soldiers were traitors, Lincoln carefully refrained from executing Confederate prisoners. Instead of calling a nation to arms he asked for 75,000 three-month volunteers. In Illinois such caution served as a frost on the exuberant foliage of radical war enthusiasm. As the war dragged on, maladministration, slowness to take vigorous action, unfortunate distribution of patronage, and — above all — the failure to win victories increased the dissatisfaction. Radical Republicans, peeved by the President's disregard of their officious advice, began to abuse Lincoln in unmeasured terms. The "imbecility of President Lincoln," announced one Illinois extremist, "has done more to aid Secessia than Jefferson Davis has done." When the presidential message of December 1861 failed to recommend immediate emancipation, it was denounced as "a tame, timid, timeserving common place sort of an abortion of a Message, cold enough with one breath, to *freeze* h—ll over." The President lacked the unctuous piety to suit these critics. "Tale-telling and jesting," frowned a Chicago preacher, "illy suit the hour and become the

[4] Herndon had used this phrase almost exactly four years before Sumter. Herndon to Parker, March 10, 1857, Herndon-Parker MSS.

[5] Herndon monograph on causes of Civil War, Herndon-Weik Coll.

[6] Untitled Herndon monograph, *ibid.*

man in whose hands the destiny of a great nation is trembling. Levees and levity in his palace indicate utter want of estimation of the proportions of this great rebellion." [7]

In this radical disaffection Herndon shared. He was an impetuous man, swept off his feet by the excitement of war, impatient of constitutional restraints and ignorant of practical political obstacles. It was irritating and perhaps a little embarrassing that the President was not following his good advice. The most exasperating blow of all came in the fall of 1861 when President Lincoln revoked the order of General Frémont freeing the slaves of Confederates in the western military district. "Good God!" Herndon exploded. "What is Lincoln doing?" "This People has got to meet this negro question face to face now or at some future time. God w[r]ites *this* in the instincts of the race. . . . Heaven or Hell must rule." The issue was plain, Herndon asserted. "The question is — Shall the union go under or shall slavery go out of sight." "Old Abe" was taking halfway measures, exhibiting a shameful want of courage. "Does he suppose he can crush — squelch out this huge rebellion by pop guns filled with rose water," jeered Herndon. "He ought to hang somebody and get up a name for will or decision — for character. Let him hang some Child or woman, if he has not Courage to hang a *man*." "[I]f I were Lincoln," Herndon shrilled, "I would declare that all slaves should be free and stand emancipated. *I would be this ages great hero.*" [8]

II

The sharpness of Herndon's tone may have some relation to his domestic unhappiness at this time. Mary Herndon had been ailing for years. She had tuberculosis — "phthisis," as the doctors of that day called it — and her illness was no doubt aggravated by the constant burden of childbearing and the drudgery of housework. In the summer of 1860 she was sent to the Falls of St. Anthony for her health, but becoming homesick for her husband and children, especially for "little Mollie," she soon returned to Springfield. One more Illinois winter was too much, and in the summer of 1861 Herndon's first wife died. [9]

[7] A. C. Cole, "President Lincoln and the Illinois Radical Republicans," *Miss. Valley Hist. Rev.*, IV, 417–436 (1918); J. G. Randall, "The Unpopular Mr. Lincoln," *Abraham Lincoln Quar.*, II, 255–280; Robert Laird Collier, *Moral Heroism: Its Essentialness to the Crisis* . . . (1862), 8.

[8] Herndon to Trumbull, November 20, 1861, Trumbull MSS.; Herndon to Caroline H. Dall, November 10, 1861, Dall MSS.

[9] *Illinois State Journal*, August 19, 1861. The date is usually given incorrectly as 1860.

This Huge Rebellion

The sincerity of Herndon's grief is not to be questioned, though he was soon looking for another wife. A sociable creature, he needed companionship; family tradition has it that before her death Mary Herndon urged him to remarry speedily. Besides, there was the practical consideration that his six children needed a mother's care. Within a few short months after his wife's death Herndon began to pay more frequent visits to Petersburg, in nearby Menard County, and he became a habitual caller in the twin parlors of Major George U. Miles's red brick house, just off the public square.

Even today in Petersburg Major Miles's youngest daughter is seldom referred to simply by name; she is always "the beautiful Anna Miles." A striking brunette with dark hair and cheeks so rosy that it was whispered — shocking thought — that she used rouge, Anna was the belle of Petersburg. She had spent a winter in Washington with Menard County's Congressman Thomas L. Harris and his wife, and, lingering tradition has it, was for a season the toast of the capital. Widespread but wholly unauthenticated rumors tell of the gay times she had at the Washington balls, murmur enviously of her beautiful gowns, and whisper excitedly of an offer of marriage by an unnamed California congressman.[10] When Harris died in 1858, Anna's triumph was over and she returned to her father's home. Well-read for her day and, as Herndon somewhat patronizingly characterized her, "a very intelligent female,"[11] Anna must have found Petersburg dull and stodgy.

Herndon was eighteen years her senior. After his wife's death, he began paying court and on Sundays would drive Anna in a rented surrey out to the Masters farmhouse for dinner.[12] Anna was apparently reluctant to let the affair progress further. A gruff, middle-aged widower with a houseful of children was no marital prize. Even at that time it was known that Herndon was not a temperate man, and his law practice, though extensive, was not very lucrative. Through association with the Harrises Anna had developed strong attachments to the Democratic party; in Menard County it was not quite socially respectable to marry a Republican.

Anna Miles's decision to accept Herndon came about in an amusing and complicated fashion. Her older sister Elizabeth had some years earlier married Charles W. Chatterton, who wanted a federal job that would offer money and adventure. To please a prospective brother-in-

---

[10] For the traditions about Anna Miles I am indebted to Dr. Ella Harris, daughter of the congressman.

[11] Herndon to Caroline H. Dall, January 28, 1862, Dall MSS.

[12] Edgar Lee Masters, *The Sangamon*, 71.

law, Herndon volunteered to secure an appointment for him. In return, Chatterton and his wife would use their good offices in convincing Anna that Herndon would make an acceptable husband.

Early in January 1862 Herndon packed up to visit his partner in the White House. He had not much difficulty in reaching the President and laid the whole story before him. Finding this roundabout courtship "wonderfully funny," Lincoln agreed to give Chatterton some inconspicuous post. Herndon was given a card bearing the President's endorsement and called on Secretary of Interior Caleb Blood Smith in the hope of finding an opening. Learning of no vacancy, he returned to the White House the following day and told Lincoln of his troubles. The President rose from his chair and said: "Let's go down to the Indian department and see Dole." The commissioner of Indian affairs, W. P. Dole, was an old friend from Paris, Illinois, and at the personal request of the President he did not find it too difficult to locate "one of Buchanan's appointees who could be spared from the service." [13] A commission was issued shortly afterward, and Chatterton was made agent for the Cherokee Indians at a salary of $1500 a year. [14]

Herndon lingered a few days in Washington, visited old acquaintances and spent much time in Lincoln's office and in the waiting room of the White House, where he watched the endless stream of office seekers who were badgering the President. Wearily Lincoln emerged from his office one evening after long hours of interviewing petitioners and prophesied dejectedly: "If ever American society and the United States government are demoralized . . . it will come from the voracious desire of office — this struggle to live without toil — work and labor. . . ." Then he thought a minute and added whimsically: ". . . from which I am not free myself." [15]

Two embarrassing episodes marred Herndon's visit. Running short of money, he had to borrow twenty-five dollars from his partner-President. [16] And Mrs. Lincoln, who had always thoroughly disap-

---

[13] The best account of this episode is Jesse W. Weik, "Lincoln in a New Role. How He is Alleged to Have Helped His Law Partner to a Young Wife," unidentified clipping from Weik scrapbook, Lincoln National Life Foundation. Weik's version, though not always accurate in detail, was based on information supplied by Herndon. See also "Lincoln's Offer of Appointment to Herndon," undated Herndon monograph, Herndon-Weik Coll.; *Illinois State Journal,* September 24, 1883.

[14] Chatterton was appointed March 6, 1862, and was engaged in caring for the refugee Cherokees who fled to Kansas from the Indian Territory during the Civil War. Rather ungratefully after all Herndon's exertions, Chatterton died in August 1862.

[15] Failing to see the humor of the overworked President's statement, Herndon remembered the remark in all seriousness and repeated it in his second lecture on Lincoln. *Abraham Lincoln Quar.,* I, 406–407.

[16] Pratt, *Personal Finances,* 135.

proved of Herndon, snubbed him. Herndon's feelings were hurt and he was bitterly resentful. "Mrs. Lincoln," he confided to a friend, "is a very curious — excentric [*sic*] — *wicked* woman." "Poor Lincoln!" he sympathized. "He is domestically a desolate man — has been for years to my own knowledge." [17] In years to come, Mrs. Lincoln would have cause to regret her rudeness.

Before leaving the capital Herndon had dinner at the White House. When he was ready to go, President Lincoln accompanied him to the rear portico of the executive mansion, where a carriage was waiting. Grasping his partner by the hand, the President bade him a hearty "Good-bye." It was the last time Herndon saw Lincoln alive. [18]

III

Back in Springfield gossips were speculating about Herndon's Washington visit. One rumor had it that Billy had gone to ask Lincoln for an appointment for himself, probably as minister to the Kingdom of Italy, which was considered peculiarly fitting because of Herndon's "fondness for classical history." Another report had it that not only Herndon but half a dozen other Springfield citizens went in person to the White House to urge such an appointment and that the President refused only because "he would be charged with paying the debts of personal friendship with public patronage." [19] When Herndon returned with nothing more impressive than a $1500 Indian agency for a prospective brother-in-law, it was whispered that the President had been about to give his law partner a major position but changed his mind when Herndon was found scandalously drunk on the streets of Washington. [20]

To understand how these tales gained currency it must be remembered that a great many of Lincoln's friends looked on his election as an opening of the door to the public treasury. Surely a President of the United States would reward his old and faithful Illinois friends. Lincoln did appoint many, but the federal patronage was not large enough to give everyone a job. There was considerable wailing and gnashing of teeth among the disappointed. Joseph Medill of the Chi-

[17] Herndon to Caroline H. Dall, January 28, 1862, Dall MSS.

[18] *Herndon's Lincoln*, III, 508; Jesse W. Weik, "Lincoln in a New Role," unidentified newspaper clipping, Lincoln National Life Foundation.

[19] Interview of Weik with James H. Matheny, May 9, 1883, in undated clipping from Indianapolis *Times*, Lincoln National Life Foundation; Whitney, *Life on the Circuit*, 417; Weik to Clinton L. Conkling, February 11, 1917, C. L. Conkling MSS.

[20] Interview of Clinton L. Conkling with John W. Bunn, December 13, 1917, C. L. Conkling MSS.

cago *Tribune* regarded the President as a kind of personal property, and when his faction seemed not to be securing its share of the patronage he raged: "We made Abe and by G— we can unmake him . . . ."[21] Jesse K. Dubois, Illinois state auditor, who had expected a lush federal job and got nothing, expressed the general attitude of resentment:

> Lincoln is a singular man and I must confess I never knew him. He has for 30 years past just used me as a plaything to accomplish his own ends: but the moment he was elevated to his proud position he seemed all at once to have entirely changed his whole nature and become altogether a new being — knows no one and the road to favor is always open to his enemies whilst the door is . . . sealed to his old friends.[22]

When Herndon received no appointment from his partner, it was naturally assumed that he would share the views of these malcontents. In Springfield parlors, under the globe-shaped lamps and the baleful stare of the daguerreotypes, the story was elaborated in minute detail. Herndon had, gossips repeated, gone to Washington with high hopes, and Lincoln had offered him only a very inferior appointment. Greatly dissatisfied, Billy was supposed to have returned to Illinois "very sour" on the President. An embittered man, he then began collecting disreputable anecdotes about Lincoln in order to be revenged for his slight.[23]

The actual facts of this matter are difficult to determine. Herndon's own version of his efforts as office seeker under Lincoln is not consistent. Very late in life, worn out by hard physical labor and a little befuddled by constant use of liquor, he would, in uninhibited moments, confide to his friends: ". . . I could have had any place for which I was fitted, but I thought too much of Lincoln to disgrace him. No, I wanted to be free, drink whiskey when I pleased." Herndon frequently repeated: "It was distinctly understood between Lincoln and myself that I wanted to hold no office under his administration. . . ."[24]

Actually this was only a half-truth. It does not seem likely that at the beginning of the Lincoln administration Herndon desired a federal job. His ailing wife, his numerous family, his extensive law practice

[21] Joseph Medill to C. H. Ray or J. L. Scripps, January 6, 1861, Ray MSS.
[22] Dubois to H. C. Whitney, copy, Herndon-Weik Coll.
[23] *Illinois State Journal*, September 1, 1883.
[24] Letter probably by Hardin Masters quoted in Rankin, *Intimate Character Sketches*, 270; *The Valuable Collection of Autographs and Historical Papers Collected by the Hon. Jas. Mitchell* . . . (1894), 102.

confined him to Springfield. He was not then poor, for in 1860 his personal property was valued at $11,000.[25] Besides, he was still a state bank commissioner, an office that made slight demands on his time but paid very well indeed — about $1000 a year. So rewarding was this position that the bank commissioners in 1861 were jittery lest the incoming Governor Yates be tempted to sweep out the incumbents and use the offices to pay some of his political obligations. It seems fair to credit Herndon's statement that at his request the President Elect visited Yates to urge that Herndon be continued in office and that at the time he regarded this position more highly than any federal appointment likely to fall his way.[26]

So far as can be learned, Herndon's 1862 visit to Washington was made solely in behalf of Chatterton and not in his own interest. But by the winter of 1862 his affairs had changed for the worse. Business was not good, and Herndon "went, like a thousand others, under pecuniarily." [27] In desperation he appealed to Lincoln for aid and was offered "a job of about a month's duration at Saint Louis, $5 a day and mileage," [28] probably on a commission investigating cotton claims. Not wishing to leave home — and possibly hoping for a more permanent position — Herndon declined the appointment and wrote a tactful letter to the President's secretary, John G. Nicolay, explaining his action.[29] Apparently no further offers were forthcoming from Washington. In 1864 Herndon still had hopes and tried a roundabout approach through congressman Shelby M. Cullom, an old personal friend. "Cullom," he wrote jocularly, "if you see Lincoln tell him for me that if he has any large, honorable, & fat office with a big salary to give away and cannot get any person on earth to take it that I'll take and run it. . . ." [30] The hint was not taken, and Herndon held no federal appointment under the Lincoln administration. If he was embittered,

---

[25] Illinois census returns, 1860 (MS., National Archives).

[26] *Illinois State Journal,* September 24, 1883.

[27] "Lincoln's Offer of Appointment to Herndon," undated Herndon monograph, Herndon-Weik Coll.

[28] Nicolay and Hay, eds., *Works,* VIII, 217.

[29] "If you preserved the letter which I wrote to you declining the office which the Prestd [*sic*] offered me please send it to me. I didn't save a Copy. Don't forget to write to me & send the letter." Herndon to "Friend Nickoly," March 3, 1863, Robert Todd Lincoln Coll. See also Herndon to Hart, December 12, 1866, Hart MSS.

[30] "Lincoln's Offer of Appointment to Herndon," undated Herndon monograph, Herndon-Weik Coll. Herndon's account dates this plea as before 1863, but Cullom was not elected to Congress until 1864. As Herndon recalled it, his letter to Cullom was supposed to be simply a jocular greeting to the President; the congressman remembered it as a serious application for office. Statement of Cullom, "Special Correspondence of the [St. Louis] Globe-Democrat," undated clipping, Lincoln National Life Foundation.

however, his contemporary letters give no inkling of his disappointment.

IV

Disgruntled or not, Herndon returned to Springfield with a promise of appointment for Chatterton, who immediately began to use his influence with Anna Miles. Under strong family urging, her reluctance crumbled and in late July 1862 she and Herndon were married.[31] The new wife brought to the Herndon home a whirlwind of energy. The house was renovated, an adjoining lot was purchased, and the grounds were landscaped for a flower garden. The Herndon house became a showplace in Springfield, and visitors at the St. Nicholas Hotel used to stroll by in the evenings to see Herndon's roses.

Marriage is at best a difficult business, and Herndon was hardly the ideal husband for Anna. His children by his first wife bitterly resented his remarriage; none of them was ever to call Anna "Mother." Herndon himself, though devoted, had his idiosyncrasies, and it must at times have been hard to get along with him. Influenced by her Petersburg friends, Anna had been an ardent Democrat and was what Herndon called "a pro-slavery girl." Soon she learned that to keep peace in the family she must adjust her political notions to suit her radical husband; her silly Southern ideas, Herndon wrote, "I took . . . out of her by fair argument & reason pretty quick after marriage." [32] Other adjustments must have been more difficult. Herndon was never accepted by the tight little clique of Springfield's ruling families. If Anna expected a brilliant social career, she must have been sorely disappointed; there was an impassable distance between Mrs. Herndon and Mrs. Milton Hay, Mrs. John Todd Stuart, or Mrs. Ninian W. Edwards.

Another problem that caused constant anxiety was Herndon's drinking. Before his second marriage Herndon swore off liquor and joined the Order of Good Templars, successor to the earlier temperance organizations. He acted in good faith, and apparently his reformation was convincing, for as late as December 1866 he lectured on the evils of alcohol.[33] To President Lincoln in 1865 he pledged: ". . . I am a sober man, and will keep so the balance of my days." [34] It was a high

[31] Marriage Record, Book A, Menard County, p. 240. The date was July 30, 1862.

[32] Herndon to Weik, January 14, 1887, Herndon-Weik Coll.

[33] Springfield *Union Herald and Everybody's Advertiser,* January 15, 1862; *Illinois State Journal,* December 8, 1866.

[34] Herndon to Lincoln, February 11, 1865, quoted in Pratt, *Personal Finances,* 134–135.

ideal, but it must have been a frequent temptation to relapse into his former bad habits.

Herndon needed both his wits and his sobriety, for he was now head of the law firm and had no senior partner to steer him right. It is a frequently repeated tradition that the Lincoln & Herndon partnership was not terminated by Lincoln's election but that it continued "until it was dissolved by the bullet of the assassin Booth." [35] In one sense their association was not interrupted, and though Herndon had "stripped the good ones pretty well" just before his partner started for Washington, he continued to send the President his half of fees collected on cases in which Lincoln had been interested.[36] The overworked President gave Herndon a free hand.

> Do just as you say about the money matter [Lincoln wrote wearily]. As you well know, I have not time to write a letter of respectable length. God bless you, says
> Your friend,
A. Lincoln.[37]

It is, however, a mistake to think of Herndon holding the fort alone in Springfield while Lincoln was in the White House. The Lincoln & Herndon shingle continued to creak above the office entrance — it doubtless had advertising value anyway — and their professional card appeared in the Springfield papers until January 1862. But months earlier Herndon entered into an informal partnership with Charles S. Zane, a younger lawyer, born in New Jersey, and like Herndon a vociferous and radical Republican. As early as July 1861 Herndon & Zane handled cases in the circuit courts and in September of that year their professional announcement was carried in a Springfield newspaper.[38] The new firm retained the old office on the public square.

Herndon handled almost all the firm's cases in the federal district and circuit courts. In 1861 he was listed as counsel in no fewer than fifty cases before the United States Circuit Court — a number exceeded only by such long-established firms as Stuart, Edwards, and Brown, or Hay and Cullom.[39] In the Sangamon County Circuit Court he received

---

[35] *Herndon's Lincoln*, II, 266.

[36] Herndon to Lincoln, August 29, 1863, Robert Todd Lincoln Coll.

[37] Nicolay and Hay, eds., *Works*, VII, 94–95.

[38] Springfield *Everybody's Advertiser*, September 1, 1861. "Upon the election of Mr. Lincoln the further existence of the firm of Lincoln & Herndon terminated without a formal dissolution, and it was succeeded by the firm of Herndon & Zane." "Judge Zane Tells of Close Relations with Emancipator," unidentified clipping, Lincoln National Life Foundation.

[39] General Docket No. 1, U. S. Circuit Court for the Southern District of Illinois.

Lincoln's Herndon

more assistance from his new partner. Neither Herndon nor Zane appeared frequently in the state supreme court.

V

During the war the practice of law became inextricably involved with political questions. Herndon met new kinds of cases: John Noelish, a minor, had run away from home to enlist in the Union army against his father's consent, and Herndon sued for a writ of habeas corpus to secure his release; Union soldiers, taken prisoner by the Confederates and later paroled, wanted protection against being drafted; five citizens of Williamsville had to be defended for attacking a too zealous Democrat who was "hurrahing for Vallandigham." [40]
The soil of Illinois saw no major armed conflict during the Civil War, yet in a real sense the state was a battleground. The war was not universally popular. In Egypt (southern Illinois) there were many who actively sympathized with the South and even more who were reluctant to join in coercive measures against the seceded states. Most of the Democrats over the state rallied behind Douglas in his stand for the union, yet there were few who could refrain from casting a backward glance at what might have been, had not a sectional, Republican President been elected. Party politics entered into every discussion of the war, and the presidential suspension of habeas corpus, numerous arbitrary arrests — including the Illinois congressman W. J. Allen — and Lincoln's emancipation proclamation were regarded by many Democrats and conservative Republicans as acts of usurpation. The President was shrilly denounced by the *Illinois State Register* as "the craftiest and most dishonest politician that ever disgraced an office in America." "*Honest Abe, forsooth!*" sneered the Copperhead editor; "*Honest Iago! Benignant Nero! Faithful Iscariot!*" "How the greatest butchers of antiquity sink into insignificance," exclaimed the newspaper in Lincoln's home town, "when their crimes are contrasted with those of Abraham Lincoln." [41] Sangamon County was dominated by Lincoln's political foes, and the subversive Order of American Knights was reported to be drilling openly with guns and knives. Elliott B. Herndon was one of the leaders in the antiwar group, but it included many another of Lincoln's neighbors and former friends. [42]
Billy Herndon was sometimes vexed with Lincoln's slowness and

[40] *Illinois State Journal,* June 20, October 7, 1863; *War of the Rebellion: Official Records . . . ,* 2 ser., I, 157–158.
[41] Civil War files of *Register* quoted in *Illinois State Journal,* April 18, 1885.
[42] *War of the Rebellion: Official Records . . . ,* 2 ser., VII, 298.

possibly he may have been disappointed in the distribution of patronage, but above all he was a Union man and a Republican. He was dissatisfied when the Lincoln government failed to act, not when it moved too quickly. After the issuance of the emancipation proclamation and the adoption of a conscription act he became increasingly convinced that the administration was doing all in its power to suppress the rebellion and to make the war a holy crusade for liberty. Both in law and in politics he vigorously upheld the wartime measures of the federal government.

In the initial burst of war enthusiasm Springfield had opened its doors to the Union volunteers stationed in the city at Camp Yates or, later, at near-by Camp Butler. At first nothing was too good for these brave heroes. In April 1861 "sojer boys" arrested for getting "a little drunk" were dismissed without punishment by the Springfield magistrate because "their country needs their services more than the city does the usual fine." But Springfield soon learned that the presence of great numbers of bawdy, brawling soldiers was no unmixed blessing, and even the Republican newspaper began complaining at the number of officers and men who loafed "from day to day on the streets, at hotels and saloons, neglecting their military duties for the sake of sporting their buttons in the eyes of the citizens." [43]

In early 1863 this prejudice between the civilians and the military was brought to a head when Lieutenant E. P. Dustan under somewhat obscure circumstances shot a Springfield citizen. Popular resentment was high and a mob threatened to hang Dustan in the street. Believing the officer would not receive a fair hearing before Springfield's Democratic justices of the peace, the commandant at Camp Butler demanded that Dustan be turned over to a court-martial and, over the protests of the city authorities, took him from jail and put him under military guard.

Springfield was outraged. The sovereignty of the state of Illinois, it was said, had been violated; law no longer had any meaning; the unconstitutional act of the military was virtually a blanket blessing for any soldiers who might "take it into their brave little heads to try some pistol or bayonet practice upon some dastardly citizen who was so utterly contemptible as not to wear Uncle Sam's uniform." [44] For months the Dustan case was a *cause célèbre*, and Democrats used it as an excuse for denouncing the conscription act, the army, and the President.

To Herndon as leading Republican lawyer of Springfield and law

[43] *Illinois State Journal*, April 26, November 21, 1861.
[44] *Illinois State Register*, March 26, 1863.

partner of President Lincoln fell the duty of defending the action of the military authorities and of placating the aroused citizens. With some justice he pointed out, in an extended address before a mass meeting, that Dustan's hearing before the justices of peace had been handled with "prejudice or extreme ignorance, or haste or fear." Vigorously Herndon defended the constitutionality of the conscription act and particularly of that section under which offenses were "punishable by . . . a general Court Martial . . . when committed by persons . . . in the military service of the United States." He concluded with a burst of spread-eagle oratory which sent "this Constitution and the Stars and the Stripes . . . over every ocean — over every land — up every line of longitude — every line of latitude — up every bay and creek — on every house top in this broad land — nay, into *every* heart, . . . until this round, pendant, swinging globle [*sic*] shall hear the tread of a Christian Democracy, a higher civilization around the equator, and from pole to pole, ending alone with the great law of gravitation that binds worlds to worlds." [45]

As a reward for his faithful and voluble Republicanism, Herndon was selected in 1864 as assistant to the United States district attorney for the southern district of Illinois. Aiding Lawrence Weldon and in many cases substituting for him, he prosecuted those who harbored deserters, defied the conscription act, resisted enrolling officers, and incited Clingman's notorious guerilla band of Copperheads. So vigorously did he act in the Union cause the federal grand jury in June 1864 passed a special resolution commending Herndon for his "gentlemanly bearing and promptness in legal counsel to this Grand Jury." [46]

VI

Before Lincoln left Springfield he promised that Herndon's letters should not be opened by his private secretaries but would be handed to him in person. Herndon wrote frequently during the war years, giving the President the latest news of Springfield and Illinois politics and occasionally "dilating on national affairs." Enthusiastically he welcomed President Lincoln's emancipation proclamation. As soon as he heard the good news he wrote to the White House: "Now Mr Lincoln you can go down on the other side of life filled with the consciousness of duty done blazing with eternal glory." The conscription measures he praised with equal ardor.[47]

[45] *Ibid.*
[46] *Ibid.*, June 10, 15, 18, and 22, 1864.
[47] *Herndon's Lincoln*, III, 505–506; undated Herndon memorandum, Herndon-Weik Coll. These letters have not been preserved in the recently opened Robert

If Herndon ever wavered in his loyalty to the Lincoln administration, if he sometimes doubted or complained, it was only in confidential letters. Throughout the war he was known as a leading Republican lawyer and orator for the Sangamon region. It was not the popular stand, but as early as 1862 Herndon was demanding all-out support for the President and "the prosecution of the war to whatever extent it may be necessary, or at whatever sacrifice may be required." [48]

The unconditional Union men of Illinois planned to hold a giant rally at Springfield in September 1863, and the President was invited to attend.

We will have a great time [Herndon reported to his partner-President] . . . and it is thought it will be the largest Crowd Ever Convened here. There is no doubt but that it will be a large meeting. I hope it will — hope it will give us confidence, back-bone vigor & energy. The Democracy are evidently organizing for Evil, but when, where & for what they will strike we are left in the dark. The Union men are busy at work all over the State to meet any Emergency. They are determined — are cool — not hasty — not rash. The English say — "God save the Queen." I say "God save the Union." [49]

There was never any doubt as to Herndon's political complexion in 1864. The Republicans (disguised under the name "Union Party") renominated Lincoln, with Andrew Johnson for vice president. At a convention in Chicago the Democrats chose General George Brinton McClellan and George H. Pendleton to run on an ambiguous platform which McClellan himself repudiated. Issues in the campaign were involved and confused, but not to Herndon. It was white against black. "Lincoln represents FREEDOM . . . ," he wrote; "McClellan represents SLAVERY. . . ." [50]

Naturally Republicans expected Herndon's aid in the 1864 campaign, partly for his own not inconsiderable influence and even more because he was law partner to the President. Several times during the fall Herndon attempted to speak for the Republican ticket but was prevented by a lingering attack of bronchitis, caused, he said, by his exertions in the "great canvasses of 1854, 1856, 1858 and 1860." ". . . I

Todd Lincoln Collection. Since Herndon made no copies and recalled his words after the passing of many years, the above quotations should not be taken as literally accurate.

[48] *Illinois State Journal*, September 25, 1862.

[49] Herndon to Lincoln, August 29, 1863, Robert Todd Lincoln Coll. Lincoln was unable to attend the mass meeting but sent an eloquent letter which was read by James C. Conkling.

[50] *W. H. Herndon on the Democratic Platform* (1864 broadside, Ill. State Hist. Lib.).

am physically broken down," he mourned.[51] Nevertheless, it was highly desirable that he be trotted out by the Republicans at least once during the campaign, and he was selected to dedicate the big new Republican "wigwam" — it was more like a barn — just finished on Sixth Street in Springfield.

The occasion was an important one, and the Republicans were anxious that all should go off well. Patriotic ladies had decorated the entire building "in the most tasteful manner" with a curious combination of flags, "Union lanterns," pictures, evergreens, and drapery, and the whole building was splendidly illuminated by gas light. Pursuant to considerable advertising ("COME ONE! COME ALL!"), an audience of about two thousand — intelligent and enthusiastic, as all audiences were described in those days — collected to hear Herndon's "most profound, philosophic and patriotic speech." Every foot of space was occupied and hundreds went away who could not obtain admittance.[52]

After a brief introduction Herndon appeared and was greeted by loud hurrahs and the waving of ladies' handkerchiefs. He had evidently prepared very carefully, for his address showed unusual attention to the embroidery of rhetoric.

> When night has usurped the blaze and realms of day [he darkly began] — when thick fogs and blacker mists roll up against our shores, baffling and cheating the eye that would fain look through, common prudence compels us, from our patriotic watch towers, to throw out the blazing, glistening calcium lights over the dark, deep waste of things below, in search of some low black craft stealthily and silently creeping along the beach, filled with bomb and shell, things intended for our common ruin.

From his patriotic watch tower Herndon espied enemies and he gave warning in his usual polysyllabic fashion. For years, he said, he and other leading Republicans had been telling the people that there was irreconcilable conflict between freedom and slavery; this was the key to the dreadful carnage of the war. "Slavery and slavery alone was the cause. . . ." Those who suggested that the election of a Republican President in 1860 had anything to do with it revealed a most lamentable ignorance of those "regular gradations of thought from the first and primal truths in nature, up to the highest and grandest principles" — all of which proved conclusively that either liberty or slavery must die. President Lincoln to save the free had struck the manacles

[51] *Ibid.*
[52] *Illinois State Journal*, September 20 and 22, 1864.

off the slave; his action was humane, just, and wise. Equally so were the provisions of the Union (i.e., Republican) platform supporting the prosecution of the war.

But by contrast, Herndon went on, how suspicious were the provisions of the Democrats' Chicago platform. There was something strange about the way it was formulated. Was not Vallandigham at the convention? Did not "Jeff. Davis" intervene to select Pendleton as McClellan's running mate? Such were the pirate craft Herndon discerned from his lookout, and he pledged his "heart's blood, if needed" to repel them. "Blow them up, my friends, with shot and shell and bomb, and send them heavenward or hellward." [53]

These explosive sentiments provoked a vicious attack from the Democratic newspaper in Springfield. Reporting that the "shoddyites" (Republicans) dedicated their temple to the worship of their "tutelar deity, Abraham Lincoln," the *Register* acidly described Herndon as "a young, able-bodied shoddyite noisily proclaiming his loyalty, shouting for abolition, for war, and for confiscation at the top of his lungs, and pointing others to the battlefields he sneaks away from himself." [54] Herndon must have been consoled when the *Journal* published his speech in full and praised it fulsomely: "No right-minded or intelligent citizen can rise from its perusal without having his views widened, his aims elevated, and his patriotism quickened." [55]

It is probable that the success of Union arms in the South had more to do with the outcome of the election than frenzied oratory in the North. Springfield went Republican by the smallest of majorities, but, as was expected, Sangamon County again repudiated Lincoln. The state as a whole endorsed her favorite son, and Lincoln was re-elected for another four years.

VII

During the winter of 1864 and the spring that followed, thrilling news kept coming in, to the accompaniment of mounting death lists. To the re-elected President, Sherman presented Savannah as a Christmas present; grimly battering away, Grant was slowly forcing Lee back. In April the break came. With Sherman moving up through the

---

[53] *Ibid.*, September 23, 1864.

[54] *Illinois State Register*, September 23, 1864. Herndon's failure to volunteer for military service was probably caused by his poor health and by his heavy family obligations. The only member of his family in the army was seventeen-year-old Beverly, who served in the Illinois Militia Volunteers for thirty days in 1862, guarding Confederate prisoners at Camp Butler. Muster rolls, National Archives.

[55] *Illinois State Journal*, September 23, 1864.

Carolinas and Grant gradually encircling Richmond, Lee withdrew to the west and, finding the odds impossible, surrendered at Appomattox. "REJOICE! REJOICE!" the Springfield papers screamed, a little prematurely, "RICHMOND AND PETERSBURG GRANT SHERIDAN AND VICTORY THE UNION RESTORED THE CONSTITUTION VINDICATED REBELLION SUPPRESSED." Copperheads, War Democrats, and Republicans united in shouting the good tidings. Disorganized processions thronged the public square. In the afternoon the Pioneer Fire Company started to parade and practically the entire citizenry fell in behind. A mule was led around the square, mounted by a straw-stuffed dummy which bore the placard "Jeff. Davis' last ride," and on the tail of the mule — perhaps the oldest pun in history — a sign read "*Lee's End.*" Twenty-gun salutes were fired as the procession marched and countermarched through the principal streets. All the Springfield worthies were there, but Old Bob, Lincoln's horse, stole the show. All evening the bands played and there were speeches by recently inaugurated Governor Oglesby, by Herndon, and others — "which were received with marked attention." Springfield went to bed drunk with joy.[56]

Only five days later came the tragic shock of Lincoln's death. From the garbled accounts that sped in over the wires, Springfield soon learned the truth. On Friday, April 14, the President had been fatally shot by John Wilkes Booth. Before eight o'clock of the following morning the news had spread over Springfield like a black pall. A Sabbath hush settled over the town, interrupted only by the mournful tolling of church bells. Business was suspended, and men gathered in tense groups around the telegraph office to hear the latest dispatches. Within a few hours every important store and most of the homes were swathed in black, sometimes "gracefully intertwined with the national colors." The cannon at the armory were draped with the American flag. High above the state house a black pennon floated. The utmost sorrow was seen in every face, and the "whole city presented a funereal aspect, as if the Death Angel had taken a member from every family. Never was there a day of such universal solemnity and sadness seen. . . ."[57]

Party differences and past disagreements were for the moment forgotten in the orgy of grief. Within a few days men were remembering Lincoln as a figure larger than life. The *Register,* which only a month before had sneered at "old Abe" as a "smutty joker" whose obscenity was his principal claim to distinction, now retracted. "We forget the

[56] *Illinois State Journal,* April 10 and 11, 1865.
[57] *Ibid.,* April 17, 1865; Chicago *Times,* April 17, 1865.

points of difference of the four years past," wrote the Democratic editor, "and think only of Abraham Lincoln, the kindly and indulgent man, beloved of his neighbors, and of the chief magistrate who has honestly followed the path that seemed to him best for the welfare of the people." Less than a week after Lincoln's death the *Register* was praising his "godlike mercifulness," his magnanimous and generous policies,[58] while the Republican *Journal* joined the chorus of eulogy for "the purest of citizens, the noblest of patriots, the most beloved and honored of Presidents, and the most forbearing and magnanimous of rulers." [59]

Herndon had a lost feeling. ". . . I did not feel like doing any business," he wrote.

> My good friend — *is gone* — yet is with us in *Spirit.* The news of his going struck me dumb, the deed being so infernally wicked — so monstrous — so huge in consequences, that it was too large to enter my brain. Hence it was incomprehensible, leaving a misty distant doubt of its truth. . . . It is . . . grievously sad to think of — one so good — so kind — so loving — so honest — so manly, & so *great,* taken off by the bloody murderous hand of an assassin.[60]

April 19, the day of the funeral ceremonies in Washington, was appointed a day of mourning in Springfield, and "Solemn and appropriate religious services" were held in all the places of worship. Overcoming his grief, Herndon spoke briefly in the Baptist church, calling up reminiscences of his partner and friend.[61]

A few days later Springfield lawyers met to pay tribute to their colleague's memory, and it was naturally Herndon who was chosen to frame the resolutions of grief and respect. Lamenting the foul crime which robbed the bar of a cherished brother, his resolutions praised Lincoln's "uprightness, integrity, cordiality and kindness of heart, amenity of manner and his strict attention not only to the rights, but to the feelings of all." In presenting his report Herndon spoke with much emotion, recalling his long personal and professional relations with the dead President. While lauding the nobility of Lincoln's character, he remarked in passing that his onetime partner "was not as broadminded as some other men." Herndon's resolutions were adopted unanimously, but his faint hint of a slur on Lincoln was at once re-

---

[58] *Illinois State Register,* March 11, April 15 and 18, 1865.
[59] *Illinois State Journal,* April 17, 1865.
[60] Herndon to Caroline H. Dall, May 26, 1865, Dall MSS.
[61] *Illinois State Journal,* April 21, 1865.

pudiated. Judge Stephen T. Logan rose to differ with Herndon, asserting that Lincoln had been "a man of very profound and comprehensive views and as free from narrowness as any man he had been acquainted with." [62] Even so early the lines of a future battle were drawn.

[62] *Illinois State Journal,* April 25, 1865; *Illinois State Register,* April 25, 1865; "Judge Zane Tells of Close Relations with Emancipator," unidentified clipping, Lincoln National Life Foundation.

CHAPTER *xii*

A True Biography of Mr. Lincoln

I

LINCOLN's death was the most important event in Herndon's life. For the first time Herndon became front-page news. He found himself described and quoted and characterized. He was interviewed by correspondents. His character was alternately extolled and traduced; he was damned and eulogized; his writings were praised and maligned. A Herndon letter, a Herndon speech, or a Herndon book drew extended quotation and lengthy comment even in New York and Boston papers. Herndon had become famous.

The explanation of this rather unexpected access of fame and notoriety lay in the immediate apotheosis of the martyred Lincoln. The carnival of death in Springfield was paralleled by countless similar funereal celebrations all over the land. At the news of the assassination the country — or at least the North — swathed itself in mourning. The nation grieved over its fallen captain. Sadness and despair did not abate in the days that followed Lincoln's death but mounted into a veritable orgy of grief as his corpse began its slow procession from the White House to its Springfield tomb. The trappings of death intensified grief. The black-draped catafalque, the silent funeral train that moved by a circuitous route over the land, the white-robed choirs that wailed a never-ceasing dirge, the silent throngs of stony-faced mourners, the tolling bells — all combined to make Lincoln's passing seem even more calamitous.

Only in death did Lincoln win universal applause. He was now a hero in a sacred cause, this holy blissful martyr, this second savior of his country. Those who in his lifetime had scorned and despitefully used him now joined in the tribute at his tomb. During the dark postwar decades men needed guidance, and they turned to the memory of Lincoln. The fallen President became the symbol of the continuing Un-

167

ion for which he and so many others had given their lives. In part this apotheosis was a deliberate manipulation by radical Republican leaders, who used the prestige of the President to promote their program of vindictive reconstruction, but their very success reveals the powerful hold the memory of Lincoln kept on the popular mind. Almost overnight he became a folk hero, a sort of mythological demigod. In contemporary correspondence Lincoln was referred to — and nearly always in capitals — as the Great Emancipator or the Great Martyr.

There was an immediate demand for more knowledge about Lincoln's career. His every word, his writings, his anecdotes were seized upon and repeated with endless variations. An avid audience looked forward eagerly to the memoirs and reminiscences that began to flood the country. To this demand for detail on Lincoln's life, few would reply as did George Spears, an old friend from New Salem days, who explained the brevity of his recollections by declaring: "at that time I had no idea of his ever being President therefore I did not notice his course as close as I should of." [1] Half a dozen Lincoln biographies were at once projected, and authors began to collect facts from those who had seen him plain.

Naturally men turned to Herndon for information, for who could have known Lincoln better than his law partner for sixteen years? (That figure of sixteen years was rapidly expanded into a full twenty and before long became a quarter of a century.) He was besieged, he said, by "enquires & interrogations by thousands of visitors as to Lincoln"; he was obliged to "write dozens of letters weekly" explaining that he had no Lincoln autographs to sell or give away; he was importuned by newspaper reporters for statements until he became, in his own words, "simply a talker — a babbler." [2]

Very quickly Herndon concluded that the demand for his knowledge was so great that he should put in writing his memories of his partner. In this decision he was fortified by the encouragement of Horace White, editor of the Chicago *Tribune* and high priest of Republican journalism, who considered Herndon "peculiarly qualified, by long and intimate association with Mr Lincoln, by knowledge & appreciation of his character, & sympathy with his personal, professional & political aims in life, to be . . . [Lincoln's] biographer." [3]

---

[1] George Spears to Herndon, November 3, 1866, Herndon-Weik Coll.

[2] Herndon to Josiah Gilbert Holland, June 8, 1865, Holland MSS.; Herndon to Hart, January 13, 1866, Hart MSS.

[3] Horace White to Herndon, May 22, 1865, Herndon-Weik Coll.

A True Biography of Mr. Lincoln

Just when Herndon finally determined to write on Lincoln it is not now possible to discover, but before May 9, 1865, he had informed friends that he proposed to publish "something about Lincoln." [4]

Herndon's somewhat indefinite plans were perhaps influenced by the visit to Springfield in late May of Josiah Gilbert Holland, who was writing a full-length biography of Lincoln. The Massachusetts visitor, editor of the Springfield *Republican*, and under the pen name "Timothy Titcomb" author of numerous, prolix, and immensely popular novels and essays, had delivered a tearful eulogy on Lincoln's death, emphasizing the President's "simple, honest, Christian heart" and portraying "that toil-worn man, rising long before his household and spending an hour with his Maker and his Bible" every morning.[5] At the suggestion of an astute publisher, Holland undertook to expand his eulogy into a life of the Great Emancipator; it was a timely enterprise, for eventually nearly one hundred thousand copies of his Lincoln biography were sold. More, one should judge, for the purpose of substantiating his own prejudices than for acquiring new insights, Holland in May 1865 made a brief tour of the West. Spending two days in his researches at Springfield, the Massachusetts author introduced himself to Herndon, who "quit for that period of time . . . [his] profession" in order to answer his questions about Lincoln. He gave Holland a list of the important dates in Lincoln's career, introduced him to Springfield residents whose memories would supplement his own, and in general served as the visitor's cicerone.[6]

During a conversation with Holland, Herndon casually mentioned that he proposed "to write & publish the *subjective* Mr Lincoln — 'the inner life' of Mr L." Doubtless the to-do made over Holland's presence in Springfield and the eager anticipation with which his biography was expected helped to crystallize Herndon's intentions. As yet Herndon's project was relatively unambitious. Believing that the world did "not begin to understand the grand full orb of Lincoln, as it swang amid the heavens of men," he planned a short biography to portray Lincoln "in his passions — appetites — & affections — perceptions — memories — judgement — understanding — will . . . *just* as he lived, breathed — ate & laughed." This writing, Herndon believed, would be

---

[4] "I am glad you design giving us something about Lincoln." John L. Scripps to Herndon, May 9, 1865, copy, Lamon MSS. There is no evidence that Herndon planned a biography or began collecting information during Lincoln's lifetime.

[5] Mrs. H. M. Plunkett, *Josiah Gilbert Holland*, 55. See also Harry H. Peckham, *Josiah Gilbert Holland in Relation to his Times*.

[6] "Holland on Herndon," undated Herndon monograph, Herndon-Weik Coll.

a *"little thing"* of no more than "50 to 75 pages, pamphlet form." Modestly he added: "I have not got the Capacity to write much at best, and not that much well." [7]

II

Herndon's undertaking soon expanded far beyond his original idea. Reading the tedious and misleading recollections that began to appear in the newspapers and studying the uncritically eulogistic biographies that described Lincoln as "the great and good man — the savior of the Republic," "so far above human approach that human envy cannot reach him," [8] Herndon became disgusted. Very soon he concluded that practically all "the stories we hear floating around are more or less untrue in part or as a whole." [9] Lincoln had already become a myth, about whom clustered a voluminous body of apocrypha.[10]

Like a good many others who had known Lincoln in his earlier years, Herndon was not pleased with this idealized portrait of the President. Only six weeks after his partner's death he had thought it necessary to inform his correspondents that Lincoln "was not God — was man: he was not perfect — had some defects & a few positive faults: [but] he was a good man — an honest man." [11] To Herndon his partner had not seemed a demigod but instead had represented the antitype of the "original western and south-western pioneer," with all his virtues and all his defects. Increasingly as the years went by Herndon felt it his duty to emphasize that Lincoln was not so much a man called of God as a natural product of the "mud flowers & mind" which he had encountered in the pioneer northwest.[12]

Having recently read Buckle's *History of England,* Herndon was impressed with the economic-geographical interpretation of history and planned to use that approach in his biography. His Lincoln should stand revealed as a natural product of the soil of the West, as "the representative American, . . . not . . . from the North or from the South, but . . . the descendant of the Anglo-Saxon and German

[7] Herndon to Holland, May 26, 1865, Holland MSS. See also the announcement of Herndon's project in *Illinois State Journal,* June 3, 1865.
[8] *Obsequies of Abraham Lincoln, in the City of New York* [vii]; Boston City Council, *A Memorial of Abraham Lincoln, Late President of the United States,* 121.
[9] Herndon to Holland, June 8, 1865, Holland MSS.
[10] I have discussed the origin of the Lincoln myth in more detail in "The Folklore Lincoln," Ill. State Hist. Soc., *Jour.,* XL, 377–396.
[11] Herndon to Holland, May 26, 1865, Holland MSS.
[12] Herndon, *Abraham Lincoln. Miss Ann Rutledge. New Salem. Pioneering, and THE Poem;* Herndon to Hart, November 28, 1866, Hart MSS.

elements of the Valley of the Mississippi." [13] Of his Eastern friends Herndon inquired the best manner in which to bring out Lincoln's fundamental "Western-ness." For use "in Mr Lincolns life" he requested from Henry C. Carey, the Pennsylvania economist whose writings he had diligently studied, a statement concerning the "rate at which the *wealth — food, population,* & *education* relatively . . . grow & multiply." [14] Obviously Herndon's biography would not be of the usual life-and-letters genre.

III

Herndon soon realized that his own store of facts would be insufficient for a real biography. He had known little of Lincoln before 1837 and had seen the President but once after 1861. Industriously he began reading everything he could lay his hands on. He devoured sermons, eulogies, and biographies. He purchased, for example, the 1865 edition of Joseph H. Barrett's *Life of Abraham Lincoln,* studied it closely, and for handy reference made a five-page index.[15] Now he read critically, attempting to test each statement. If an author asserted that Lincoln had read Plutarch and Aesop, Herndon immediately had to know when these classics were first published in America and to what editions Lincoln might have had access.[16]

Herndon's original researches began in Springfield. He set himself the tedious job of leafing through the files of the *Sangamo Journal* and of its successor, the *Illinois State Journal,* and compiled a list of Lincoln's speeches which had appeared in print. To supplement his own knowledge of Lincoln's law career, he raided the files of county and circuit courts of central Illinois, from which he was permitted to "borrow" records — pleadings, demurrers, judgments, etc. — of cases in which Lincoln had been interested.[17]

At every opportunity he badgered his fellow citizens in Springfield, as well as those whom he encountered on the law circuit, for reminiscences of Lincoln. Herndon talked nothing but Lincoln and asked so many questions that he earned the reputation of being "*a little off*" on the subject.[18] Frequently the results of his inquiries were disappoint-

[13] *Illinois State Journal,* November 30, 1865.
[14] Herndon to Carey, June 15, 1865, E. C. Gardiner Coll.
[15] Herndon's copy of the Barrett biography is now owned by Mrs. Bertie Trainer of Springfield, Illinois.
[16] James Miller to Herndon, July 5, 1865, copy, Lamon MSS.
[17] Copies of Herndon's newspaper gleanings are preserved in the Lamon MSS. The court records which he borrowed are in the Herndon-Weik Collection.
[18] Herndon to Weik, September 25, 1887, Herndon-Weik Coll.

ing. Men who had been intimate with Lincoln for thirty years could recall that "Mr. Lincoln was a tall man & a funny one" — and nothing else.[19] When he did come upon a more rewarding source of information, Herndon tried to arrange a formal interview. Herndon's memoranda of these interviews are, for the most part, clear and informative. He began by asking the full name, age, and personal history of his informant; he ascertained what opportunities the subject had had for firsthand knowledge of Lincoln; and then by skillful questioning he proceeded to evoke detailed reminiscences. Terminating the interview, Herndon on many occasions apparently read back to his subject the notes he had made and asked for amendments and for approval.

At the outset Herndon received full cooperation from Lincoln's Illinois associates. Springfield opinion, as revealed in these confidential interviews, was surprisingly cool towards its martyr President; Herndon soon learned that "Mr. Lincoln was not at all times *the* popular man in Sangamon County." [20] Possibly his rise to power had excited the jealousy of his contemporaries. Mary Todd Lincoln, of the excitable temper and sarcastic tongue, was even less popular. A public show of veneration for the President was coupled with private gossip and rumor-mongering of an unfriendly character.

John Todd Stuart, for example, who had been Lincoln's law partner, but who had been alienated from him politically for many years, speculated on Lincoln's physical organism. "Lincoln . . . was a kind of vegetable," he concluded, "the pores of his flesh acted as an appropriate organ for . . . evacuations &c." He added, rather needlessly, that Lincoln "differed with other men about this." Mary Lincoln's brother-in-law, N. W. Edwards, who had been disappointed in his hope of securing a major appointment from the federal government, told Herndon that "Lincoln was not a warm hearted man — seemed to be ungrateful." James H. Matheny, best man at Lincoln's wedding, contributed a spicy account of an episode in 1841 when Lincoln was said to have jilted Mary Todd and added: "Mrs. Lincoln often gave L[incoln] Hell in general — . . . *Ferocity* — describes Mrs L's conduct to L." Not all of Springfield's memories of the Lincolns were of the sensational kind, though most were — to say the least — remarkably unflattering. James Gurley, who lived next door to the family on Eighth Street, recalled his years of association with the Lincolns, declared that "Lincoln & his wife got along tolerably well, unless Mrs L got the

[19] Herndon to Mrs. Leonard Swett, March 14, 1890, Swett MSS.
[20] Herndon to Weik, February 11, 1887, Herndon-Weik Coll. Compare Holland, *Life of Abraham Lincoln*, 241.

devil in her," characterized Mary Lincoln as a good woman, and concluded: "Mrs & Mr Lincoln were good neighbors." [21]

IV

To all his friends and acquaintances Herndon sent letters of inquiry. "Judge," he questioned Senator Lyman Trumbull, "I wish to Know 2 questions — 1st What were the *strong* points of Mr Lincoln's Character as a *statesman* & *executive:* 2dly What were the *weak* points of Mr Lincoln's Character as to his *Statesmanship*. . . ." The senator's own opinion was requested first, and then Trumbull should gather a consensus of "a majority of senators, on these 2 questions." When a satisfactory answer was not forthcoming, Herndon kept after the senator. "I promise to get through asking you questions in about 3 centuries," he pledged in his third letter.[22]

Along with these personal letters, Herndon made a broadside plea for information. First he announced his biography and explained his plans. Later newspapers carried his appeal imploring all who were "disposed to aid in preparing . . . a true biography of Mr. Lincoln" to send Herndon copies of any Lincoln manuscripts in their possession, "however short and apparently unimportant." [23]

Though Herndon's letters and notices brought in a large number of answers, his gleanings about the years of Lincoln's presidency were meager. If Sumner, Trumbull, or Yates responded to his questions, their replies have been lost. Apparently many treated his letters as did Orville H. Browning, a White House intimate of the Lincolns, who filed away Herndon's queries as "Unanswered." [24] Justice David Davis, badgered by hundreds of requests for statements, reluctantly declined to write his recollections for Herndon, though he consented to a series of interviews at Bloomington.

The most important source material Herndon collected on the presidential years pertained to the Baltimore plot and to Lincoln's famous night ride into Washington in February 1861 to avoid threatened assassination. He was permitted to examine the papers of Allan Pinkerton, the private detective whose agents had uncovered the alleged plot, and he had a long transcript made of Pinkerton agents' reports,

[21] For these comments, in the order given, see Herndon's interviews with John Todd Stuart [July 21, 1865?], with N. W. Edwards, September 22, 1865, with J. H. Matheny, May 3, 1866, and with James Gurley, undated — all in Herndon-Weik Coll.
[22] Herndon to Trumbull, January 11 and August 19, 1866, Trumbull MSS.
[23] *Illinois State Journal*, November 13, 1866.
[24] Herndon to Browning, January 30 [1866?], Browning MSS.

of frantic correspondence in code carried on with headquarters, and of the hush-hush negotiations with the Philadelphia, Wilmington, & Baltimore railroad for the delivery of the presidential "package" safely in the capital.[25]

Herndon was most successful in collecting data on Lincoln's earlier years in Kentucky, Indiana, and Illinois. Addressing "Some Good *Union* Lawyer," he would write to those localities where facts might lurk, and frequently his letters would fall into the hands of garrulous old men of long memory who delighted in retailing all the local gossip and lore about the martyr President. It was, after all, rather flattering to be addressed by the partner of so great a man as Lincoln. Many of these correspondents proved to have disappointingly scanty stores of information. Most tended to write in the general terms of stereotyped, though genuine, eulogy about Lincoln's character. "through my Long Acquaintance With him of near on quite forty years," declared one old settler, "his friendShip Was undying It Was Eternal All Ways Standing [o]ut in Bald Reliefe It Was Truly freindShip in Marble." [26]

Sometimes Herndon's questions would heat the cauldron of local gossip to such frenzied boiling that the point of his inquiries would be forgotten. He asked his friends the date when some of the early settlers arrived at New Salem, and George Spears reported the fruitless results of his effort to secure the information:

> I took my horse this morning & went over to the Neighbourhood of Newsalem among the Potters & Armstrongs & made all the enqirys I could but could learn nothing the Old Ladys would begin to count up what had happened in Salem when such a one of their children was born & such a one had a Bastard but it all amounted to nothing I could arive at no dates only when those Children wer Born.[27]

When it was announced that Herndon was preparing a biography of Lincoln, he was flooded with mail from the lunatic fringe, from those who had axes to grind (or to use), from some who hoped to see their names in print, and from many who simply liked to write letters. One correspondent, thinking of the "pleasant notoriety" of being "a teacher of the late President," volunteered the information that Lincoln had attended his school in Preble County, Ohio, in 1827.[28] Captain Joseph Artus of Quincy, Illinois, a retired riverboatman with noth-

---

25 Herndon's transcripts of the Pinkerton reports are in the Lamon MSS.
26 William Engles to Herndon, June 10, 1865, Weik MSS.
27 George Spears to Herndon, November 3, 1866, Herndon-Weik Coll.
28 J. G. Montfort [to Edgar Conkling?], August 10, 1867; and Richard H. Collins to Herndon, August 19, 1867, copies, *ibid.*

ing else to do but write long and illegible letters, contributed accounts of an occasion when he thought Abraham Lincoln had ridden on his Mississippi river steamer. He was not at all sure of the place or the date, nor was he certain of the name and appearance of his passenger, but he clung firmly to this his one encounter with greatness.[29] Probably the most tedious of the whole lot was Cyrus Wick, a Union soldier of Indianapolis, who sent Herndon a long poem on Lincoln, "written in Spencer's stanza yet . . . in a studied simplicity of style so as to correspond with the man described" and having what the author correctly described as "a peculiar arrangement of rhymes." [30]

V

Digging through this rubbish, Herndon occasionally unearthed some real ore, and he assiduously worked each vein of information that opened up. Learning that Mrs. Sarah Bush Johnston Lincoln, the President's stepmother, was still living at an advanced age, and fearing that the old lady might pass away before he could interview her himself, Herndon asked his friend H. P. H. Bromwell, Republican congressman from Charleston, Illinois, to select "some young — shrewd lawyer who is veracious, honest & truthful" who would "go to Mrs Lincoln at his *Earliest possible Convenience.*" Herndon was not content with asking in general terms what the old lady remembered about her famous stepson; he prepared an elaborate syllabus of questions which the interviewer was to put to Mrs. Lincoln. His queries were pointed and concrete, beginning:

> 1st What was your maiden name before you were married — to whom were you first married — what year — where & how many children did you have by your first husband — where were you born — & when — in what State & County.
> 2d When did you marry Thos Lincoln — where — when — in what County & State —. When did Mrs Lincoln [die?] — what year — what County.

Herndon continued for two and one-half closely written pages, asking what Lincoln had done "year after year consecutively — Year regularly following year by year," and concluding with an admonition: "Be positive — clear — explicit & do not state any [thing] that you do not know to be true." [31] Similar lists of questions were sent to other in-

[29] Joseph Artus to Herndon, June 13, and 21, October 31, 1865, and November 3, 1866, *ibid.*

[30] Cyrus Wick to Herndon, January 23, 1867, *ibid.*

[31] Herndon to H. P. H. Bromwell, June 1865, Bromwell MSS.

formants who promised to have facts of Lincoln's life. Frequently their replies are interesting; sometimes they are of real historical significance.

Herndon's selection of Kentucky correspondents was on the whole unfortunate. As he did no research for himself in Kentucky, Herndon came to place heavy dependence on these statements of elderly men whose minds were sometimes warped by the lingering bitterness and hatred of war times. His most reliable informant was the aged Samuel Haycraft, who had corresponded with Lincoln himself and who was something of an authority on Kentucky history. Most of Herndon's other Kentucky correspondents, with such names as Creel, Burba, and Pirtle, made very brief and uninformative statements. As a result, Herndon was forced to rely heavily on the letters of John B. Helm, whose reminiscences were as inaccurate as they were colorful and detailed. A merchant in Hannibal, Missouri, Helm had been born in Kentucky and claimed to have known the Hanks-Sparrow-Lincoln family intimately in his early days; as a clerk in his father's store he had, he declared, frequently given little Abraham Lincoln "a lump of home made sugar." Helm described the Lincoln-Hanks clan in Kentucky as "rough, uncouth, uneducated, beyond any thing that would seem credible now to speak of." It was apparently from this source that Herndon first heard the gossip, which modern scholarship has proved groundless, that Nancy Hanks was "of low character" and that Abraham's real father was one "Abe Enlow . . . as low a fellow as you could find — you need not try to find any thing under his circle."

To illustrate the depravity of the Hanks connections in Kentucky Helm wrote of a camp meeting he had attended in 1816 at which a scantily clad "Miss Hanks" and her young man embraced publicly, shouting: "I have my Jesus in my arms — sweet as Honeycomb and strong as bacon ham." He went on to add: "The Hanks' were the finest singers and finest shouters in our country. The only drawback on them was, that, some nine months after these interesting meetings some of them were likely to have babies."[32] It appears doubtful whether Helm could possibly have remembered seeing Abraham Lincoln as a boy, and certainly the camp meeting which he so graphically described was not attended by Nancy Hanks or Thomas Lincoln. A historian would have difficulty in accepting Helm's reminiscences as anything more than gossip, but Herndon believed him.

[32] John B. Helm to Herndon, copy, Lamon MSS. On the now exploded rumor of Lincoln's illegitimacy, see W. E. Barton, *The Paternity of Abraham Lincoln.*

A True Biography of Mr. Lincoln

VI

One of Herndon's best, as well as most amusing, informants was Lincoln's country cousin, Dennis Friend Hanks. A "Base Born Child," as he himself admitted,[33] Dennis was the illegitimate son of Nancy Hanks's aunt, and he so closely resembled his famous kinsman as to be almost a caricature. It was a resemblance which he carefully cultivated — even to the point of wearing a stovepipe hat — and the combination of Lincolnian mannerisms with Dennis's shambling gait and countrified accent was a ludicrous spectacle. Dennis had been raised in close connection with Thomas Lincoln's family, had been one of the first to look at that red, squirming infant to be named Abraham, and had moved with the Lincolns to Indiana and then to Illinois. He married one of Abraham Lincoln's stepsisters and settled in Coles County, Illinois, near the last home of the President's father. Even during the Civil War Lincoln did not lose sight of this rural relative, for Dennis made a visit to the White House in 1863 in behalf of anti-war rioters of Coles County, and, as he reported when he returned home: "Abe gethered me in his arms." [34]

During Lincoln's lifetime Hanks had been pumped for information and he acquired a reputation as an inexhaustible source of anecdote. After the assassination Dennis became something of a celebrity, and his picture appeared in Holland's biography of Lincoln. In June 1865 Dennis attended the Sanitary Fair in Chicago to exhibit the Lincoln log cabin originally erected in Macon County, Illinois, and to spin his yarns about the early years of the martyred President. Here Herndon first found him and copied down his recollections in a nineteen-page statement, which he had Dennis sign. This was followed by another long interview in September 1865 and by an extended series of letters and questionnaires.

Very proud of his knowledge of Lincoln, Dennis was not inclined to minimize his own importance. Herndon had been warned that Dennis was likely to stretch the truth — one wonders why a warning was necessary — and he noted that Hanks was something of a "blow," and that when he became "gloriously tight" his facts acquired remarkable elasticity.[35] It was at such times that he would make his most exaggerated claims. "I taught Abe his first lesson in spelling — reading & writ-

[33] Dennis Hanks to Herndon, February 22, 1866, Herndon-Weik Coll.
[34] Sandburg, *The War Years*, I, 616.
[35] Herndon's memorandum on his interview with Dennis Hanks, Charleston, Ill., September 8, 1865, copy, Lamon MSS.

ing," he asserted, "I taught Abe to write with a buzzards quill" [36] —
and, looking at Dennis's unorthodox spelling and almost illegible
scrawl, one wonders what kind of lesson it was. Not unlike Herndon himself, Dennis came to think of himself as having a monopoly on
facts concerning Lincoln's early years. He became a little peeved when
Herndon tried to check up on his recollections by writing to John Hall
of Charleston, Illinois, for supplementary facts. When he heard about
Herndon's letter, Dennis immediately questioned: "what was it Billy
that you wanted to No of him." Hall, he reported, did "Not No Much
a Bout the old Man Lincoln" and besides — this from Dennis! — "he
cant write very well." "he has Nothing to Do with writing to any one
a Bout the Life of Lincoln," Dennis advised Herndon; "it Dependes on
Me to Do all this." [37]

Yet with this harmless egoism Dennis was enthusiastic in sharing
his information. "William," he would conclude his letters, "A[s]k all
questions you want I am very cirtin I can answer them." Cheerfully
he responded to repeated questioning. "friend Billy," he replied, "those
questions that you proposed to me is the Easiest for Me to answer of
all the Rest I give it in full Noing what I say." Sometimes he had to
write in pencil because his "Ink was frose," but his cheerful generosity showed no trace of ice. Dennis wrote with difficulty; his orthogra-
phy was all his own; he shared the universal complaint that when trying to spell a word "Webster Dont No any thing you want to No."
Still, and rightly, Herndon appreciated the valuable nature of the
Hanks recollections.[38]

Dennis's memories of the Lincolns in Kentucky were relatively
brief, but on the Indiana years he knew all the particulars. After all,
he had helped build the little cabin where the Lincolns had lived on
first moving to Pigeon Creek; he had assisted Thomas Lincoln in clearing the "Knobby — Knotty" soil of the new farm, while little Abraham
performed the chores; he had seen his cousin shoot a turkey gobbler
through a crack in the log cabin.[39]

Herndon, with surprisingly good judgment, did not concentrate his
questions on the Lincolns alone but tried to get a general picture of

[36] Dennis Hanks to Herndon [in Herndon's writing], Sanitary Fair, Chicago,
June 13, 1865, Herndon-Weik Coll.

[37] Hanks to Herndon, January 6, 1866, *ibid*. Cf. Herndon to Squire Hall, January 22, 1866, MS., collection of Mr. Oliver R. Barrett.

[38] Quoted phrases are from Hanks's letters to Herndon dated August 2, December 24 and 27, 1865, and January 26 and February 10, 1866, all in Herndon-
Weik Coll.

[39] All these incidents are related in great detail in Hanks to Herndon, June 13,
1865, *ibid*.

pioneer life in early Indiana. Dennis was just the man to help him. The scenes around Pigeon Creek were still vivid in his mind. Dennis had firsthand knowledge of the "Bar Deer Turkeys and coon wilecats and other things and frogs" in southern Indiana.[40] Even more helpful was his recollection of social life among the pioneer Hoosiers. For hymns, Dennis said, the early settlers had sung "O When Shall I Se Jesus and Rain with him a Bove" and "How teageous [tedious] and tasteless the hour when Jesus No Longer I See." He could not be persuaded to relate the "Smutty Songs" which had been popular, but he did recall singing "Hail Collumbia Hap[py] Land if you aint Broke I will Be Damned." One of Lincoln's favorites was a ballad which Dennis remembered as: "the turpenturk [turban'd Turk] that Scorns the world and Struts a Bout whith his whiskers curld for no other man But him Selfto See."[41] "Abe," said Dennis, "youst to try to Sing pore Old Ned But he Never could Sing much."[42]

On one matter only was Dennis's testimony badly confused. Around 1850 Lincoln had hinted to Herndon that his mother had been the illegitimate child of a Virginia planter, and Herndon's memory of the statement had been refreshed by the biased comments his Kentucky correspondents had sent him on the general state of the Hanks family's morals. In his very first interview he tackled Dennis on the subject and was firmly informed that all such reports were untrue and were "only got up by base political enemies & traittors to injure A. Lincoln reputation."[43] But suspicion kept gnawing away in Herndon's brain; the problem of Nancy Hanks's legitimacy became almost an obsession with him. He kept recurring to the basic question: If Lincoln's mother was legitimate, why did she bear only her mother's name (Hanks) and not that of her mother's husband (Sparrow)?

Repeatedly he grilled Dennis on this point, and, lying like a gentleman to preserve his family's reputation, Hanks squirmed under the questioning. Dennis was uneducated, but he was no man's fool. "Billy," he questioned, "it Seames to me from the Letters that you write to me

[40] Hanks to Herndon, May 4, 1866, *ibid.*
[41] The song was titled "None Can Love Like an Irishman," and modern readers may prefer the original version as given by Carl Sandburg (*The American Songbag*, xiii):

> The turban'd Turk, who scorns the world,
> May strut about with his whiskers curled,
> Keep a hundred wives under lock and key,
> For nobody else but himself to see;
> Yet long may he pray with his Alcoran
> Before he can love like an Irishman.

[42] Hanks to Herndon, December 24, 1865, Herndon-Weik Coll.
[43] Hanks to Herndon, June 13, 1865, *ibid.*

askin questions that you ask the same questions over Severl times how is this Do you forget or are you Like the Lawyer trying to Make Me Cross my path or Not." Firmly and repeatedly he insisted that Lincoln's mother had really been named Nancy Sparrow and that she was called Nancy Hanks only as a sort of nickname. Herndon was off on a false lead. "Now Billy," Dennis insisted, "this question is all gamon." [44] The present-day reader is inclined to agree with Dennis, but the legitimacy of Nancy Hanks, completely unimportant as it is, has excited a vast amount of pen swinging among Lincoln specialists, and even today conclusive evidence is lacking. Herndon was probably wise in distrusting Dennis's testimony on this subject, for, as he said: "Dennis has got things mixed up: he purposely Conceals all things that degrades [*sic*] the Hanks." [45]

But on other points Dennis could and did give remarkably accurate recollections; his two interviews with Herndon constitute one of the best accounts of Lincoln's Indiana years. Dennis was boastful and sometimes he made mistakes, but most of his statements have the authentic ring of truth. Quite correctly he informed Herndon: "I will Say this Much to you if you Dont have My Name Very frecantly in you[r] Book it wont gaw [i.e., go] of at all. . . ." [46]

[44] Hanks to Herndon, February 10 and March 7, 1866, *ibid.*
[45] Herndon to Weik, April 14, 1885, *ibid.*
[46] Hanks to Herndon, December 12, 1865, *ibid.*

CHAPTER xiii

Solid Facts & Well Attested Truths

I

Herndon transferred his transcendental intuition into the realm of biography. Letters with conflicting opinions and versions of an event upset him mightily. Lacking a working knowledge of the techniques of historical research, when statements were at wide variance he could arrive at "no fixd opinion." On the hotly debated issue of Nancy Hanks's illegitimacy, for example, his reports showed so much confusion that for a time he was at a total loss. His solution was to call in his "mud instinct," his ability to read the "faces & features of men." He needed, he asserted, "to see men's & women's faces when they talk" so that he could "read their motives &c." [1]

In the summer of 1865 Herndon began to plan an interview trip to Kentucky, southern Indiana, and Coles County, Illinois; in this way he could closely watch his informants as they talked and could at last determine where lay truth and where error. It was not until September 1865 that Herndon was able to shake off his business and set out on his quest. For some unexplained reason he found it necessary to shorten his itinerary and he decided not to go to Kentucky. Never again did he have the opportunity. In both 1866 and 1867 he again planned trips "to *Ky* . . . to search for, hound down some facts," but they too fell through. [2] Soon afterward financial disaster overwhelmed him and he had "no time to go to Kentucky . . . and no money to go on." [3] In 1887 Herndon sadly confessed: "I never was in Ky . . . since the assassination of Mr. Lincoln." [4] The importance of Herndon's failure to

[1] Herndon to Mrs. Caroline H. Dall, December 20, 1866, Dall MSS.
[2] Herndon to Hart, April 13, 1866, and January 12, 1867, Hart MSS.
[3] Herndon to Mrs. Dall, March 3, 1874, Dall MSS.
[4] Herndon to Weik, February 9, 1887, Herndon-Weik Coll. In view of this statement of Herndon's it is difficult to explain how Weik made the erroneous assertion that "Scarcely a month had elapsed after . . . April, 1865, before Herndon had set out for Kentucky . . . and begun an investigation so vigorous, con-

investigate Kentucky sources on Lincoln can hardly be overemphasized, and it must be stressed that his later accounts of Lincoln's birth
and Kentucky childhood were not based on original research.

But Herndon did go to eastern Illinois and southern Indiana, and
there he crammed his notebook with information. His first stop was
Charleston, Illinois, the county seat near which old Thomas Lincoln
had had his last home. Here Herndon again interviewed Dennis Hanks
and questioned him closely and critically.[5] Then he rode out to the
Lincoln farm, some eight miles in the country, in order to question Mrs.
Sarah Lincoln, Abraham's stepmother. At first Herndon "did not Expect to get much out of her — she seemed so old & feeble." Mrs. Lincoln asked his name two or three times and also where he lived. When
he told her, she would say: "Where his friend too Mr Lincoln lived
once." "She breathed badly at first," Herndon noted, "but She seemed
to be struggling at last to arouse her self — or to fix her mind on the
subject." Beginning with simple questions about her age and her marriage, Herndon was able to focus her attention and she became "as it
were a new being — her eyes were clear & calm." Then she began talking about her famous stepson. When she had married Thomas Lincoln
and had come to Indiana, she remembered, she "dressed Abe & his
sister up — looked more human."

> Abe [the old lady continued] was a good boy: he didn't like physical
> labor — was diligent for knowledge. . . . He was the best boy I ever
> saw. He read all the books he could lay his hands on — I can't remem-
> ber dates nor names — am about 75 yrs of age — . . . when he came
> across a passage that struck him he would write it down on boards if
> he had no paper. . . . He cyphered on boards when he had no paper
> . . . and when the board would get too black he would shave it off
> with a drawing knife and go on again. . . . As a usual thing Mr Lin-
> coln never made Abe quit reading to do anything if he could avoid it.
> He would do it himself first. Mr Lincoln could read a little & could
> scarcely write his name: hence he wanted . . . his boy Abraham to
> learn. . . . Abe never gave me a cross word or look . . . He was
> kind to every body and to everything. . . . His mind & mine — what
> little I had seemed to run together — move in the same channel . . .
> He was here after he was Elected President of the U.S. ["Here," re-
> corded Herndon, "the Old lady stopd — turned around & cried — wiped
> her eyes — and proceeded"] . . . I did not want Abe . . . elected

scientious, and exhaustive that the world will always be deeply in his debt."
(Weik, *Real Lincoln*, 13–14.) Most other writers have followed Weik in this serious error.

[5] Interview of Herndon with Dennis Hanks, September 8, 1865, Herndon-
Weik Coll.

. . . — felt it in my heart that something would happen [to] him. . . . Abe & his father are in Heaven I have no doubt and I want to go to them. . . .

At the end of the interview when Herndon rose to leave, Mrs. Lincoln got up, took his hand, cried a little, and said: "I shall never see you again — and if you see Mrs Abm Lincoln & family tell them I send them my best & tenderest love — Goodby my good son's friend — farewell." [6]

II

From Charleston Herndon headed toward Indiana and the scenes of Lincoln's youth. From Rockport, on the Ohio River, he struck out for the Lincoln farm on Pigeon Creek, near Gentryville, Indiana, a region almost as backwoodsy in 1865 as when the Lincolns had migrated from Kentucky. For a guide in all his researches in Spencer County Herndon had Nat Grigsby, whose brother had married Abraham Lincoln's sister and who, despite ailing health, was eager to do anything toward preserving "the history of that great and good man." [7]

Together Herndon and Grigsby rode out to the site of the Lincoln homestead. The original cabin had been destroyed, but there were some gnarled apple trees which Herndon liked to think had been planted by the President's father. About half a mile from the house was the grave of Abraham Lincoln's mother, Nancy Hanks. The sight of the unmarked grave, now only a sunken hollow almost indistinguishable in the undergrowth, aroused in Herndon all those emotions dear to his sentimental generation. Hitching his horse to a tree, he paused for a moment of silent meditation. Here, he mused, "lies buried Mrs Lincoln. God bless her if I could breathe life into her again I would do it. Could I only whisper in her ear — 'Your son was Presdt — of the U S from 1861 to 1866 [*sic*],' I would be satisfied. . . . I stood bare headed in reverence at her grave. I cant say why — yet I felt in the presence of the living woman translated to an other world. . . . After looking at the grave and contemplating in silence the mutation of things — death — immortality — God, I left, I hope, the grave, a better man — at least if but for one moment." [8]

For several days Herndon lingered in Gentryville, collecting statements from those who remembered Lincoln as a boy. His choicest sub-

[6] Interview of Herndon with Mrs. Thomas Lincoln, September 8, 1865, *ibid.*
[7] Nat Grigsby to Herndon, July 4, 1865, copy, Lamon MSS.
[8] Herndon's memorandum headed "Lincoln Farm Septr. 14th 1865," Herndon-Weik Coll.

ject was Mrs. Elizabeth Crawford, widow of the Josiah Crawford from whom Abraham Lincoln had borrowed Weems's *Life of George Washington.* When it was damaged in an unexpected rainfall that soaked through the chinks in the Lincoln cabin, Abraham had "pulled fodder a day or two for it." Herndon found the widow "a lady at first blush . . . easily approached, quite talkative — free — and generous." She bubbled over with information and told him all about the flowers and trees and birds of early Indiana days, recalled curious frontier customs and ways, and remembered the hymns and songs the pioneers sang. "Abe was a moral & a model boy," she assured Herndon, "and while other boys were out hooking water melons and trifling away their time he was studying his books — thinking and reflecting." Then Mrs. Crawford got started on Lincoln's poetry, satirical verses he had written about two of the Grigsby boys, to whose wedding the Lincolns were not invited. These "Chronicles" she began to recite to Herndon, but then she blushed and concluded: "The Poem is Smutty and I can't tell it to you — will tell it to my daughter in law: she will tell her husband and he shall send it to you." [9] In this roundabout fashion both historical truth and Victorian modesty would remain inviolate.

III

Herndon's most fruitful source of information about Lincoln was Menard County. In May 1865 while attending court in Petersburg, the county seat to which many of the inhabitants of New Salem had moved, Herndon began to ask old-timers "for *the facts & thruths* [sic] of Lincoln's life — not fictions — not fables — not floating rumors, but *facts — solid facts & well attested truths.*" His findings were exciting. Then as today Petersburg was a village of the elderly and the retired. Its old people loved to relive the past, to recall the good old days, and to stir up memories of gossip long dead. Herndon talked with Hardin Bale, Uncle Jimmie Short, N. W. Branson, T. W. McNeely, Mrs. Elizabeth Abell, Mentor Graham, Mrs. Bowling Green, and dozens of others. They told him everything. "I have been with the People," he reported breathlessly to J. G. Holland, "ate with them — slept with them, & thought with them — cried with them too. From such an investigation — from records — from friends — old deeds & surveys &c &c I am satisfied, in Connection with my own knowled[ge] of Mr L. . . . that Mr L's whole early life *remains to be written.*" [10]

[9] Interview of Herndon with Mrs. Elizabeth Crawford, September 16, 1865, *ibid.*
[10] Herndon to Holland, June 8, 1865, Holland MSS.

Solid Facts & Well Attested Truths

Many around Petersburg retained remarkably precise memories of Lincoln. One friend related his first sight of the future President, clad in "a pair of mixed blue jeans pants — a hickory shirt and a common chip hat." [11] Still others remembered Lincoln as "a good — obliging clerk & an honest one: he increased Offuts business much by his simplicity — open — candid — obliging & honest [ways?] — Every body loved him." [12] Recalling Lincoln's early efforts toward self-education, Mentor Graham perhaps overemphasized his own role in that development and proudly concluded: ". . . I think I may say he was my schollar [sic] and I was his teacher." [13] From the notes and letters Herndon collected in Menard County emerged with remarkable clarity and photographic detail the picture of life in a frontier Illinois village during the 1830's.

Herndon was interested in all these accounts, but he was fascinated by some episodes in Lincoln's early career which had hitherto escaped notice. It was a romantic age, this heart of the Victorian era, the day of the dyspeptic poets and the lachrymose novelists. They were sentimental years, and everybody was reading George Eliot or the Brontë sisters, or their American cousins, Caroline Lee Hentz and Augusta Jane Wilson. The feminine fifties were gone, but they were followed by the sentimental sixties and the saccharine seventies. These were the days of the romantic novel with its stereotyped plot of true love that never did run smooth.

If Herndon read Emerson and Parker, he also devoured Dickens and Mrs. Hentz. But his romanticism was not so much a matter of conscious filching from the novelist's stockpile of tricks as it was an attitude of mind. Herndon had never quite understood his partner. There had been things about him that were strange — i.e., different from Herndon. His gusty outbreaks of humor had alternated with moods of deep depression. In spite of an endless repertoire of tales and jokes, Lincoln seemed to the effervescent Herndon singularly reticent about his early life. Perhaps there was some secret shadow over his soul, some tragic romantic blight that had settled over his spirit in his youth. At times Herndon attributed Lincoln's moodiness to constipation; more frequently he wondered if it could be love.

As early as May 1865, interviewing old settlers in Menard County, Herndon thought he discovered the solution to the problem. In his

[11] W. G. Greene to Herndon [in Herndon's writing], May 30, 1865, Herndon-Weik Coll. Many of the letters in Herndon's Lincoln files are in his own writing though signed by another. These should probably be understood as his memoranda of oral interviews, which were read back to and approved by his informants.

[12] Henry McHenry to Herndon [in Herndon's writing], May 29, 1865, *ibid.*

[13] Mentor Graham to Herndon, May 29, 1865, copy, Lamon MSS.

rambling recollections about early days in New Salem, Hardin Bale told Herndon of "a Miss Ann Rutledge — a pretty & much accomplished girl . . . living in New Salem" with whom Lincoln fell in love. "It was said," gossiped Bale, "that after the death of Miss Rutledge and because of it, Lincoln was locked up by his friends . . . to prevent derangement or suicide — so hard did he take her death." [14] The next day Herndon's crony, W. G. Greene of Tallula, gave him the story in detail:

> He [Lincoln], in the years . . . 1833 & 4 was in love with a young lady in New Salem by the name of Mis[s] Ann Rutledge. She accepted the overtures of Lincoln and they were engaged to be . . . married. This young lady was a woman of exquisite beauty, but her intellect was quick — sharp — deep & philosophic as well as brilliant . . . a short time before the marriage was to be she took sick with the brain fever and died in 4 or 5 days. Lincoln went & saw her during her sickness — just before her death. Mr Lincolns friends after this sudden death of one whom his soul & heart dearly & [?] loved were compelled to keep watch and ward over Mr Lincoln, he being from the sudden shock somewhat temporarily deranged. We watched during storms — fogs — damp gloomy weather Mr Lincoln for fear of an accident. He said "I can never be reconcile[d] to have the snow — rains & storms to beat on her grave.[15]

One suspects that Greene, like Herndon, was a reader of novels.

Herndon was delighted with the story. Here was the key to the secret of Lincoln's silence, his melancholy, his sadness. Assiduously Herndon set himself to digging out the details of the story. He found that it had been for years a matter of common gossip in Petersburg, since as early as 1862 the tale of the "love-sick swain" who became President had appeared in the *Menard Axis*.[16] It was not hard to ferret out two or three other suitors for Ann's lily-white hand, so that his classic love story could have the additional interest of the eternal triangle. Learning that the Rutledge family had removed to Iowa, Herndon followed them with a barrage of questions and (what family would not have been proud of so intimate a connection with a martyr President?) surviving brothers and cousins of Ann gave him long and detailed accounts of the Lincoln-Rutledge romance.

By his very persistence Herndon gave undue importance to the episode. He repeatedly questioned old settlers on the Ann Rutledge af-

[14] Hardin Bale to Herndon [in Herndon's writing], May 29, 1865, Herndon-Weik Coll.

[15] W. G. Greene to Herndon [in Herndon's writing], May 30, 1865, *ibid.*

[16] Jay Monaghan, "New Light on the Lincoln-Rutledge Romance," *Abraham Lincoln Quar.*, III, 138–145.

fair. When he heard, for example, that his old friend Abner Y. Ellis had information on Lincoln's love life, he immediately demanded: "I want to know all about it from beginning to end — from top to bottom — *in-side* and outside." [17] One letter of inquiry followed another, and the more often old men and women repeated their tales the surer they became of the whole story. The hundreds of papers, letters, and interviews on the Ann Rutledge theme preserved in the Herndon-Weik Collection show that the legend grew in color and in detail and that over the years the story crystallized from a floating rumor into a fixed romance.[18]

I V

In interviewing Menard County pioneers, Herndon unearthed another story only slightly less romantic than the Lincoln-Rutledge affair. If the tale of Lincoln's courtship of Mary Owens lacked something of the sentimental appeal of the legend of blue-eyed Ann, its authenticity was perhaps a compensation.[19] Petersburg retained a distinct memory of a Kentucky visitor who had appeared in New Salem in the 1830's, Mary Owens, sister of Mrs. Elizabeth Abell, polished, well-educated, and superior to anything ever before seen on the bluffs of the Sangamon. Thirty years afterward Menard County was still rustling with gossip. Mary, remembered one impressionable male informant, "had large blue eyes with the finest tr[i]mmings I ever saw." "None of the Poets or Romance writers have ever given to us a picture of a heroine so beautiful as . . . Miss Owens in 1836," he warbled.[20] She had visited in the Sangamon country, tradition said, had been wooed by Lincoln, and had rejected his suit.

Herndon jumped at the tale. Here perhaps was another incident as satisfactory as the Ann Rutledge romance. From Mrs. Abell and from Mentor Graham he wormed out the information that Mary Owens, now Mrs. Jesse Vineyard, was still alive and that she resided in Weston, Missouri. At once he besieged her with letters. No man's fool, Herndon apparently stressed his own Southern birth in addressing this Kentucky lady, and his tact was rewarded. Repeatedly questioned, she eventually yielded. "After quite a struggle with my feelings," she wrote Herndon, "I have at last decided to send you the letters in my

[17] Herndon to A. Y. Ellis, March 24, 1866, copy, Lamon MSS.

[18] For a detailed examination of the evidence on the Ann Rutledge story, see Randall, *Lincoln the President*, II, 321–342.

[19] The best study of the Lincoln-Mary Owens courtship is *Lincoln's Other Mary*, by Olive Carruthers and R. Gerald McMurtry.

[20] L. M. Greene to Herndon, May 3, 1866, Herndon-Weik Coll.

possession, written by Mr. Lincoln, believing, as I do, that you are a gentleman of honor. . . ." [21] The enclosed letters revealed Lincoln's side of a rather unimpassioned courtship and showed that the impecunious fledgling lawyer half wished, half feared, to link his shaky fortunes with a lady so accustomed to culture and refinement.

Herndon was not yet satisfied. He plagued "Lincoln's other Mary" with another flock of questions. "Really," she bridled, "you catechise me in true lawyer style, but I feel that you will have the goodness to excuse me if I decline answering all your questions in detail, being well assured that few women would have ceded as much as I have, under all the circumstances." But she went on to explain that, though congenial in many ways, "Mr. Lincoln was deficient in those little links which make up the great chain of womans happiness," and it was for that reason that she finally refused his hand. Years afterward Mary had had a final message from Lincoln. When her sister, Mrs. Abell, was about to visit in Kentucky, Lincoln had said jokingly: "Tell your sister, that I think she was a great fool, because she did not stay here and marry me." "Characteristic of the man," snorted Mrs. Vineyard.[22]

V

Armed with the knowledge of these two earlier romances, Herndon was ready to tackle his old enemy, Mary Todd Lincoln. Herndon and Mary Todd had never got along. When Mary came to Springfield in 1837, Herndon had met her at a ball given by Colonel Robert Allen. He had asked the belle for a dance, and, thinking to compliment her, this youth just back from college tactlessly observed that the lady "seemed to glide through the waltz with the ease of a serpent." Miss Todd, never distinguished by a sense of humor, flashed back: "Mr. Herndon, comparison to a serpent is rather severe irony, especially to a newcomer" — and she left him on the dance floor.[23] Neither ever forgot that episode. When Lincoln was courting Mary Todd, Herndon strongly opposed this marriage into the wealth and aristocracy of Springfield; he was not invited to the wedding.

Mrs. Lincoln doubtless disliked her husband's choice of Herndon as a law partner; unquestionably she would have preferred someone more acceptable socially, John Todd Stuart, for example, or Orville H. Browning. For his part Herndon was sure that there was something radically wrong in the Lincoln household. According to his phi-

---

21 Mary Owens Vineyard to Herndon, May 1, 1866, copy, Lamon MSS.
22 Mary Owens Vineyard to Herndon, May 23 and July 22, 1866, copy, *ibid.*
23 *Herndon's Lincoln,* II, 209.

losophy, all men acted upon the same psychological laws, and by introspection he thought he could explain any human behavior. Comparing the Lincoln family with his own, Herndon soon concluded that there was not much love lost in the house on Eighth Street. For example, Herndon hated to spend a night away from home, while Lincoln would sometimes stay out on the circuit for weeks at a time. Surely, thought Herndon, his partner must lead an unhappy domestic life. Herndon would invite friends in for meals without giving his wife any warning; Lincoln had guests only when Mary specially asked them. Herndon nodded sagely; clearly his partner's wife had a shrewish and inhospitable disposition.

During his partner's lifetime, Herndon managed to avoid hostilities with Mary Lincoln. There are no contemporary accounts of Mrs. Lincoln's cutting Herndon in Springfield or of her refusing to speak to him in the law office; such tales were spread by Mary's self-appointed defenders in the postwar period after she and Herndon had come to an open rupture. So far as can be judged from existing evidence, during Lincoln's Springfield years Herndon and Mary maintained restrained, if distant, relations. But Mrs. Lincoln never invited her husband's partner to her house for a meal.[24]

During the Civil War Herndon's interest in the Lincolns' domestic arrangements had been stimulated by the scandalous and libelous rumors spread by a hostile press about the wife of the President and by the snubbing Mary Lincoln had administered to him on his 1862 visit to the White House. After the assassination, collecting facts, reminiscences, and gossip about the Lincolns, Herndon accumulated evidence which convinced him that Mary Todd had been, after all, the third — or perhaps the fourth or fifth — woman Lincoln had wooed in ten years; he dug up a rumor of the alleged occasion in 1841 when Lincoln was said to have jilted Mary at the very altar; and he built up a collection of tales concerning Mrs. Lincoln's unfortunate displays of temper. Already there was shaping in his mind a theory of the Lincoln marriage.

Herndon now wrote to Robert Todd Lincoln, the President's oldest son, explaining his projected biography and requesting information and assistance. In his letter Herndon included one enigmatic paragraph:

Robt — I want to give a sketch — a short life of your mother in my biography up to her marriage to your father — or say up to 1846 — or

---

[24] "Lincoln's domestic life," undated Herndon monograph, Herndon-Weik Coll.

1858 — . I wish to do her justice fully — so that the world will understand things better. You understand me. Will she see me.[25]

Swathed in widow's weeds, Mary Lincoln was then living in absolute seclusion in Chicago. Her mind had already begun to show the effects of the tragedies which had so blighted her life — first the loss of two dearly loved sons, and then the assassination of one more than life itself to her. Her action was probably injudicious, but, seeing Herndon's letter, she graciously answered it herself. "The recollection of my beloved husband's, *truly,* affectionate regard for *you,*" she wrote with a feminine superfluity of commas, "& the knowledge, of your great love & reverence, for the best man, that ever lived, would of *itself,* cause you, to be cherished, with the sincerest regard, by my sons & myself." "I have been thinking for some time past," she continued, "that I would like to see you & have a long conversation"; and she arranged for an interview at the St. Nicholas Hotel in Springfield. Her visit to her former home was to be kept sacredly private, as she was coming "to visit the tomb — which contains my All, in life — my husband."

Mary then clipped from Herndon's letter the paragraph quoted above and enclosed it with her own communication, asking just what Herndon's cryptic suggestion implied. "With the remembrance of years of *very very* great domestic happiness — with my darling husband & children — my sons & myself, fail to understand your meaning," she said. "Will you be pleased to explain — ." [26] Herndon was pleased to explain, but his explanation took the form of public letters, broadsides, lectures, and books.

In September 1866 Mrs. Lincoln came to Springfield and Herndon kept his appointment. Explaining the general purpose of his investigations, he asked for "some facts — a short history of herself to insert in the biography." In that day of reticules and reticence, it was customary for a biographer to note merely that his hero married a beautiful and charming lady and that his domestic life was invariably felicitous. It was highly improper for a woman's name to be bandied about. The etiquette books ruled "that a lady's name should appear only twice in

[25] Fragment of Herndon letter, undated, *ibid.*
[26] Mary Lincoln to Herndon, August 28, [1866?], *ibid.* It has been impossible to fix positively the date of this letter, though it was obviously written in 1865 or 1866. Mary Lincoln made her appointment with Herndon for "Wednesday week, Sept 4th" — but in neither year did that date fall on a Wednesday. No mention of Mrs. Lincoln's visit appears in Springfield newspapers under either date. In his biography (*Herndon's Lincoln,* III, 510–511) Herndon quoted portions of the letter, supplying the year as 1866, and for lack of better evidence Herndon's memory must be trusted.

the paper — first, at her marriage, and, second, at her death . . . and
. . . if it appeared at any other time her nearest male relative was under a moral obligation to shoot the editor." [27] Mrs. Lincoln, therefore,
was distressed at Herndon's suggestion and only after some argument
did she consent to give some memories of herself and of her husband.

"I was born on the 13th day of December, 1823," she began, but perhaps every woman is entitled to postdate her birth five years. The rest
of Mary Lincoln's reminiscence was characterized by accuracy of statement and dignity of phrase. Her mind went back to the closing days
of the war, when peace and happiness had seemed so close, only to
be shattered so disastrously. The President, she recalled, had been like
a boy during those last months, "cheery, funny, . . . in high spirits."
Mr. Lincoln had been "the kindest man and most loving husband and
father in the world." Always "exceedingly indulgent to his children,"
he was proud that they were "free, happy and unrestrained by paren-
tal tyranny," yet he could be "a terribly firm man when he set his foot
down." Not "a technical christian," he "was a religious man always."
"Mr. Lincoln had a kind of poetry in his nature," his widow recalled;
"he rose grandly with the circumstances" of the crisis. In her comment
lay perhaps a quiet pride at her own share in that rise: "I never saw
a man's mind develop itself so finely — his manners got quite polished." [28]

In later years the Herndon-Mary Lincoln feud broke into open warfare — and for good reason — but the historian can rejoice that for this
brief interlude after Lincoln's death they had called a truce. The reminiscences of Mrs. Lincoln, as committed to writing by Herndon, are
source material of invaluable historical importance. The Chicago
Tribune justly observed in 1874 that Herndon's memoranda of this interview give "in a very few words, the best photograph of Mr. Lincoln's real life and character that has yet been produced." [29]

VI

As he secured letters and statements Herndon carefully preserved
them for his files, and he was vastly proud of the extent and complete-
ness of what he termed the "Lincoln Record." The present-day biog-

[27] Mary Day Winn, *Adam's Rib*, quoted in W. A. Evans, *Mrs. Abraham Lincoln*, 87–88.
[28] Herndon's battered and fragmentary notes of this interview (dated for some
reason by Weik as November 14, 1871) are in the Herndon-Weik Collection. Quotations in the above paragraphs are from Herndon's published account of the interview, *Mrs. Lincoln's Denial and What She Says*.
[29] Chicago *Tribune*, January 17, 1874.

rapher who travels in streamlined luxury from one carefully indexed collection to another, who constantly has expert librarians to assist him, who takes his notes on a typewriter, or, preferably, secures for himself microfilm or photostatic copies of source materials, may easily underestimate the money and labor Herndon expended in his historical researches.

Never a wealthy man, for nearly two years Herndon neglected his business to collect information about Lincoln. His advantages were not inconsiderable, it is true, but he encountered correspondingly large obstacles. Many of his informants lived in the remote, inaccessible backwoods. Some were happy to help him out of a love of truth; others cooperated for a price. On the back of many statements collected by Herndon one finds such a notation as: "Col. A. H. Chapman of Charleston wrote this He is a relation of Mr Lincoln and handed me this paper — Sept 8th 1865 at the Union Hotel Charleston Ills — Cash $43.00." [30] By the time his records were gathered, copied, and bound, Herndon calculated that he had spent $1536 "in money actually paid out" on the project [31] — and this at a day when the governor of Illinois received only $1500 a year.

By the end of 1866 Herndon's principal researches were completed. Fearing that his office might be gutted by fire, he determined to have his entire Lincoln file copied and employed a clerk, John G. Springer, to transcribe the whole mass of letters and memoranda in his clear round hand. Word for word Springer copied from the originals, and every morning Herndon helped him "read & compare &c." [32] After careful proofing (which did not, however, always preserve eccentricities of spelling) Herndon was by the first of December ready to consider his work finished. The copies were arranged roughly by geographical subject-headings (i.e., letters on the Lincoln family in Kentucky separated from those on Indiana, and so on) and were sent to Bradford & Johnson, Springfield's best bookbinders, where they were made up into three volumes "each the size of Websters dictionary on legal cap." The binding was of "excellent heavy leather — spring back — strongly done &c." [33] Some few documents were not included in these bound copies, but by and large they included practically all the data Herndon had collected about his partner.

[30] Herndon's endorsement on Chapman's statement, September 8, 1865, Herndon-Weik Coll.

[31] Herndon to Hart, December 12, 1866, Hart MSS.

[32] Statement of John G. Springer, December 8, 1866, Herndon-Weik Coll.; Herndon to Lamon, October 29, 1869, Lamon MSS.

[33] Herndon to Hart, December 12, 1866, Hart MSS.

Only a very few years later, in desperate financial need, Herndon was forced to sell these copies of his Lincoln Record. Needing money very badly, he was naturally not over-modest in describing the contents of his three volumes. In his attempt to get the highest price the market would bear, he emphasized his superior advantages in interviewing Lincoln's intimates, stressed the amount of time and money spent in building up his records, and hinted of spectacular rewards that could be reaped by using the manuscripts. His record, he urged, was "broad — sweeping & critical — looking at good sides — & bad ones," and it was made up of undoubted facts, not fancies. "I think I may say," he wrote in one effort to promote the sale, "that no man can write a lasting Life — a good standard Biography of Presdt Lincoln without my memoranda &c." The lucky biographer who purchased his Lincoln files would surely win "Fame & the $." "I'll make the world pay for these records sometime," he vowed; "they are the most perfect of any living or any dead man — probably Johnson's Biography by Boswell excepted." [34]

Herndon's services to Lincoln biography have frequently been appraised at his own valuation. At his death the New York *World* carried Herndon's obituary under the caption, "Abraham Lincoln's Boswell." [35] If Billy could have seen it, he would certainly have been pleased. During the years after Herndon's death, when his manuscripts were not available to historians, a tradition grew up as to their inestimable value. The late William E. Barton, author of countless Lincoln monographs, is said to have written about a hundred letters seeking access to Herndon's files.[36] When Senator Albert J. Beveridge was permitted to use Herndon's collection in the preparation of his monumental but unfinished Lincoln biography, he was overjoyed. "I do not," he wrote after examining them, "recall another case in history where, immediately after the death of a great personage, the facts of his personal life were collected so carefully, thoroughly and impartially by a lifelong friend and intimate professional associate, as the facts about Lincoln were gathered by William H. Herndon." [37] "I do not hesitate to say," opined Chauncey F. Black, ghost-writer of the Lamon biog-

[34] For these bits of self-promotion see Herndon to Hart, February 24, 1869, *ibid.;* Herndon to Mrs. Dall, January 24, 1873, Dall MSS.; Herndon to Lamon, February 17 and 26, 1869, Lamon MSS.

[35] The obituary began: "For the better part of its knowledge of Abraham Lincoln posterity will stand indebted to William H. Herndon. . . ." New York *World,* March 23, 1891.

[36] Hertz, *Hidden Lincoln,* 14.

[37] Beveridge, "Lincoln as His Partner Knew Him," *Literary Digest International Book Review,* I, 33 (September 1923).

raphy, "that without Herndon *no Life of Lincoln* could ever have been written." [38]

Much of this praise was well deserved. Herndon willingly sacrificed time, money, and personal comfort to accumulate his Lincoln Record. At the risk of ridicule, he set himself the task of interviewing those who had known Lincoln best. Without formal historical training, he worked out for himself a system of notetaking and of evaluating his source materials. To a large extent Herndon's personal history disappeared after 1865; from that time he really existed only as a student of Lincoln. He thought, he talked, wrote nothing but Lincoln. If by the term is understood an indefatigable biographer, Herndon may rightly be called Lincoln's Boswell.

VII

Yet while appreciating the magnitude of Herndon's labors and the genuine value of his findings, one must make some reservations in judging his Lincoln Record. James Boswell, it will be remembered, during his twenty years of association with Samuel Johnson had the project of a biography constantly in view. His plan was known to his subject; he repeatedly questioned Johnson for details of his early history; he daily recorded his notes, observations, and recollections of the great man's pithy sayings and epigrammatic remarks. As a result, Boswell's records of the arbiter of English letters are authentic, firsthand source materials. Aside from a vague family tradition, there is literally nothing to indicate that Herndon had contemplated a biography during Lincoln's lifetime; that came only with the death and deification of the Martyr President. Except for a handful of personal letters to Herndon, the manuscripts in the Lincoln Record (or the originals in the Herndon-Weik Collection) begin with 1865. They are valuable; they contain much significant information — but they were not written in Lincoln's lifetime.

When praising the diligence of Herndon's search for facts, one should not overplead his case. To assert that "Until 1888 Herndon gave practically all his time to . . . assiduous research" [39] is arrant nonsense. With inconsequential exceptions the statements and memoranda collected by Herndon (as distinguished from letters containing his own personal reminiscences) date before 1867. Springer completed copying the Lincoln Record in December 1866. A careful

[38] Black to Lamon, March 8, 1870, copy, Herndon-Weik Coll.
[39] Hertz, *Hidden Lincoln*, 6.

searching of the manuscripts fails to reveal any important letters written to Herndon or interviews recorded by him after that date. It is true that Lincoln was Herndon's major, almost his only, interest from 1865 to the time of his death, but his researches on the subject — in contrast to his introspective brooding about Lincoln, combined with a pre-Freudian variety of psychoanalysis — were completed in less than two years after his partner's death.

The Lincoln biographer should realize the uniqueness and the prime value of Herndon's stock of information, but he should at the same time be aware of its serious limitations. The statements Herndon collected on the Virginia forebears of the Lincolns are few and of no great importance. His Kentucky "evidences" are the generally unreliable reminiscences of a small number of old men. Research among the legal documents in Kentucky might have altered Herndon's conception of the alleged backward and poverty-stricken condition of the Lincoln family; certainly he could have found the marriage bond of Lincoln's parents and put a quietus on the rumor of the President's illegitimacy.[40]

On the Indiana and Illinois years Herndon's records are much more complete. It is doubtful whether any other biographer of his day had equal opportunities to gather these invaluable reminiscences; certainly no one else collected anything of comparable significance. Without the statements of Dennis Hanks, Mrs. Thomas Lincoln, David Davis, Joseph Gillespie, James Gurley, and a score of others — all given at Herndon's urgent solicitation — our knowledge of Lincoln would be incomparably poorer.

Even for the Illinois period of Lincoln's career, however, there are certain objections to Herndon's records. To collect historical data through oral interviews, though sometimes necessary, is always hazardous. The reminiscences of a graybearded grandfather have to be guided or they are likely to become incoherent rambling. Yet in controlling an interview, it is very difficult not to influence the informant. To ask some questions is to suggest the answers desired. Herndon was a distinguished Illinois lawyer; old-timers, especially some of the more rural and less literate, were anxious to please him. Herndon's records of interviews give the answers he collected but not the questions he asked. (Or rather they give some of the answers, for he did not note down any information which he considered "inconsistent with the

---

[40] Using just such documents Dr. Louis A. Warren was able in *Lincoln's Parentage and Childhood* to make many significant revisions in the Lincoln story and to rehabilitate the reputation of Thomas Lincoln.

nature of the man — foolish — idiotic — nonsensical — Childish — or bad." [41]) From a knowledge of Herndon and from the extant letters in which he quizzed witnesses, it may be assumed that he harped on certain episodes in the Lincoln story — tales of the President's domestic infelicity, for example — to the neglect of other, and perhaps more important, points.

Finally, it should be remembered that nearly all of Herndon's Lincoln Record pertains to Lincoln's pre-presidential career. Except for the long transcript of Allan Pinkerton's dossier on the 1861 plot to assassinate Lincoln, Herndon's data virtually terminate with the departure of the President Elect from Springfield. It is with no wish to belittle Herndon that one remarks the deficiencies in his records, and it would be both unhistorical and ungrateful to criticize him for failing to follow canons of historical method which in 1866 were hardly known in the United States. It is because Herndon's Lincoln Record is so valuable that one regrets all the more its undeniable weaknesses.

[41] Herndon, "A Statement — Memoranda," January 8, 1886, Herndon-Weik Coll.

CHAPTER xiv

My Queer Lectures

I

Dʉʀɪɴɢ the Civil War patriotic speeches were preferred in Springfield to philosophical lectures. Sanitary fairs took the place of social entertainment. Men's thoughts had been with the armies advancing into the South. But when the war was over, there was a reawakening of interest in things of the spirit. Responding to popular demand, the proprietors of Bryant, Stratton & Bell's business college planned during the winter of 1865 "a rich treat" for Springfield in the form of a lecture series, intellectual entertainment which would surely bring the most pleasant and beneficial results to the community. Governor Richard Oglesby headed the list of speakers, and addresses were promised on literature, science, history, and on "general useful knowledge." Among the gentlemen of distinction who would participate Herndon was listed.[1]

This particular series of lectures was never given, largely, it seems, because the rival Practical Business College of Rutledge & Davidson demonstrated its practicality by engaging all the speakers. The elliptical second-story hall at Rutledge & Davidson's was fitted up as an auditorium, and Herndon, always ready with a speech, was asked to initiate the lecture course. On the evening of November 29, 1865, he delivered a free address before the business college students and the assembled townspeople on "American Nationality." It was the kind of high-flown oratory Springfield liked. "Every American citizen present," the newspaper reporter was positive, "must have felt his heart thrill at the splendid future of his native land, as he followed the picture of its future greatness and glory, with its teeming population on all its hill sides and verdant vales, described in the elegant periods of the eloquent lecturer." In the sixties there could be no higher tribute than to characterize a speaker as both elegant and eloquent in the

[1] *Illinois State Journal,* November 18, 1865.

same sentence. In part the success of Herndon's lecture was due to his frequent "allusions to our Martyr President, Lincoln, as the best type of the American citizen," for his every mention of the Great Dead was "received in such a manner as showed the reverence felt for his memory by every person present." [2]

So successful was this first address that Herndon was immediately scheduled for two additional lectures before the business college in December. It was a busy time with him. Herndon was attending court, collecting his Lincoln records, leading a fight against Springfield's flourishing houses of prostitution, and heading a committee which planned removal of the county courthouse. There was a new and ailing baby at the Herndon house, who might, it was feared, die any moment. During all this confusion William Lloyd Garrison paid Springfield an unsolicited visit and was invited to stay with the Herndons. But it could never be said that Herndon refused an opportunity to make a speech, and, realizing the considerable interest in his Lincoln collection, he titled his lectures "Analysis of the Character of Mr. Lincoln."

The two lectures, delivered on December 12 and December 26, 1865, were really one, divided because of extreme length. Both were free, and both received considerable newspaper publicity. Both, it was announced for the benefit of Springfield's Democratic element, would be "free from prejudice or bias, and made as popular as the nature of the subject admits of." The audiences for the lectures were large and highly intelligent — they were always that in the newspaper reports. For the first the crowd was overflowing; for the second, appreciative and refined. It must have annoyed Herndon that his lectures had to wait while the Reverend Albert Hale, the Presbyterian preacher, gave a long invocation, and while Miss Lizzie Bennett rendered "some choice selections upon the piano." [3]

When he was finally introduced, Herndon made up for lost time. If the Springfield elite expected a repetition of the usual vapid sentimentality and cloying eulogy of which Lincoln addresses in 1865 — and today as well — mostly consisted, they were to be rudely surprised. Herndon had no use for uncritical praise. His lectures were intended to be just and truthful, without "humbug statements, & fussy flourishes." "I dearly loved — and now reverence the memory of my good dead friend," he wrote to one of his correspondents.[4] To tell the truth about Lincoln was his duty to himself, to the dead, and to mankind.

---

[2] *Ibid.*, November 30, 1865.
[3] *Ibid.*, December 11 and 27, 1865; Chicago *Times*, December 14, 1865.
[4] Herndon to Hart, January 8, 1866, Hart MSS.

Besides, he added, "the Eulogies delivered by men on Mr. Lincoln's character made me sick sometimes." [5] As "a human and hence an imperfect — a very imperfect man," Herndon was attempting to present his own knowledge of the dead President "without coloring or evasion." "In writing and delivering these lectures," he pledged, "I have searched myself and have literally [*sic*] stript myself of all *friendships* & all *hates*, if I ever had any of either." [6]

It was perhaps well that Herndon's audience had been informed in advance of his subject, for he was so busily engaged in stripping and searching and in enunciating "truths and general broad principles" during the first thirty minutes of his lecture that he hardly mentioned Lincoln at all. Instead he got a long running start with a philosophical argument about the nature of biography, observations on the rule of natural law in the universe (not forgetting to boost his theory of creative activity as the law of the mind), remarks about the endless chain of Providence, oracular statements on the desirability of being baptized in the common blood of the collective democratic life, animadversions on fathers who ruined their sons' lives by accumulating gold, and miscellaneous other nuggets of philosophy and psychology.

One suspects that some in Herndon's audience after a half hour of such introductory verbiage were becoming restive. Even more, one should imagine, were so bewildered by his philosophical jargon that they missed the major point he was trying to prove. "Not a world spins on its axis in the immensity of infinite space that does not spin & whirl by a law. The great deep ocean rises & sinks . . . according to law. Spirit & matter are . . . governed by law." In short, "Law is ruler — King." And law, "in reference to the infinite purposes & plans," was producing "a motion and a rush of the Race Godward." A part of this divinely directed progress was the rise of great men. The hero, said Herndon, is great in proportion to the opposition he overcomes. Early settlers of Kentucky and Illinois had certainly encountered difficulties enough; those who did triumph over "the *in* and out pressing influence of nature" emerged with resilience of character. Lincoln was one of these. He "grew out of the dark low horizon of common democratic life" and moved "calmly — slowly — cautiously — surely — strongly — certainly and up to the stars." He had the "gravity breaking power in him." This power derived from Lincoln's personality. He was, said Herndon, "*predominantly* — material — sensuous — that is reading the

[5] Herndon to Trumbull, January 4, 1866, Trumbull MSS.

[6] Quotations in the following paragraphs are from the *Abraham Lincoln Quarterly*, I, 343–383, where the complete text of Herndon's first lecture is published from the original manuscript in the Henry E. Huntington Library.

world through the senses — cool — selfish, practical — patient — firm —
apparently indifferent — cautious — true — not warm — not cold — having no love & no hates — generally 'having malice toward none & charity for all,' and without great faith & hope." Having classified Lincoln
by personality type, Herndon felt he could deduce his characteristics.

Before beginning this work of philosophical biography, the lecturer
fortunately paused to give a physical description of Lincoln. It is probably Herndon's best literary effort, and it has never been excelled as
a word portrait of his partner. His characterization of this "rail in
broad cloth," this "thin — tall — wirey — sinewy, grisly — raw boned
man" has the precision of a Brady photograph. Herndon caught the
man in action. Lincoln's appearance, he recalled, was distinctive.

> When Mr Lincoln walked he moved cautiously, but firmly, his long
> arms — his hands on them hanging like giants hands, swung down by
> his side. He walked with even tread — his toes — the inner sides of his
> feet were parallel, if not a little pigeontoed. He did not walk cunningly
> — Indian like, but cautiously & firmly. In walking Mr. Lincoln put the
> whole foot flat down on the ground at once, not landing on the heel.
> He lifted his foot all at once — not lifting himself from the toes, and
> hence had no spring or snap or get get [*sic*] up to his walk. . . . Mr.
> Lincoln walked undulating up & down, catching and pocketing tire —
> weariness & pain all up and down his person, preventing them from
> special locations.

"Thus," Herndon concluded, "stood and walked — and looked this
singular man. He was odd; but when that eye and face and every feature were lit up by the inward soul or fire of emotion, *then it* was that
all these apparently ugly features sprang to organs of beauty. . . .
Sometimes it appeared to me that Lincoln's soul was fresh . . . from
the presence of its God."

After this digression Herndon returned to the analysis of Lincoln's
"faculties" in the fashion approved by the psychologists of his day. To
sneer at this approach is a little unkind; biographical styles are as
quickly outmoded as ladies' hats. One cannot avoid remarking, however, that in the remainder of Herndon's lecture (the second took up
the analysis where the first left off) there is surprisingly little concrete
information about Lincoln. To those who knew both Herndon and
Lincoln it may have been illuminating to learn that the former considered his partner a remorseless analyzer who perceived things in ri-
gidity; to a modern reader these remarks are something less than
revealing.

Lincoln's perceptions, asserted Herndon, were cold, slow, precise, and exact — but not sharp (whatever the distinction may be). He tended to see things as "less than they really were." Here lay his fault, for Lincoln "saw what no man could dispute, but he failed to see what some others did see." But, the speaker added, no error went by Lincoln undetected. The greatness of Lincoln, Herndon informed his audience, which had now been listening for about an hour, derived not from a study of other men's thinking but from his own original ideas. "The truth about this whole matter is, that Mr. Lincoln read *less* and thought *more* than any man in America." Cool, cautious, concentrated, Lincoln was not creative. He was "causative" by nature. He reasoned logically through the use of analogy. In short, he was a self-reliant and "a self helpful man."

Other faculties of his partner Herndon could not praise so highly. Lacking a quick, discriminating mind, Lincoln might form faulty hasty judgments; given time to think things through, however, he would arrive at sound opinions "as omnipotent and all control[l]ing as Joves thunder." The President had had "no more than ordinary common sense." To tell the truth, he "could not by the face tell a pirate from a gentleman — : scarcely a woman from a man by the features & conformation of the face." His judgment of human motives was, therefore, fearfully weak. "It will not do," Herndon advised, "to let Mr. Lincolns fame rest on his judgements — on his . . . common sense . . . — nor on his judgement of human nature."

Instead, the lecturer pointed to Lincoln's four "grand and predominating elements": (1) "his great capacity and power of Reason," in which he was unparalleled; (2) his excellent understanding; (3) his "exalted idea and sense of Right & Equity"; and (4) "his intense love and worship of what was true & good." Those who considered Lincoln "warm, & all heart," Herndon emphasized, were absolutely incorrect. It followed as an inescapable deduction from his premise that Lincoln was a cool, material man that reason should be the dominant trait in his personality. His "general life was cold — not warm." But, by following the natural law of his own soul, Lincoln personified the Golden Rule.

II

At this point Herndon concluded his first lecture. In the second, delivered on a bitter winter evening after Christmas, he resumed his theme and completed his analysis of Lincoln's mind. His audience, the newspapers related, somewhat inconsistently, was both large and select. Displaying much care and preparation, the address "commanded the close attention of his audience, and was listened to with marked interest throughout." The lecture lasted about an hour and one-half, and its conclusion was greeted with the heartiest applause.[7]

In his second lecture Herndon turned his attention to Lincoln's will, selfishness, simplicity of mind, humor and gloom, religion, domestic life, sociability, self-reliance, legal ability, and eloquence. All received extended discussion. It is not necessary here to follow the involved convolutions of Herndon's thought on these points; the lectures have recently been published in full, and one appearance in print is quite sufficient recognition of their merits.[8] Abstract, wordy, and metaphysical, the lectures concealed in an astonishing number of words a disappointingly meager content.

The lectures were vague throughout largely because Herndon rejoiced in such "philosophical" prolixity. Some sections were deliberately made obscure in order to avoid criticism. In his original draft Herndon included a passage affirming that Lincoln did not believe in miracles, discredited supernatural revelations, and doubted the divinity of Jesus. These words were crossed out as "more suited to his *life* than a *lecture*," and to his audience Herndon merely remarked that Lincoln, though not "a technical Christian," had been a deeply religious man, whose creed consisted of practically applying the principles of "Truth . . . Justice & Right — Tenderness and Kindness." The same discretion was applied in Herndon's discussion of Lincoln "domestically."

Sprinkled through these lectures there are some surprisingly bitter judgments on Lincoln. Frequently Herndon gave faint praise; sometimes he actually seemed to attack the memory of his dead partner. Though in general "rightfully entitled to the appellation — 'Honest Abe,'" the lecturer informed his audience, Lincoln "was not always — to all persons & at all times *absolutely* Honest." "He was an exceedingly ambitious man — a man totally swallowed up in his ambitions . . . ." "Rouse Mr. Lincoln's peculiar nature in a point where he deeply felt — say in his ambitions — his general greed for office . . . then Mr. Lincoln preferred Abm Lincoln to any body else." If a friend and an enemy applied to President Lincoln for an office, he would give the appointment to the one "who bored him the most." His apparent simplicity was a guise under which he promoted his ambitious, cautious, secretive, and complex schemes.

[7] *Illinois State Register,* December 27, 1865; *Illinois State Journal,* December 27, 1865.
[8] The original manuscript of Herndon's second lecture is in the Henry E. Huntington Library. It was published in full for the first time in the *Abraham Lincoln Quarterly,* I, 403–441.

My Queer Lectures

It is doubtful whether Herndon intended these judgments to sound as harsh as they now do, wrenched from their context. In the introduction to his lectures he had announced the purpose of divesting himself of all friendships and hates in the analysis; perhaps these belittling remarks about Lincoln were intended as a measure of his impartiality. Disgusted by the undiscriminating flattery heaped upon the deified Lincoln, Herndon was leaning backward to avoid apotheosis. His lectures were prepared *"solely* for the purpose of putting . . . [Lincoln] where he in fact and truth & justice belongs." "I felt it my duty," he confided to Senator Trumbull, "to place Mr Lincoln on his true stand point, and if I have pointed out where the world may find the true greatness of the man I am Content." [9]

One may conjecture also that some of Herndon's anthology of abuse was included largely for rhetorical purposes. There is, for example, his often quoted statement: ". . . Mr. Lincoln read *less* . . . than any man in America. No man in this audience . . . can put his . . . finger on any great book written in the last or this century that he read." Herndon's remark was obviously false, and both he and his audience knew very well that it was an untruth. This great exaggeration was made in order to emphasize the other half of Herndon's proposition: "that Mr. Lincoln . . . thought *more* than any man in America." The same is true of many another of Herndon's seemingly derogatory comments. Lincoln, he said, was not "a bold, generous, brave, courageous man" — but "he never willingly and knowingly went with the wrong [side] — popular or unpopular." Secretive Lincoln "led mankind by a profound policy" — but he "was not a hypocrite — he used no tricks — no base arts — committed no frauds to accomplish his ends." Not *"absolutely* Honest," Lincoln kept honesty as his "great Polar star for which he drove all his manhood."

It is difficult to determine precisely what shade of meaning Herndon intended to convey in these statements. The turn of a phrase, the inflection of voice, the emphatic gesture might give his hearers an impression entirely different from that conveyed to the reader of his manuscript lectures. Herndon never published these addresses in full. They exist today in his hastily written first draft, which served as a sort of text from which he departed frequently in public delivery. ". . . I paid no close attention *to the paper* when I delivered them," he recalled. "In delivering my lectures I did not always follow the written words — but as ideas would come up I would orally state the ideas

[9] Herndon to Hart, January 8, 1866, Hart MSS.; Herndon to Trumbull, January 4, 1866, Trumbull MSS.

in unwritten words." [10] These alterations made during the presentation of the lectures may have been minor, but they may have determined the impression given by his words. A careful reading of Herndon's handwritten drafts, avoiding the interpretation of phrases outside their context, conveys the intent of sincere though moderate praise for Lincoln.

III

Herndon's first two lectures were enthusiastically received. They doubtless sounded better than they now read. After twenty-three years one man in his audience remembered the addresses well; they were stimulating and provocative, he recalled — "enough to keep me awake all night." The *Journal* correctly predicted: "These lectures of Mr. Herndon will be of importance to the historian who would prepare a faithful life of the greatest and best of America's sons." [11]

Herndon was very fortunate in the newspaper accounts of these lectures. Perhaps because their shorthand was inadequate to catch his outpouring of words, the reporters eliminated about half of Herndon's adjectives and nearly all of his philosophy, leaving a brief, straightforward analysis of Lincoln's mind. It was not editing that Herndon liked; the newspapers, he grumbled, gave only "a kind of blind mysty [*sic*] idea of the real thing." [12] But this unauthorized pruning did a great deal for Herndon's lectures. Not many readers could have pushed their way through the thicket of adjectives and the low-hanging branches of philosophy that cluttered the unabridged manuscript.

Shortened, they caught on immediately. Herndon was famous. Local papers, of course, gave extensive extracts, and a broadside, printed without Herndon's knowledge but probably not against his wishes, circulated the lectures in an abridged form. The Chicago *Tribune,* the Cincinnati *Commercial,* the St. Louis *Democrat,* the Philadelphia *Press,* the New York *Times,* and other metropolitan papers carried long stories. The Washington *Chronicle* requested permission to publish Herndon's lectures in full. [13]

Francis B. Carpenter, a self-trained artist from Homer, New York, during the Civil War had burned with the desire to paint the signing of the Emancipation Proclamation. Through the intercession of Republican friends, he was given free run of the White House for six months

[10] Herndon to Lamon, February 25, 1870, Lamon MSS.; Herndon, "A Statement — Memoranda," January 8, 1886, Herndon-Weik Coll.

[11] *Illinois State Journal,* December 27, 1865; Frank Marshall Eddy to Herndon, March 21, 1888, Herndon-Weik Coll.

[12] Herndon to Hart, January 25, 1866, Hart MSS.

[13] B. J. James to Herndon, November 28, 1866, Weik MSS.

in 1864, and the young artist's undisguised hero-worship made him a favorite with the Lincolns. After the assassination Carpenter was urged to write out his reminiscences of his stay in the Executive Mansion, and he began an unassuming, chatty little book which he appropriately titled *Six Months at the White House*. Just as he was completing his work, Carpenter ran upon a newspaper account of Herndon's first lecture and "was as much impressed with the power and originality shown in *it*, as by anything . . . [he] ever read of *Lincoln's*." "It was in my mind," the painter wrote Herndon, "that artists and sculptors would be likely to refer to my book for a personal description of Lincoln, and I desired to make this as *full* as possible, and what you had given was so immeasurably beyond any thing I could say or write, that I made very little attempt . . . at anything of my own beyond a record of incidents." [14] Liking Herndon's description of Lincoln so much, Carpenter, without a by-your-leave to the author, incorporated the lecture into his book, where this "masterly analysis" which had "scarcely an equal in the annals of biographical literature" occupied twenty-eight printed pages. Over thirty thousand copies of *Six Months at the White House* were sold, and through this deservedly popular little book Herndon's name became familiar to thousands of Northerners who took their Lincoln-worship very seriously.

Everywhere these reports of Herndon's first two Lincoln lectures were "approved . . . by all honest & candid minds as true and honest vindications of the good man's nature &c." [15] Senator Lyman Trumbull felt that the lecturer had presented Lincoln "as he really was." Leonard Swett, long associated with Lincoln in law and in politics, considered the lectures "the first analysis of Mr Lincoln's character . . . worthy of any man's consideration or thought." Shelby M. Cullom, the Republican congressman from the Springfield district, whose fancied — and carefully cultivated — resemblance to Lincoln was to make him a perennial Republican presidential aspirant for the next three decades, asked for copies of the lectures to distribute to his friends. Monumentally upright Isaac N. Arnold of Chicago, plugging away himself at a Lincoln biography, exclaimed that Herndon's lectures were "the most appreciative, discriminating & *just*" estimate of the President yet published. Illinois Governor Richard Oglesby, ex officio a high priest in the Lincoln cult, gave verdict that Herndon had dissected Lincoln "most fairly and with Thorough correctness" by "enter[ing] into the wavy sinews nerves and vaines [*sic*] of all there was of him and unravel[ling] hold[ing] up and expos[ing] each . . .

[14] Carpenter to Herndon, December 4, 1866, Herndon-Weik Coll.
[15] Herndon to Caroline H. Dall, January 1, 1866, Dall MSS.

faithfully and faultlessly." Even the pompous and misanthropic Robert Todd Lincoln, the President's oldest son, was moved to admit that the lectures contained nothing "at which to take umbrage." [16]

On only one point was there criticism, the forecast of a future bitter debate. Herndon's rather general remarks on Lincoln's religion ran afoul of editorial censorship. His statement that the President had not been "a technical Christian man" was suppressed. The Cincinnati *Commercial,* for example, gave a long summary of Herndon's second lecture under the caption, "Abraham Lincoln as he was." Paragraph by paragraph Herndon's analysis of Lincoln's imagination, will, ambition, and humor was summarized. Then the report was interrupted: "The lecturer devoted a chapter to the religion of Mr. Lincoln, which, viewed through his own peculiar theological lens, presents a picture differing . . . materially from that generally conceded as characterizing Mr. Lincoln's later years. . . . For these . . . reasons, a report of this portion of the discourse is omitted." [17]

Such censorship embittered Herndon. Newspaper editors were unseeing hero-worshipers. "I," Herndon protested loudly, "love Mr. Lincoln dearly — almost worship him, but that can't blind me." [18] Some of his readers also regretted this muzzling of the speaker. The trouble was that while many urged Herndon to reveal his whole knowledge of Lincoln, each really wanted to learn only facts and anecdotes which would blend into a preconceived portrait of the President. Chauncey Goodrich, for example, scion of the distinguished Connecticut family, acting editor of Webster's dictionary and son-in-law of the great lexicographer, begged Herndon to give to the world everything he knew about Lincoln — but to say nothing "which would belittle him in our eyes." Leonard Swett had much the same feeling. Warning Herndon against what would now be called debunking, he cautioned that truth was palatable only in small doses; then he requested confidentially to learn what the secret cancer was which had gnawed at Lincoln's brain.[19] "The task you have [entered] upon is a difficult one," correctly

[16] For these verdicts, in the order quoted, see: Trumbull to Herndon, December 27, 1865, Trumbull Coll., Ill. State Hist. Lib.; and Swett to Herndon, December 23, 1865 (letter is torn and conjectural emendation has been applied); Cullom to Herndon, January 6 and 28, 1866; Arnold to Herndon, December 31, 1865; Oglesby to Herndon, January 5 and February 5, 1866; R. T. Lincoln to Herndon, January 8, 1866 — all in Herndon-Weik Coll.
[17] Cincinnati *Commercial,* January 29, 1866.
[18] Herndon to Edward McPherson, February 4, 1866, MS. in collection of Mr. C. N. Owen.
[19] Chauncey Goodrich to Herndon, November 13, 1866, Weik MSS.; Swett to Herndon, February 14, 1866, Herndon-Weik Coll.

judged Herndon's Petersburg friend, Congressman T. W. McNeely. "He is a bold man who undertakes [a] true biography of a public man especially of one called by the world — a Martyr." [20]

IV

On December 27, 1865, the Philadelphia *Press* devoted a full column of its front page to a report of Herndon's first Lincoln lecture. Young Charles Henry Hart, a law student at the University of Pennsylvania, read it and was greatly interested. Wishing "very much to peruse it en‑tire," he wrote Herndon asking where copies could be obtained. Also, did Herndon have any Lincoln autographs to spare? [21]

In this rather abrupt fashion began one of the lasting friendships of Herndon's life. One is always a little astonished by Herndon's lack of reticence with complete strangers. Hart in 1866 was only nineteen years old and had not yet been admitted to the Pennsylvania bar. Without any kind of introduction save his flattering interest in Herndon's lectures, he wrote to Lincoln's law partner, who immediately adopted him as a correspondent to whom he could reveal his most private thoughts. It happened that Herndon's intuition proved good, for Hart became distinguished as a lawyer and achieved a quiet but reputable fame as an art critic.

To Hart's first letter Herndon replied that his lectures had never been printed in full. "I am an extremely lazy man," he confided to this complete stranger, "and have to be kicked to act." He had no Lincoln autographs left; months ago he gave them all away. But on second thought, Herndon advised that, though he had "no letters with the signature of Mr Lincoln attached to them," he could spare a legal document written and signed by the great man. "It is now the best thing I can do," he apologized, "probably the best thing you will get of any one at any time." He "could have given it away a *thousand* times," but somehow he preferred Hart as the recipient.[22]

In the long correspondence that followed, there was always a strange note of deference in Herndon's letters to the bright young Easterner. It was that defensively self-deprecatory attitude often assumed by Westerners. Thinking of publishing "my queer Lectures . . . poor as they are," Herndon promised Hart a copy but asked the Philadelphian "to excuse what is odd in me and my language." "We

[20] McNeely to Herndon, November 28, 1866, *ibid.*
[21] Hart to Herndon, January 3, 1866, Hart MSS.
[22] Herndon to Hart, January 8 and 13, 1866, *ibid.*

are rough and ready out here," Herndon explained, "rather than Educated & polished." [23] Though doubtless intended as a compliment, Hart's reply was somewhat gauche. In none of Herndon's writing had he found anything "which the most fastidious could object to" — but he rendered his praise nugatory by adding: "I am a great admirer of any thing which is outré in composition. . . ." [24]

Late in January 1866 Herndon could report to his new friend that he was about to give a third lecture on Lincoln. His first addresses had been "purely analytic . . . of Mr Lincoln's mind"; this new effort was intended to demonstrate the "abstract mind applied — Mr Lincoln's mind working on Love of Country & Statesmanship." [25] On the evening of January 23, after considerable drumming and advertising, a sizable crowd assembled in the hall of Bryant, Stratton & Bell's Commercial College to hear Herndon's free lecture on "The Patriotism and Statesmanship of Abraham Lincoln." This time his audience was not only large and intelligent but also elite and fashionable. The lecture was described as able and eloquent, and his hearers gave marked attention throughout — "the highest compliment an assembly can pay to an orator." [26]

By literary standards this third lecture of Herndon's was markedly inferior to his previous addresses.[27] It lacked structure; its ideas straggled aimlessly. By way of compensation it contained a number of anecdotes and reminiscences about Lincoln, of which some were true and even more were interesting. The human brain, began Herndon from his profound knowledge of philosophy, is prone to speculation. It cannot peer into the infinite, but even an inferior mortal brain, given an adequate supply of facts, can understand the finite mind. (This presumably meant that the lesser beings in his audience might not fathom the mind of God but they could, with his help, understand that of Abraham Lincoln.) The problem Herndon posed was whether Lincoln had been a successful and patriotic statesman. "By the Constitution," the lecturer opined, "the President has two chief duties — namely 1st to give information . . . to Congress of the state . . . of the Nation — : 2d That he will execute the laws and preserve the Constitution. . . ." Though desirable, it was not an "indispensable neces-

[23] Herndon to Hart, January 13, 1866, *ibid.*
[24] Hart to Herndon, January 18, 1866, *ibid.*
[25] Herndon to Hart, November 28, 1866, *ibid.*
[26] *Illinois State Register,* January 24, 1866; *Illinois State Journal,* January 24, 1866.
[27] Quotations in the following paragraphs are from the *Abraham Lincoln Quarterly,* III, 178–203, where Herndon's third lecture has been published in full from the original manuscript in the Henry E. Huntington Library.

sity that he should have any creative capacity — organizing ability or commanding power." Lincoln had had "the wise and sagacious quality to a preeminent degree of giving information . . . to Congress"; he "impartially executed the laws; and . . . preserved and defended the Constitution; and therefore he fulfilled his ends — this great Peoples' purposes."

It would thus seem that at the very outset of his lecture Herndon had solved his problem of appraising Lincoln's statesmanship. Apparently the speaker had somewhat the same feeling, for he abruptly began a series of anecdotes which for the most part had little relation to what had preceded or to each other. First he related how Lincoln's house-divided speech of 1858 had been written in order "to take the winds out of Sewards Sales." (Of course, Herndon was in error on this matter, as the house-divided speech was delivered several months before Seward enunciated his irrepressible-conflict theory.) Similarly Lincoln's Freeport questioning of Douglas in 1858 had been intended to kill the Little Giant as a presidential possibility for 1860. These incidents proved to Herndon that Lincoln had policy, will, "strong self determination" and "that he was secretive — cautious, complex minded and *morally courageous.*"

But in spite of the courage of the house-divided doctrine, it seemed to his partner that Lincoln did not fully comprehend the implications of his theory. "I know that Mr. Lincoln did not thoroughly understand human nature," declared the lecturer, "and I do not think he understood to the bottom, and end of the tap root of his ideas — namely the never ending antagonisms between slavery & freedom." Why otherwise had he been so long in advocating wartime abolition of slavery? Why, when war did come, had he made the "sad & fatal error" of summoning only 75,000 short-term volunteers to the Union colors? His proclamation of amnesty and his revocation of Frémont's and Hunter's emancipation orders had given the impression of pusillanimity and had encouraged the enemies of freedom. Herndon himself had wished: "O for the iron hand of a Napoleon, or a Cromwell; or for the quick iron will of a Jackson."

Despite mistakes Lincoln ultimately demonstrated that he was the right man in the right place. Confessing ignorance of the secrets of state, Herndon concluded that Lincoln's policies had succeeded. The President had saved the country, emancipated the slaves, kept the peace with Europe, and met a glorious death "without a blemish or spot of corruption on his character." Lincoln had been triumphant because he "was seized, *as it were insanely,* with *one* idea and one purpose — namely the Union and its preservation." To this central idea he sacrificed friends and foes alike. In its pursuit he was cool, remorseless, unfeeling.

Approaching his peroration, Herndon now became highly rhetorical. Lincoln "called for 75 thousand men — 500 thousand men — 300 thousand men; he called for millions of dollars — hundred millions of dollars — thousand millions of dollars — : made seas of blood — used mountains of wealth: he could gaze on the starving stalking forms of his brave & gallant soldiers at Andersonville and feel not — feel not much more relatively speaking than you would, when you demanded a plate of oysters at a saloon or smoke a cigar on the pavements of this city's walks." If Lincoln had had a heart, he "would have lost — *lost,* all, *all.*" Here was proof of the main idea running through all of Herndon's lectures: that Lincoln was cool, material, patient, and practical, not warm, tender, and sympathetic. It was because of Lincoln's hardness that the Union had been preserved. When "the dead soldiers all over the land shall dryly stalk before our President's eyes — he can Justly & Truthfully say — 'Thou canst not say I did it — : slavery, that would pull down heaven's high Thrones, and forge them into chains to fetter mankind, *did it* — killed and starved you: it deserved death, and death I gave it. I willingly gave it death and hurled it into *Hell* as I passed from Earth to Heaven.' "

What Herndon's Springfield listeners were thinking as they rose and stretched at the end of his ninety-minute address is not a matter of record. Those who approved probably congratulated the speaker in person, while those who did not — and by this time there were doubtless many — made unflattering remarks as they emerged from the auditorium and trudged over Springfield's frozen streets to their homes.[28]

V

Herndon sent a report of his third lecture to Hart, with a suggestion that some publicity in the Philadelphia newspapers would not be displeasing. Hart complied by having inserted in the *Press* and the *Bulletin* a flowery and highly flattering notice of Herndon's projected biography. Mr. Herndon, Philadelphians read on April 1, 1866, was "a genius of no ordinary kind." His lectures indicated "a very rare combination of delicate examination and a strict conscientiousness, allied with a happy appreciation of all that is characteristic and interesting" about Lincoln. A "writer of Mr. Herndon's sagacity and collective dis-

[28] Some weeks later Herndon repeated this lecture in Jacksonville. For comments see Jacksonville *Sentinel,* February 23, 1866; Jacksonville *Journal,* February 22, 1866; Louis H. Jenkins to Herndon, February 19, 1866, copy, Lamon MSS.

position, aided by twenty years of the most intimate personal relations" would surely produce a most valuable biography.[29]

Herndon was greatly pleased, and the warmth of his letters to Hart increased noticeably. He found it more and more easy to depend on the young Philadelphian for all sorts of little research tasks. He would be "a thousand times obliged" if Hart would write out an account of an interview Hart's father had had with the President. Perhaps his young Eastern friend would "clip out & send . . . from the leading Ph[a] papers the account of Mr L's arrival and doings [in Philadelphia in 1861] . . . from his entrance to his final departure." And it would be well to have the same done for the Harrisburg papers, too.[30]

For a time it almost seemed that Hart was going to be a joint author of the projected Lincoln biography. Even before corresponding with Herndon the young law student had begun to collect books and pamphlets about the Great Emancipator. In March 1866 he asked Herndon: "How would you like to have an appendix to your volume in the shape of a 'Bibliography of Lincolnian[a]' containing the full title and size of every Eulogy, Sermon &c. which has appeared since his death."[31] Herndon was highly pleased with the idea; such an appendix would be eminently proper. "The Eulogies — Sermons — Lectures &c. delivered on a man's death are an index of the nations Estimate of the man," he correctly observed. "This historic fact is a Eulogy — a fine Eulogy of the dead in itself. . . ."[32]

Though Herndon usually spelled the word "bigliography" and once inserted an announcement of Hart's "Bilibographia" in the Springfield papers,[33] he really was interested. But his court work, the need for collecting additional Lincoln data, and the time required to write an occasional lecture made sustained literary production on the Lincoln biography impossible. Like many another historian he found it "extremely hard to get time — place & circumstances truly — correctly — exactly as they were." His standards were high. "I wish to write Mr L's life just as he thought it and acted on this earth in his flesh & blood, and bones. I must take my own time and do it honestly, truthfully — fairly & manly — not otherwise."[34] He would be glad to use the "Bib Lin" (as he abbreviated those difficult words), but Hart had time on time for completing his share of the work.[35]

[29] Philadelphia *Bulletin*, quoted in Newton, *Lincoln and Herndon*, 294–295.
[30] Herndon to Hart, February 12, April 13, and September 1, 1866, Hart MSS.
[31] Hart to Herndon, March 2, 1866, Weik MSS.
[32] Herndon to Hart, September 25, 1866, Hart MSS.
[33] *Illinois State Journal*, November 28, 1866.
[34] Herndon to Caroline H. Dall, September 3, 1866, Dall MSS.
[35] Herndon to Hart, March 9, 1866, Hart MSS.

The young Philadelphian had already compiled a bibliography of several hundred items, and he soon began wondering about Herndon's publishing arrangements. It would be well, he suggested, for the Lincoln biography (and his bibliography) to appear "in the *East,* e.g. *New York, Philada.* or *Boston,* for the reason it will cause it to be better and sooner known than if pub. in the West, and it will be brought out in finer style." "Western publishers unlike everything else in the 'Great West,'" Hart added a little superciliously, "are very slow . . . ."[36] Herndon liked this advice about his "poor littl[e] book" and agreed to have the "Biog published in Philda or N Y."[37] At this time he could have picked his publisher. The sedate old Boston company of Tichnor & Fields, publisher for Emerson, Hawthorne, and James Russell Lowell, was begging for the manuscript, expressing the "desire . . . shared by every member of our house to become the publishers of . . . [Herndon's] work."[38] Now all that was lacking was the biography to publish.

VI

While Herndon was working away, Holland's *Life of Abraham Lincoln* appeared and was snapped up by a hundred thousand readers. The popularity of its subject, the physical attractiveness of the book, the overt Republican bias of the author, the sustained tone of eulogy, the mixture of homey anecdote and unblushing platitude — all combined to make the biography the best seller of its day. It was by far the best of the early Lincoln biographies and even today it has a quaint flavor of the era. Herndon had to admit the book had merit. "There is much in Holland's life . . . which is true," he grudgingly confessed, "as I gave him much, though he did not record what I said correctly."[39] But Herndon had little liking for the biography. This was not the Lincoln he had known so well. The picture was too refined, too ladylike. Holland seemed to Herndon a literary old maid with a passion for prettifying and tidying.

Another thing that bothered Herndon was Holland's constant harping on Lincoln's belief in Christianity. When the Massachusetts editor visited Springfield in the spring of 1865, he asked Herndon: "What about Mr Lincoln's religion."

[36] Hart to Herndon, April 2, 1866, Herndon-Weik Coll.
[37] Herndon to Hart, April 13 and June 29, 1866, Hart MSS.
[38] J. S. Clark to Herndon, October 12, 1866, Weik MSS.; Mass. Hist. Soc. *Proceedings, 1917–1918,* 498.
[39] Herndon to Lamon, March 6, 1870, Lamon MSS.

"*The less said the better,*" replied Herndon, well aware of local gossip on the subject.

"*O never mind,*" Holland said with a wink. "*I'll fix that.*" [40]

When the *Life of Abraham Lincoln* appeared, Herndon learned that Holland had done just that. A sincerely devout man himself, the Massachusetts author had at the very outset decided that the deified Lincoln must have been "a true-hearted Christian." He incorporated into his biography all sorts of improbable anecdotes to emphasize Lincoln's religiosity. The book concluded with an invocation to the shade of the Great Departed:

> Humble child of the backwoods . . . we receive thy life and its immeasurably great results, as the choicest gifts that a mortal has ever bestowed upon us; grateful to thee for thy truth to thyself, to us, and to God; and grateful to that ministry of Providence and grace which endowed thee so richly, and bestowed thee upon the nation and mankind.[41]

Extended space was given in Holland's book to the recollections of Newton Bateman, Illinois superintendent of education, on the question of Lincoln's Christian faith. From Bateman, whose offices had adjoined those used by Lincoln in the Illinois state capital, Holland received an eight-page memorandum detailing a remarkable conversation held with the Republican presidential nominee in October 1860. It was a moving scene, recalled the Illinois schoolman, one filled "with deep emotion & many tears." "I am not a Christian," Lincoln was reported to have confessed; "God knows I would be one. . . ." "I know there is a God & that he hates injustice & slavery. . . . I know that liberty is right, for Christ teaches it and Christ is God. . . . The future would be something awful, as I look at it, but for *this rock* on which I stand, (meaning the Bible, which he held in his hand). . . ." Then, according to Bateman's recollection, Lincoln "repeated many passages of the Bible," "referred to his conviction that the day of wrath was at hand," "said he believed in divine providence & . . . in the duty, privilege, & efficacy of prayer," and "dwelt much upon the necessity of *faith* . . . in . . . the Christian's God."

By his own testimony Bateman was not a little surprised to hear such religious sentiments from Lincoln, a man generally reputed in Springfield to be an agnostic. When the superintendent remarked how strange it was that intimate friends should be ignorant of Lincoln's

[40] Herndon to Arnold, December 27, 1882, Arnold MSS.
[41] Holland, *Life of Abraham Lincoln*, 544.

change of heart, the Republican candidate had confided: ". . . I am obliged to appear different to them, but I think more on these subjects than all others, & have done so for years, & I am willing that *you* should know it." All these words of "Dear noble heroic Lincoln" Bateman vouched for as exactly as he uttered them.[42] Holland was greatly pleased, and he devoted four pages of his biography to this touching revelation of Lincoln's belief in Christianity.

When Herndon came across this narrative, he nearly exploded. Decidedly unorthodox in his own religious views, he was not willing to have his partner canonized as a Protestant saint. Besides, the Bateman statement made Lincoln appear cowardly and hypocritical. Herndon had little personal knowledge of his partner's religious beliefs,[43] but in collecting his Lincoln records he had formed an opinion decidedly different from Holland's. Joshua F. Speed, one of Lincoln's most intimate friends during the early Springfield years, had written Herndon that Lincoln "was skeptical as to the great truths of the Christian religion"; Lincoln's first law partner, John Todd Stuart, considered him an infidel; Isaac Cogdal, a Menard lawyer who rode the circuits in central Illinois, affirmed that Lincoln gave no credence to "the orthodox Theologies of the day"; Mrs. Lincoln herself stated that her husband "was not a technical christian." [44]

Some of Herndon's informants discussed this subject more fully. Hardin Bale and other New Salem survivors asserted that Lincoln had read Volney and Paine during his Menard County period and had written "a work on infidelity, denying the divinity of the Scriptures." James H. Matheny, best man at Lincoln's wedding, also knew of this "pamphlet attacking the divinity of christ — special inspiration Revelation &c." From John Hill, editor of Petersburg's Democratic newspaper, Herndon learned the sequel to the story. His father, Sam Hill, he remembered, had read the "infidel book" and realizing how it might damage Lincoln's political career had "morally compelled Mr Lincoln to burn the book, on account of its infamy &c." [45]

[42] Bateman to Holland, June 19, 1865, Holland MSS.

[43] Lincoln "Never let me know much about his Religious aspiration[s] from 1854 to 1860." Herndon to Lamon, March 6, 1870, Lamon MSS.

[44] Speed to Herndon, January 12, 1866; interview of Herndon with Stuart [July 21, 1865?]; interview of Herndon with Cogdal, undated; interview of Herndon with Mrs. Abraham Lincoln [1866?] — all in Herndon-Weik Coll.

[45] Bale to Herndon, May 29, 1865; interview of Herndon with Matheny, May 3, 1866; John Hill to Herndon, June 27, 1865 — all in *ibid.* The truth or falsity of the "infidel book" story is not the main point here. It has never been proved or disproved. Charges of infidelity were made against Lincoln in his own lifetime. During the campaign of 1846 these became so damaging that the Whig candidate for Congress was obliged to issue a public statement on the subject of his religious opinions. Lincoln admitted having unorthodox views and confessed that he had

With such testimony in mind, Herndon stamped into the office of the superintendent of education and charged: *"Bateman,* in order to make Lincoln a technical christian — *you have made him a hypocrite."* Looking "puzzled — or ashamed," the school superintendent backed down from his statement as quoted in Holland's biography. His recollection of Lincoln's words, he confessed with embarrassment, was "not precise — didn't write out in particular and full till after Mr. L. was assassinated." [46] In later conversations with Herndon (records of which are now lost) Bateman apparently retracted even further — but prohibited Herndon from publishing his statement. [47]

Herndon's major concern in this argument was not to prove Lincoln's religious unorthodoxy. His principal objection to the Bateman narrative (and to other such tales) was that it made Lincoln appear two-faced and weak-kneed. If Lincoln really was a Christian, Herndon shrewdly pointed out, there was no conceivable reason why he should have felt obliged to conceal his change of heart, for to reveal his hidden conversion would have won influential political and social support. The ultimate effect of Bateman's rather flimsy testimony was to show up Lincoln as insincere and even a little foolish. [48]

Herndon's wrath was not directed against Bateman, whom he shrugged off contemptuously as "a good man, but a mistaken one," but against Holland. Like most Lincoln scholars up to the present day, Herndon was ignorant of Bateman's detailed written account of the confessional interview; he assumed that Holland had been drawing heavily on his own imagination. The Massachusetts editor, thought Herndon, was overdoing the eulogy. He was trying to build up for the President "a superhuman fame — . . . make Lincoln a perfect — unblemished — spotless angel of God a part of the godhead." Such apotheosis might lead to a dangerous reaction. So extreme a stand was playing into the hands of those who hated Lincoln and who wished to "paint him a perfect hellion — a high criminal — a tyrant — despot — a child of the Devil." [49] Already the Chicago *Times,* arch-Democratic and pro-secessionist, had rumbled editorial threats. The extravagant eulogies of Lincoln by the Republicans seemed to the *Times* motivated by "a hope that they will shelter the follies and criminalities of

---

on occasion ("with one, two or three, but never publicly") attempted to uphold his opinions in argument, but he firmly denied ever having scoffed at religion. (Lacon [Ill.] *Gazette,* August 15, 1846, quoted in *Abraham Lincoln Quar.,* II, 4.)

[46] Herndon to Arnold, December 27, 1882, Arnold MSS.; interview of Herndon with Bateman, undated copy, Lamon MSS.

[47] Barton, *Soul of Abraham Lincoln,* 121–123.

[48] Herndon to Holland, February 24, 1866, Holland MSS.

[49] Herndon to Arnold, November 30, 1866, copy. Herndon-Weik Coll.

the party which elected him." Too much praise of Lincoln, it was hinted, might "provoke inquiry into his own character and that of his administration which would not else have been made." [50]

Herndon shuddered to think what damage could be done to Lincoln's fame if his enemies were to reveal certain episodes in his early life: the illegitimacy of Nancy Hanks, the absence of a marriage record for Abraham Lincoln's parents (it was not discovered until 1878), Lincoln's "derangement" after Ann Rutledge's death, or his 1841 "jilting" of Mary Todd and his subsequent "insanity." What if Lincoln's "infidel book" should be "slumbering — to be sprung . . . when we are dead and gone, and no defence being made — he — L — will go down all time as a writer on Infidelity — Atheism &c — !" [51] Herndon had come to believe strongly in such a possibility, for it would be impossible to hush these incidents up. "I know human nature," he boasted; "hide a mouse in a crack, and shade it, and it will in the minds of men — grow and expand into an Elephant." [52]

This "persevering boring — digging — inquiring — sifting age" would surely ferret out these secrets, and, publicized by Lincoln's detractors, they could do irreparable harm to the fame of the Great Emancipator.

> You need not suppose [Herndon informed a correspondent] . . . that the world will not hunt up — run down and dig out all these things though ten thousand timids should howl against the search & pursuit. . . . Sacred lies will not protect us. Hence as Mr Lincoln's friend I propose to sink and cut a counter mine. I propose to throw overboard in other words all things now & avoid the whale & the shark. . . . Suppose all these things — Lincoln's faults magnified by time through a want of the exact truth at the right moment — mankind in time & during the ages would magnify them — swell them out to immense dimensions and pray — who would be at fault — . . . Lincoln's friends or who? Why Lincoln's friends, who know the truth & told it not. Mr Lincoln has bitter enemies — bitter deeply & thoroughly malicious ones and they are I know biding their time. I propose to cut and clip that by telling how all things are, so that no future lie will have any Effect on mankind.[53]

To minimize the effects of possible future revelations Lincoln's true friends must sink countermines. On Nancy Hanks's (reputed) illegitimacy, for example, Herndon thought it would be best to make an indirect statement. He would perhaps declare that there had been a

[50] Chicago *Times*, December 12, 1865.
[51] Herndon to Arnold, November 20, 1866, copy, Hart MSS.
[52] Herndon to Hart, November 26, 1866, *ibid.*
[53] Herndon to Mr. Hickman, December 6, 1866, copy, Herndon-Weik Coll.

great deal of moral laxity in early Western society, and "in very indirect language — by hint," would add "that some of the near and dear relatives of L. so acted as to crush the soul of Abrm." These statements would be balanced by emphasizing the significance of Lincoln's ascent from lowly origins as an illustration of "the Power of the Individual Man to rise above Conditions & of Democratic Institutions as guardians of fair play in the Eternal Right." [54] By such tactics, Herndon felt, Lincoln's fame could be defended from the most scurrilous Democratic attacks.

[54] Herndon to Hart, December 26, 1866, and January 12, 1867, Hart MSS.

Abraham Lincoln. Miss Ann Rutledge. New Salem. Pioneering, and The Poem

I

O N November 16, 1866, Herndon detonated his first countermine. His high-explosive charge had been prepared with great care. In October, after the adjournment of the Menard County Circuit Court, Herndon had ridden out toward New Salem to see John McNamar, fiancé of Ann Rutledge, whose long absence in the East had reportedly led to her engagement to Lincoln. At once he came to the point of his visit. "Did you know Miss Rutledge?" he asked McNamar. "If so, where did she die?"

Through the open window the old Scotchman pointed a trembling finger toward the west. "There, by that," he began but seemed to choke up with emotion; "there, by *that* currant bush, she died." Romantic Herndon was so moved by the display of feeling that he immediately jumped to the conclusion that McNamar had purchased this farm "in part, if not solely, because of the sad memories that cluster over and around it." [1] Actually the closefisted Scotchman had owned the land before he went East in 1832 and had since buried one wife and married another near that same currant bush.

At McNamar's suggestion Herndon went to see S. C. Berry, from whom he hoped to learn more about the Rutledges. It was a Sunday morning, and he found both Berry and Uncle Jimmie Short, who had known Lincoln since the first day he drifted down the Sangamon, in the Concord church. They directed him to Ann's grave, in the near-by cemetery, a clearing almost lost in the timber.

Herndon, like most of the romanticists of his day, had a fondness

---

[1] Quotations in this and the following paragraphs are from Herndon's fourth lecture, *Abraham Lincoln. Miss Ann Rutledge. New Salem. Pioneering, and THE Poem* (subsequently cited as *Abraham Lincoln. Miss Ann Rutledge*). All citations are to the original newspaper-size broadside published in 1866.

for graveyards. They brought to mind misty but satisfying thoughts of Life, Immortality, and the Transience of Things. Had not Gray's elegy been written in a country churchyard? Here "in the presence of . . . Ann Rutledge, remembering the good spirit of Abraham," Herndon pulled out pencil and paper to record his profound emotions. This Milton might be inglorious, but never mute. He was inspired by "the immediate presence of the ashes of Miss Ann Rutledge, the beautiful and tender dead." Never before had he felt so poetic. "The village of the dead," he mused in somber mood, "is a sad, solemn place, and when out in the country, especially so. Its very presence imposes truth on the mind of the living writer. Ann Rutledge lies buried north of her brother [David Rutledge], and rests sweetly on his left arm, angels to guard her. The cemetery is fast filling with the hazel and the dead."

As court was over, Herndon was free the next day to pursue further his biographical investigations. The morning was "misty, cloudy, foggy and cold," but he got up early and went with a single guide to the abandoned site of New Salem. The town had vanished; its inhabitants were scattered or dead; a forlorn weather-beaten cabin, standing lonely on the high bluff above the Sangamon, was all that remained of the village so intimately identified with Lincoln. Believing in the value of on-the-spot observation, Herndon "sat down to write amid the ruins." It was a hushed day. Over the hill he could hear "the ring of a lone cow-bell, rattling, tapping and sounding here and there." From the east came the monotonous "roll and roar of the Sangamon" pouring over the old milldam. It was fall in Illinois, a time for melancholy and pensive musing. "The frost had scorched the leaves of the forest, and they hung dry, curled and quivering in the winds as they sighed and moaned." It was in an autumnal mood that Herndon pondered over the past, reconstructed in his mind the picture of New Salem as it had once been, and with a tranquil sadness brought life for a moment to the ghosts of yesterday. "Death rides everywhere," he brooded, "but life has begun every where before death comes. Death is a natural condition of life, and life a condition of death. Which is the normal one? Are death and life normal?"

When Herndon returned to Springfield he planned to use his New Salem notes in an exposé-defense of his partner. He proposed to deliver another lecture which would recreate the past, place the New Salem pioneers in their proper light, and unfold "one of the world's most classic stories." In short, he would tell all about "Mr. Lincoln. Miss Ann Rutledge. New Salem. Pioneering, and THE Poem." He was jittery. Already the "Eds & Devils of the *Chicago Times*" had threatened: "Be ware, you Lincoln men! I'll spoil your Hero." They must have the "bad side of these facts" concerning Lincoln's early life.[2] It was urgently necessary that precautions be taken to prevent irreparable damage to Lincoln's fame from these bitter, partisan enemies. Herndon's new lecture was intended to anticipate hostile revelations, to "explain things" about Lincoln in a sympathetic manner, to serve as a countermine against his traducers.

For example, if some day pages from Lincoln's "infidel book" should turn up (and Herndon was sure this was a real possibility), he would already have explained away any unpleasant significance by showing that Lincoln had written the pamphlet in a deep fit of depression — indeed, almost insanity — after Ann Rutledge's death.[3] Or, if the various tales of Lincoln's troubled courtship of Mary Todd in 1841 and of his later domestic difficulties should be published, enemies could not point to Lincoln as a heartless husband or to Mrs. Lincoln as a hopeless termagant. Herndon would have forestalled such criticism by showing that all this unhappiness was the result of Lincoln's earlier infatuation. In this way, he thought, no blame would attach to either of the Lincolns; all would be understood if the world but knew that Abraham's heart lay buried in Ann Rutledge's grave. One of the principal objects of Herndon's lecture would be to put Mrs. Lincoln "properly before the world." "She hates me," Herndon knew, "yet *I can* and *will do her justice.* . . . Poor woman! The world has no charity for her, and yet justice must be done her — being careful not to *Injure* her husband. All that I know ennobles both, and their difficulties sprang from human nature. . . ."[4]

Herndon's thinking on this subject was a muddle. His ideas may have been an unconscious rationalization of his dislike for Mary Lincoln, but there is no reason to think him insincere in believing that the Lincoln-Rutledge romance must be disclosed by a friend of the President in order to prevent hostile revelation at some later day. He was probably incorrect in crediting any systematic plan to debunk Lincoln by exposing his personal or marital difficulties. If the Chicago *Times* had any serious idea of attacking Lincoln's reputation — and that is doubtful — it would probably have tried to expose wartime fraud and corruption in the national government. But nothing that any anti-Lincoln newspaper could publish about the Great Emancipator would

[2] Herndon to Hart, December 28, 1866, Hart MSS.

[3] Herndon's flimsy evidence placed the writing of the "infidel book" before Ann Rutledge's death, but this did not at all suit his plans. "The dates as I have them make *the book* before the crazy spell but my knowledge of Lincoln and my reason tell me that the book was written in 1836." Herndon to Arnold, November 20, 1866, copy, *ibid.*

[4] Herndon to Hart, November 26, 1866, author's draft, Herndon-Weik Coll.

ever have reached the wide audience and achieved the general credence that inevitably attached to any statement made by Lincoln's
law partner and intimate friend. For once Herndon did not realize his
own importance.

II

A Massachusetts visitor hastened the delivery of Herndon's lecture.
Mrs. Caroline Wells Healey Dall had been writing to Herndon since
1860 on woman's rights, abolition, and other reform isms and ologies.
Born in Boston, Mrs. Dall had been a schoolmarm at Miss English's
select seminary for young ladies in Georgetown, D. C., before she
married Charles Henry Appleton Dall, a young Unitarian minister.
After one year of married life, her husband felt an irresistible call to
go as the first Unitarian missionary to India, and he left for the Far
East, depositing his wife in Boston and returning to America only
once in every five years. A glance at Mrs. Dall's photograph perhaps
explains her husband's missionary zeal. This hatchet-faced female
fiercely drew her straggly hair into a bun on the back of her head,
leaving a high forehead as conspicuous as an exposed knoll on the
prairie. With inquisitive eyes, a sharp nose ready to smell out gossip,
a mouth irrevocably fixed in a humorless line, Caroline Dall threw
herself into the business of crusading. Her favorite cause was woman's suffrage, and she made tedious addresses, wrote heavily didactic
books, and for a time edited *Una,* the Boston woman's rights magazine.

In 1866 Mrs. Dall began an extended lecture tour into the Middle
West, and she wrote her old friend Herndon that it would not be difficult to persuade her to speak in Springfield. She could talk about almost any subject, she declared, suggesting — though it would probably be far too radical — a bit of theological criticism titled "Moses &
his Law." [5] Her letter was a calculated blend of flattery and snobbish-
ness, and Herndon was easily taken in. It was almost insulting that
Mrs. Dall should think her Moses lecture too unorthodox for Springfield. With some of the other liberal citizens he would see to it that
the lecturer had a hall, and the more iconoclastic her address the
better.[6]

When Mrs. Dall invaded Springfield, she descended in full force on
Herndon's house and made herself quite at home. Herndon was
charmed with the visitor; Mrs. Herndon's reactions are not on record.
Herndon found in Mrs. Dall the perfect audience, and he expatiated

[5] Mrs. Dall to Herndon, August 28 [1866], *ibid.*
[6] Herndon to Mrs. Dall, September 3, 1866, Dall MSS.

221

at great length on all sorts of subjects: the geological structure of the Mississippi valley; the superiority of Southern poor whites to lesser breeds of men; the brave, bold days of the pioneers; the hardships of the frontier — including "gallinippers" (mosquitoes) with "stings three quarters of an inch long" — and a score of other wild tales.[7] She believed everything he said. Carried away by his own verbosity, Herndon revealed to his visitor the whole sad story of Ann Rutledge's death with the tragic consequences which he believed it had entailed. He could soon say of his Boston guest: "No one in the world but you so well knows my trials — plans — schemes &c. . . ."[8]

Herndon was a brilliant conversationalist — or rather monologist — and Mrs. Dall was deeply impressed. A true provincial Easterner, she was amazed to find in this man who had no drop of New England blood in his veins, who even boasted that he came *"from 'Poor White trash,'"* [9] an observer so keen, so perceptive, so philosophical. It seemed to her that Herndon and his Western associates belonged to a tribe of men different from the Bostonians — "a race desperate, peculiar, undescribed, careless of legal restraints, scarce conscious of family centres, emigrating in hordes, kind-hearted." [10] A woman of freakish romantic enthusiasms, Mrs. Dall was swept away by Herndon's ebullience. "It is well," she reflected in the savage wilds of Illinois, "to be born in Boston, . . . where 'prunes and prisms' form part of one's elementary discipline, but it is also well to go away from Boston, to be purged utterly of provincial egotism and moral bigotries. . . ."[11]

One day when Herndon was busy in court, this prying Bostonian was left alone in his study. Rummaging through his papers, Mrs. Dall discovered two little black notebooks in which Herndon had recorded rumors of a doubtful character (mostly pertaining to Lincoln's alleged illegitimacy) and in which he had jotted down some of Lincoln's off-color ancedotes. Mrs. Herndon surprised the visitor busily reading away. Herndon himself learned of the incident only after Mrs. Dall left for Wisconsin, and he generously said it was all right for her to peep into the books but that she should be warned that many of the "facts" she read were simply memoranda of interviews and many were "false — perverted & maliciously colored." [12]

---

[7] Mrs. Dall, "Pioneering," *Atlantic Mo.*, XIX, 403–416.

[8] Herndon to Mrs. Dall, December 20, 1866, Dall MSS.

[9] "My mother prides herself on her descent — so does my father. . . . I, on the other hand, claim that I have come *from 'Poor White trash.'* . . ." Herndon to Mrs. Dall, December 8, 1866, *ibid.*

[10] *Atlantic Mo.*, XIX, 404.

[11] Mrs. Dall in Boston *Advertiser*, December 15, 1866.

[12] Herndon to Mrs. Dall, November 30, 1866, Dall MSS.

Abraham Lincoln. Miss Ann Rutledge

After his visitor left Herndon began worrying. Mrs. Dall was, after all, a professional writer who might feel tempted to reveal the Ann Rutledge story. At once he requested that she keep Lincoln's love life *"sacredly private,"* but, though she agreed to silence, Herndon doubted whether any woman could keep so delicious a morsel of gossip.[13] Fearing that Mrs. Dall might burst into print at any moment, he hastened the composition of his fourth lecture, incorporating bodily the notes he had made during his visit to New Salem and Concord cemetery. This was such an important lecture he wanted no more partial reports in the newspapers to distort his meaning. Five hundred copies of the entire lecture were printed in advance on newspaper-size broadsides and Herndon secured a copyright.[14]

III

November 16 was Herndon's big day. Those in his courthouse audience who had attended Josh Billings's lecture on "Putty and Varnish" the previous night were now served a very different, though perhaps equally sticky, fare. If Herndon's address was amusing, the humor was not intentional. Attracted by his fancy title (the *Journal* announced it as "A. Lincoln — Miss Ann Rutledge, New Salem — Pioneering, and the poem called Immortality — or, 'Oh! Why should the Spirit of Mortal be Proud'") and by the absence of admission charge, a quite large audience assembled to hear Herndon and listened throughout with most marked attention.[15] Few realized it was a historic occasion.

After repeating his elaborate title, Herndon began bluntly: "Lincoln loved Anna Rutledge better than his own life. . . ."[16] The facts of the sad tale of Lincoln, Ann, and the poem called "Immortality" were drawn from "the memories of men, women and children all over this broad land," now collected, the speaker said, "in fragments in the desk at my office, in the bureau drawers at my home, and in my memory." This "long, thrilling and eloquent story" was too long to relate in a single lecture (even one of fifteen thousand words). No other person, he modestly believed, understood "the many delicate wheels and hidden springs of the story of Lincoln, Miss Rutledge, the Poem, and its relation to the two, in time and place" so well as himself. Since human

[13] Herndon to Mrs. Dall, October 28, 1866, *ibid.;* Herndon to Hart, November 1, 1866, Hart MSS.

[14] "Copy-right Record, Illinois Southern District," II, 100 (MS. records, Lib. of Cong.); Herndon to Hart, November 23, 1866, Hart MSS.

[15] *Illinois State Journal,* November 16 and 17, 1866.

[16] Quotations in the following pages, unless otherwise identified, are from the broadside of Herndon's fourth lecture, *Abraham Lincoln. Miss Ann Rutledge.*

life is most uncertain and the thread of existence might be suddenly snapped, he had consented to speak, write, and utter what he alone knew in order to "put these fragmentary facts and historic events . . . beyond danger." It was his sacred duty to mankind to relate what was "as to artistic beauty, one of the world's most classic stories."

Anticipating criticism, Herndon promised not to "awaken or injure the dead, nor . . . wound or injure the feelings of any living man or woman." He made his defense in advance. "If any man or woman . . . after hearing this lecture, still doubts what is here told, let him or her come to my office and have all skepticism wiped out at once. . . . I am willing that my character among you may stand or fall by the substantial truthfulness of this lecture, *in every particular*." The facts he was about to relate, with the addition of one other set of facts "a little older than . . . [Lincoln] was — some a little younger" (a veiled reference to Herndon's belief in Nancy Hanks's unchastity), would "throw a strong foot-light on the path of Abraham Lincoln, from New Salem, through Springfield, to and through Washington, to the grave." "They . . . throw their rays all over Mr. Lincoln's thoughts, acts, deeds, and life, privately, domestically, socially, religiously and otherwise." "This is my apology for the publication of these facts *now*, and I appeal to time for my defense."

After this preface, Herndon began in earnest the romantic story of Ann, the "beautiful, amiable, and lovely girl of nineteen," who had been courted by three gentlemen of New Salem — Samuel Hill, John McNamar, and Abraham Lincoln. In his printed lecture Herndon discreetly blanked out all the names but Lincoln's. "Circumstances, fate, Providence, the iron chain of sweeping events, so willed it that this young lady was engaged to Mr. Lincoln and Mr. [McNamar] at one and the same time." Without blame in the matter, she suffered from a Victorian "conflict of duties, love's promises, and womanly engagements," which made her "think, grow sad, become restless and nervous." "She suffered, pined, ate not and slept not," and soon she died of a raging fever.

Thus was the whole of Herndon's tragic tale told in the first ten minutes of his lecture. But this was only his point of departure. He then read the notes of his October interviews with McNamar and Berry, not forgetting his musings in the Concord churchyard. Next followed a detailed description of what Lincoln probably saw when he first came to New Salem. Lincoln "*must* have been struck with the beauty of the scene," the speaker conjectured, and this rather tenuous hypothesis afforded the excuse for giving a running picture of the rivers, peaks, and bluffs of the Sangamon country at enormous length.

Abraham Lincoln. Miss Ann Rutledge

Passionately devoted to nature himself, Herndon firmly believed that the climate, terrain, fauna and flora of New Salem had a significant part in shaping Lincoln's personality. This lecture was intended to demonstrate "the influence, & power of mud flowers, & mind *on mind* — Lincoln's mind," showing how environment during adolescence had patterned the life of the future President.[17] Anyway, such a description of New Salem gave the lecturer ample opportunity for demonstrating his eloquence in a "set piece" so popular with the audiences of the grandiloquent days.

Here, began Herndon dramatically, was "the eternal Sangamon, casting and rolling sand and clay, flint and lime-stone, animal and vegetable *debris*, on either shore as it half omnipotently wills, sometimes kissing the feet of one bluff and then washing the other." Here were the plains and bluffs of Illinois, now dotted with barns, orchards, and wheat fields, "where once probably floated the shark or other monster of the deep, or browsed the mastodon and other beasts." Here was New Salem, dead village of the dead. Much of Herndon's oratory sounded like a lawyer's description of a land title: "The only and main street was about 70 feet wide, and the backbone of the hill is about 250 feet across — sufficiently wide for a street, with lots 180 feet deep. . . ." At other points he became extremely "poetic" and dragged in lush purple passages: ". . . the sun was just climbing upward out of the forest in the east, hanging over the timber like a fire-wheel, climbing and rolling up the deep unmeasured immensities above me." Interspersed were philosophical meditations: "Oh! what a history." "And oh! how sad and solemn are New Salem's memories to me. . . . May the spirits of the loved and loving dead here meet and embrace, as they were denied them on earth."

Though at times incoherent, Herndon's description was not inaccurate. He knew this country. Standing on the high bluff above the Sangamon he had seen "the lands . . . covered with rich meadows, wheat, oat and barley fields . . . and as the wings of the wind gently move over the plains and fields, varied shades and colors, deep green, pale green, ripening into straw, salmon, dark straw and bright, in long, wide, wild waves, chase and follow each other as wave runs on and rolls after wave, in the ocean's sport and play." He enumerated at length the flowers of the New Salem region: the wild asters "trembling on their wiry stem in the wind," the blue lobelia, the morning and evening primrose, the mullen, "the blue and purple johnny," the "blue-bell . . . bending in beauty and humility to ground," the "lady-slipper, called the whipporwill shoe," the Judas tree. "All, all these flow-

[17] Herndon to Hart, November 28, 1866, Hart MSS.

225

ers come, bloom, have their passions, form and bear their seeds, and perish; and yet come again . . . ," the lecturer grieved, "and yet, and *yet* how few, oh! how few men and women ever look upon and study these beauties of valley and hill."

IV

From Lincoln's physical surroundings, Herndon turned to his human climate. He took as his text two unfortunate sentences which Holland had employed in relating Thomas Lincoln's many migrations: "When inefficient men become very uncomfortable, they are quite likely to try emigration as a remedy. A good deal of what is called 'the pioneer spirit' is simply a spirit of shiftless discontent." [18] Herndon had little use for Holland's book anyway, and this particular passage seemed to him a deliberate slur on the President's father, indeed, almost an insult to Herndon's own parents. Far better than the Massachusetts editor Herndon understood the epic significance of the frontier in American history. He knew that the pioneers were not inefficient men but rather "Men of capacity, integrity and energy." They had migrated to the new West not because they were too lazy to compete with their Eastern neighbors, "but rather *because they refuse*[d] *to submit to the bad conditions at home.*" The westward movement was a part of "a glorious rebellion for the freedom of man."

One of the basic articles in Herndon's creed was a fixed faith in the Western migrant as archetype of Young America — strong, manly, democratic. Holland's statement revealed to Herndon a complete misunderstanding of the most important current in American history, and, in terms which anticipated the writings of Frederick Jackson Turner, Herndon set about explaining his own theory of the frontier. The Mississippi valley, he began, had been peopled by "four distinct and separate waves — classes of men." First came the Indians. Second were the "bee and beaver hunter, the embodied spirit of western . . . pioneering, . . . wandering Gipsies of the forests." The third class came "as a triple wave": "the religious man, . . . preaching in the wilderness"; the "honest, hardy, thrifty, active and economical farmer"; and the "wild, hardy, honest, genial and social man — a mixture of the gentleman, the rowdy and roysterer." Finally the fourth wave had poured in from the East, the Middle States, and the South, Scotch, Irish, English, German, French, Scandinavian, Italian, Portuguese, and Spanish immigrants, with "the universal, the eternal, indomitable and inevitable 'Yankee,' victorious over all."

[18] Holland, *Life of Abraham Lincoln*, 24.

Abraham Lincoln. Miss Ann Rutledge

At some length Herndon defended the second and third waves of settlers from such calumniators as Holland. His characterization was vivid and precise; he knew these men well. The early Westerner, he told his audience was

> a long, tall, lean, lank man; he is a cadaverous, sallow, sunburnt, shaggy-haired man; his face is very sharp and exceedingly angular; his nose is long, pointed, and keen . . . ; his eyes are small . . . keen, sharp and inquisitive . . . ; he is sinewy and tough . . . ; he is all bone and sinew. . . .

This Westerner "is physically powerful, is cunning, suspicious, brave and cautious," "swifter than the Indian," "a man of acts and deeds, not speech," "stern, silent, secretive and somewhat uncommunicable," "hard to cheat, hard to whip, and still harder to fool."

Herndon did not idealize his pioneers; he knew well their failings.

> These men [he said] could shave a horse's main [*sic*] and tail, paint, disfigure and offer him for sale to the owner in the very act of inquiring for his own horse, that knew his master, but his master recognizing him not. They could hoop up in a hogshead a drunken man, they being themselves drunk, put in and nail down the head, and roll the man down New Salem hill a hundred feet or more. They could run down a lean, hungry wild pig, catch it, heat a ten-plate stove furnace hot, and putting in the pig, could cook it, they dancing the while a merry jig.

But their very defects were virtues, and Herndon burst into a prose poem of praise.

> What! are Grant and Jackson, Douglas and Benton, Clay and *Lincoln,* *inefficient men, coming west from the spirit of shiftless discontent!* . . . *the pioneers,* with their brave hearts and their defiant and enduring souls, are and were efficient men and women — . . . they consumed and burnt the forest and cleared and cleaned it. They had and have energy and creative activity, with capacity, honesty and valor. They created states and hold them to the Union, to liberty and to justice. They and their children after them can and do point with the highest pride and confidence to the deep, broad-laid, tolerant, generous, magnanimous foundations of these mighty several western states, whereon our liberty and civilization so proudly and firmly stand. . . .

"My defence has ended," Herndon calmed down after his outburst. The first two waves of inhabitants had almost completely disappeared; only a few of the third were left, "leaning like grand, gray old towers, with lights on their brow, quietly inclining . . . almost dipping in the deep, the unknown, the unknowable and unfathomable deeps of the future." The fourth class was now abroad in the land. "We thus come and go, and in the coming and the going we have . . . progressed. . . ."

After this long digression Herndon returned to his main theme. "Abraham Lincoln loved Miss Ann Rutledge with all his soul, mind and strength." "They seemed made in heaven for each other. . . ." But after a last pathetic interview, Ann died, and Lincoln's heart was sad and broken.

If Herndon had stopped at this point, he might have avoided much abuse; his story (though not acceptable to modern scholarship) was simply a youthful idyll in picturesque surroundings. It contained nothing discreditable to Lincoln, nor would it have reflected on Lincoln's family. But Herndon was intent on placing his countermines; he was going to put Mrs. Lincoln's domestic difficulties right in the eyes of the world. He went on to conjecture what effect Ann's death must have had on Lincoln. After Ann's demise, he speculated (incorrectly), Lincoln "*never* addressed another woman . . . 'yours affectionately'; and . . . abstained from the use of the word '*love.*' . . . He never ended his letters with 'yours affectionately,' but signed his name, 'your friend, A.Lincoln.' " [19]

After Ann's funeral, said Herndon, Lincoln "slept not, . . . ate not, joyed not." "His mind wandered from its throne. . . . walked out of itself along the uncolumned air, and kissed and embraced the shadows and illusions of the heated brain." It was not exactly the truth to say Lincoln had been totally insane, but certainly he behaved peculiarly. Though "not now discussing the complicated causes of insanity in a scientific method," Herndon thought he could give a probable example of Lincoln's thoughts during this dark period, and he proceeded to invent an imaginary soliloquy — mostly misquotations from Hamlet and King Lear — which Lincoln might have uttered "sharply and incoherently, sadly and wildly."

> What a time for joy to-day in town [Herndon imagined Lincoln probably said]; the men and women looked so happy all through the village. Ah! me. No, not to-day; its night. There's a trick in it, and where's the fallacy? Does nature deal unjustly? I thought not. I'll see and tell myself. 'Tis a rude wind that blows no man joy. Where am I? What strange woods are these. . . . Oh! immensities above me, below me, and around me. The dogs, the very dogs bark at me. . . . What's that

[19] Herndon's statement was unjust and incorrect. Lincoln's letters to his wife were concluded "Affectionately" or "Most affectionately." Sandburg and Angle, *Mary Lincoln, Wife and Widow,* 186–194.

in the mill pond, going splash, splash? 'Twas a fish, I guess. Let's go and feed it, and make it joy, and be happy. . . . She's dead and gone — gone forever. Fare thee well, sweet girl! We'll meet again.

Under the care of Mrs. "Bolin" Green, Lincoln slowly recovered. Wandering over New Salem hillsides, Lincoln must have "walked in daylight — at night time — under the forest tree and beneath the moon's pale, sad glance, contemplating all human life, its laws and springs, its mysterious ways and ends, his own insignificance, the utter insignificance of all men and things, the follies, foibles, ambitions and corruptions, as compared with nature, laws and principles, all embodied in the permanent, and it in the never beginning and never ending Absolute, unconditioned and illimitable." In this mood, Herndon told his hearers, Lincoln gloomily burst forth into the doleful stanzas of the poem "Immortality" (written by one William Knox). So far as can be determined Herndon had no evidence to show that Lincoln even knew this jingle in 1835, but a long quotation of verse made an effective conclusion to a lecture, and he recited it in full. It was a tedious dirge that took fourteen long stanzas to assert that the grave was the common ultimate habitation of infant and maid, king and sage, saint and sinner. It concluded with the mournful reflection:

> 'Tis the wink of an eye, 'tis the draught of a breath,
> From the blossom of health to the paleness of death,
> From the gilded saloon to the bier and the shroud —
> Oh! why should the spirit of mortal be proud?

V

Springfield newspapers discreetly omitted notice of Herndon's address "as the lecture has been published, and is for sale at the news depots in this city." [20] Silent censure in Herndon's home town was coupled with a storm of abuse abroad. Herndon's name became a reproach and a hissing. Few challenged the accuracy of his facts — that was the work of a later generation of historians — but many doubted the propriety of his revelations. These disclosures about Lincoln's love life, these insinuations about his mental collapse, these inferences as to his domestic infelicity were greeted with horrified surprise and shocked incredulity. To Americans Lincoln had become an ideal, almost a religion, very nearly a man who became god. Now it was revealed, from a seemingly indisputable source, that Lincoln had been mere mortal. The vandal had shattered the idol. Even Herndon's artist friend Fran-

[20] *Illinois State Journal*, November 17, 1866.

cis B. Carpenter was distressed by the Ann Rutledge lecture. "It seemed to me," he explained, "an invasion of a sacred *chamber* — a tearing away of the veil which conceals the 'holy of holies.'" [21]

On November 28 the Chicago *Tribune* devoted a full column to the lecture. Feeling a kind of proprietary pride in the apotheosized Lincoln, the Republican newspaper launched into a scathing indictment of the sacrilegious Herndon. Unable to refute his facts, the *Tribune* quoted the more lurid passages from his address, commenting that the whole was "very long and very curious, not so much for its contents as for its character; not so much for the facts it narrates . . . as for the state of mind it reveals on the part of the lecturer in regard to the subject of his discourse." Others agreed that Herndon was prying into the privacy of the dead, that he was attacking a partner who could not defend himself, that he was carelessly handling "the fame of the greatest, & . . . the best man, our country has produced." [22]

Some at once saw how Herndon's lecture reflected on Mrs. Lincoln. "Mr. Wm. H. Herndon is making an ass of himself," Robert Todd Lincoln wrote in panic to Justice David Davis. Aloof and sensitive to publicity, Robert became seriously annoyed and strongly felt "the impropriety of such a publication even if it were . . . all true." Herndon's lecture, he sneered, would be very ludicrous but for the fact that "he speaks with a certain amount of authority from having known my father so long." Could Davis do anything to shut off this running tap of revelation? [23]

Early in December 1866 Robert made a special trip to Springfield in an attempt to hush up the Ann Rutledge story. He had never liked Herndon, and his antipathy was now reciprocated. When Robert was a student at Harvard, Herndon had written him "absurd pseudo philosophical letters" which Lincoln's down-to-earth son ridiculed as insane.[24] Hurt, Herndon came to regard Bob as "a little cold soul — his mother's Child" — and in Herndon's vocabulary there could be no more damning phrase. The air was tense when Robert invaded Herndon's law office. "I think Bob wanted to fight," Herndon recalled later, "but I kept my temper and he couldn't fight, because he had no one to fight with." [25] Apparently the President's son took a high tone. He declared that he never had any doubt of Herndon's good intentions, but since everyone else understood the lecture as a slur on Mrs. Lincoln, he felt quite "justified in asking you to change your expression."

21 Carpenter to Herndon, December 4, 1866, Herndon-Weik Coll.
22 Arnold to Herndon, November 16, 1866, *ibid.*
23 R. T. Lincoln to Davis, November 19, 1866, Davis MSS.
24 R. T. Lincoln to C. L. Conkling, December 17, 1917, C. L. Conkling MSS.
25 Herndon to Weik, undated but written about 1888, Herndon-Weik Coll.

It was the worst possible approach. Stubborn and self-righteous, Herndon could not be browbeaten. Robert's lofty manner made him all the more resolute. Belatedly Lincoln's oldest son appealed to Herndon's better nature. "All I ask," he begged, after returning to Chicago from his fruitless mission, "is that nothing may be published by you, which after *careful consideration* will seem apt to cause pain to my father's family, which I am sure you do not wish to do." "I hope you will consider this matter carefully, My dear Mr Herndon," he entreated, "for once done there is no undoing." [26]

Herndon had already opened the Pandora's box; the evil spirits were out and not even the scientific historians have been able to exorcise them. The Ann Rutledge story spread rapidly. All the papers carried stories, and most scolded or spoke harshly of the daring author. Only a few old-timers from New Salem days approved. Though he had corrections to make on details, Ann's brother, R. B. Rutledge, praised Herndon's address as "bold manly and substantially true." George Spears, who confessed that he was ignorant of much of the story, was sure the lecture had "nothing in it but what is strictly true." Many of the Menard County pioneers, believing themselves that it was impossible to overdraw the picturesque characteristics of "New Salem in its palmyist [*sic*] days," lauded Herndon's effort as "a master success." [27]

"Regarded as an effort to interest, flatter and, possibly, surprize the people of New Salem," John A. Andrew, war governor of Massachusetts judged, Herndon's lecture was doubtless very good. "But, if regarded as addressed to the world at large, with the design to throw a strong light into the hidings of a great man's heart," the governor continued, "the lecture is a failure." It was "too scattering, lacking in unity, closeness both of thought & style." And Andrew coined an epigram which the lecturer could well have borne in mind: "It speculates on the man, instead of walking with him his own way." [28]

Many of Herndon's correspondents were brutally blunt in their criticism. Judge Theophilus Lyle Dickey, one of Lincoln's best friends in the old days, though more recently a political opponent, wrote curtly to the author:

> Thank you for copy of that fancy lecture — Romance is not your forte — The few grains of history stirred into that lecture — in a plain narrative would be interesting — but I dont like the garnishments.[29]

[26] R. T. Lincoln to Herndon, December 13 and 24, 1866, *ibid.*

[27] Rutledge to Herndon, November 18, 1866; Spears to Herndon, November 21, 1866; W. G. Greene to Herndon, November 21, 1866; T. W. McNeely to Herndon, November 28, 1866 — all in *ibid.*

[28] Andrew to Mrs. Dall, December 26, 1866, Dall MSS.

[29] Dickey to Herndon, December 8, 1866, Herndon-Weik Coll.

A long warning letter came from Grant Goodrich, the Chicago law-yer associated with Lincoln in the sand-bar case. "In my opinion," he boldly informed Herndon, "you are the last man who ought to attempt to write a life of Abraham Lincoln." Herndon was too close to the great man to understand him. The Ann Rutledge lecture Goodrich feared to be the portent of worse to come. Surely Herndon did "not realize what an injury & injustice you did to the memory of your dead friend, & mortification you caused his friends, but especially his widow & children." For good measure the Chicagoan added that Herndon's style was purely legal and ill suited for a literary project. The lecture, Goodrich stated frankly, "reads as if it had been jerked out, word by word — it gives one the sense that you have in riding in a lumber wagon over a frozen road — or the noise made in machinery when a cog has been broken." [30]

Even Mrs. Dall, whose prying had in a sense precipitated the lec-ture, regretted that Herndon had published. As a confidential revela-tion from his own lips the Lincoln-Rutledge romance had been most instructive, but now, in cold print before a hostile world, it "would give a false impression of the *proportion* of things." Herndon should have sent her his manuscript for revision; after all, he did not under-stand the universal mind.[31] But as Herndon's friend — and as an in-veterate publicity seeker — Mrs. Dall felt a certain obligation, and when Massachusetts papers carried a bitter attack on Herndon with the insinuation that he was Ann Rutledge's disappointed lover, now venting his jealousy on his successful rival, she sprang to his defense. In a long public letter to the Boston *Advertiser* Mrs. Dall strongly sup-ported the truth and the propriety of the Ann Rutledge story as Hern-don had revealed it. "It could," she thought, "no more be left out of a true life of Lincoln than Dante's love for Beatrice, or Petrarch's love for Laura. . . ." Boston criticism of Herndon was misinformed, for in her venture into the wild west she had "found that the life of Abra-ham Lincoln was something very different from what we at the east had imagined." "We must trust Mr. Herndon," she emphasized, "be-cause Abraham Lincoln trusted him." "He is a man of genius, and we shall have to be patient with his individualities. . . . The wilderness had educated him. The wilderness must pronounce upon him." [32]

When a copy of that letter reached the wilderness of Springfield, one of Herndon's fellow townsmen lost no time in pronouncing on

[30] Goodrich to Herndon, December 9, 1866, *ibid*. Stung, Herndon retorted that his critic was "an exceedingly weak headed brother." Herndon to Goodrich, De-cember 10, 1866, copy, *ibid*.

[31] Mrs. Dall to Herndon, December 15, [1866], *ibid*.

[32] Boston *Advertiser*, December 15, 1866.

both Mrs. Dall and Herndon. "With no disposition to depreciate Mr. Herndon, or to wound his feelings," the anonymous correspondent began meekly enough, "respect for my own State and for the memory of Mr. Lincoln compels me to say, that Mr. Herndon's lectures are regarded here as caricatures upon the life, habits and manners of the late President, and there can be no doubt whatever that if Mr. Herndon ever completes his biography it will be characterized by the same rambling, conceited qualities that are so conspicuous in his lectures." All of Lincoln's Springfield friends, continued the writer, deplored Herndon's efforts. "If you have read the sketches of Mr. Herndon's lectures, you have seen a fair picture of the man. He is 'Bill Herndon,' a man *sui generis*, but neither entitled to be a representative of Springfield or the West, nor a biographer of any other man than himself." "His lectures are *Bill-iania*," the letter concluded viciously, "and his book will be Billy-Herndoniana — neither more nor less." [33]

VI

When Leonard Swett visited Boston in December 1866, he found everybody talking about Herndon, Lincoln, and Ann Rutledge. People were asking: Who is Herndon? What is he trying to do? [34] Herndon's name now had news value, and war correspondent George Alfred Townsend, lecturing in the Middle West on "Europe Armed," was not a man to overlook this chance. Townsend was an old hand at ferreting out "inside" stories. His sharp eyes, his prying nose, his long prodding fingers went well with an insatiable appetite for off-the-record interviews and behind-the-scenes revelations. Signed with the pseudonym "Gath," his syndicated columns appeared in all the important papers, giving the low-down on the great and the near-great. During the Civil War as correspondent for the New York *Herald* Townsend had roamed at large with the Union army, reporting human incidents and poignant soldier anecdotes, later collected in his *Campaigns of a Non-Combatant*. After Lincoln's murder he had written vividly of the escape, capture, and death of the assassin Booth. Early in 1866 "Gath" had gone abroad to report the Austro-Prussian war; when that conflict had lasted only a disappointing seven weeks, he had returned to America for a lecture series.

Springfield was on his itinerary, and "Gath" was a little amused at the countrified Illinois capital, "a market town, where eggs were duly

[33] Letter dated January 25, 1867, clipped from Boston *Advertiser*, Lincoln National Life Foundation.
[34] Swett to Herndon, December 22, 1866, Herndon-Weik Coll.

exchanged for calico, and the father of the family reported himself twice a year to get stone-drunk." In such a place he was surprised to find a man like Herndon. In the dreary law office with its view "of stable-roofs and dingy back yards," of "ash-heaps and crowing cocks and young Americans sledging or ball-playing," Townsend discovered this "saffron-faced, blue-black haired man . . . , bearded bushily at the throat, disposed to shut one eye for accuracy in conversation, his teeth discolored by tobacco, and over his angular features, which suggest[ed] Mr. Lincoln's in ampleness and shape, the same half-tender melancholy."

During his two days in Springfield Townsend spent half his time with Herndon. Never a reticent man, Lincoln's partner told his interviewer enough about the Great Emancipator to "stagger all . . . [Townsend's] notions of the dead President's character." The reporter was not so staggered as to forget to take notes, and "Gath" reported his long conversations with Herndon in a letter that spread over two and one-half columns of the front page of the New York *Tribune*. Townsend enthusiastically praised Herndon, and he drew on his recollections for incidents of Lincoln's "moccasin days," his law practice, and his political career. Having asked particularly about Lincoln's "tenderness of nature," Townsend learned all the details of the Lincoln-Rutledge romance, to which he added some trimmings of his own invention. So interesting was "Gath's" letter that it was republished in the weekly *Independent* and later was issued in pamphlet form as *The Real Life of Abraham Lincoln. A Talk with Mr. Herndon, His Late Law Partner.*[35]

Mrs. Dall felt she was missing out on a good thing. If Townsend after two days with Herndon could produce a pamphlet, surely an account of her visit in Herndon's own home would have far more news value. She whipped out a long, wordy, and extremely flattering article about Herndon and Lincoln which appeared in the *Atlantic Monthly* for April 1867 under the title "Pioneering." In fourteen closely printed pages Mrs. Dall reproduced almost verbatim the conversations she had had with Herndon. Her memory was as accurate as her judgment was weak. She believed every improbable tale Herndon had told, and she revealed to her readers an embellished epic of two men of Springfield, "prepared, it would seem, by the Divine Hand, . . . who were to love each other with such passion, trust each other with such implicit faith." On and on the Massachusetts author went, extolling Herndon as the best representative of this new, strange race of Westerners.

---

[35] New York *Tribune*, February 15, 1867; *Independent*, February 28, 1867.

She had examined Herndon's Lincoln records unashamed of "the tears that started as . . . [she] read." From their perusal she now understood that the key to Lincoln's life lay in "those facts of his history which transpired before his own birth" (an allusion to the rumors of Lincoln's illegitimacy which she had surreptitiously learned from Herndon's little black notebooks) and in his tragic devotion to Ann Rutledge. This tale of "the only girl he ever loved" was recounted in sickly-sweet detail. All through the article Mrs. Dall stressed the importance of Herndon's influence on his partner. With Herndon as mentor Lincoln had been guided to the pinnacle of power. "He had been led by a hard, dark way; he had expiated in his own person, not only his own sins, but those of all his ancestry, as he was hereafter to expiate those of his nation." When better saints were made, Mrs. Dall would make them.

VII

Townsend's and Mrs. Dall's articles kept Herndon and the Ann Rutledge story before the reading public. A few ardent defenders appeared. The Rochester *Express* exalted Herndon as "one of the noblest representatives, intellectually and morally, of the America which is to be." His book on Lincoln, the editor felt, was "a great history in the hands designed by Providence to do the work, for, in all that goes to make up the highest manhood, the biographer is probably the superior of the subject." [36] The Indiana congressman-spiritualist, Robert Dale Owen, found in the Ann Rutledge lecture "the key-note to all Lincoln's after-life." After the first shock wore off, Francis B. Carpenter decided that "Lincoln's love for Ann Rutledge, may yet loom up in history like Dante's for Beatrice, or Petrarchs for Laura." [37]

These were exceptions. To most men Herndon appeared a mocker, an iconoclast, a defiler of the dead. One irate soul advised Carpenter to expunge the report of Herndon's first lectures which had been included in *Six Months at the White House;* even Herndon's name was anathema. [38] It is difficult to recapture the intensity of this feeling. It

[36] Rochester *Express*, November 24 and December 21, 1866. "If you are offended at being called the 'probable' superior of L. I can only say that the 'probably' was put in for the public, but that my own opinions would not have even that qualifying word." D. W. Wilder (editor of the *Express*) to Herndon, December 21, 1866, Herndon-Weik Coll.

[37] Owen to Herndon, January 22, 1867; Carpenter to Herndon, December 24, 1866, *ibid.*

[38] Carpenter to Herndon, February 15, 1867, *ibid.*

can be understood only if one remembers that Lincoln to his country-men was more than a man with mortal failings; he had become in a real sense an American demigod.

The most devastating public attack on Herndon came from Scot-land. The Reverend James Smith had been minister at Springfield's First Presbyterian Church in the fifties. Mrs. Lincoln and the children had regularly attended his services, and Abraham Lincoln had rented a pew in the church. President Lincoln had appointed Smith American consul to Dundee, Scotland, where he was still stationed in 1867. When the Dundee newspapers published an account of Herndon's Ann Rutledge lecture, Smith became indignant. His anger grew red hot upon receiving shortly afterward an impertinent letter from Hern-don. Having heard that Smith claimed to have converted Lincoln dur-ing his Springfield ministry, Herndon addressed to the preacher a most impudent inquiry. Did the Reverend James Smith have "any writings — letters or other such like evidence" to show that Lincoln was won to a "belief that the Bible was God's *special miraculous revelation*"? If Lincoln had been converted as it was claimed, Herndon jeered, "why didn't he join your Church, the 1st Presbyterian Church of the city of Springfield?" "I knew you as a gentleman in this city for several years," Herndon concluded his letter. "I knew you as a Christian. As you were a gentleman before you were a Christian, I ask you in that capacity *first* to answer these questions, if you *please,* and then I ask you ditto as a Christian to answer the questions — if you please." [39]

The insolence of Herndon's letter put Smith into a veritable rage. He vowed to unmask this monster who dared attack the memory of the Great Martyr. Lincoln "did avow his belief in the Divine Author-ity and Inspiration of the Scriptures," he informed Herndon, and as Lincoln's pastor he could tell many interesting incidents connected with his conversion. He added stiffly: "I am constrained however most respectfully to decline choosing you as the medium through which any such communications shall be made by me." The reason was Ann Rut-ledge. Smith had read "with feelings of mingled indignation and sor-row" this base effort "calculated to do the character of that great and good man an incalculable injury, deeply to wound the feelings of his heart broken widow and her orphan boys, and to place that whole family . . . in a most unenviable light." Herndon's statements would show that Lincoln had never loved the bride whom he had led "to the hymeneal Altar"; he was trying to brand the Lincoln children as "sons

[39] Chicago *Tribune,* March 6, 1867, quoting Herndon's letter to Smith, De-cember 20, 1866.

of a man who never loved their mother." The lecture was "a most cruel and . . . malignant attack upon his heart stricken widow."

"Oh! Sir," the irate preacher continued, "was it not enough that . . . [Mrs. Lincoln] should be overwhelmed and stricken to the earth by the dreadful . . . blow which had fallen upon her, in the Cruel death of her husband, but you must Come on the scene and mingle your poisoned chalice into that cup of woe which she must drink even to the dregs?" "The assassin Booth," Smith concluded with a flourish, "by his diabolical act unwittingly sent the illustrious martyr to glory, honor and immortality, but his false friend has attempted to send him down to posterity with infamy branded on his forehead, as a man who . . . was destitute of those feelings and affections without which there can be no real excellency of character."[40]

Herndon filed the preacher's letter away unanswered, making only the marginal note: "Foolish This man left a base Character here." Doubtless fearing just such silence, the parson had taken the precaution of publishing his letter in the Dundee *Advertiser*, "hoping its circulation will place our beloved President and his family in a proper light before those who have read the shameful attack made upon them by the author of the Ann Rutledge romance." As Smith had hoped, the Chicago *Tribune* copied his bull against Herndon and it was republished in most of the major American newspapers.

Widowed Mary Lincoln, alone now in the world, her diseased mind already beginning to give way under her troubles, had secluded herself in Chicago. Her only interests in life were the love of her sons and the memory of their father. Herndon's Ann Rutledge lecture came as a stunning blow of vindictive cruelty. She understood it as a covert attack upon herself. Urgently she begged Justice David Davis, administrator of her husband's estate, to direct Herndon's "*wandering* mind" to the impropriety of his remarks. Ann Rutledge, she was convinced, was only a myth, invented to suit the diabolical plans of Herndon. "This is the return for all my husband's kindness to this miserable man!" Mrs. Lincoln raged. "Out of pity he took him into his office, when he was almost a hopeless inebriate and although he was only a drudge, in the place — he is very forgetful of his position and assumes, a confidential capacity towards Mr. Lincoln."[41]

When the Chicago *Tribune* printed Smith's denunciad of Herndon, Mrs. Lincoln almost wept for joy. "W. H. may consider himself a ruined man," she exulted; "in attempting to disgrace others the vials of

[40] Smith to Herndon, January 24, 1867, Herndon-Weik Coll.
[41] Mary Lincoln to Davis, March 4, 1867, Davis MSS.

wrath will be poured upon his own head." Smith's letter would make
him rue his lies about Lincoln. "[I]f W. H. utters another word and is
not silent with his infamous falsehoods in the future," Mary stormed,
"*his* life is not worth living for I *have* friends, if his low soul thought
that my great affliction had left me without them. In the future he
may well say his prayers. 'Revenge is sweet,['] especially to womankind, but there are some of mankind left who will wreak it upon him.
He is a dirty dog. . . ." [42]

VIII

Herndon squirmed under criticism. It was so unjust, he felt, so un-
called for. If people understood the whole situation, he was sure critics would see that he was really defending both Lincoln and Mrs. Lincoln. Publicly he remained surprisingly silent. Smith's attack went by
unanswered, since a reply would "drag Mrs Lincoln into the field, because Smith took refuge under her — fought from behind her." [43]

He made no public defense of himself or his lecture. "I never stoop
to defend my motives — purposes, & plans," he told Governor Andrew,
"and never authorized others so to do — *never;* and will not." [44] Mrs.
Dall was almost frantic in her wish to fire another volley at his assail-
ants, but Herndon discouraged her.

> I know all [he modestly wrote her] and what is best for Mr L. & the
> great ever living universal head & heart. I shall do no one wrong but
> in the end liberal & enlarged Justice. I cannot now open my ideas —
> plans — purposes — schemes &c. . . . but I can well bear scolding —
> angry words made hastily. . . . I have never yet defended myself
> from any charge. I generally sit down and bide my time — the good
> people's returning reason. A true man cannot be more than momentarily
> injured. If I had my way I should say to all my friends "Be silent — vic-
> tory is yours to-morrow." [45]

Outwardly calm, Herndon was really deeply hurt. Everywhere he
fancied slights and imagined insults. For several months he had been
corresponding with Charles Godfrey Leland, author of the "Hans
Breitmann" ballads. For some days after the publication of the Ann
Rutledge lecture Leland was too busy to write, and Herndon struck a
martyr's pose. "I fear — *suspicion* — that I have wounded beyond heal

[42] Mary Lincoln to Davis, March 6, 1867, *ibid.*
[43] Herndon to Lamon, March 6, 1870, Lamon MSS.
[44] Herndon to Andrew, December 29, 1866, Andrew MSS.
[45] Herndon to Mrs. Dall, December 20, 1866, Dall MSS.

. . . my good friend Chas. G. Leland. The Lecture did it, I suppose, for I have been as kind to him as I know how to be to any man . . . if such things must be, so be it. I cannot be *liar* — I must be brave, and keep my own self respect, or sink." [46]

"I am the only man on the world who knows how to defend Lincoln," Herndon complained to Hart, "and yet I am 'cussed' by those who are his friends." "When you hear men scolding me," he requested, "*please* say to them — 'Do you know what you are talking about? Have faith in the only man who knows what to do to hedge — dodge — explain — modify, or deny &c.'" "No true man ever lived that was not abused," Herndon consoled himself. "Why should I hope to escape." But he would be brave; he would suffer. And above all, "My Records of Mr. Lincoln *shall go down* the files of time, if I have to send them to England — Russia, unless confiscated by false men and burned before landing &c." [47]

Only to a few friends did Herndon explain the real motives behind his Ann Rutledge lecture. "You will now begin to detect a purpose in my 4th — late, Lecture, not guessed at before," he wrote Hart; it was to show up Mrs. Lincoln in her proper light. He went on to explain his theory of countermines which friends of Lincoln ought to lay in order to defeat future attack. [48] A similar defense went to Carpenter. "I acknowledge that what I said [in the Ann Rutledge lecture] is calculated to create a twinge of nerve," Herndon admitted, but "I have weighed results — fully — fully; and I bide my time." [49]

Since 1864 a close friend of Lincoln's, Isaac N. Arnold, had been writing a biography of the President. This tall, blue-eyed Republican, a former congressman from Chicago, represented the best type of New England stock in the West. A serious, stiff man, it was said by a witty reporter, not altogether fairly, that his greatest delight was "the daily reflection that he is Isaac N. Arnold, of Illinois." [50] If pompous, Arnold was also a sincere man of indisputable integrity. He had known Herndon for years, and, though he failed to acknowledge his indebtedness, had drawn on Lincoln's partner for many of the facts used in *The History of Abraham Lincoln, and the Overthrow of Slavery,* which he published in 1866.

Herndon liked Arnold's book and he liked its author. He sent the Chicagoan an advance copy of his Ann Rutledge lecture, and his

[46] Herndon to Hart, December 12, 1866, Hart MSS.
[47] Herndon to Hart, December 28, 1866, January 12 and March 2, 1867, *ibid.*
[48] Herndon to Hart, November 26, 1866, author's draft, Herndon-Weik Coll.
[49] Herndon to Carpenter, December 11, 1866, author's draft, *ibid.*
[50] "Castine" [Noah Brooks], in Sacramento *Union,* April 22, 1864.

friend was fascinated by this "strange chapter in Mr Lincoln's history." "You verify what I have said of Mr Lincoln," Arnold wrote, "that had he lived in the days of mythology he would have been placed among the gods." He admired the lecture — but he warned the author that the Ann Rutledge story would be misunderstood. Some would think Herndon was maligning his dead partner, but "I know you could not intentionally do him injustice." [51]

Arnold was an acquaintance of long standing, and Herndon thought his friendship worth saving. In a rather peculiar fashion he set about removing Arnold's apprehensions. Again Herndon explained his theory of countermines. Those who considered the revelations in the Ann Rutledge lecture extreme, Herndon informed his shocked correspondent, did not realize that the situation was really "much worse than I painted it." Did Arnold know that "Lincoln wrote a work — a book on *Infidelity*" which might any day turn up to expose Lincoln "as a writer on Infidelity — Atheism &c — !" Had he heard that "Mr. Lincoln was '*as crazy as a loon*' in *this city in 1841*" over his engagement to Mary Todd? Did he realize that "Lincoln told his wife that he did not love her; she was cognizant of the fact that Lincoln loved an other. Did you know that the *Hell* through which Lincoln passed was caused by these things?" "Did you know that Mr. Lincoln was informed of *some facts* that took place in Kentucky *about the time he was born* . . . that eat [*sic*] into his nature. . . ." All these truths would sooner or later out; people would learn them somehow, if not from Lincoln's friends, then from his enemies. Anyway, what real biographer would "have Mr. Lincoln a sham — . . . a symbol of an unreality?" "Mr. Lincoln must stand on truth or not stand at all." [52]

Aghast at Herndon's hints and insinuations, Arnold could only give a lame warning against using gossip for facts. Now that Lincoln was dead and could no longer defend himself he feared Herndon's writings would be used to attack the fame of the Great Emancipator. [53] Herndon welcomed the chance for another explanation of his motives. The North, he believed, was trying to "make Mr Lincoln a perfect being — a supernatural man"; the South and Southern sympathizers were saying he was a devil. Lincoln would "travel down all time misapprehended . . . and pray whose fault will it be? Lincoln's friends." Between vilification and eulogy lay the proper course for a biographer. Those who attacked Lincoln most viciously were no worse than those "Blind bat eyed hero worshipers — timid creatures, orthodox theolo-

[51] Arnold to Herndon, November 16, 1866, Herndon-Weik Coll.
[52] Herndon to Arnold, November 20, 1866, copy, Hart MSS.
[53] Arnold to Herndon, November 22 and 23, 1866, Herndon-Weik Coll.

gians, and other frigid souled men" who were trying to idealize the President. This plaster saint was "a sham — a lie — a fraud & a cheat." Herndon was sure his partner, scorning all subterfuge and suppression, would have said: " 'Write my life truthfully as I . . . *acted it out.* Come no shams.' " [54]

[54] Herndon to Arnold, November 30, 1866; Herndon to Carpenter, December 11, 1866; Herndon to Mr. Hickman, December 6, 1866 — all author's drafts, *ibid.*

CHAPTER *xvi*

Several Hells

I

NOTHING so infuriated Herndon as a challenge to his omniscience. When the accuracy of his memory was questioned, he took honest dissent as a personal affront. If his recollections were doubted, he did not question his own facts but the motives of his assailant. He felt himself "above all just attacks — all truthful assaults." [1] As the years passed, Herndon came to consider himself the sole authority on all things Lincolnian. There is the bitter taste of truth in an unfriendly characterization that Herndon "proclaimed himself as the only living man who knew all about Lincoln, [and] assumed that he had been Lincoln's conscience-keeper." [2]

From those he aided, Herndon demanded unquestioning acceptance of his version of events. He had greatly assisted J. G. Holland, who acknowledged his indebtedness. Though he followed Herndon on many matters, the Massachusetts editor felt obliged to reject some Herndonian interpretations. On one point he thought that his Springfield informant had made a factual error. According to Herndon, in the senatorial campaign of 1854 after a joint debate at Peoria Lincoln and Douglas had agreed to observe a truce on public speaking for the remainder of the canvass. Herndon believed that Lincoln had withdrawn from the campaign but that Douglas, having secured the silence of his principal rival, had continued to speak in defense of the Kansas-Nebraska act. Holland found evidence that both Lincoln and Douglas had been active all during the remainder of the 1854 election, and in his biography he rejected the Peoria truce story related by "One authority" — identified in a footnote as Herndon. [3] (Holland was

---

[1] Herndon to Mrs. Dall, February 23, 1867, Dall MSS.
[2] Milton Hay, quoted in Barton, *Paternity of Lincoln*, 361.
[3] Holland, *Life of Abraham Lincoln*, 141.

probably correct, for modern scholars do not accept Herndon's account.[4])

For Holland to doubt the accuracy of his memory struck Herndon as a blow in the face. When he cooled off enough to write coherently, Herndon was still almost boiling. "What I told you in every-thing I *know* to be true," he railed at Holland. "But suppose I was mistaken, *you should have written to me*, requesting me to look up the matter &c. and explain before you denied what I said, leaving me on the record in *rather an unpleasant* fix I assure you: it stings." The circumstances called for a public apology, but Herndon declared he would be content with a private "letter, so that I shall *feel* cleared at all events." [5]

Courteously Holland promised to study Herndon's evidence and to make a revision if a new edition of his biography was published. When months went by and no retraction appeared, Herndon became more and more enraged. Holland had treated him shabbily.[6] He would have some vindication. In December 1866 Herndon published an open letter in the newspapers to answer the infamous slur on his veracity. Holland's widely circulated biography had placed Herndon "wrongly on a particular record." He repeated his evidence on the Peoria truce (all belated reminiscence, none contemporary). "Feeling that I have been badly treated, and misplaced, as it were, wantonly, on the record," he concluded, "I am compelled in self-defense to publish this letter." [7]

This rather aimless shot of Herndon's was a trifling matter, yet it marked the beginning of a Herndon-Holland feud that was to have a decisive influence on the pattern of Lincoln biography. As editor of *Scribner's Monthly,* Holland was one of the literary pundits of his day; he was not a man to be offended lightly or denounced over a quibble. Herndon's absolute conviction of infallibility transformed a former friend into an outright opponent.

II

With Herndon indiscretion was almost a habit. For some months the distinguished Boston house of Ticknor & Fields had been angling to publish his Lincoln biography. It was an association that could have been mutually profitable. For Herndon it would have meant a reputa-

[4] Angle, "The Peoria Truce," Ill. State Hist. Soc., *Jour.,* XXI, 500–505; E. E. East, "The 'Peoria Truce': Did Douglas Ask for Quarter?" *ibid.,* XXIX, 70–75.
[5] Herndon to Holland, February 24, 1866, Holland MSS.
[6] Herndon to Hart, January 12, 1867, Hart MSS.
[7] *Illinois State Journal,* December 28, 1866.

ble, widely known publisher; for Ticknor & Fields, an important addition to their list of writers. A representative of the firm made a special trip to Springfield to visit Herndon, ascertain his plans, and secure his cooperation.

Publishers were awake to the possibilities of the Lincoln market. After the assassination there had been an immense demand for steel engravings of the Great Emancipator to hang in solemn state above the parlor mantels in a million Northern homes. During the President's lifetime few if any engravings had been made, and publishers were caught unprepared for his death and deification. The first answer to the need was to engraft Lincoln's head on the body of other notables of whom plates and lithograph stones had already been prepared. There is a series of amusing engravings in which Lincoln's head is superimposed on the shoulders of Buchanan, Van Buren, and Calhoun.[8] At the time of Lincoln's death William E. Marshall, a New York artist, had been studying in Paris, but he caught the first boat for America in order to paint the martyred President. An engraving was quickly made from his portrait, and Ticknor & Fields arranged to publish and distribute it. As the Lincoln expert on Ticknor & Fields's list, Herndon was sent proof of the engraving and — as the firm thought, at any rate — seemed to endorse it as the best likeness of Lincoln.[9]

At the same time Francis B. Carpenter was preparing a competing portrait of Lincoln. From his experience in painting the signing of the Emancipation Proclamation, Carpenter was able to give his picture literal accuracy, though to some it seemed "to lack emotion, to lack character." [10] Engraved by Halpin, Carpenter's Lincoln was put on the market as a rival to Marshall's painting. Critical opinion was sharply divided, and the conflicting claims of the two artists became the subject of an unseemly newspaper squabble.

It was not Herndon's fight, and self-interest would have taught him to abide by his tacit endorsement of the Marshall portrait. But Carpenter had a winsome way of asking advice, and Herndon was very susceptible to flattery. When Carpenter sent proofs of his engraving and humbly begged suggestions and criticisms, Herndon injudiciously replied: "It looks to me, and *is* a better portrait — and likeness than Marshall's." Stung by newspaper criticism of his painting, Carpenter, without asking Herndon's consent, published these private letters in

---

8 W. E. Baringer, "The Birth of a Reputation," *Abraham Lincoln Quar.,* IV, 218–220.

9 John Spencer Clark to Herndon, October 12, 1866, Weik MSS.

10 New York *Tribune,* December 28, 1866.

the New York *Tribune*,[11] and Herndon was spread on the record as endorsing the engraving issued by a rival to his own publisher. Ticknor & Fields not unnaturally felt aggrieved and dropped negotiations for publishing Herndon's life of Lincoln.[12]

In spare moments Herndon still attempted to work on his biography. During December 1866 he began writing a projected fifth lecture concerning Lincoln's childhood, and he hoped it would "scribble itself out this month — or die attempting to be born." [13] This new effort was "*to be* on [Lincoln's] . . . infant & boyhood Education — *the means — methods, & struggles* of . . . his mind — to know & to develop itself." At one time Herndon seems to have toyed with the idea of publishing his five lectures as an analytical study of Lincoln. They had not been written in chronological order, but if rearranged he thought the five would form a brief outline of Lincoln's intellectual development. As the author of these penetrating lectures and as the compiler of Lincoln records "*worth one million* of *dollars,*" Herndon felt he could rest in the comforting assurance that he had "rendered mankind some 5 cents worth of service." [14]

But he had trouble with the lecture on Lincoln's childhood. He made jottings, even wrote out some paragraphs, but he could not finish it. His Kentucky evidences were so flimsy, so incomplete. He lacked so many important details. Perhaps he ought to go to Kentucky and find firsthand information. He made plans for the trip, but something always interfered. The notes for his fifth lecture were stuffed into his bureau drawer, where they gathered dust as Herndon turned his thoughts to other subjects.[15]

After 1867 Herndon lost interest in his biography. He found writing difficult, he had no publisher, and, after his Ann Rutledge lecture, the press was sharply hostile. Charles H. Hart kept nagging at him to finish his book. The young Philadelphian had come to think of Herndon's work chiefly as a vehicle for the publication of his own Lincoln bibliography. Herndon needed, as he himself confessed, "kicking — scolding — 'Kussing' &c in order to make [him] . . . trot along briskly with head and tail up, gaily snorting along the great road of life." [16] He still talked grandly about his Lincoln biography, and he spent much time

[11] *Ibid.,* January 16, 1867.
[12] Carpenter to Herndon, January 16, 1867, Herndon-Weik Coll.
[13] Herndon to Hart, December 4, 1866, Hart MSS.
[14] Herndon to Hart, November 26, 1866, author's draft, Herndon-Weik Coll.
[15] "I never completed my 5th lecture — was . . . too lazy — the notes of it . . . now lie in my drawer." Herndon to Lamon, February 25, 1870, Lamon MSS.
[16] Herndon to Lamon, February 26, 1869, *ibid.*

in showing off his manuscripts and relics. But though he rather irritably assured Hart that he had not "given up *all* or 'any notion' of writing the life of Presd Lincoln," talking was as far as Herndon ever got. Finally Hart got tired of waiting and entered into a partnership with Andrew Boyd for the publication of a joint Lincoln bibliography.[17] There was no one left who urged Herndon to make the race, and he put his projected biography out to pasture.[18]

III

By 1865 whatever fondness Herndon once had for the law had disappeared. He still had to spend tedious hours greeting clients, digging out precedents, and drawing up briefs, but his mind was elsewhere. For a time after Lincoln's death Herndon's association with Charles S. Zane was continued, and with Herndon as senior partner, the law practice went along a monotonous but declining way. Zane was popular and able, but his mind was on politics. Herndon, too, was competent, but he dreaded the laborious work of the law office. When court adjourned, he rejoiced that he could be "free, at least for *one* day." [19] Herndon's dwindling interest was reflected in the firm's business. During the war years Herndon had averaged more than twenty cases each year in the federal circuit court at Springfield; in eight years after 1865, he appeared in a total of only twelve.[20] In the Sangamon circuit court, where Zane was the more active, the partners were able to keep a steady practice, though most of their suits were of a petty sort — minor divorce cases, partition of estates, collection of small debts.

After 1860 few lawyers rode the circuits, but to keep up his income Herndon regularly attended the court at Petersburg. He could live with his brother-in-law, and any fees that came his way would be clear profit. He hung around the Petersburg courthouse, often tipsy, or lounged on the grass of the courthouse yard, telling tales grave and obscene.[21] The record of Herndon's Menard practice tells its own story: [22]

[17] Herndon to Hart, January 6, 1869; Hart to Herndon, November 8, 1869, Hart MSS.

[18] The rumor that Herndon published a biography during this period which was "suppressed" by Republican politicians is examined in a note at the end of this chapter.

[19] Herndon to Hart, April 13, 1866, Hart MSS.; *Abraham Lincoln. Miss Ann Rutledge.*

[20] Statistics compiled from Chancery Record, United States Circuit Court for the Southern District of Illinois, Springfield.

[21] Edgar Lee Masters, *The Sangamon*, 65, 73.

[22] Statistics compiled from Judge's Dockets, Menard Co. Cir. Court.

In 1864	Herndon	had	26	cases	in	the	Menard	County	Circuit	Court.
" 1865	"	"	18	"	"	"	"	"	"	"
" 1866	"	"	8	"	"	"	"	"	"	"
" 1867	"	"	14	"	"	"	"	"	"	"
" 1868	"	"	12	"	"	"	"	"	"	"
" 1869	"	"	12	"	"	"	"	"	"	"
" 1870	"	"	5	"	"	"	"	"	"	"
" 1871	"	"	1	"	"	"	"	"	"	"
" 1872	"	"	0	"	"	"	"	"	"	"
" 1873	"	"	0	"	"	"	"	"	"	"

By 1868, tired of his unprofitable partnership, Zane set up in practice alone. For his new associate Herndon chose young Alfred Orendorff, just back from legal training in Albany, New York.[23] From the start the firm of Herndon & Orendorff was handicapped by the general knowledge that law bored the senior partner. When their professional card appeared in the *Illinois State Journal* in September 1869, it was felt necessary to assure prospective clients that Herndon, "one of the oldest and best practitioners at the bar," would "in the future . . . give his entire attention to the practice of his profession." [24]

At first Herndon had neglected his professional duties to pursue his Lincoln researches. After 1866, when the Lincoln Record was copied, bound, and stored away, he became more and more absorbed in another hobby. Shortly before his death in 1867 Archer Herndon deeded to his oldest son a farm of nearly six hundred acres along the Sangamon, some six miles north of Springfield.[25] The farmhouse stood on the steep bluff called Chinkapin Hill and looked out across flat, rich bottom lands along the meandering river. Herndon called his place "Fairview," for he had a grand sweep of the countryside — the dusty road that wound from Springfield toward Petersburg, the gray of the cypress trees along the river, an occasional dull glint of sunlight reflected in the sluggish stream, the level fields of corn, green-black under an August sun.

Tired of the law and discouraged with literature, Herndon turned

[23] The statement is sometimes made that Orendorff joined Herndon and Zane to form Herndon, Zane, & Orendorff, a firm which is alleged to have continued until Zane's election as circuit judge in 1873 (Ill. State Hist. Soc., *Trans., 1910,* 35). I have examined the files of all the Springfield courts for this period and did not find a single case in which the firm name Herndon, Zane, & Orendorff was used or even a case in which all three attorneys appeared. The *Springfield City Directory for 1869–70* (pp. 96, 182) lists Herndon & Orendorff and Charles S. Zane as two distinct firms.

[24] *Illinois State Journal,* Sept. 24, 1869.

[25] Sangamon Co. Deed Record, XXIX, 447.

enthusiastically to agriculture. He spent much of his time walking about on his farm and boasted that the exercise had made a new man of him. In the back of his mind there had been a gnawing worry about the future of his children. He had not been able to give his sons a college education, and they had no jobs, no training, no security. Herndon thought he could best provide for his family by training his three sons to be farmers.[26] He plunged vigorously into the project of improving his inheritance. To correspondents who pestered him with queries about Lincoln, he replied after a long delay: "I have been *busy* — BUSY BUSY at Law — Agriculture &c. &c." He had no time to waste on writing.[27]

Herndon knew nothing about practical agriculture, but he had read books on the subject. He had the notion of being a fancy farmer, raising blooded cattle and fine fruits. In his first year of ownership he "planted . . . some 500 grape vines — 400 apples — peach — plum — cherry — pears &c . . . got 60 cattle — 12 horses — 100 hogs &c." [28] Once thoroughly equipped, he thought, his farm would almost manage itself. Charmed by the idea of being a gentleman farmer, Herndon spent more and more time on his estate and sometimes remained at the farmhouse for weeks at a time rusticating. Herndon enjoyed his farm, but he never became a good farmer. "He could tell any one how to plant seeds to produce the best results," an old neighbor pithily remarked, "but he could not raise any thing but Hell." [29]

IV

Herndon's farming turned out to be a flat failure. It was not entirely his fault. He bought machinery and stock at inflated postwar rates. In the late sixties when a general depression struck, farm prices fell. Between 1868 and 1872 the price of corn on the Chicago grain market dropped almost fifty per cent. Other farm commodities declined in similar ratio, but the cost of manufactured goods remained obstinately high. Bitterly Herndon resented the injustice. "[I]t is too hard," he complained, "to give fifty bushels of corn (an acre of corn) for a pair of boots, simply to satisfy . . . monopolists." [30] Caught in the depression cycle, Herndon was helpless. He had invested all his savings in

[26] Herndon to Mrs. Dall, February 1, 1868, Dall MSS.; Herndon to Hart, February 10, 1868, Hart MSS.
[27] Herndon to Hart, November 12, 1867, and February 10, 1868, Hart MSS.
[28] Herndon to Mrs. Dall, February 1, 1868, Dall MSS.
[29] J. J. VanNattan, quoted in Louis Obed Renne, *Lincoln and the Land of the Sangamon*, 42–43.
[30] Herndon's letter in *Illinois State Register*, February 19, 1873.

his farm. He had bought when prices were high; now, when he had produce to sell, his market was gone.

Herndon was always a poor financier. He was extravagant, accustomed to careless spending and prodigal hospitality. During the years after Lincoln's death he welcomed one visitor after another, taking days off from his work to entertain the curious, the inquisitive, and the morbid who wanted to learn all about the Great Dead. No visitor left without a memento — a letter, a legal document, or a book of Lincoln's — given by an impecunious partner.[31] In other respects Herndon was equally generous. He signed other men's bonds, he endorsed their notes, he gave credit on his fees, he loaned money even when he knew there was no chance for repayment. While he had a steady income as state bank commissioner, he could afford to be liberal, but after 1865 his salary stopped though his generosity continued.

When depression came, Herndon was ruined. His debts mounted, his creditors were pressing, but his income slumped. Desperately he sought money, good money to throw after bad. He sacrificed his library, the joy of his life. Apparently a portion of his home in Springfield was rented to a German widow and her numerous family. He tried to borrow in Springfield but as security he could offer only land — land which depression had made almost worthless. As a last resort in December 1868 Herndon approached his Philadelphia friend Hart. "I want to borrow — say 8 thousand dollars on 5 years time — interest payable annually — or semi-annually if it *must* be so." The loan would be secured by a mortgage on his farm, which was really "worth $50 thousand dollars." Would his friend kindly see "some . . . monied men — institutions — trustees — guardians &c and ascertain if the money can be had." But times were hard in the East too, and Hart reported that "the monied men will not let go their grip on the dollar." [32] The mortgage on Herndon's home in Springfield was foreclosed, and in 1871 he and his family moved out to the farmhouse on Chinkapin Hill.[33] Herndon was no longer a gentleman farmer. At the age of fifty-

---

[31] Herndon to Hart, December 15, 1869, Hart MSS.; Herndon to J. T. Fields, January 1, 1867, MS., Harvard Univ.

[32] Herndon to Hart, November 27, 1868, and January 6, 1869, Hart MSS.

[33] It is difficult to determine precisely when Herndon moved to the country. He was living in Springfield on August 3, 1870, when the census was taken. In April 1870 he had been obliged to deposit title papers for his town lot as security for a debt of $448 to John P. Fixmer, a wholesale liquor merchant. On January 16, 1871, both his house lot and the adjacent plot occupied by his rose garden were mortgaged, and Herndon apparently moved out shortly afterward. Sangamon County Mortgage Record, XXIX, 325, 404. "I . . . moved in[to] the Country in 1871. . . ." Herndon's "A Statement, Memoranda," January 8, 1886, Herndon-Weik Coll.

three, for the first time in his life, he was forced to do physical labor in his fields. The flood tide of disaster had come, and Herndon was left stranded high on the bluffs above the Sangamon, with a few blooded cattle, a row of pear trees, and a bitter memory.

V

In 1869, just as Herndon was about to give up hope, a visitor came into his office. Herndon had known Ward Hill Lamon since the pre-war days when lawyers used to ride the circuit together in central Illinois. Since that time Virginia-born, abolitionist-hating Lamon had gone to Washington with President Lincoln as marshal of the District of Columbia, where he had engaged in violent and flamboyant feuds with practically everybody in the national government. Lamon was as rococo as the bric-a-brac that littered the whatnots of the gilded age. His oiled hair, carefully disarranged for theatrical effect, his walrus moustache, his sagging jowls, his protuberant paunch made him look like the living caricature of an American senator. In Washington as in Illinois Lamon was famous for his rendition of Southern songs, for his wide assortment of smutty jokes, for his vocabulary of profanity, and for his capacity for liquor.

After Lincoln's death Lamon, like Herndon, was a ship without a rudder. He wandered aimlessly from one project to another. First he wanted to become governor of the Territory of Idaho. Then he decided to return to the law and became the partner of Jeremiah Sullivan Black, Buchanan's attorney general and secretary of state. He practiced for a time in the District of Columbia but soon abandoned that project for another. Lamon became closely attached to his partner's son, Chauncey Forward Black, a young man of undoubted abilities but, like his father, eccentric, high-tempered, and unpredictable. Lamon and Chauncey Black proposed to prepare a biography of Lincoln. Lamon would provide his intimate knowledge of the President, and Black, in addition to using his father's voluminous papers, would do the actual writing.

When he began gathering materials, Lamon quickly found that Herndon had everywhere preceded him. Visiting his father-in-law, Stephen T. Logan, in Springfield, Lamon went to see Herndon's records. He was so impressed that he offered to buy Herndon out. Herndon was frankly taken aback.[34] Some months earlier he had tried to sell his manuscripts to Robert Dale Owen, the Indiana congressman who planned a biography of Lincoln, but when Owen proved reluc-

[34] Herndon to Lamon, February 17, 1869, Lamon MSS.

tant to propose any cash terms, Herndon had come to think his documents were unsalable.[35] Now, at the time of his greatest need, they proved to be a negotiable asset. Herndon gave Lamon no categorical answer but wrote frantically to Hart in Philadelphia, describing his collection of Lincolniana and begging: "Give me your opinion — after consulting friends — book makers & sellers among others, as to the value of the memoranda — what a man ought to pay for them or the use of them." [36]

He stalled Lamon off by giving him an elaborate sales talk on the value of the Lincoln Record. Probably Lamon did not "know the content — value & importance of the Records." Herndon claimed that he had had unique advantages in collecting facts, as he knew what strings to pull; that he had paid out "more than a thousand dollars" (which he quickly raised to $1800) in the accumulation of his manuscripts; and that he had spent "about 3 years in collecting — comparing & analyzing the facts of Mr L's life." "I think — in fact I know that my Records — facts — manuscripts &c of Mr Lincoln are the most perfect on record. He who writes a biography of Mr Lincoln from my facts writes the only true life of the good & great man that can by any possibility be written now or in the future." Herndon knew Lamon's weak spot. There was "a fortune in the Records," he confided; "there is fame in it — there is money too my good friend." [37]

Lamon nosed around the bait very cautiously. At first he thought Herndon had the completed manuscript of a Lincoln biography to sell. Herndon explained that while he had written "no biography as yet of Mr Lincoln — only sketches — manuscripts — lectures — facts — opinions &c.," his records were so complete and so perfectly arranged that all a biographer would have to do was to "open them and read — know — analyze & recombine the facts &c &c. & write." Fearing to seem overeager, Herndon posed as reluctant. "I want money — money," he confessed, but he was not so sure he would sell his documents. ". . . I probably shall finish my biography in a year or so — can do it — wish to do it." Still, it was not impossible that Lamon could persuade him to sell out "horse foot &c." [38]

In March 1869, after he received Hart's advice, Herndon became specific. He would sell his records, copies of lectures, his entire store of materials, and agree not to publish anything on Lincoln, "probably reserving a right to deliver a lecture or two to our people here." His

[35] Carpenter to Herndon, February 12, 1867; Owen to Herndon, July 26, 1867, Herndon-Weik Coll.

[36] Herndon to Hart, February 24, 1869, Hart MSS.

[37] Herndon to Lamon, February 17, 1869, Lamon MSS.

[38] Herndon to Lamon, February 26, 1869, *ibid.*

price was "four thousand dollars for my facts — memoranda — manuscripts &c — that is to say *their use* till you finish your biography." Two thousand must be paid in cash, but he would accept a note for the remainder, bearing ten per cent interest. Lamon must agree "that no word is to be erased — changed — no leaf torn no mutilations — no alterations — interlineations &c of the records — want them returned to me when you are done . . . in the exact order & condition you receive them." This was a high price, Herndon knew, yet the manuscripts would be worth ten thousand dollars to the lucky Lincoln biographer who secured them. Lamon could proudly announce the purchase to the world, and that would "give your biography value &c. &c." Herndon concluded craftily: "others will take the records if you do not want them." [39]

Herndon made his proposition and nothing happened. A month passed, and Lamon did not even answer. Herndon began to worry. There was "an other gentleman in _____" who wanted to buy the records; wouldn't Lamon make up his mind? Still no answer. Herndon tried again with a calculated indiscretion. ". . . I desire to give the *Hon Isaac N. Arnold* of Chicago — now you have the man's name — an answer which I am withholding on your account." There was also an anonymous biographer in Boston who might purchase the manuscripts. Lamon would please have the kindness to state his intentions. [40]

If Lamon was hesitant, Herndon's other prospects were more so. In fact, if either Arnold or the mysterious biographer from Boston approached Herndon on the subject, their inquiries as well as his replies have been lost. During the summer Lamon reached a decision, and in September he returned to Springfield to complete the transaction. Sore pressed financially, Herndon was obliged to give up some of his conditions when he made out the bill of sale:

Springfield Ills. Septr. 17th 1869

I have this day sold to W H Lamon of Washington D C my Lincoln Records in three vols. for the consideration of Four thousand Dollars Cash in hand paid. He is now the sole owner and possessor of said Records and is Empowered and authorized by me to sell — publish — use or dispose of said Records as he wishes or will. Lamon promises to use discretion & good judgement as to what shall be published — sold — or made public at the present time.

W H Herndon [41]

[39] Herndon to Lamon, March 17, 1869, *ibid.*
[40] Herndon to Lamon, April —, and April 29, 1869, *ibid.*
[41] The bill of sale is in the Lamon MSS.

The sum of two thousand dollars was apparently paid to Herndon in cash, as he had demanded, and the remainder by a note, which was to mature in two years. Herndon was so poor he had to put the note up as collateral on December 29, 1869.[42] Money was the principal thing with him. He did not even bother to keep a copy of his contract with Lamon.

V I

After purchasing Herndon's manuscripts, Lamon took the bound copies of the Lincoln Record back East and drew up a contract with Chauncey Black for the publication of "a just, full, and impartial biography of Abraham Lincoln." Lamon agreed to supply Herndon's records and other papers, while Black was "to write the text of the book and arrange the materials for publication." For $1,500 Black secured half ownership of the Herndon manuscripts and of the copyright on the biography, though his name was not to appear in the published work.[43] James R. Osgood & Company, successors to Ticknor & Fields, were still looking for a standard life of Lincoln, and the Lamon-Black partnership seemed to offer the ideal opportunity. The publishers agreed to issue "Lamon's" biography and to advance the joint authors $5,000.[44]

The Lamon-Black biography was planned in two volumes, and the collaborators commenced work on the first, covering Lincoln's career before 1861. Lamon's stock of facts about the pre-presidential years turned out to be very meager, while Black could supply information from his father's papers only about the secession crisis. Herndon's Lincoln Records began to assume a new importance for the biography.

[42] Lamon's note, endorsed by D. T. Littler and Milton Hay, was paid by his father-in-law, Stephen T. Logan, on December 2, 1871 (Stuart-Hay MSS.). The precise amount Lamon paid Herndon for the records has been a matter of controversy. Herndon asked $4,000; Lamon always claimed he had paid that amount (C. F. Black to James R. Osgood & Co., undated author's draft, Black MSS.); the bill of sale found among Lamon's papers would indicate that this was the amount agreed upon. Herndon kept no copy of his bill of sale. When asked three years later on what terms he had sold to Lamon, he replied: "He paid me 2 thousand Dolls — no more and no less." Herndon's memory at this time was not too good. He was "not certain as to what I sold Lamon *in the Records.*" (Herndon to C. F. Black, January 4, November 19 and 30, 1873.) Herndon's tottery reminiscence is more than counterbalanced by evidence of the bill of sale, turned over to Lamon with the documents in 1869.

[43] Memorandum of agreement between Lamon and Black, December 10, 1869, Black MSS.

[44] On Lamon, Black, and "Lamon's" biography see the thorough study by A. V. House, Jr., "The Trials of a Ghost-Writer of Lincoln Biography," Ill. State Hist. Soc., *Jour.*, XXXI, 262–296.

When Lamon and Black examined together the copies which Lamon had brought from Springfield, they were at first immensely pleased. Black was sure that "without Herndon *no Life of Lincoln* could ever have been written." The collaborators could hardly praise highly enough Herndon's "astonishing collection of materials — the richest, fullest, rarest . . . ever conceived." [45]

On closer examination, Herndon's manuscripts raised problems. Obviously the records were fragmentary and Herndon must certainly have "much, very much evidence relating to particular parts of Mr. Lincolns life which is no where to be found in the bound volumes of manuscripts." Lamon wrote Herndon in just criticism that the Lincoln Record was frequently obscure in meaning. He begged for elucidation. "In addition to . . . the possession of all your documents," he entreated Herndon, "I want to possess myself of your *mind* in regard to Lincoln — your theories respecting disputed points and facts, and your plan or scheme of life, and the influence of particular incidents on his subsequent character." [46]

At first Lamon was keenly interested in the biography, and he studied Herndon's memoranda critically. He had little patience with some of Herndon's wild theorizing. "You say he [Lincoln] was told 'certain facts' . . . regarding his birth and his mothers chastity — When? By whom? Exactly *what* was he told? Give me the reasons for your conviction that the melancholly [*sic*] of his spirit was founded originally on this knowledge." "And as to L's mother having done the world so great a favor by receiving the embraces of somebody other than her husband," Lamon replied to one of Herndon's pet notions, "the theory might do well enough in a private correspondence . . . but would look damned ugly in print for general circulation." On other points Lamon pointed to Herndon's jumping at conclusions, his frequent inconsistencies, his unwarranted inferences. For every report he asked: "Is this proved? When and by whom?" [47]

Herndon replied that his records were a collection of documents and that he personally was responsible for their accuracy only "to the extent that the copies are true — faithful & genuine — made out from the originals." He could not "guarantee . . . that every man or woman in that Record tells the truth." It was Lamon's job to "Reconcile all" if he could by following his own good judgment. Herndon would prefer not to obtrude his own ideas, lest he seem "a blow — boast — or fool

[45] Black to Lamon, March 8, 1870, copy, Herndon-Weik Coll.; "Preface of Lamon's Life of Lincoln as originally written by C F Black," February 1, 1872, Black MSS.
[46] Lamon to Herndon, February 18, 1870, Herndon-Weik Coll.
[47] Lamon to Herndon, February 18 and March 9, 1870, *ibid.*

who wishes to be noticed." But since Lamon requested his opinion, he would do all he could to help.[48] He sent Lamon the manuscripts of his first three Lincoln lectures, a copy of his broadside against Holland, and the printed version of his Ann Rutledge lecture. He scrawled out letter upon letter, giving all his opinions and memories and impressions. He elaborated and explained and defended. He wrote long disquisitions on Lincoln's legitimacy, the Ann Rutledge romance, the jilting of Mary Todd, the composition of the house-divided address, the formation of the Republican party in Illinois, and every other subject remotely related to Lincoln. Herndon did his best to tell all.

VII

For three years Herndon's memories had been stored in silence. When he began to pump out his reminiscences for Lamon and Black, a significant alteration occurred in Herndon's thinking about Lincoln. It was not that Herndon's basic conception of his partner's character had changed; now as always he regarded Lincoln as a man, human, lovable, perplexing. As Lord Charnwood has said, Herndon's was always "the task of substituting for Lincoln's aureole the battered tall hat." [49] In 1870 as in 1865 Herndon thought of his partner as a typical Western figure, with the defects of his race, but all in all "a hero — having lived a grand good life." [50]

Herndon's memory of events did not undergo material change during his years of silence, but there was a gradual alteration of perspective, of which Herndon himself was not aware. In the years immediately after Lincoln's death even when striving to be impartial Herndon considered himself the President's defender. Very early he doubted the legitimate descent of Lincoln. He had what he considered indisputable authority for believing that "A Lincoln's mother FELL — *fell* in Ky about 1805 — *fell* when an unmarried [woman] — *fell* afterward" and that "Thomas Lincoln left Ky [in 1816] on THAT account; and for no other." But in 1866 Herndon was unwilling to accept the worst interpretation of these reports. "There . . . *is room for mistake,*" he wrote Hart, and he planned an expedition to Kentucky in order to get his evidence "*absolutely* Right." "There is some mistake as to identity," he kept repeating, "and I'll find it out and expose those engaged in it." [51] If Lincoln was proved illegitimate, Herndon in 1865 thought it

[48] Herndon to Lamon, December 18, 1869 [misdated by Herndon 1867], and February 25, 1870, Lamon MSS.
[49] Charnwood, *Abraham Lincoln,* 102.
[50] Herndon to Lamon, March 6, 1870, Lamon MSS.
[51] Herndon to Hart, December 28, 1866, and January 12, 1867, Hart MSS.

best to publish the fact in indirect language so as to prevent future revelation by the malicious enemies of the Great Dead. "Mr Lincoln," he was convinced, "can stand unstaggeringly up beneath all *necessary or other truths.*" [52] But he did not advocate a ruthless revealing of the truth whatever the cost; his idea was to put a bad case in the best light possible.

Herndon did not go to Kentucky. He did not acquire new facts of any import. Instead, he stored away his Lincoln records and began farming. Then in 1870, prodded by Lamon, he thought back over the subject of Lincoln's legitimacy. In 1866 a study of his evidences had produced doubt; in 1870 a rehashing of his memories produced conviction. "I now & have for years believed [Lincoln] . . . the son of [Abraham] Enloe," he informed Lamon. He reviewed his shaky evidences on the subject — reminiscences marred by animus, confused recollections, and Herndon's own "inferences springing from [Lincoln's] . . . acts — from what he said, and from what *he didn't* say." "*The evidence is not Conclusive*," he granted, "but men have been hung on less evidence." Even more radically changed was Herndon's opinion as to publishing the "fact" of Lincoln's illegitimacy. ". . . I should tell the truth as I saw it," he advised Lamon. "I should suppress no truth & suggest no falsehood. If I thought Mr Lincoln an illegitimate I should so state it." [53]

Precisely the same change was noticeable in Herndon's ideas about Lincoln's religion. When Holland visited Springfield in 1865, Herndon merely advised as to Lincoln's faith "*the less said the better.*" The President had never been a technical Christian, he was sure, but Lincoln had never attacked the Christian church. "Some men," Herndon remarked in 1866, "think that Mr. Lincoln did scoff and sneer at the Bible. This is not so; he had no scoff — nor sneer, for even a sacred error; he had charity for all and everything." His "infidel book," of which some old settlers had fuzzy memories, was not a mockery of the Bible but "a lofty criticism — a high spiritual rationalistic criticism." [54]

By 1869 Herndon had changed his tune. "On Mr Lincoln's Religion," he advised Lamon, "be bold. Tell the truth — that Mr. Lincoln was an infidel — a Deist — wrote a book . . . in favor of Infidelity &c. — that sometimes . . . he was an atheist. . . . He held in contempt the Idea of God's Special interference &c. &c. . . . Tell the truth and

[52] Herndon to Hart, November 26, 1866, author's draft, Herndon-Weik Coll.
[53] Herndon to Lamon, February 25 and March 15, 1870, Lamon MSS. Though Herndon spelled the name "Enloe," he probably referred to one Abraham Enlow (1794–1861), who lived in Hardin County, Kentucky. See Barton, *Paternity of Lincoln*, 156–185.
[54] Herndon to Mr. Cronyer, December 3, 1866, copy, Lamon MSS.

shame 'old Nick.'" Lamon should declare that Lincoln ridiculed the virgin birth and "scorned the idea that God seduced, even by a shadow, a lovely daughter of His own." [55] Carried away by his own advice, Herndon dashed off a long letter to Francis E. Abbot, editor of a Toledo free-thought journal, *The Index,* in which he termed Lincoln an infidel. Lincoln "held many of the Christian ideas in abhorrence" and "was living on the borderland between theism and Atheism — sometimes quite wholly dwelling in Atheism." "I never heard him use the name of . . . Jesus," wrote Herndon, "but to confute the idea that he was the Christ." [56]

VIII

Lincoln writers have frequently speculated on the causes of Herndon's somewhat irreverent attitude toward the President. Without much investigation, biographers have repeated the stereotype that Herndon was a drunkard, a drug addict, a wastrel, an embittered failure. It is worth remembering that the proof of a pudding is not in the cook but in the eating. The change in Herndon's attitude toward Lincoln is of central importance in his own biography, but it is of minor significance in the study of Lincoln. Lincoln students have sometimes emphasized alleged weaknesses in Herndon's personality because it is easier to discredit Herndon than to disprove his reminiscences.

It was natural that Herndon's thinking about Lincoln should change. One obvious explanation is the passing of time and the fallibility of human memory. Herndon put away his manuscripts for almost three years; when he returned to the Lincoln subject, he found many of his memories hazy. Ann Rutledge, he dimly recalled, had had a fiancé, but he had forgotten his name. McNamara, had it been? Dates he telescoped in a bewildering fashion. He vouched for Lincoln's desertion of Mary Todd at the altar in 1841 as a thing absolutely proved; he claimed to know all about the incident because he was then sleeping above Speed's store and "heard Lincoln talk about the matter." Actually Herndon married and moved to his own home in March 1840, nine months before the incident was supposed to have occurred. [57]

But Herndon's altered view of Lincoln was something more than a lapse of memory; it was almost a revolution in his orientation. Some have attempted to show that Herndon's jaundiced view of Lincoln was of the same color as the corn liquor he drank. Billy Herndon was a

[55] Herndon to Lamon, December 16, 1869, and February 25, 1870, *ibid.*
[56] *The Index,* I, 5–6 (April 2, 1870).
[57] Herndon to Lamon, February 25 and March 23, 1870, Lamon MSS.

drinking man. Even before the war he had sometimes gone on sprees, and at one time his drunkenness seemed so chronic that friends urged Lincoln to drop him from the law partnership. After Lincoln left for Washington, Herndon at first managed pretty well. But when he was excited, in the middle of a political campaign or a lecture series, he felt the old craving again.[58] Still, during the war years he kept a fairly steady course and could write his White House partner: "I am toddling on tolerably well. . . . *Above* all I am a sober man, and will keep so the balance of my days. . . ."[59]

Lincoln's death came as a crushing blow. It was followed soon by the universal opprobrium which attached to the author of the Ann Rutledge lecture. Next occurred a series of financial reverses, a time when it seemed that God himself was against Herndon. Everything he did turned out wrong. His law practice virtually vanished. He lost money at farming. He went into debt. His fruit trees died, his potatoes were eaten by beetles, his cows were mutilated by a vicious dog, his mule was killed, his hogs had the cholera. Bit by bit he was obliged to sell off the desirable pieces of his farm. He was not even well enough to work what land remained, for the nagging bronchial trouble that had afflicted him in 1860 hung on, making him increasingly susceptible to colds and influenza. Year after year he would drearily report to his friends that he had been "sick during this summer — fall & winter."[60] Truly Herndon could say: ". . . I have passed through several Hells since 1866 & 7."[61] Everywhere he had a record of failure, and as a solace he again took to drink.

Anecdotes concerning this phase of Herndon's life are not pleasant. Neighbors remembered seeing "him hauled home from town just like you would haul a hog on hay in the back end of the wagon . . . they unloaded him with his jug of whiskey — he would lay up stairs drunk for a week."[62] John Hill, editor of the Petersburg newspaper, reported that Herndon would go "on sprees lasting for weeks, although his friends constantly tried to sober him up."

> . . . I was one night in a restaurant [Hill recalled] . . . when Herndon came in, full, and set [*sic*] down across the table from me and called for oysters for a stew. The pan with the oysters in it was set on the chafin[g] dish before him, . . . and the usual pitcher of milk set beside. Herndon moved the milk away, and reached for the salt cellar

---

[58] Herndon to Weik, February 5, 1891, Herndon-Weik Coll.
[59] Herndon to Lincoln, February 11, 1865, quoted in Pratt, *Personal Finances,* 135.
[60] Herndon to Mrs. Dall, December 26, 1872, Dall MSS.
[61] Herndon to Lamon, March 23, 1870, Lamon MSS.
[62] Renne, *Lincoln and the Land of the Sangamon,* 42–43.

ANNA MILES HERNDON

"The beautiful Anna Miles," they called her, but the only likeness we have of the second Mrs. Herndon is this unskillful crayon drawing, badly battered and damaged by water. Reproduced through the courtesy of her nephew, Mr. James S. Miles.

I HAVE PASSED THROUGH SEVERAL HELLS

This late photograph of Herndon shows the effect of years of hard labor, poverty, and illness. "Jesse," he wrote to Weik, "it's a bad thing to be poor aint it?"

and dumped the whole contents into the oysters: then off with the top of the tin pepper box, and in that went, followed by the whole contents of the mustard pot, the liquor of the home grown pepper sauce bottle, and final[l]y all the vinegar in the cruet. He stirred all together, boiled up, and then calling for pickles, which there and in those days meant *pickles*, he swallowed down the whole, without crackers with relish, and was about to duplicate, when I persuaded him to go with me to the Hotel, and final[l]y put him to bed. This is only one of many instances. . . .[63]

That Herndon drank excessively during this period is undeniable, but the main point of the inquiry is not to determine Herndon's drinking habits but to ascertain what effect alcohol had on his mind. A day-by-day examination of the newspaper files reveals that until at least 1874 Herndon retained an upstanding leadership in Springfield affairs. In the decade following 1865 he was in constant demand. It is hard to find a single month in that period when Herndon was not called on to head some committee, promote some reform, speak for some civic cause. In every public meeting of importance held in Springfield during the decade (except church gatherings) Herndon was asked to speak. He made addresses on the rights of American citizens abroad, on the establishment of the Third French Republic, on securing better prices for Illinois cattle, on promoting a railroad, on awarding agricultural prizes, on reducing the tariff.[64] Every year Herndon was chosen to give the Fourth of July address and the Emancipation Day oration. In 1866 (after the Ann Rutledge lecture was delivered) Herndon was the principal speaker at a major Springfield temperance banquet.[65]

Springfield citizens were not fools. Everybody knew that Herndon drank, but everybody realized that drink had not impaired his undoubted mental ability. Throughout the decade following Lincoln's death, Herndon's handwriting remained steady. His vocabulary, always direct and colorful, lost nothing of its energy. His sentences were as coherent as they had ever been. His public addresses were "delivered with . . . fervor and eloquence," and he handled his subjects "with that ungloved hand and 'coatless' style peculiar to him." [66] By 1875 Herndon seemed to the younger people in Springfield rather quaint. He was a grand old relic of the early days, not a sodden drunkard in the gutter.

[63] John Hill to Ida M. Tarbell, July 9, 1896, Tarbell MSS.
[64] For examples, see *Illinois State Journal*, December 21 and 22, 1867, August 17, 1868, March 21, 1870, January 17, 1873.
[65] *Ibid.*, December 8, 1866.
[66] *Illinois State Register*, February 25, 1875.

IX

During these postwar decades when malicious rumor had him besotted with drink or drugs, Herndon actually achieved on some subjects a greater mental clarity than he had ever before attained. Before the war Herndon's thinking had been shaped by other men — Lincoln, Parker, Carey, Sumner, Greeley. Now some of his idols were dead; others were shattered. Poverty helped Herndon think for himself. His sentiments had always been for the oppressed, but now, ruined by the remorseless operation of economic machinery over which he had no direction, he came to understand that oppression was not merely a matter of Negro bondage in a slave state. The greatest tyranny, he learned from skimping poverty, was "the unjust abuse — the unholy use of the almighty dollar." [67]

Like many another high-minded soul, Herndon belonged to the Republican party before the war because it seemed the only practical way to oppose slavery. The emancipation he desired for the Negro was no limping freedom; he would have absolute "justice . . . done the negro everywhere under our flag." [68] President Andrew Johnson's moderate program of postwar reconstruction Herndon denounced as an invitation for unshrived traitors to return to the Union.[69] Johnson's claim that he was really carrying out Lincoln's program for peace he branded as a "wilful and premedi[t]ated lie." [70] In 1868 Herndon was one of the principal Illinois supporters of Grant and Colfax and of radical reconstruction.

Once the Negro was free Herndon hoped his party would go forward in a general campaign of economic and social reform. His hope was not so futile as it might seem in retrospect. Illinois Republicans were united by only three factors: the memory of Abraham Lincoln, the support of a harsh policy of reconstruction, and the desire to continue in office. On other points there were drastic cleavages within the party. Reformers demanded civil service, aid for the farmers, anti-monopoly legislation. A strong group of Republicans, led by Horace White of the Chicago *Tribune*, opposed the protective tariff. But these protestants found little support in the high counsels of the party, dominated by Eastern capitalists, by corrupt rings, and by oligarchical

67 Herndon to Black, January 21, 1874, Black MSS.
68 Herndon to Zebina Eastman, February 6, 1866, Eastman MSS.
69 Herndon to Yates, March 3, 1866, photostat in collection of Mr. Thomas I. Starr.
70 Chicago *Tribune*, October 3, 1866. Herndon was in error. Johnson was very closely following the Lincoln program of reconstruction.

cliques. Those who dared favor reform were either whipped into con-
formity or were gradually ousted from the party.

Herndon followed an inevitable course. In 1870, when he still had
hope for reforming the Republican party, he gave a speech titled
"Free Trade vs. Protection" before a usual large audience in Representatives' Hall in the state capitol. It was probably the most effective
argument he ever presented. In a sense his address was a confession;
he wished publicly to repudiate his past. He was sorely ashamed that,
misled by Lincoln,[71] he had once advocated a protective tariff. "My
excuse is that I was then too young to investigate this difficult, abstract
and complex question." Now he was convinced that protection was
both unconstitutional and inexpedient. The tariff was "false and cruel
to the honest toiler," because it was really "taxation . . . for the sole
benefit of the capitalist." On and on Herndon went in a cogent summary of the anti-tariff position. "I am willing to admit that Tariffs do
some people good," he granted, "while it strikes a quick, heavy blow
at all men; causing consumption to be less through taxation – causing
stint or starvation, . . . causing nakedness . . . ignorance and pau-
perism . . . to live and breed." [72]

This "young and small-fisted farmer" was speaking from personal experience. As a city lawyer he had read books about monopolies; as a
destitute farmer he knew the trusts and rings in operation. He had had
to sell corn in Springfield for twenty-two cents a bushel, only to pay a
dollar at the Chicago stockyards for the same corn to feed cattle sent
to the market. Poverty taught Herndon. He repudiated his former economic theories; he expressly repented of his former thoughtless following of Lincoln. "Your tariffs for protection," he concluded, "your exclusive banking system – your monopolies – your granted exclusive
privileges – your building up of classes at the expense of the general
man, and all your other unjust laws, are violations of the greater laws
of nature – and, oh, how we suffer. . . ." [73]

No fair observer can read Herndon's 1870 anti-tariff address with-

---

[71] In this discussion one must distinguish between what Lincoln actually
thought and the ideas that were attributed to him by others. Lincoln's own thinking about the tariff was not clear, and he seems to have entertained some doubts
about the advisability of high protective rates. Randall, *Lincoln the Liberal Statesman*, 177–178. See also Reinhard H. Luthin, "Abraham Lincoln and the Tariff,"
Amer. Hist. Rev., XLIX, 609–629. But after his death Lincoln was claimed as an
ardent advocate of protection. *Illinois State Journal*, November 12, 1869. The liberal elements of Lincoln's thought were forgotten during the postwar decades.

[72] *Address on Free Trade vs. Protection . . . at Springfield Illinois, January
28, 1870.*

[73] *Ibid.*, 36.

out concluding that this man had a vigorous and alert mind. His thinking was straight and it was sound. Sad experience knocked much of
the wind and some of the high-flown words out of Herndon. For the
first time he spoke in terms of down-to-earth economic realism. This
free-trade speech of Herndon's was delivered at almost the same time
he was writing Lamon: "I . . . have for years believed [Lincoln] . . .
to be the son of Enloe." The mind that produced Herndon's tariff lecture
also produced the sensational revelations about Lincoln. Neither was
the product of a brain muddled by drink; both were the expression of
a revolt against the practices of the postwar Republican party.

After 1870 Herndon left the party he had helped found. In 1872 he
joined the Liberal Republican schism and as "the old law partner and
life-long friend of Lincoln" urged the election of Horace Greeley.[74]
When Grant was again successful, Herndon became discouraged with
political action. The Democrats were divided; the Republicans were
reactionary. For a time he entered vigorously into the independent
farmers' movement in Illinois and was made president of the Chinkapin Hill farmers' club. Not a Granger himself (probably because he
could not afford the initiation fee), Herndon strongly sympathized
with the ideas of the Patrons of Husbandry. In public letters (printed
significantly enough in the Democratic *Register* but not in the Republican *Journal*) he announced he was "down on railroads and rings, and
conspiracies, and monopolies, and *treason* against the general welfare." He offered to help organize "farmers, gard[e]ners, horticultur-
ists, laborers and all others struggling to better their condition." "Resistance to all monopolies, rings and conspiracies against the public
good and general welfare," he pledged, "shall be my sworn duty — my
most sacred obligation to man." [75]

At the outset the farmers' clubs and Granges in Illinois were nonpolitical, but since the dominant Republican party was controlled by
hacks and monopolists, the farmers inevitably drifted into active politics. In 1873 Herndon helped sponsor an independent anti-monopoly
party.[76] The next year Herndon, who had supported Grant in 1868,
was reviling the President as "an obstinate fool [who] . . . will die at
the mouth of a jug while smoking a cigar and driving of fast horses
and faster women." [77] But the independent movement in Illinois split
over the "rag baby," the greenback issue. Herndon was a hard money
man, favoring immediate resumption of specie payments for the green-

[74] *Illinois State Register*, October 7, 1872.
[75] *Ibid.*, February 12 and 19, 1873; Herndon to Black, January 21, 1874,
Black MSS.
[76] *Illinois State Register*, September 25, 1873.
[77] Herndon to Black, January 26, 1874, Black MSS.

backs issued during the Civil War. When the majority of the Illinois independents and anti-monopolists favored greenbacks or other inflationary programs of currency reform, Herndon went over to his old enemies, the Democrats.

In 1874, denouncing "the corruptionists who congregate at the national capital, including the president himself," Herndon urged the selection of Democratic (as opposed to both Republican and Independent) nominees.[78] Two years later Herndon himself contended unsuccessfully for the Democratic nomination for district attorney in Sangamon County.[79] Within ten years after his partner's assassination, Herndon had repudiated the economic theories and the political practices of the party which had elected Lincoln President.

It is in this altered economic and political orientation that one finds the most satisfactory explanation of Herndon's changed view of Lincoln. It is not just a coincidence that some of the most unfavorable judgments on Lincoln have come from men who were closely associated with him before 1861 but who during the postwar years turned in shamed loathing from the party they had helped create. For every critical comment by Herndon there is a parallel in the writings of David Davis, Orville H. Browning, John M. Palmer, Lyman Trumbull, Leonard Swett, or Ward Hill Lamon. All these men had been ardent Republicans before the war; all left the party during the reconstruction period.[80] By 1870 Lincoln to the popular mind typified the Republican party, and by 1870 the Republican party to these men had come to represent reaction. In the years immediately after Lincoln's murder, when they thought of him as the Great Emancipator and the Great Martyr who laid down his life for the Union, it was easy to speak in terms of eulogy. On later, cooler thought, when the Lincoln administration was regarded as the opening of the door to corrupt and sinister economic forces, it was easy to take a less favorable view of the wartime President.

Any explanation of motives can, of course, be only partial. It is not suggested that Herndon deliberately redrew his picture of Lincoln in the light of his changed political affiliation, but rather that an altered economic perspective made for a new and less flattering portrait of the Civil War President. Other factors helped in this reappraisal. Herndon always stiffened under criticism; the attacks on his Ann Rutledge lecture and later on his other writings made his opinions the

[78] *Illinois State Register,* October 22, 1874.
[79] *Ibid.,* July 8 and 11, 1876.
[80] Josephine Louise Harper, "Post-Lincoln Party Attitudes of Lincoln's Friends" (MS., master's dissertation, Univ. of Ill., 1943).

more positive. One cannot omit the possibility of unconscious jealousy toward the memory of the partner who had been successful, nor the effect of Herndon's admitted animus against Mrs. Lincoln. Age had its part in distorting the remembered image. Perhaps alcohol had some share. But his reduced economic status, his shift of occupation, the reorientation of his economic thought, and his slow drift into the Democratic party best explain Herndon's acid etching of Lincoln.

A Note on the "Suppressed Edition"

The legend that Herndon actually wrote and published a harshly realistic biography of Lincoln in 1866 or 1867 has gained considerable currency. The book was supposed to have been so shattering to "the effigy which had been hurriedly gotten up by the [Republican] apotheosizers" of Lincoln, that politicians sent out agents, bought up all the copies, and destroyed the plates of the book.[81]

The only person who claimed actually to have seen this "suppressed edition" was Mrs. Elizabeth A. Meriwether of Memphis and St. Louis, author under the pseudonym "George Edmonds" of *Facts and Falsehoods Concerning the War on the South* (1904), a little book intended as a reply to "the injustice and falsity of many accusations hurled at her beloved South."[82] She declared she found this sensational early book by Herndon in a St. Louis library, but when she returned to verify her extracts from it, this copy, too, had been suppressed. The familiar work published in 1889 as *Herndon's Lincoln* Mrs. Meriwether believed to have been written entirely by Jesse W. Weik, whose intent was "to concoct a book which would just give enough truth to interest, and not enough to offend the Republican apotheosizers." For financial reasons Weik was supposed to have concealed the fact that "over twenty years previous" to the publication of the 1889 biography Herndon "had written and published [a life of Lincoln], . . . and had witnessed its destruction by those he had imagined would set a high value on it."[83]

This tale of a "suppressed edition" has fascinated Lincoln collectors. The only remaining copy of such a work would, of course, be a veritable treasure. But the evidence is conclusive that Herndon did not write or publish a biography of Lincoln before 1889. There is no known reference to such a work in Herndon's own correspondence, in

[81] Mrs. Elizabeth A. Meriwether ("George Edmonds"), *Facts and Falsehoods Concerning the War on the South, 1861–1865*, 38.
[82] Lee Meriwether (son of the author of *Facts and Falsehoods*) so wrote me, December 6, 1944.
[83] *Facts and Falsehoods*, 40–41.

the letters of his contemporaries, or in the newspapers of the period.[84] No copyright was issued on such a biography. No one but Mrs. Meriwether claims to have seen the book. The librarians at the St. Louis Mercantile Library and at the St. Louis Public Library have no record of its existence.[85] No Lincoln collector, bibliographer, or book dealer has ever seen a copy.

Mrs. Meriwether did not make her story up out of the whole cloth. The "quotations" she furnished from the "suppressed life" (and a check on other verifiable citations in her book reveals how inaccurate was her copying) are closely similar to statements in Herndon's first two lectures. She probably used Carpenter's *Six Months at the White House* or O. H. Oldroyd's *The Lincoln Memorial: Album-Immortelles* (both of which contain long extracts from Herndon's lectures) or the Lamon biography of Lincoln. When she returned and asked for the same book as "Herndon's Life of Lincoln," the librarians were unable to produce it and, having heard a garbled rumor of the expurgation of the 1889 Herndon biography, Mrs. Meriwether concluded that the book she had been using had been suppressed.

Jesse Weik, Herndon's collaborator in the 1889 biography, wrote confidentially at a time when the revelation of a "suppressed edition" could have had no financial ill effects: ". . . *I have seen the Edmonds pamphlet and I do not hesitate to pronounce it and its allegations regarding Herndon as pure* BOSH." [86]

[84] When Herndon was desperately trying to get the highest price possible for his Lincoln records, he had to confess: ". . . I have no biography as yet of Mr Lincoln." Herndon to Lamon, February 26, 1870, Lamon MSS.

[85] Mr. Clarence E. Miller of the St. Louis Mercantile Library and Mr. Charles H. Compton of the St. Louis Public Library at my request searched their records in December 1944 and found no trace of such a book.

[86] Weik to W. H. Townsend, September 25, 1922, MS. used through the courtesy of Mr. Townsend. On this whole subject see W. E. Barton, "An Old Lincoln Tale is Revised," New York *Times*, May 6, 1928.

CHAPTER *xvii*

Judas in Springfield

I

LAMON had trouble with his biography. Herndon himself was one big problem. Now that he had sold out to Lamon, Herndon began to have scruples about the use of his records. Suddenly he remembered that many facts and statements had been given him in strict confidence. The names of his informants must not be used. "I do not say this simply because I can say it," he assured Lamon, "but because it is probably true." Lamon would have to "walk discreet" or he would "blow this social American world wide open." He might quote Dennis Hanks or Mentor Graham if he pleased, but when it came to questions of Lincoln's legitimacy, his domestic relations, or his religion, Lamon would have to write each informant and request permission to quote his statement, but the better plan would be to give Herndon and his records as authority throughout. Herndon's attitude was not unlike Dennis Hanks's egotistical faith: "if you Dont have My Name Very frecantly in you[r] Book it wont gaw of at all." "You are at perfect liberty," Herndon assured Lamon, "to . . . quote me as often as you see proper." [1]

At the outset Lamon was keenly interested in the Lincoln biography, but when the tedious work of composing a connected narrative began, he quickly became bored. Lamon could never keep his mind on one subject for very long. His close friend Justice David Davis was a prominent candidate for the Liberal Republican presidential nomination, and in 1871 Lamon turned from literature back to politics. His ghost-writer, Chauncey F. Black, was left to finish off the life of Lincoln as best he might.

Black was probably the most unfortunate choice possible for a Lincoln biographer. By birth an Easterner, by inheritance a Buchanan Democrat, by temperament an anti-Lincoln man, Black was the last

[1] Herndon to Lamon, March 6 and 23, 1870, Lamon MSS.

person to deal intelligently with Herndon's jumble of gossip, fact, and speculation. Lamòn had strongly suspected some of Herndon's wilder theories; Black believed anything unfavorable to Lincoln.

Herndon found Lamon a most unsatisfactory correspondent. After the first month or so Herndon's long, gossipy letters went unanswered. As Lamon became bored, Black took over the correspondence. At first he suggested questions for Lamon to ask Herndon; then he wrote out letters for Lamon to sign; finally he began questioning Herndon himself. Herndon conceived a great attachment for the young Pennsylvanian. Black answered letters promptly, he respected Herndon's intuitions, and he never asked embarrassing, critical questions. "Write to me as often as you please," Herndon urged; "your letters shall always rec[e]ive respectful attention, I assure you." [2]

Black was equally pleased with Herndon. He longed to know Herndon's ideas on all sorts of subjects. "Was not Lincoln's inordinate love of the lascivious, of smut, something nearly akin to lunacy?" he asked. "Didn't he love it for its own sake, when there was neither wit nor humor in it? Was he not a man of strong erotic passions, which conscience prevented him from indulging physically, and which therefore revelled in the creations of a diseased imagination?" [3] Whatever Herndon answered, Black regarded as unquestioned truth.

As Black drafted "Lamon's" biography, Herndon was quoted on nearly every page. He kept turning up at every critical point in the story. According to Black (and according to Herndon), it was he who gave Lincoln sage advice, who managed his political fortunes, who guided him to the presidency. All of Herndon's less probable theories and the more disreputable bits of gossip found in his Lincoln records were related in elaborate detail. The so-called Lamon biography was Herndonian throughout, but it failed to show the real affection and respect which Herndon always retained for his partner.

II

The Lamon-Black partnership was not a happy one. James R. Osgood & Company, stout Republicans of a conservative turn, were far from pleased with the manuscript of the biography.[4] Under great pressure from Lamon and from the publishers Black deleted some of his more extreme statements about Lincoln's personal history, but the final chap-

[2] Herndon to Black, December 27, 1870, Black MSS.
[3] Black to Herndon, February 27, 1871, Herndon-Weik Coll.
[4] On the Black-Lamon-Osgood negotiations see A. V. House, Jr., "The Trials of a Ghost-Writer of Lincoln Biography," Ill. State Hist. Soc., *Jour.*, XXXI, 262–296.

ter of his book remained a venomous indictment of Republican policies during the secession winter of 1860–1861.

Rumors of Lamon's debunking biography spread back to Illinois, where they caused panic. One of the strongest arguments in favor of David Davis's selection as the Liberal Republican presidential candidate in 1872 was his intimate friendship with Lincoln. The Liberal Republicans, and not the Radicals, would appear as the true followers of the first Republican President. But now Lamon, one of Davis's closest associates, was about to publish a book critical of Lincoln. Davis's managers were upset. "You can never make the world believe that our mutual friend Judge Davis did not know the contents of your history," S. C. Parks argued with Lamon. "His friendship for you has been so great so long continued & so well known that nearly every body will believe that he could have prevented its publication & would not do it." [5] Others urged Lamon to withhold his book, at least until the Cincinnati convention of Liberal Republicans decided Davis's chances. According to one account, a group of Davis supporters met Lamon in Boston and, supported by his publishers, pressed him to suppress, expurgate, or delay the publication of his biography. When Lamon proved intractable, these "parties from the West" are supposed to have locked him in a room with the assurance that he would never be released till he consented to the censorship of offensive passages. [6]

However it came about, in early 1872 Lamon, without asking the consent of his collaborator, agreed to revise many small matters and to suppress the entire last chapter of Black's manuscript. Thus mutilated, "Lamon's" *Life of Abraham Lincoln from His Birth to His Inauguration as President* appeared in June 1872, a fat and expensive volume of 547 pages. It was a sensation. After all the deletions and revisions, this was probably the most harshly critical biography that had appeared in America. It combined ruthless revelation and flippant cynicism to give a devastating caricature of Lincoln. At the time of Abraham's birth, the biography began, his parents "are supposed to have been married about three years," but for this belief "there exists no evidence but that of mutual acknowledgment and cohabitation." This was but the start. For the first time the stories about which Herndon had been gossiping for years in his "indirect language" were now revealed in their ugly nakedness — the illegitimacy of Lincoln's mother, Lincoln's "infidel book," the jilting of Mary Todd, domestic difficulties

---

[5] Parks to Lamon, June 12, 1871, Black MSS.

[6] There are several variant accounts of this incident. Leonard Swett is alleged to have been active in securing the expurgation of the Lamon biography. Horace White to Weik, April 15, 1909, Herndon-Weik Coll.

in the Lincoln household, Lincoln's "shrewd game" in deceiving preachers by pretending to be a Christian. Throughout the emphasis was on Lincoln the schemer and the politician, cunning, ambitious, unprincipled. Black had charity for none.

From any chapter in the Lamon biography one could compile a vocabulary of vituperation. Lincoln's engagement to Mary Todd was termed "one of the great misfortunes of his life and of hers" — this at a time when the President's widow was still alive. Lincoln was "singularly inconstant and unstable in his relations with . . . women." "His mind was filled . . . with extravagant visions of personal grandeur and power." "He would go a long way out of his road to tell . . . a broad story," for "his humor was . . . chiefly exercised in . . . telling stories of the grosser sort." Lincoln "did nothing out of mere gratitude, and forgot the devotion of his warmest partisans as soon as the occasion for their services had passed." He had an "overweening ambition" and pursued political office with breathless eagerness. Though at heart an infidel, this "by no means . . . unselfish politician," this wily politician, "did not disdain to regulate his religious manifestations with some reference to his political interests." "To be popular was to him the greatest good in life." On and on Black's book went, quoting the less savory reminiscences from Herndon's records, adding some of Herndon's less favorable judgments, and citing Herndon as authority throughout.

Newspaper reviewers who skimmed the volume in order to meet a deadline were not unduly critical, but critics in the influential monthly periodicals were severe. Few questioned the veracity of the Lamon-Black biography; most doubted its propriety. Horace White of the Chicago *Tribune* examined the biography "with the most painful feelings" and pronounced it a book for gossips. "Even if every word of it were true," he ruled, "no excuse can palliate the atrocity of its publication." [7]

The most unfavorable review appeared in *Scribner's Monthly*, edited by J. G. Holland. Herndon had gone out of his way to offend the Massachusetts editor, and Black repeatedly ridiculed the eulogistic Lincoln biography which Holland published in 1866. The *Scribner's* editor now had his chance to retaliate. He found grave objections to the new life of Lincoln. "The violent and reckless prejudice, and the utter want of delicacy and even of decency by which the book is characterized," Holland concluded, "will more than counterbalance the value of its new material . . . and will even make its publication (by the fa-

---

[7] Chicago *Tribune*, June 4, 1872. For a summary of other critical opinions, see the article by A. V. House, Jr., cited above.

mous publishers whose imprint imparts to it a prestige and authority which its authorship would fail to give) something like a national misfortune." [8]

Reviewers did not fail to note Herndon's share in the Lamon-Black biography. "Mr. Herndon," Holland pointed out, "is accredited by Colonel Lamon with a share in the authorship . . . which makes it very largely his own." Throughout Herndon was quoted; he was repeatedly eulogized; he was played up as the guiding force in Lincoln's career. "The theory on which [the Lamon biography] . . . is written," Holland added witheringly, "seems to be that Mr. Herndon was the Pumblechook of the great President, his guide, philosopher, and friend, the architect of his fortunes. . . . No doubt the book makes an effective portrait of what Mr. Lincoln would have been . . . if Mr. Lincoln had become what Mr. Herndon would have had him . . . become."

Herndon was shrilly denounced by the *Galaxy*. Lamon had merely fathered the gossip about Lincoln which Herndon "had ineffectually hawked about in Illinois as a . . . course of lectures, until friends of the great President compelled him, for the sake of decency, to desist." Herndon was too thorough an egotist with too unbalanced a mind to be a reliable informant on any subject. The "Herndon and Lamon narrative" was characterized by "vulgar incapacity to understand, and the . . . gross conceit to misrepresent . . . the plainest history." "Perhaps we should add," the reviewer sneered, "that we do not accuse Herndon and Lamon of intending to tell untruths about Mr. Lincoln. . . . they are too ignorant and conceited to know untruth from truth." [9]

III

While this war of words was being fought, Herndon on his farm along the Sangamon knew little of the great stir in the world of letters. Lamon, taking his bound copies of Herndon's manuscripts with him, holed up at Martinsburg, West Virginia; he answered no critics, wrote no letters, and drank much whiskey. Chauncey Black had the heady feeling of being left alone in a hostile world. His position was awkward, for as Lamon's anonymous ghost-writer (though that secret had leaked out) he could not defend himself. He was bitter at the critics who dared assault his book. He was outraged at the cowardice of his publishers in mutilating his manuscript. He was furious at Lamon for permitting the expurgations.

He had paid out $1,500 in cash; he had spent months in preparing his manuscript; and for his investment he received precisely nothing.

[8] *Scribner's Mo.*, IV, 506–510.   [9] *Galaxy*, XIV, 566–569.

Osgood & Company reported that in spite of all the furor over the biography fewer than two thousand copies were sold during the first six months after publication. Black understood that he had purchased half-ownership of Herndon's records, but Lamon carried the bound copies off with him and would agree to no settlement. Black considered legal action against his former partner and asked Herndon just what the terms of his contract with Lamon had been. Herndon, who had kept no record at all of the transaction, replied that the original manuscripts were his own property; Lamon, he reported incorrectly, had paid him only $2,000 for the *use* of the copies of his Lincoln Record. Generously Herndon would permit Black to look at his records if he ever came to Illinois.[10] Black was disheartened. As ghost-writer for Lamon, he had no opportunity to promote the sale of his own book. His mutilated biography was a total loss, and he did not own the materials from which to prepare a revision or a new volume.

Just as public interest in the Lamon life was declining, a new outbreak of criticism offered a chance to stimulate interest in a revised, but unexpurgated, edition of the life of Lincoln. One of the things in the Lamon-Black biography that had most outraged readers was its insistence that Lincoln "was never a member of any church, nor did he believe in the divinity of Christ, or the inspiration of the Scriptures"; that as a youth if "he went to church at all, he went to mock, and came away to mimic"; that in his New Salem days he wrote a book "deriding the gospel history of Jesus"; that in later years, though politics made him more discreet, he never changed his religious views.[11] Eighteen pages were devoted to the question of Lincoln's Christianity, and extensive extracts were quoted from Herndon's interviews with David Davis, John Todd Stuart, James H. Matheny, Mrs. Abraham Lincoln, and other intimates to prove the President's unorthodoxy. Black also included the full text of Herndon's letter to Francis E. Abbot, free-thinking editor of the *Index,* in which Lincoln was positively classified as an infidel.

These slurs had not gone unnoticed by reviewers of the Lamon biography. Holland, whose own life of the President was dedicated to proving that Lincoln had been a "true-hearted Christian," took immediate exception. He considered Lamon's book an assault on Christianity "under cover of the good name and great fame of Abraham Lincoln." Holland was not injudicious. "The religion of the Lord Jesus Christ," he pointed out, "is no more in need of the patronage of a great man than it is in danger from the disparagement of a small

---

[10] Herndon to Black, January 4 and February 24, 1873, Black MSS.
[11] Lamon, *Life of Abraham Lincoln,* 486–487.

one. . . ." But Lamon's "offence against good taste and . . . outrage on decency" raised a question of historical truth. The basic issue, as Holland saw it, was "not whether Abraham Lincoln was a subscriber to the creeds of orthodoxy, but whether . . . he was used to do those things which Jesus Christ exemplified." [12]

Holland's views were those of the devout and the Republican all over the nation. The political aspects of the quarrel over Lincoln's religion must not be overlooked.[13] This was no mere tempest among crackpots; it was a major political struggle to determine the status of a national hero. Republicans, realizing that the untarnished name of the Great Emancipator was one of their strongest political assets, directed violent abuse against Lamon, against Black, whose share in the biography had become known, and against Herndon, who was considered a sort of joint author. The reputed author and his collaborators were denounced by the *Illinois State Journal* as vile vermin, drawn "from the mud of the festering pool." [14]

The Reverend James A. Reed, pastor of Springfield's First Presbyterian Church, in which the Lincolns had rented a pew, a fundamentalist and a fighting Republican, took it upon himself to answer the "infamous charges made in Lamon's book." [15] A humorless, intolerant man who took this whole affair very seriously, Reed considered himself a sort of self-appointed defender both of Christianity and of the Republican party. The minister had not personally known Lincoln, but he assiduously gathered up statements and reminiscences concerning the President's faith and combined them in a lecture titled "The Later Life and Religious Sentiments of Abraham Lincoln." Delivered first in Springfield on January 4, 1873, Reed's lecture was immensely popular; he said precisely what his audience wanted to hear. He was asked to repeat his address in other parts of Illinois, in Minnesota, and in Pennsylvania, and, at Holland's urging, published it in full in the July 1873 issue of *Scribner's Monthly*.

Reed's lecture was an effective piece of pleading. His basic point had considerable validity. Whatever his early religious views (and in this whole controversy it is well to remember that neither side had any knowledge of Lincoln's 1846 declaration: "That I am not a member of any Christian Church, is true; but I have never denied the truth of the Scriptures . . . [or] spoken with intentional disrespect of religion . . ."), there was abundant evidence to show that in the pres-

[12] *Scribner's Mo.*, IV, 509.
[13] A. V. House, Jr., "The Genesis of the Lincoln Religious Controversy," Middle States Assoc. of Hist. and Soc. Sci. Teachers, *Proceedings*, XXVI, 44–54.
[14] *Illinois State Journal*, June 18, 1872.
[15] Reed to I. N. Arnold, December 12, 1872, MS., Chicago Hist. Soc.

idential years Lincoln thought much about religion and acted as a Christian. Reed's fundamental proposition was sound, but the manner in which he supported his argument left much to be desired. At the outset he promised that the sentiments imputed to Lincoln by the "latest biography . . . published under the name of . . . Lamon, but with the large co-operation of Mr. W. H. Herndon" would "not go down unchallenged to posterity." He then introduced a side issue — singularly inappropriate in view of his title — by discussing the irrelevant question of Lincoln's illegitimacy, at which the Lamon biography had hinted.

Most of Reed's lecture-article was devoted to the testimony of various witnesses as to Lincoln's religious views. Public opinion in Springfield was highly wrought up, and under pressure John Todd Stuart and James H. Matheny, whose statements to Herndon had been heavily emphasized in the Lamon biography, recanted and denied that they had been correctly quoted. The evidence of Bateman and of the Reverend James Smith as to Lincoln's devout religiosity was repeated, along with reminiscences by various Springfield and Washington preachers in the same tone. All in all, Reed gave an effective performance. The expert might doubt some of his testimony, might note the careful phrasing of certain statements, or might challenge the interpretation of others, but the general reader, with a disposition to idealize Lincoln, was likely to consider the case settled for all time.

Republicans rejoiced that Herndon, Lamon, and Lincoln's other traducers had been so thoroughly discredited. The national ideal was safe; the party hero was once more firmly enshrined as a model of Christianity.[16] Democrats, none too well pleased with the apotheosis of a Republican President, scoffed: "When will this nonsense cease?" "What is the object of these persistent efforts to prove that [Lincoln] . . . was a sanctimonious christian, when the world . . . knows that he was not?" [17]

I V

Chauncey Black saw in the widespread publicity given Reed's lecture a chance to revive interest in his Lincoln biography. He himself concocted a reply to Reed, which was published in the New York *World,* the Chicago *Tribune,* and other papers. Black cross-examined the Springfield preacher, challenged him to produce Lincoln's name on the roll of any Christian church, and asked just when the President's

[16] *Illinois State Journal,* January 10, 1873.
[17] *Illinois State Register,* June 25, 1873.

reported conversion occurred.[18] By this anonymous public letter, phrased in a tone of irritating superiority, Black hoped to provoke a retort either from Reed himself or from Holland. If this occurred, a newspaper war could be prolonged indefinitely, and to "a publisher who had the heart in his work" such publicity would offer many broad opportunities to sell countless copies of the Lincoln biography. The whole controversy was well "calculated to promote the sale of the book." [19]

But Black needed reinforcements. In a panic he wrote Herndon about Reed's lecture which "paints *Lamon* as a mercenary libeller, and you [i.e., Herndon] as the forger of the documents paraded in support of the libels." "The substance . . . of Mr Reeds elaborate performance," Black panted, "is that you, being an infidel and therefore an immoral man, yourself have resorted to the basest means of proving that Mr Lincoln was like you." The lecture-article was "a flimsy, libellous, fraudulent concern," but was "well calculated to deceive the public mind . . . and unless it is answered and exposed it disgraces us all." "The responsibility of meeting this flood of falsehood and calumny," Black urged Herndon, "rests . . . upon you, who are of all men the most competent to repel the lie and maintain the truth." [20]

Tied to his little farm north of the river, Herndon apparently had not heard Reed's lecture and did not know of its publication in *Scribner's* until Black's letter arrived. Prompted by Black and prodded by Mrs. Herndon, he came to think of the Reed article as a personal assault upon himself. Vowing to "write an article or deliver a Lecture . . . on Lincoln's religion from childhood up to 1860," Herndon promised to "Crush the scoundrels." [21] Black was delighted and wrote his publishers that Herndon's reply would doubtless sell incalculable copies of the biography.

Black had been alternately threatening and persuading James R. Osgood & Company since the publication of the "Lamon" book. He tried to convince the skeptical publisher that a cheap, unexpurgated edition of his biography would have enormous sales; failing that, he demanded that Osgood, having mutilated his manuscript, should release all rights in the work and permit Black to find another publisher. Claiming a loss of over seven thousand dollars in the venture, Osgood & Company probably would have been willing to sell the plates of the Lincoln biography for a reasonable sum, but Lamon owned half of

---

[18] Black's letter is reprinted in Douglas C. McMurtrie, ed., *Lincoln's Religion*, 89–98.
[19] Black to J. R. Osgood & Co., July 8, 1873, author's copy, Black MSS.
[20] Black to Herndon, June 23, 1873, Herndon-Weik Coll.
[21] Herndon to Black, July 27, 1873, Black MSS.

the copyright. Black and his former friend were no longer on speaking terms, and, to spite his ghost-writer, Lamon was playing "the dog in the manger and very *snappy*"; he would not give up his rights, would not agree to any terms, would not even write to Black.[22]

Stumped, Black had a bright idea. Since Herndon proved so compliant in the matter of answering Reed, the Pennsylvania lawyer conceived the plan of having Herndon round up some reliable Western publisher who would buy out Osgood's interests in the plates and purchase Lamon's share of the copyright for Herndon.[23] Though "sour and sulky and ugly-tempered" toward Black, Lamon might yield to the blandishments of his old Illinois crony. When this transaction was completed (and Herndon was to take all the risk and do all the work), Black proposed to publish a new, revised edition of the Lincoln biography, "making it a light, rapid sketchy book, for sale on railroads, &c.," with Herndon as reputed author. Of course, he added, both he and Herndon had "other than a pecuniary interest" in such a work, but it would doubtless have an enormous sale. The newspapers could be "made to ring with this Holland, Reed, Herndon, Black controversy about Mr Lincolns religion, and thus indirectly advertise the book indefinitely." [24]

Poor as he was, Herndon was amenable to any suggestion that promised cash. He was green, but he liked Black's project. In all innocence he asked: "Why buy out any body? Why not write a Biography from my originals?" [25] Black pointed to the danger of infringing on the copyright of the "Lamon" biography. It would be much less risky to purchase the plates of the earlier work if Lamon would only sell his interest. Lamon, Black thought, feared exposure; he would say: "if it comes out that *Herndon* furnished all the materials [in the Lincoln biography] and *Black* wrote the book where in the hell will *I* be?" Still, Black figured he would probably sell out cheaply to his old friend Herndon.[26]

Obediently Herndon began looking about for a publisher west of the mountains. By now Black had another idea. If his final offer to Osgood & Company was not accepted, he would claim lawful title to his manuscript and, using the original Lincoln Record, he and Herndon could run whatever legal risks were involved and produce another biography of the President. But to bolster a shaky legal situation it

[22] Black to Herndon, August 18, 1873, Herndon-Weik Coll.
[23] For a sprightly account of the Herndon-Black negotiations see Benjamin P. Thomas, *Portrait for Posterity*, 65–83.
[24] Black to Herndon, August 18, 1873, Herndon-Weik Coll.
[25] Herndon to Black, August 25, 1873, Black MSS.
[26] Black to Herndon, September 3, 1873, Herndon-Weik Coll.

should appear that Herndon had had no hand in the production of the earlier "Lamon" biography. Black enclosed the draft of a "short, sharp terse Card" which Herndon ought to publish in the Chicago *Tribune,* positively denying that he had participated in the writing of Lamon's book. A fling at Holland and Reed was inserted, designed to provoke a retort, which would "furnish a first class opportunity" for more publicity.[27]

Herndon, who had previously endorsed the Lamon-Black biography as "the standard one — one to which all future authors will make their appeal," [28] now discovered that there were numerous faults in that work. He meekly sent to the *Tribune* the public letter drafted by Black, affirming loudly: "*I never wrote a chapter, a page, a paragraph, a sentence, or a word* for the [Lamon] book, except . . . where I am quoted as authority." [29] (Herndon's statement was, of course, irrelevant. Though he did not perform the actual writing of the Lamon biography, he furnished the materials for its composition, read proof on the volume, and vouched for its correctness. As Black wrote Herndon, the Lamon book was "in a peculiar sense *your* book . . . . written on your plan, from your materials, and largely on your authority." [30])

V

The publication of this open letter was a very important move, Black assured Herndon, one that would place him "in an independent position, . . . as the proper person to revise and correct the present volume or to prepare a new one." Meanwhile, what had happened to that lecture Herndon promised? Holland, Reed, and the clericals had been silent now for months on end; they needed to be goaded into a reply and more publicity.[31] Thus spurred, and with Mrs. Herndon nagging at him to defend his besmirched name, Herndon in December 1873 dropped his farm work for five days to write out a lecture which he titled "Lincoln's Religion." He had not attempted anything "literary" since 1866 and the writing "ran hard." It was, he feared, a poor, trashy thing, one that smelled "of the corn field or barn yard." [32]

Herndon could always draw a crowd in Springfield, and notwithstanding the inclement weather the announcement of his lecture for

[27] Black to Herndon, September 26 and November 3, 1873, *ibid.*
[28] Herndon to Black, January 24, 1873, Black MSS.
[29] Chicago *Tribune,* November 20, 1873.
[30] Black to Herndon, August 18, 1873, Herndon-Weik Coll.
[31] Black to Herndon, September 26 and November 22, 1873, *ibid.*
[32] ". . . *my good wife* . . . has been at me for months to answer Reed." Herndon to Black, December 15 and 20, 1873, Black MSS.

December 12 called out "a crowded auditory of intent listeners" at the courthouse.[33] At the very outset Herndon announced his thesis, "that Mr. Lincoln was an unbeliever." [34] ". . . I could state facts about Mr. Lincoln's jokes on and gibes at Christianity . . . that would shock a Christian people." Herndon made these revelations with no little misgiving and only because his own veracity had been impugned by "the most Reverend James A. Reed, 'defender of the faith' of Honest Abe."

As a critique of Reed's article, Herndon's lecture showed considerable skill. One after another he tested Reed's witnesses and showed that they were prejudiced, badly informed, or imperfectly quoted. The minister had cited letters from John Todd Stuart and James H. Matheny denying that they wrote the statements attributed to them in the Lamon biography. Quite true, answered Herndon; they did not *write* the words. He himself had written the statements during his interviews with these men. Their denials were just a quibble over words. Actually, he went on to reveal, Matheny did not write the retraction which Reed quoted; "it was prepared for him by Mr. Reed, and Matheny is old enough to have known that deception and wrong . . . were intended."

As he continued, Herndon lost his temper. He was unwilling to accept the possibility that his opponents could be honestly mistaken; if they did not accept his point of view, they must be deliberately lying. The "Rev. James Smith of Scotland" was publicly branded as "a very able man, but a great old rascal," and one not above lying. Reed had published a letter from Thomas Lewis, a prominent Springfield resident, affirming that Lincoln had expressed admiration for a book written by Smith. Herndon tore into the witness viciously. "Mr. Lewis' veracity and integrity," he jeered, "in this community need no comment. I have heard good men say they would not believe his word under any circumstances, especially so, if he was interested. I hate to state this of Tom, but if he will obtrude himself in this discussion, I cannot help but say a word in self-defense." Lincoln, Herndon declared, detested this man, and it was absurd to think he would have confided his private beliefs to such a fool.

All in all, the lecture on Lincoln's religion revealed Herndon at his worst. It was characterized by the dogmatic conviction of his own righteousness, by intolerance for the opinions of others, and by loose reasoning. Throughout were sprinkled those owlish remarks of which Herndon was so fond. Lamon had suggested that Lincoln was illegiti-

[33] *Illinois State Register,* December 13, 1873.
[34] Quotations in this and the following paragraphs are from Herndon's lecture, conveniently reprinted in McMurtrie, ed., *Lincoln's Religion,* 13–44.

mate, because no marriage record had then been found for his parents. In reply Reed had produced a (spurious) record. Herndon now hinted heavily of things too shocking to be revealed unless his enemies pressed him beyond endurance. There was no record of the Lincoln wedding; perhaps Thomas Lincoln and Nancy Hanks were married only "by mutual consent and agreement . . . , somewhat after the fashion of the free-lovers." Herndon cryptically suggested that there was "one link in the chain of evidence in favor of those who thought . . . that Mr. Lincoln was illegitimate — the child of Abraham Enloe." (Thus for the first time the name of Lincoln's putative father was revealed in print.) Having disclosed his secret, Herndon added cautiously: "I wish it distinctly understood that I give no opinion of Mr. Lincoln's legitimacy or of the marriage of Thomas and Nancy."

As a constructive argument, Herndon's lecture was pitifully weak. He had two basic propositions, both untenable. First of all, his whole case revolved around a definition of terms. He admitted that Lincoln made "addresses at Bible and Sunday school societies," used the Christian "ideas, language, speech and forms" in his presidential proclamations, and had many Christian sentiments. But Lincoln, according to Herndon, did not believe in the literal truth of the Bible and did not join any Christian sect; therefore, no matter how *religious* he may have been, he was not a *Christian*.

Herndon's second main point was essentially negative. Reed and Holland (and most other writers previous to the recent discovery of Lincoln's 1846 statement as to his religion) admitted that Lincoln had been a freethinker in his youth. Herndon thought it the duty of these "defenders of the faith" to establish some occasion on which Lincoln expressly repudiated his old views and formally adhered to Christianity. As Herndon ripped into Reed's witnesses and demolished their testimony, he established only that many persons in Springfield considered Lincoln to have been an unbeliever in his youth. For the President's mature years Herndon had but two authorities. A rather ambiguous letter from John G. Nicolay, one of the President's secretaries, stated that while in the White House Lincoln "gave no outward indications of his mind having undergone any change" in regard to religion. From the record of his interview with Mrs. Lincoln, Herndon quoted Mary Lincoln's statement that her husband "was not a technical Christian."

Thus in logical structure Herndon's address betrayed hasty composition and slovenly reasoning. Black had prescribed a lecture, and Herndon supplied it. He concluded his argument by declaring that he had reviewed all the testimony on the subject fairly and that "the whole weight of the evidence . . . is in favor of the idea that Mr. Lincoln died an unbeliever." This debate, Herndon declared, had great significance.

> 1st. It settles a historic fact. 2nd. It makes it possible to write a true history of a man free from the fear of fire and stake. 3rd. It assures the reading world that the life of Mr. Lincoln will be truly written. 4th. It will be a warning forever to all untrue men, that the life they have lived will be dragged out to public view. 5th. It should convince the Christian pulpit . . . that it is impossible . . . to daub up Sin, and make a hero out of a fool, a knave or a villain, which Mr. Lincoln was not. . . . 6th. Its tendencies will be to arrest and put a stop to romantic biographies, and now let it be written in history and on Mr. Lincoln's tomb — "He died an unbeliever."

VI

Printed in full in the *Illinois State Register*[35] and in broadside form, Herndon's lecture quickly spread over the country. The St. Louis *Globe-Democrat,* the Chicago *Tribune,* the New York *Herald,* the New York *Tribune,* and a score of other papers carried long extracts. The Republican press was uniformly hostile. "JUDAS IN SPRINGFIELD," screamed the New York *Herald.* The lecture "proved that Colonel Herndon had the heart of Judas beating beneath an exterior of friendship; . . . that beneath the cunning pretention of seeking after truth, Colonel Herndon could disguise a horrible avidity for raking amid the ruck of infamous scandals. . . . No words can adequately describe the blackness of such treachery."[36]

Springfield itself was in a dither of excitement. "Perhaps no one Speech was ever deliv[ere]d in Springfield that has caused so much comment," reported one of Herndon's friends.[37] Public opinion divided along party lines. The Republican *Journal* coldly rebuked Herndon for "obnoxiously thrusting his views before the general public" in a discussion which must necessarily be profitless. The Democratic *Register,* unhappy at the canonization of a Republican as the national hero, retorted that Herndon's remarks had been called forth in self-defense, since Herndon had been "assailed and his facts contradicted by several prominent christian ministers." The *Sangamo Monitor,* an independent Democratic scandal sheet, rejoiced that Herndon had crushed Reed. "[H]ad it not been for an itching for notoriety by con-

[35] December 13, 1873.
[36] New York *Herald,* December 15, 1873.
[37] James H. Matheny to Herndon, January 10, 1874, Herndon-Weik Coll.

necting the name of a very obscure parson with that of a very distinguished dead president, the particular belief of Mr. Lincoln, as well as the missing links in the genealogical table of his legitimacy, would have remained with his body in the . . . sepulchre." As it was, "Mr. Reed has entered the arena of debate with vastly his superior, intellectually," and, according to the *Monitor,* the petty parson had been slain.[38]

Isolated by winter weather and impassable roads, Herndon got the reaction only through friends in the city. Those "who cannot be made to believe any thing else, than . . . that Mr. Lincoln was a perfect Saint" were denouncing the lecture bitterly. Those "ready and glad to believe . . . everything that could be said against him" were rejoiced at Herndon's boldness. Perhaps a majority of "the earnest seekers after truth" deplored the lecture as "a powerful blow, at a very beautiful 'air castle' which men were gazing upon, with a great deal of gratulation — they do sincerely regret, that that 'castle' is in danger of crumbling beneath your determined assaults — . — They ask . . . '*What good*' — Why disturb a beautiful faith, which, 'tho unfounded was still a pleasure to hold and enjoy." [39]

Republicans in Springfield were doing all in their power to prevent the air castle from crumbling. The *Journal* quoted in full the New York *Herald's* "Judas in Springfield" editorial. Some saw the weak link in Herndon's argument: his dependence on Nicolay's equivocal letter and on a conversation with Mrs. Lincoln to prove Lincoln's continued unorthodoxy during the war years. Nicolay could be interpreted away, but Mrs. Lincoln's statement needed more than an explanation. That pitiful widow, about to be committed to a mental sanitarium, was prevailed upon to denounce Herndon and to repudiate the interview in which she had declared that Lincoln "was not a technical Christian." The *Journal* could proudly announce on its first page that Mrs. Lincoln denied "unequivocally that she had the conversation with Mr. Herndon, as stated by him." [40]

It was the signal for Herndon to loose all his long stored-up hatred for Mary Lincoln. For once he had caught this most vulnerable and most detested of his enemies in a factual error, and he produced a public letter to show Mrs. Lincoln up as an irresponsible liar. He transcribed in full the notes of his conversation with Mary Lincoln in the St. Nicholas Hotel shortly after Lincoln's death. Here was the record.

[38] *Illinois State Journal,* December 13, 1873; *Illinois State Register,* December 13, 1873; *Sangamo Monitor,* December 18, 1873.

[39] William Jayne to Herndon, December 19, 1873; James H. Matheny to Herndon, January 10, 1874, Herndon-Weik Coll.

[40] *Illinois State Journal,* December 19, 1873.

If Mrs. Lincoln denied it, what did she mean? Did she intend to say that no such interview had ever occurred? Or that Herndon did not correctly record her words? Or that her recorded statements were not true? Did Mrs. Lincoln assert that her husband "was a technical Christian and joined a church"? If so, where was her proof? Herndon gloated over his trapped enemy. He was sure that Mary Lincoln's friends, knowing of her mental condition, "would not let her answer these questions." Her reckless charges revealed her "spasmodic madness." [41]

In justice to Herndon, it must be recalled that he was writing under provocation. His facts were correct. He had had the interview with Mary Lincoln, and she had doubtless said what he noted in his records. But his public attack, "Mrs. Lincoln's Denial, and What She Says," was a cruel blow against a sick woman. It was issued as a broadside, was hawked about the streets, and was republished in Chicago, St. Louis, and New York papers. Before many months Mary Lincoln was committed to an asylum, and Herndon could celebrate a final victory over his old foe.

Herndon's cronies congratulated him on his success. Mary Lincoln had never been popular in Springfield. More than one who had felt the sharp edge of her tongue rejoiced when Herndon humbled her. "It is always unfortunate to get into a controversy with a woman," William Jayne knew, "but you seemed to be pushed into this one & could not avoid after her denial some kind of reply." Herndon had "managed it very well." "In this affair with the 'First Lady of the Land,'" Jayne complimented him, "you do not like a clod hopper call her a d — d old liar & hussey — but like a courtly gentleman & lawyer you say that the good poor woman crushed beneath a mountain of woe . . . is not altogether a competent & trustworthy witness   William, your intellect & diplomacy does not seem to have rusted by a few years of country life . . . every one I have heard speak of it pities the woman for again obtruding herself before the public." [42] Hearing only from those who agreed with him, Herndon was convinced that "Every intelligent man and woman says I said just enough and in the right spirit &c. &c." [43]

The controversy over Lincoln's religion now deteriorated into a kind of farce. Republican papers searched around frantically to find some witness to bolster the theory that Lincoln was a Christian. Testimony

[41] Herndon's open letter appeared in the *Illinois State Register*, January 14, 1874, in the *Illinois State Journal*, January 15, 1874, and in the Chicago *Tribune*, January 16, 1874. It was printed also as a broadside, a copy of which, titled *Mrs. Lincoln's Denial, and What She Says*, is preserved in the Mass. Hist. Soc.

[42] Jayne to Herndon, January 19, 1874, Herndon-Weik Coll.

[43] Herndon to Black, January 21, 1874, Black MSS.

of the most improbable sort was adduced to "prove" the President's adherence to any one of a half-dozen sects. The *Illinois State Journal* induced an old friend from New Salem days, Ben F. Irwin of Pleasant Plains, Illinois, to reply to Herndon. While not questioning Herndon's candor or veracity, Irwin believed that Herndon "never knew or understood what the faith of Lincoln was." He reviewed the familiar evidence and then added a sensational feature. While at New Salem, Irwin asserted, Lincoln had written a book about religion, but it was not "an argument of the Thomas Paine variety" but a manuscript in favor of Christianity and a defense of universal salvation. As for the writing alleged to have been burned by John Hill, that was not really an "infidel book" at all but a love letter addressed to Ann Rutledge! That, claimed Irwin, finished off Herndon; Lincoln was actually a Universalist.[44]

The Democratic papers made merry over these conflicting claims. Pointing out that within a few weeks speakers had attempted to show that the Sixteenth President had been an infidel, a Presbyterian, a Congregationalist, a Methodist, a spiritualist, a Universalist, and "both a theoretical and practical free-lover, and . . . really the father of the Oneida community," the editor of the *Illinois State Register* humorously threatened "to prove by indisputable documentary evidence that he was a Mormon, and the boon companion of Joe Smith." [45]

VII

Black was vastly pleased with all the to-do created by Herndon's lecture. The address was mighty bold, and if Parson Reed had any self-respect he "must rise to explain, and confess or justify." That meant more publicity, and more publicity would mean more sales. "Don't let the subject get cold," he kept urging Herndon. But on second thought Black found one weakness in Herndon's lecture. It was, after all, rather negative. "It would have been more effective if [Herndon] . . . had inserted a broad eulogy upon Mr Lincoln['s] character as a patriot and a man." [46]

Receptive to Black's every suggestion, Herndon ground out a tribute to Lincoln, so eulogistic that it was published in the Republican *Journal* but not in the Democratic press. One would be a little more impressed by this tribute to Lincoln if it was not in sharp contradiction to Herndon's previous utterances, made when he had no financial

44 *Illinois State Journal*, May 16, 1874.
45 May 16, 1874.
46 Black to Herndon, December 18 and 19, 1873, Herndon-Weik Coll.

interest at stake. Upon Black's advice, Herndon now decided that Lincoln had been "a kind, tender, and sympathetic man," "of unbounded veracity and unlimited integrity," "bold and manly in his denunciation of wrong, however and by whoever done," "a man of great fidelity to what he believed was right . . . true to friends, never deserting them till they deserted virtue, veracity and integrity," "true to his trust, true to his country, and true to the rights of man." "Washington was America's creator; Lincoln was its savior . . . take him all in all, he was as near a perfect man as God generally makes." [47]

Black approved Herndon's made-to-order eulogy as "a capital piece of work," which would help sales of the projected Lincoln biography. [48] This proposed life of Lincoln was the thread that connected all these squabbles and arguments and lectures and public letters and broadsides. The object was to keep interest in the Lincoln subject alive until Herndon and Black could secure a good publisher. Plans for the book went smoothly for a time — but then Herndon struck a snag. He was enthusiastic about the projected biography, but "thinking over and over" his agreement with Lamon he remembered hazily, "I *think* I did engage not to write a life of Lincoln for five years." "I do not say that I did so agree & yet it seems I did." He anxiously asked Black whether five years had elapsed since the sale. "What I state about the 5 years time &c is not even a decided opinion," he hazarded, "it only *seems* — a kind of dream &c." [49]

If that was the case, Black replied, there was only one course open. Since Osgood & Company had mangled his manuscript, he would inform the publishers that he intended to take his book and put out a new, unexpurgated edition. The publishers would complain but could do nothing. A copy of Black's letter would be sent to Lamon, who would "curse himself black, drink himself blind, and go to bed under a heap of blankets to sweat out his wrath." "He will probably write me a courtly letter," Black conjectured, "containing two separate and distinct propositions — (1st) that I may kiss his backside and go to hell, and (2) that he will upon sight give me a much deserved 'body-beating.'" But neither would happen, for at that psychological moment Herndon would write Lamon "Stating that you believe the five years aforesaid have about expired; that his book (to your great regret) seems to have met with no favor; . . . that a new Life is demanded; that you intend to write it; . . . and in short will he now sell

[47] *Illinois State Journal*, February 14, 1874. Herndon's letter was reprinted in the New York *Tribune* and the Pittsburgh *Chronicle*. Black to Herndon, February 22, 1874, Herndon-Weik Coll.

[48] Black to Herndon, February 22, 1874, Herndon-Weik Coll.

[49] Herndon to Black, November 19 and 30, 1873, Black MSS.

you . . . his copyright." Lamon, thinking to foil Black, would probably accept Herndon's terms — and only then would discover that Herndon and Black were partners.[50]

Negotiations proceeded along these lines for some months. Herndon wrote Lamon precisely as Black had suggested. He offered to purchase Lamon's copyright of the Lincoln biography. "Has any other person, except yourself, any interest in the Book. . . ?" he asked in seeming ignorance.[51]

While waiting for Lamon's decision, the would-be collaborators were daydreaming about their biography. The main thing, they both agreed, would be to make some money out of the book. Herndon wanted to delete all the speeches and long quotations in the Lamon biography and to exclude "all speculation — all hits spats &c at any and all persons." He would "dodge no well authenticated fact . . . evade no truth . . . make nothing by suggestion — nor unmake anythink by suppression." But the principal object was to publish "a *very cheap life* — one to be read on cars — boats — stages — One to be read[i]ly [available to] all everywhere and anywhere — night or day — *cheap* to all. — good for old or young, but CHEAP — CHEAP." [52]

No word came from Lamon. Herndon fussed and fretted. His former tactful inquiry was now followed by a very saucy letter, which he hoped would make Lamon "mad — 'Cuss' & write me." His old friend, whom he had praised for telling the truth and for standing straight before the facts, Herndon now condemned as "a great ass — an obstinate fool — suspicious, jealous and ungrateful — a very — very curious man." By May 1874 Herndon had still done nothing toward finding a publisher, for Lamon's silence created a horrid doubt. He had to secure a copy of his bill of sale for the Lincoln Record. "I may in that writing," he timidly confessed to Black, "have said I would *never* write a life of Linon [*sic*]." [53]

That was the end of the proposed Herndon-Black biography. Black could do nothing alone. Herndon could not move until he knew "what to do lawfully." Lamon would not write. In disgust, Black gave up the project and turned to politics; a few years later he was elected lieutenant governor of Pennsylvania. Lamon sank into silent obscurity. And Herndon, his hopes dashed, his projected book buried, his vision of a fortune vanished, hobbled back to his pears and his pigs — and his whiskey.

[50] Black to Herndon, November 19, 1873, Herndon-Weik Coll.
[51] Herndon to Lamon, January 8, 1874, Lamon MSS. Herndon sent a copy of the letter to Black for approval.
[52] Herndon to Black, January 26, 1874, Black MSS.
[53] Herndon to Black, May 29, 1874, *ibid.* Italics supplied.

CHAPTER *xviii*

A Dead Flat Failure

I

For five years after 1875 Herndon dropped almost out of sight. He came to Springfield so rarely that his infrequent presence was noted in the newspapers.[1] His declining business in the Sangamon courts was almost entirely abandoned. Late in 1875 Herndon announced he was going to confine himself to practice in Menard County and promised to "be present at each term of court, and [to] . . . attend to all business entrusted to him."[2] Regularly he went to Petersburg, but he found few clients — only those who could not afford a better lawyer.

Most of his days were spent in hard work on his farm six miles north of Springfield. Bit by bit his six hundred acre inheritance had been sold to pay debts and taxes until hardly more than a garden plot remained. In 1873, probably to prevent foreclosure for debt, Herndon deeded to his wife his house, his barren acres, and his pitifully few belongings — twenty-five Berkshire hogs, one roan colt, a cow and a calf, and one mule named Tom.[3]

During these bitter years Herndon aged rapidly. He became stooped and thin, for he ate "no more than a canary bird."[4] Repeatedly he suffered from colds or influenza, and each attack was followed by weeks of painful neuralgia. With his wife and the three children of his second marriage, Herndon lived alone on the ridge above the Sangamon.[5] Isolated by bad roads and poverty, Herndon lost touch with affairs in the world. The few letters he wrote were no longer proudly addressed from "Fairview" estate but from the plebeian "Chinkapin P. O."

Herndon was lonely. He had sold his library; he had lost his best friends; he had no one to talk to. The farmers in the community jeered

[1] *Sangamo Daily Monitor,* February 19, 1878.
[2] Petersburg *Democrat,* September 11, 1875.
[3] Sangamon Co. Deed Record, XLVIII, 349–350.
[4] Statement of Mr. James S. Miles, Sr., to me, November 14, 1944.
[5] Herndon's children by his second marriage were Nina Belle, born 1865; William M., 1870; and Minnie, 1875.

Lincoln's Herndon

at him as impractical, improvident, inebriate. Herndon's passion for reading, his unorthodox religious views, and his advocacy of greenbacks (for he changed his monetary politics after 1875) caused him to be strongly distrusted in this rural, fundamentalist, Republican neighborhood. Once or twice a month to buy groceries — those few indispensables his clay hills would not grow — Herndon trudged on foot the six long miles into Springfield, and his neighbors watched him pass thinking: "There goes Bill Herndon, the old drunkard, he lights his cigars with greenbacks." [6]

The chance visitors who came his way were welcomed with open hands. In 1879 young George Washington Smith, later a familiar and loved professor at Southern Illinois Normal University, was visiting a friend north of Springfield. When conversation drifted around to Abraham Lincoln — as it always seems to do in Sangamon County — his host asked if Smith would not like to meet "a man who knew more about Lincoln than anyone else." About sundown the two called on Herndon and found him at home. After introductions were made, Herndon led his young visitor into the house.

Mr. Herndon appeared to me at the time [Professor Smith remembered] as a worn out lawyer. He was dressed as you would expect to find a farmer who was just knocking around seeing that things about the farm were going well. There was no one else in the house . . . except Mr. Herndon. He was thin, not plump. His face was covered with a ragged beard, hair not abundant, and somewhat "towsled." I would not say he looked decrepit, but he moved about cautiously, slowly. He offered me a plain kitchen chair. We sat about the cook stove. . . . When we got it straightened out that I was a visitor to his home just because I was interested in Lincoln and because of his relation to Lincoln, we began our conversation about Lincoln. . . . In all his expressions, he spoke in great respect of Lincoln. . . .

When Mr. Herndon and I had talked quite a while in the kitchen he suggested we go into the Library to look at Lincoln's picture. We walked through the "dog trot" into the library. This room was about 16 x 16 ft., a big strong table in the center, chairs, and as I remember a sort of "day bed." . . . On the walls . . . were cases full of books. . . . But the chief thing in the room was a life size portrait, in oil, of Abraham Lincoln. It was the work of "Conant" [Alban Jasper Conant], a portrait painter of considerable prominence of the last century. It seemed to me at the time that his attentions to the picture were very tender. In fact he seemed to feel different when we went into the Library from what he did in the kitchen. I think I did not stay more than an hour and a half. When I said I must go he urged me to stay

6 Renne, *Lincoln and the Land of the Sangamon,* 41.

A Dead Flat Failure

longer and seemed to be affected much as if I were a dear relative whom he did not often get to see. I thought it odd.

Herndon seemed so reluctant to see his guests leave that Mr. Smith guessed "he was hungry for a kind of association which he did not get from his hired help or from his neighbors." [7] That phrase summarizes Herndon's lost years.

II

Though Herndon was out of sight, he was not forgotten. His reputation lingered, like the smell after a sulphur match burns out. Vicious rumors were whispered in Springfield parlors and were repeated on the streets. Herndon was a scab, a malcontent, a shiftless tramp, a theorist. "Herndon is in the lunatic asylum, well chained," gossips said. "Herndon is a pauper." "Herndon is a drunkard." "Herndon is a vile infidel and a knave, a liar and a drunkard." [8]

Tired and ill as he was, Herndon had still enough energy to denounce a lie and nail a falsehood. In September 1877 the New York *Tribune* carried a notice that he had attempted to commit suicide by taking an overdose of laudanum. When the story reached Springfield it created a big sensation until Herndon's explicit denial quashed the tale: "I never attempted to commit suicide; never took laudanum; am well, happy, hearty, doing well, and hope to live just one hundred years, and to do good to my fellow-man to the end." [9]

But there was always a new crop of rumors. In 1882, for example, a Kansas newspaper carried the report:

Lincoln's Old Law Partner a Pauper

Bill Herndon is a pauper in Springfield, Ill. . . . It is said that he worked hard with Lincoln in preparing the memorable speeches by the man who afterward became President, during the debates . . . in 1858, and in constructing the Cooper Union address. . . . Herndon, with all his attainments, was a man who now and then went on a spree, and it was no uncommon thing for him to leave an important lawsuit and spend several days in drinking and carousing. This habit became worse after Lincoln's death, and . . . Herndon went down step by step till his old friends and associates point to him as a common drunkard.[10]

[7] Professor George Washington Smith kindly supplied me this account of his visit in a letter dated November 15, 1944.

[8] *Sangamo Daily Monitor*, October 2, 1877; Herndon's *A Card and a Correction.*

[9] New York *Tribune* (semi-weekly ed.), September 14 and 28, 1877.

[10] Cherryvale (Kansas) *Globe-News*, September 1882, quoted in *A Card and a Correction.*

In "a *mad* FIT" Herndon refuted these charges by issuing *A Card and a Correction,* a printed broadside sent to his few friends. Emphatically he announced that he "was not a pauper, never [had] . . . been and expect[ed] never to be." "I am working on my own farm, making my own living with my own muscle and brain, a place and a calling that even Christianity with its persecution and malignity can never reach me to do me much harm." He had never been a common drunkard, Herndon claimed, but for years was an ardent and enthusiastic temperance man. "It is a fact," he confessed, "that I once, years ago, went on a spree; and this I now deeply regret. It however is in the past, and let a good life in the future bury the past. I have not fallen, I have risen, and all good men and women will applaud the deed, always excepting a small, little, bitter Christian. . . ." Herndon swore that he had never left a client "during the progress of a trial or at other times for the causes alleged, drunkenness." His broadside concluded with a venomous fling at his defamers; his reply was bitter, he admitted — "but it is true nevertheless." [11]

"Why," asked Herndon, replying to the rumor mongers, "is all this libelling of me? I am a mere private citizen, hold no office, do not beg the good people to give me one often." These malicious attacks he was convinced were the work of his old enemy, "the Right Rev. pastor and liar of this city." Herndon never forgave an affront. In 1873 James A. Reed in a public lecture had challenged Herndon's statements about Lincoln's religion. Ten years later Herndon was still convinced that the minister was "an eager, itching libeller," who spread lies "because [Herndon] . . . did assert and affirm . . . that Mr. Lincoln was an infidel, sometimes bordering on atheism." "These charges," Herndon complained, "have been scattered broadcast all over the land, and have gone into every house, have been read at every fireside, till the good people believe them, believe that I am nearly as mean as a little Christian, and *all because I told the truth and stand firm in my convictions.*" [12]

It was true that much of the abuse against Herndon was caused by his controversial statements on Lincoln's unbelief. If the earlier stages of this somewhat ghoulish quarrel had political implications, the latter phases of the dispute over Lincoln's religion were important skirmishes in the fierce war waged in the seventies and eighties between orthodoxy and freethought.

Darwin's evolutionary theories and the higher criticism applied to

[11] Herndon to Arnold, December 27, 1882, Arnold MSS.
[12] Herndon's *A Card and a Correction.*

the Bible shattered the cast-iron fundamentalism of American religious thought. Many tried to cling to a literal interpretation of the Scriptures and battled science as the spawn of the devil. Moderates slowly shifted to an emphasis on a social gospel. The left wing of the Protestant movement drifted into various systems of freethought.[13] The most important of these dissenting groups was the Free Religious Association formed in Boston in 1867 with such distinguished members as Octavius Brooks Frothingham, Robert Dale Owen, Charles Eliot Norton, Francis E. Abbot, and Lucretia Mott. The tenets of the Free Religious Association combined the religious philosophy of Theodore Parker with the neo-rational creed of social Darwinism. These radicals abandoned all sects and creeds. Christianity, they held, was but a local, temporary aspect of religion — just as Buddhism, Confucianism, or Judaism. A true faith constructed rationally and in accordance with the latest findings of archaeology, biology, geology, and astronomy, would combine the best elements of all these earlier beliefs into a universal religion of humanity — "free religion."

Others went beyond the ideas of the Free Religious Association. Some, like Robert G. Ingersoll, hardly waited for Huxley to coin the word before becoming agnostics. More radical disbelievers professed themselves atheists. Regardless of the shade of disbelief, all carried on a militant campaign against orthodox Christianity. All delighted in puncturing its unhistorical traditions, in deriding its prescientific cosmology, and in mocking its inconsistent ethic. The freethought movement was more than a theological argument; it was part of a general effort to transform American religion from a sterile, individualistic fundamentalism into a philosophy for social reform.

Herndon applauded all these freethought movements. Not an atheist himself, nor even an agnostic, he considered himself "a progressive and advanced little thinker . . . an altruist, believing in an infinite Energy — Universal soul — God — in universal inspiration, revelation — [all men the] sons of God." [14] Most of his views were shared by members of the Free Religious Association. "Evangelical Christianity is fast departing," he hoped, and he was eager to speed the day. "I am glad to see free thought come to the front everywhere," he cheered.[15]

The Christian religion seemed to Herndon an obstacle to social progress. He strongly urged civil marriage and "an easy, inexpensive,

[13] For a thorough and objective study of this intellectual current, see Sidney Warren, *American Freethought, 1860–1914.*

[14] Herndon to Weik, January 15, 1886, Herndon-Weik Coll.

[15] Herndon to Editor of the *Liberal Age*, October 26, 1882, clipping in Lincoln National Life Foundation.

and quick method of getting a divorce" on the ground of incompatibility, but he saw this reform thwarted by people who considered marriage "a religious — a *Christian* institution."

> Christians . . . believe, or pretend to believe [he sneered], that the Bible is a personal God's divine special revelation, fully inspired, and that it contains all the necessary truths for man in this world, even to planting corn and reaping it. This Christian idea rises like a huge mountain before the progress of the human race, and this credulous, fanatical, and bigoted idea must be wiped out, sponged out, of the mind of man, before we can march upward and onward. Is there any book in the world that does half the damage to man that this book does? It does more harm than all the vulgar, filthy, and obscene books and prints in the world.[16]

With this hatred for organized Christianity Herndon entered wholeheartedly into the freethinkers' campaign against orthodoxy. He was a valued recruit, because he could — and did — speak not for himself alone but for his dead partner. The martyred Lincoln had advertising value. As early as 1870 Herndon had informed Francis E. Abbot, editor of the *Index,* the voice of the Free Religious Association, that Lincoln was an unbeliever in Christianity. His letter was published with a great deal of fanfare, and it was reprinted as an anti-Christian tract.[17] The freethought press gave much attention to the sections of Lamon's biography dealing with Lincoln's religious, or irreligious, views, and Herndon's 1873 lecture on *Lincoln's Religion* was widely quoted.

This was one subject Herndon was unwilling to drop. Even during the five lost years after 1875 he managed to keep up some connection with freethought leaders. In 1883 he roused himself to continue his discussion of Lincoln's religion in a series of communications addressed to the new "brave, reading, intelligent, and searching generation" who might have missed his earlier pronouncements on this touchy subject.

Herndon had a mind like a weathercock; he pointed in whatever direction his correspondents blew. By 1880 most of his friends were confessed atheists, and Herndon's statements accordingly became more extreme. "I affirm at the outset that Mr. Lincoln was an Infidel of the radical type, sometimes bordering on Atheism," Herndon wrote in the *Truth Seeker,* the atheist periodical. Repetitiously he reviewed his evi-

[16] Herndon to Editor of the Boston *Investigator,* December 29, 1882, clipping in Lincoln National Life Foundation.
[17] Reprints of this "document of great historical value" were offered for sale at $3.50 a hundred. *Index,* I (March 12, 1870), 4.

dences on this subject; he had added nothing since his quarrel with Newton Bateman in 1866. Lincoln, Herndon claimed, usually believed in a God, but he derided special inspiration, the direct revelation of the Bible, the divinity of Christ, and the efficacy of prayer. Those who tried to prove the President was a Christian were really making him seem "a fool, an ass, or a hypocrit[e], or a combination of them." "The tendency of Mr. Lincoln was to a scientific Materialism — evolution — though . . . without denying soul, heaven, God. His idea of God was a kind of 'Sufficient Cause'. . . ." All these statements Herndon swore were positively and unshakably correct.[18]

Along with these public communications Herndon kept up an active correspondence with freethought leaders.[19] Again and again he elaborated Lincoln's religious views, explained and defended his interpretation, and reviewed the course of the controversy since 1865. His letters, public and private, were welcome ammunition for the anti-Christians. The *Index,* the *Iconoclast,* the Boston *Investigator,* and the *Truth Seeker* published and republished his statements. A Kansas atheist leader, John E. Remsburg, used Herndon's communications as a principal source in writing *Six Historic Americans: Paine, Jefferson, Washington, Franklin, Lincoln, Grant, the Fathers and Saviors of Our Republic, Freethinkers.*

There was only one way the devout Christians could snatch the shroud of the martyred Lincoln from these infidels. They denounced Herndon. The bitterness of the abuse measures the importance attached to his statements. Rumors about Herndon's private life were circulated. It was whispered that he was a drug addict.[20] His fondness for drink was widely publicized. Even among his neighbors he became known as "old Bill Herndon, the drunkard," or "Herndon the infidel."

III

In 1881, after years of virtual silence, Herndon's voice was again heard in Springfield. He tried to make a fresh start. He stopped drinking. His new policy was one of absolute abstinence from liquor,[21] and it is

---

[18] "Abraham Lincoln's Religious Belief," *Truth Seeker,* X, 114–115; "Lincoln's Religion," *ibid.,* X, 148–149.

[19] See, for example, Herndon's long letter to Eugene MacDonald, editor of the *Truth Seeker,* December 7, 1883, collection of Mr. W. H. Townsend.

[20] The charge that Herndon was a drug addict is unfounded. I have unimpeachable evidence on this point. The rumor probably rose through a confusion of identity, since another member of the Herndon family did use narcotics.

[21] Cyrus O. Poole to Herndon, December 24, 1885, Weik MSS.

doubtful that Herndon was ever intoxicated again. He boasted: "I live a sober — manly and moral life." [22]

With this unexplainable reformation Herndon tried to turn back time to 1865, but Springfield remembered well the past fifteen years. His sins were not lightly forgiven. At every door he tried, this tired, broken old man was refused. Rather pitifully he attempted to get back into politics and in 1882 announced as a Democratic candidate for the state legislature. When the votes in the primary were counted, Herndon received only 121 ballots in all of Springfield. From the city ward where he resided for thirty years he got not a vote. [23]

Herndon tried also to pick up his law practice again. After 1876 his name had been dropped from the Springfield directory of attorneys. For years Herndon had hardly a case in the Sangamon courts. In 1884 he reopened an office in the city, choosing for his new partner G. W. Murray, a young Democrat from Ohio. [24] The Herndon & Murray office on North Fifth street drew a piddling business, and Herndon resorted to advertising:

> I have taken up my old profession, the prompt and vigorous practice of the law in this city . . . [he announced]. I will, speedily and cheaply, do all the law business given over or entrusted to me. No person shall complain of my want of care to his best interests, nor to the fees, nor to the value of the labor. Strict and close attention to all business matters given to my charge, and cheapness of fees shall be my invariable rule. [25]

None of these attractions were quite enough. In law as in politics Springfield repudiated Herndon. Of more than two hundred cases heard before the Sangamon County Circuit Court in 1885 Herndon was listed as attorney in three; the next year he had only two. In the 1880's when Herndon wrote that he was busy in court, his words had a special meaning: ". . . I am still in Court and am somewhat busy watching my cases and attending to my practice befor[e] Justices of the peace." [26]

The partnership with Murray lasted less than a year. The struggle was too heavy for a man with broken health, failing sight, and impaired hearing. One day Herndon slammed his book on the office desk

[22] Herndon to Mrs. Dall, October 14, 1881, Dall MSS.
[23] *Illinois State Register,* June 4, 1882. Primaries were not established under Illinois statute until 1885 but were employed as an extra-legal device in Springfield some years earlier.
[24] *Illinois State Journal,* December 22, 1884.
[25] Unidentified clipping, dated May 20, 1885, in Joseph Wallace Scrapbooks.
[26] Herndon to Weik, November 15, 1885, Herndon-Weik Coll.

and cried out: "My God! I can't see; I can't hear! I am going to quit." He picked up his hat and left the office. This time he did not return.[27]

Another venture was equally unsuccessful. Invited to address the old settlers of Menard County in 1881, Herndon dug out a copy of his Ann Rutledge lecture and repeated his eulogy of the pioneers and pioneering.[28] It was so well received that he had the notion of making a lecture tour, talking on Lincoln and earning enormous amounts of money. There was a certain timeliness in Herndon's project, for it coincided with a revival of public interest in Mrs. Lincoln. In 1875 Mary Lincoln had been committed to a sanitarium, but a few months later she was released and, after some rather aimless traveling, came to live with her sister, Mrs. N. W. Edwards, in Springfield. Her mind was still disordered and she fretted feverishly over her finances. In response to her frequent letters and demands, a measure was introduced into Congress increasing her pension and making her an outright gift of $15,000.

At just this moment Herndon provocatively announced his "newly prepared Lecture" which would reveal for the first time "the true and real facts of Abram [sic] Lincoln's Life and Character, his studies, methods of education, struggles and triumphs, his domestic life, his courtship with various women, his marriage with Miss Mary Todd, and what came of it, his nature and qualities, together with facts not generally known." [29] On January 10, 1882, Herndon made his debut in Petersburg, where a "select and very appreciative audiance [sic]," paid out twenty-five cents each to hear him. There is no record of what Herndon said, but the local newspaper was kind to the old man. "Mr. Herndon is a lawyer and public speaker of ability," it was reported; "his lecture gives his audience the true picture of the life and times of this great character." [30]

Herndon now employed a lecture agent, one John B. Barnhill of Meadville, Pennsylvania, who had handbills and circulars printed, announcing:

The pages of Plutarch or of Herodotus contain no such wonderful romance as the story of Abraham Lincoln's rise to the Presidency. . . . [I]f there be one man better qualified than another to tell it, that man is Lincoln's old law partner, Hon. W. H. Herndon. Mr. Herndon can

---

[27] G. W. Murray, quoted in Barton, *Paternity of Lincoln*, 362.

[28] *Illinois State Journal*, September 2, 1881; *History of Sangamon County, Illinois* (1881), 206–212.

[29] Broadside (1882), Herndon-Weik Coll.

[30] Petersburg *Democrat*, January 14, 1882, quoted in *Abraham Lincoln*, a printed card advertising Herndon's lecture, Lincoln National Life Foundation.

tell you more about the inner man within two hours than all the biographies that have been written will give you.

The circulars quoted the Petersburg *Democrat's* "blurb" about Herndon and concluded with the hint: "Lecture Associations can now arrange a date for Mr. Herndon's Lecture on Lincoln, by addressing his agent. . . ." [31]

There was no great rush to fill Herndon's dates. Freshly fitted out in top hat and patent-leather shoes he waited expectantly for invitations to speak. Schuyler Colfax was delivering a Lincoln lecture that brought him $2,500 a night; he spoke in Chicago, Boston, and New York. Herndon's tickets cost twenty-five cents each, and he was asked to lecture in Pana, Pekin, and Havana, Illinois.[32] Once again he was defeated, and the projected speaking tour turned out to be "a dead flat failure." [33]

I V

If Herndon's unsuccessful lecturing expedition did nothing else, it reawakened his interest in the Lincoln subject. His Lincoln Record lay neglected under the dust of sixteen years. Some papers had been destroyed in an office fire; mice and rain had damaged others. A few of his memoranda were at his house in the country, but most were crammed into pasteboard cartons and carelessly stored behind the old Lincoln & Herndon office. But for Isaac N. Arnold Herndon might never have gone back to his collection. That indefatigable writer, who had already produced four books on Lincoln, was planning a full-length biography of the President, and he needed Herndon's aid and suggestions. All of Arnold's writings turned out to be highly eulogistic, and he rejected many of Herndon's thoughts and fancies and suppositions. But, unlike most people, Arnold could get along with Herndon even when he disagreed with him. He knew just how to manage the cantankerous old lawyer by a shrewd mixture of silence and flattery. "You & I can differ without offence," Arnold assured Herndon, "& I like you because you say what you think." [34]

He also liked Herndon because he furnished information. Arnold fired all sorts of questions: When did Lincoln get up in the morning?

---

[31] *Abraham Lincoln,* printed folder announcing Herndon's lecture, Lincoln Memorial University.

[32] Letter of Mr. Neal D. Reardon to me, October 31, 1944; *Illinois State Journal,* January 12 and February 24, 1882. Herndon's lecture at the village of Pana was canceled because of a railroad washout.

[33] Herndon to Weik, February 21, 1891, Herndon-Weik Coll.

[34] Arnold to Herndon, October 23 and November 6, 1882, *ibid.*

A Dead Flat Failure

What did he eat? What did he read? How did he dress? Herndon answered in colorful detail. Some of Arnold's queries brought back amusing memories. "Could Lincoln Sing? Can a Jack ass whistle . . . ?" "What Lincoln dance? Could a sparrow imitate an Eagle. Barnum could make more money on Lincoln's dancing than he could on Jumbo." Along with much information Herndon furnished shocking hints and cryptic observations. "You have never asked, 'Did Lincoln love *women?*'" he suggested. "Friend — it wouldn't do to be inquisitive on these points to one who *knows* Mr L." Arnold had inquired whether Lincoln had any pets about his home. Herndon replied: "I do not think that Mr Lincoln was *fond* of horses — dogs — cats — rats — or other such animal[s], *unless* they could be of service to him. I do not think that he was very *fond* of men, unless he could utilize them somehow & for some purpose." [35]

Besides giving opinions and memories, Herndon permitted Arnold to come down from Chicago and inspect his Lincoln collection. For several days Herndon worked at his manuscripts, trying to "arrange things, so as at [*sic*] to be 'comeatable,'" [36] and Arnold found a considerable treasure. He brought along a clerk, who copied Herndon's list of speeches by Lincoln published in the *Sangamo Journal*. Herndon claimed that he saved his visitor a month's toil, and in those days before Lincoln's writings had been collected the statement was hardly an exaggeration. Faithfully Arnold swore that full acknowledgment would be made for this valuable assistance, but when his book appeared Herndon was hardly mentioned and the obligation was forgotten.[37] But by this time Herndon was used to ingratitude.

[35] Herndon to Arnold, October 24, 1883, Arnold MSS.
[36] Herndon to Arnold, February 10, 1883, *ibid.*
[37] Herndon's "A Statement — Memoranda," January 8, 1886, Herndon-Weik Coll. Arnold died before his volume was published and it is possible that, had he lived, he might have acknowledged his indebtedness to Herndon.

CHAPTER *xix*

I Could Read His Secrets

I

SCRATCHING through his disorderly papers, Herndon came upon an unanswered letter. In 1875 an Indiana college boy named Jesse William Weik had asked him for a Lincoln autograph. Herndon had promised that he would try to oblige if he ever had time to sort out his papers. Now, six years after the original request, he remembered his promise and succeded in finding something "more sacred . . . than a mere autograph." To this complete stranger Herndon sent a long account of his interest in Lincoln biography and of his efforts to preserve facts concerning the Great Emancipator. Shortly after Lincoln's death he had "determined to gather up all the facts of his life — truly — honestly — & impartially," Herndon wrote, but as the age was "not ready to meet its own great truths" he had been abused. The past he connected with the present in the recent assassination of President Garfield. "Here is the name of *Lincoln* before me & in my mind; and the news papers overflowing with the sad intelligence of Garfields death —. The mind remembers Socrates and Jesus — *double* stars of the Old World — Lincoln and Garfield *twin* stars of the New."

Along with his letter Herndon sent Jesse Weik a leaf from Abraham Lincoln's copybook, on which was written in a boyish hand the jingle:

> Abraham Lincoln
> his hand and pen
> he will be good but
> god knows When.[1]

In 1881 Jesse Weik was a rather ponderous young man of twenty-four, cultivating the beginnings of a goatee which later disappeared and of a paunch which did not. The son of a sturdy German immi-

[1] Herndon to Weik, October 8, 1881, Herndon-Weik Coll.

grant who had settled in Greencastle, Jesse had graduated from Indiana Asbury University (later DePauw) in his home town in 1875. His teachers were impressed by this "energetic, thorough-going, industrious, persevering" youth,[2] and he in turn developed a great admiration for John Clark Ridpath, professor of literature, history, and political philosophy at the university, a tireless author of books on James Otis and South Africa, banking and universal literature.

Under Ridpath's inspiration Jesse became an enthusiastic student of the Civil War. Too young to have known the horrors of battle himself, Weik grew up during the decades when age was gilding the memories of veterans and when recollections of slaughter, vermin, and disease were being replaced by those of courage and daring. Greencastle was the center of a strongly Republican region and the young man early became a devotee of the Lincoln cult. At Professor Ridpath's suggestion Weik had written to Herndon for a Lincoln autograph.

By the time Herndon answered, Jesse Weik had graduated from college, but he was still young enough to be enormously flattered by a personal communication from Lincoln's law partner. He thought Herndon's letter very significant and asked permission to publish it in the local newspaper. Weik had found the surest way to Herndon's heart, for the discredited old lawyer doted on praise. Doubtless, he agreed, he had "said some new thing in that letter which may please or instruct &c." [3] On November 24, 1881, a special supplement to the Greencastle *Banner* featured Herndon's communication.

A desultory correspondence between Greencastle and Chinkapin Hill was kept up during the next year or two. Weik's interest in history did not diminish, but he had the practical problem of making a living. He made several false starts. He studied law with the Republican boss of the community and was admitted to the bar; then he opened a real estate office in Greencastle; later he returned to his alma mater and earned a highly prized master's degree.[4] A faithful Republican, Jesse tried to secure an appointment as secretary to the governor of the Territory of New Mexico but, though his application was backed by the governor, lieutenant governor, and both senators from Indiana, he did not receive the job: he was not a Civil War veteran. Finally his influential friends had Weik made pension agent in the Department of Interior, assigned to investigate the numerous disability claims made

[2] John Clark Ridpath to the President of the United States, February 21, 1881, Department of Interior Records, National Archives.

[3] Herndon to Weik, November 5, 1881, Herndon-Weik Coll.

[4] Information supplied through the kindness of the registrar of DePauw University; *Asbury Monthly*, I, 62, and II, 285; *Forty-fifth Year-Book of DePauw University . . . for the Year 1883–84*, 197.

by war veterans. On November 9, 1882, Weik was told to make his headquarters in Springfield, Illinois.[5]

He was delighted. In Springfield, heart of the Lincoln country, he could earn his living and learn history at the same time. As soon as he secured a room at the Revere House Jesse hunted up Herndon. Together they went to the back room of the old Lincoln & Herndon office, where Herndon's papers were jumbled together in paper cartons. Herndon had not looked at them for so long they were almost as new to him as to his visitor. Delightedly they rummaged through the boxes, and each new bundle of papers brought new stories and reminiscences to Herndon's mind. He laughed when he dug out a package of letters bearing Lincoln's notation: "When you can't find *it* anywhere else look into this." [6]

From the very first Weik seems to have had the idea of writing something about Lincoln — newspaper stories, magazine articles, or perhaps even a book. Wherever he went, Jesse talked to old-timers about Lincoln. He interviewed Dennis Hanks and Mrs. Ninian Edwards, Mary Lincoln's sister; he visited the courthouses in central Illinois and drove out to the abandoned site of New Salem. Weik's duties kept him away from Springfield much of the time, and he saw little of Herndon for over a year after their first interview. But that one conversation made a deep impression. When Weik began writing a series of articles for the Indianapolis *Times,* he started one: "Boswell's love for Johnson finds its modern parallel in the devotion of William Herndon to the memory of his illustrious friend and law partner, Abraham Lincoln." [7]

Not until March 1885 did Weik's diary note another meeting with Herndon; then the young pension agent "spent an hour or two at the office of W. H. Herndon and listened to him telling about Lincoln." [8] Nothing so pleased Herndon as an audience, and he was charmed by this young man's excellent manners and sympathetic attention. Given a very little encouragement, Herndon could become embarrassingly confidential, and he told his visitor all sorts of startling information — his "Theory of Lincoln's [illegitimate] paternity," for example, which Weik must not under any circumstances divulge, "as it will be liable to misconstruction." [9]

---

[5] Many letters of recommendation and some autobiographical information are found in Weik's personnel file, Department of Interior Records, National Archives.

[6] Weik Diary, November 25, 1882; Weik, *Real Lincoln,* 5–12.

[7] Letter signed J. W. W[eik]., July 1, 1883, clipped from the Indianapolis *Times,* Lincoln National Life Foundation.

[8] Weik Diary, March 3, 1885.

[9] Herndon to Weik, April 14, 1885, Herndon-Weik Coll.

Weik, for his part, told some secrets, too. About to resign from the pension service because of ill health, he proposed to take up writing as a career. At first he thought of preparing a series of sketches on Lincoln for the Cincinnati *Commercial Gazette*, but after he returned to Greencastle he had a more ambitious idea. He proposed to submit an article to *Harper's Monthly*, and he invited Herndon to collaborate with him.

For some months Herndon had been thinking, rather hazily, of trying again to write something about Lincoln, and Weik's suggestion came at exactly the right moment. "If I can help you in any way," he agreed, "I will do so at all times willingly." "If you come up here and wish my assistance and advice I will freely give it to you — hear your article read with patience too." But Herndon was very generous with this young friend. He would help in preparing the article if Weik wished it, though he cautioned, "the world would rob you of the credit of the article and *give it to me*, if my name were used." [10]

Weik decided to run that risk, and he begged Herndon to supply him information. Herndon obliged. Between the last of October 1885 and the following January he sent thirty-five long letters, chock-full of information and anecdote about Lincoln. In a rambling fashion he discussed virtually every aspect of Lincoln's pre-presidential career. "You *know* that I am fighting the wolf at the door," Herndon explained the lack of sequence in his letters. He told about Lincoln's dislike for glittering generalities; he related how Mary Lincoln refused to receive a poor relation; he detailed Lincoln's alleged ingratitude to his friends; he analyzed the question of Lincoln's legitimacy; he characterized Mrs. Lincoln as the spur that sent Lincoln from his "home hell" out to seek office. Lincoln would sprawl out all over the office with "his body on the Sofa — one foot on one chair and one foot on the table " and read the newspapers aloud. On the circuit Lincoln "took *Euclid* around with him . . . and of nights and odd times he would learn Euclid's problems," reading by candlelight. The future martyr told his partner: "I feel as if I should meet with some terrible End." "Lincoln sometimes drank liquor — was a good chess player — loved 'fives' — ie to play ball, knocking it up against a wall with the hand."

Many of his stories Herndon recounted in elaborate detail, reconstructing long speeches which he claimed Lincoln had uttered. About 1854 he had purchased a biography of Edmund Burke. "Do you not wish to read a most excellent life of Burk[e], the English statesman?" he had asked Lincoln.

[10] Herndon to Weik, August 5 and September 9, 1885, *ibid.*

No, I do not wish to read his life, nor any mans life as now written [his partner was supposed to have replied]. You and I have talked over life writing many and many times and you know that biographies are eulogistic — one sided — colored and false. The dead man's glories are painted hugely — brightly & falsely; his *successes* are held up to eulogy, but his *failures* — his shortcomings — his negatives — his errors — slips & foibles and the like are kept in the dark. You dont get a peep at them — You don't get a true understanding of the man — only see one side and that colored and hence false. I have no Confidence in biographies — Why do not book sellers have blank biographies ready printed and piled on their shelves and published for sale — so that when a man dies his heirs . . . can find a life of the dead ready made and at hand; and all that has to be done is to buy the eulogistic thing — fill up the blanks and call it the life & writings of the . . . loved dead. This would economize time and save strains on the brain. This is my opinion of biographies as now written. I want none of them and will not read them.

Or so Herndon remembered Lincoln's words thirty years after they were spoken.[11] On and on Herndon spun out his thoughts and recollections. Presently he grew tired. He hated the mechanics of writing, and he groaned about having to push his pen across so many sheets. Besides, he was running short of reminiscences. "I am about pumped dry," he confessed, "dry as a sand desert." When he thought back over all the long letters he had written to Weik, he had an idea to suggest. "It seems to me that I have written to you enough matter to make a respectable life of Lincoln. . . . Had you not better change your plans and issue a little life of Lincoln yourself?"[12]

Weik jumped at the idea, and the two men began to plan a series of articles, to be collected later in book form. This time Herndon was cautious about approaching publishers before the biography was actually written. "When the thing is finished or about to be then it *will* be time to write to publishers," he advised. "We better agree first as to what shall be done, and then how to do it; and lastly who shall . . . publish &c &c." He had definite ideas as to what the book should contain. "The world is full of the lives of Lincoln," he told Weik, "and the people are tired of them, as I think." They should not attempt a formal, full-length biography (though "facts — dates &c. &c of his life might be strung along unartistically — unthoughtedly as it were"); their book should be unassumingly be called, "Reminiscences of Lincoln at home."[13]

11 Herndon to Weik, December [21], 1885, *ibid.*
12 Herndon to Weik, December 23, 1885, January 1 and 15, 1886, *ibid.*
13 Herndon to Weik, January 19, 1886, *ibid.*

I Could Read His Secrets

II

Starting with full force in October 1885, Herndon's stream of letters continued without interruption until his death. During the spring and summer Herndon's deluge of correspondence slacked off, for he had farm chores to do, but in the long winter evenings, beneath the picture of Lincoln in his library, his mind turned back to times long past. As he wrote, Herndon kept one eye on posterity. "I am glad that you save and have saved all things written to you by me," he told Weik. "I want them saved, because they will have much in them probably that the world will want. I am willing to be tested by them during all coming time, by the severest criticism. If I misrepresent wilfully the world will know it, & if I am honestly mistaken the world will know that; & if I am true they will know that too. We Cannot escape Criticism if we are worthy of it." [14]

As digested by Weik, these letters became the ingredients of *Herndon's Lincoln*. When that biography finally appeared in 1889, it was Herndonian in every line — but it was not all of Herndon. In the writing, Weik selected and sorted and rephrased; the final product (though perhaps an improvement) fails to represent the full processes of Herndon's thinking. To understand Herndon's own rather peculiar approach to Lincoln biography, one must go back to his letters.

Herndon's correspondence during the 1880's gives, first of all, the impression of inextricable confusion. If this is a portrait for posterity, it is certainly the work of a cubist. In one letter Herndon might give a photographically precise description of Lincoln on the stump; in the next, some preposterous tale concerning Lincoln's (wholly fictitious) visit to a prostitute; in a third, a philosophical disquisition on the causes of Lincoln's melancholy; and in a fourth, a detailed and accurate account of how the first inaugural was prepared. For almost any statement in one of Herndon's letters there is a contradiction in another. Lincoln, he confided, told the "very nastiest and vulgarest stories that possibly Could be told" — but he also said that Lincoln "was not a vulgar nor nasty minded man by any means." Lincoln, he whispered to his confidants, "had a strong if not a terrible passion for women, which sometimes *slopt* over" — but he insisted that Lincoln was absolutely faithful to his wife. [15]

The lack of coherence is partly explained by the way Herndon wrote, in the late hours of the night, when rain made it impossible to

[14] Herndon to Weik, January 16, 1886, *ibid.*
[15] Herndon to Weik, January 10 and 12, 1886, *ibid.;* Herndon to James H. Wilson, September 23, 1889, copy, *ibid.*

work outside, or on an occasional visit to Springfield. He had to think as well as write in short snatches. Another factor was his almost pathetic eagerness to please his correspondents. "You ought to tell me to take a different turn — a different cut," he urged, "if things [i.e., in his letters] don't suit you." [16] Sometimes Herndon's ambiguity was the result of his painful effort to arrive at a balanced judgment. Sometimes he sent his friends a hasty judgment which he later corrected. In any case, the result is a queer hodgepodge of fact and fancy. One of the secrets of Herndon's popularity among later Lincoln students is his peculiar ambivalence. He can be quoted on all sides of any question.

Events which he himself had witnessed Herndon still remembered distinctly. He could, of course, make mistakes. After thirty years he sometimes confused names, dates, and places. But when one allows for an old man's garrulity, it must be admitted that Herndon's recollection of men whom he had known and of events in which he himself participated remained startlingly accurate. He was at his best when describing Lincoln's physical appearance and mannerisms. Herndon had thought much about this man; "he was so good & so odd a man, how in the hell could I help study him." [17] He remembered vivid glimpses, like candid camera shots, of his noble friend. "Mr. Lincoln was exceedingly fond of apples, & fruits generally — : he ate apples peculiarly — he clasped his finger — fore finger, and his thumb around the Equatorial part of the apple — the stem end being toward his mouth: he never peeled apples — peaches — pears &c." [18] Or he described how Lincoln appeared on the platform:

When Mr Lincoln rose up to speak, he rose slowly — steadily — firmly: he never moved much about on the stand or platform when speaking, touching no desk — table — railing: he ran his eyes slowly over the crowd, giving them time to be at ease and to completely recover himself, *as I suppose.* He frequently took hold with his left hand, his left thumb erect, of the left lapel of his coat, keeping his right hand free to gesture in order to drive home and clinch an idea. In his greatest inspiration he held both of his hand[s] out above his head at an angle of about fifty degrees — hands open or clinched according to his feelings and his ideas. If he was moved in some indignant and half mad moment against slavery or wrong in any direction and seemed to want to tear it down — trample it beneath his feet and to eternally crush it, then he would extend his arms out, at about the above degree — angle with clinched big, bony, strong hands on them — . If he was defend

16 Herndon to Weik, January 10, 1886, *ibid.*
17 Herndon to Lamon, February 25, 1870, Lamon MSS.
18 Herndon to Arnold, October 24, 1883, Arnold MSS.

ing the right — if he was defending liberty — eulogizing the Declaration of Independence, then he extended out his arms — palms of his hands upward somewhat at about the above degree — angle, as if appealing to some superior power for assistance and support; or that he might embrace the spirit of that which he so dearly loved. It was at such moments that he seemed inspired, fresh from the hands of his creator. . . . Such was this great man *to me*. . . .[19]

III

But along with his own memories Herndon repeated the recollections of others. It should not be imagined that he was doing extensive research during the eighties; he merely reported the gossip current in Springfield. Every time he visited the capital he talked to his old cronies — James H. Matheny, William Jayne, Governor Richard Oglesby, and the like — and came away with a new crop of improbable tales.

By this time Herndon had lost touch with his more authentic sources who in the 1860's had so enriched his Lincoln records. Mary Owens Vineyard had been Herndon's prize discovery, and her well authenticated romance with the future President in his New Salem period was one of Herndon's major contributions to Lincoln biography. By 1886 Herndon had forgotten her name. "Mrs Vincent," he vaguely remembered it, "Mrs Vincent of Mo." His one reliable Kentucky informant had been Samuel Haycraft of Elizabethtown. Herndon had forgotten him too; he thought his name might be Winterbottom.[20]

As he lost touch with his reliable sources, Herndon became increasingly willing to accept wild legends about Lincoln. Where his personal friends were concerned, he had always been a little credulous; now he was truly gullible. Springfield was — and still is — buzzing with rumors about Lincoln's widow. Mary Lincoln had never been popular in her home town, and not even the tragedy of mental illness had softened that enmity. Mrs. Lincoln died in July 1882, but Herndon's hatred for this woman lived on. In 1866 he had spoken of her as a poor woman, for whom "the world has no charity." But since 1874 there had been in Herndon's mind no question of charity; he believed anything about Lincoln's wife that was bad. Some of his comments were unprintable. Mary was the "she wolf of this section," "soured . . . gross . . . material — avaricious — insolent," "a tigress," "like the tooth ake [*sic*] — kept one awake night and day," "terribly aristocratic . . .

[19] Herndon to Bartlett, July 19, 1887, Bartlett MSS.
[20] Herndon to Weik, December 10, 1885, and January 19, 1886, Herndon-Weik Coll.

and haughty," "as cold as a chunk of ice," *"the female wild cat of the age."* [21]

Herndon's receptivity to any malicious rumor about Mrs. Lincoln was heightened by his complete lack of a sense of humor. There was (so Springfield said thirty years after the incident was supposed to have occurred) "a man by the name of Tiger" who got into an argument with Mrs. Lincoln. Gossip had it that she "abused Tiger shamefully, calling him a dirty villain — a vile creature & the like" and that Tiger demanded satisfaction from her husband for these insults. With a twinkle in his eye the unchivalrous Lincoln asked: *"Friend* Tiger, can't you endure this one wrong done you . . . for old friendship's sake while I have had to bear it without complaint and without a murmur for lo these last fifteen years." [22] Herndon credited such tales as recitals of sober fact; he never knew a joke unless it was labeled.

Herndon was not content with relating his own reminiscences and with retailing those of others. He felt a necessity for "explaining" Lincoln, and he brushed up his best fancy psychological language for the job. "You are aware that I love the science of the mind quite over all studies," he wrote Weik. [23] From a description of Lincoln's body he could easily be diverted to an analysis of his mind. Lincoln "was a great big — angular — strong man — limbs large and bony: he was tall and of a peculiar type." That made Herndon sure that "his mind was tough — solid — knotty — gnarly, more or less like his body: he was angular in body and angular in thought. . . . The convolutions of his brain were long: they did not snap off quickly like a short thick mans brain: they had to have their time, but when those convolution[s] opened and threw off an idea it WAS an IDEA, tough — solid — gnarly — big — angular." [24]

All along Herndon had had the idea of a subjective life of Lincoln, analyzing the thought patterns and motives of the President. He took this study very seriously indeed. Perhaps the funniest thing in the Herndon manuscripts is a grave, long-winded inquiry as to why Lincoln had laughed at amusing stories. Herndon solemnly concluded that the President had told jokes because they served as a "stimulant, sending more blood to the brain, [which] aroused the whole man to an active consciousness — sense of his surroundings." [25]

[21] Herndon to Weik, December 1, 1885, and January 8, 12, 15, and 16, 1886, *ibid.*
[22] Herndon to Weik, January 1887, *ibid.*
[23] Herndon to Weik, February 21, 1891, *ibid.*
[24] Herndon to Bartlett, August 7, 1887, Bartlett MSS.
[25] Herndon to Weik, December 22, 1888, Herndon-Weik Coll.

Lincoln's biography he regarded as a challenge to his best efforts in speculative biography. The Sixteenth President was "the Ideal Man of America." This most noble man had led his nation through the gravest crisis in its history. His career should be studied by every schoolboy as an inspiration, by every statesman as a lesson in policy. His motives, thoughts, and actions must be explained, even if this meant digging into the deepest reticences of his mind. "The *whole* of the man, objectively and subjectively, should be truthfully and fully, without suppression, suggestion — or evasion — or other form of falsehood, stated — generously written out." [26]

Lincoln was hard to get at, Herndon knew. He was "a kind of Enigma." [27] He was the "most reticent & mostly [*sic*] secretive man that ever existed"; [28] "he did not trust any man with the secrets of his ambitious soul." [29] "[H]e was a hidden man and wished to keep his own secrets." [30] Moreover, Lincoln "was a man of opposites — of terrible contrasts." He was " a many mooded man." [31] There were "*great contrasts* in Lincoln's life — mysterious ones — Sometimes Lincoln was great — very great, and sometime[s] small. He was strong and he was weak — he was sad and cheerful by turns. . . ." [32] "Mr. Lincoln thought too much and did too much . . . to be crammed into an epigram or shot off with a single rocket." [33] Sometimes Herndon feared that even he might not know the whole of Lincoln; sometimes he was willing to concede: ". . . I cannot say I comprehended him." [34] "Lincoln," he feared, "is unknown and possibly always will be." [35]

But this was only in Herndon's more modest moods. More frequently he was quite sure that Lincoln operated "*under his own law*," [36] and that he, above all others, was most capable of comprehending that law. "I am somehow or other quite intuitive," he proudly informed his friends. [37] By intuition he felt he could arrive at the essential elements of Lincoln's personality. He explained his biographical method after he had attained that high point of insight: "You had

[26] Herndon to Weik, January 10, 1887, and October 22, 1888, *ibid.*
[27] Herndon to Bartlett, August 16, 1887, Bartlett MSS.
[28] "Miss Rutledge & Lincoln," undated Herndon monograph, Herndon-Weik Coll.
[29] Herndon to John W. Keys, April 14, 1886, MS., Hist. Soc. of Penn.
[30] Herndon to Bartlett, August 22, 1887, Bartlett MSS.
[31] Herndon to H. C. Whitney, July 17, 1887, MS., Henry E. Huntington Lib.
[32] Herndon to Bartlett, July 8, 1887, Bartlett MSS.
[33] Herndon to C. O. Poole, January 5, 1886, copy, Herndon-Weik Coll.
[34] *Herndon's Lincoln*, III, 585.
[35] Herndon to Bartlett, September 22, 1887, Bartlett MSS.
[36] Herndon to Whitney, July 17, 1887, MS., Henry E. Huntington Lib.
[37] Herndon to Weik, November 29, 1890, Herndon-Weik Coll.

to take some leading — great leading and well established fact of Lincoln's nature and then follow it by accurate & close analysis wherever it went. This process would lead you correctly, if you knew human nature and its laws." [38] Herndon considered himself an expert at this game. "I knew the man so well that I think I could read his secrets & his ambitions." [39]

In his analysis Herndon attached central significance to Lincoln's spells of gloomy melancholy, which had been noticed both in Springfield and in Washington. Herndon was not alone in this emphasis. Many of Lincoln's friends had wondered: "What has made this joyous, merry man so sad? What great sorrow lies at his heart?" [40] But Herndon intuitively concluded that Lincoln's sadness was more than an oddity; it was his principal hold upon the hearts of the people. ". . . Mr. Lincoln was a sad man — a man of suffering — a man of sorrow. These were written on his face and deeply cut in every organ of that face: they were in his little sad gray eyes. The people saw that and sympathized with the man. This made him friends, through sympathy." [41]

Herndon regarded it as his principal function as a Lincoln biographer to explain the causes of that melancholy. He concocted an elaborate speculative analysis of factors which he believed had influenced Lincoln's development. First of all, Lincoln's sadness sprang from his organization and structure. Herndon was convinced that his partner was of tubercular build and that like "most male consumptives," he was a man of "goatish passions." In addition, Lincoln suffered from chronic constipation and had to take "blue mass pills," which upset both his digestion and his disposition. Another cause of gloom, according to Herndon, was Lincoln's knowledge of "the origin of his own mother — the low and vicious family out of which he came — the very lowest of the lowest." Then there was Lincoln's knowledge of "his own origin or suspected origin" — an allusion to the rumor that Lincoln was illegitimate. Another link in this gloomy chain was the courtship and untimely death of Ann Rutledge and, as Herndon suggested weightily, "what grew out of it." Herndon was also convinced that Lincoln's marriage and "his domestic misery" gave him the blue devils. And finally Lincoln had had a premonition "now and then that he

[38] Herndon to John E. Remsburg, September 10, 1887, MS., collection of Mr. Alfred W. Stern.
[39] Herndon to John W. Keys, April 14, 1886, MS., Hist. Soc. of Penn.
[40] Arnold, *Life of Abraham Lincoln*, 445.
[41] "Lincoln's Power over the People," undated Herndon monograph, Herndon-Weik Coll.

would meet with some terrible end." This, then, was Herndon's final unveiling of Lincoln.[42] "I would risk my chances in heaven on this long settled opinion, founded on long years of observation — Experience, and reason," Herndon boasted of his analysis. "I need not say . . . that I have studied the sciences somewhat relating to these questions, and think I am fully supported by them."[43]

IV

If Herndon were not taken so seriously, both by himself and by later Lincoln biographers, one would dismiss his analysis with a smile. In all these matters he was speculating, inferring, guessing; in none did he have any real data to support his conclusions. One can take the tiresome question of Abraham Lincoln's legitimacy as an illustration of Herndon's mental processes during his latter years. During the Civil War political enemies had whispered that Lincoln was a bastard.[44] As early as 1865 Herndon heard the gossip. At first he repudiated it and threatened to expose the perpetrators of the lie. Later this monster of so frightful mien was endured and finally embraced. There were several reputed candidates for the honor of being the President's real father, but Herndon's favorite was one Abraham Enlow (or Enloe).

Herndon's "evidences" on this point may be briefly summarized. Lincoln had told his partner that Nancy Hanks Lincoln was the illegitimate daughter of a well born Virginia planter, and from this recital Herndon inferred that Lincoln had doubts about his own descent. Dennis Hanks in his cups confided to Herndon that Thomas Lincoln had "*had the mumps*" and "was incapable of getting a child."[45] From Kentucky gossips Herndon heard the report that Thomas Lincoln had found Abraham Enlow at his house under suspicious circumstances, that the men quarreled, and that Thomas "bit off Enloes nose in the terrible fight." Furthermore, Herndon claimed that Nancy Hanks Lincoln had "bred like a rat" while in Kentucky (actually she had three children in twelve years of married life), while no children were born to her in Indiana, where she was away from the Enlow influence. And

---

[42] Herndon repeated this analysis in letters to all his friends. Quotations in these paragraphs are from Herndon to Weik, January 23, 1890, and from "Lincoln's Domestic Life," undated Herndon monograph, *ibid.*

[43] Herndon to Weik, February 9, 1889, *ibid.*

[44] "Abraham, the son of Inlow, whose mother was of the Ethiopian tribe of Hanks." Richard Grant White, *Book of the Prophet Stephen, Son of Douglas. Wherein Marvelous Things are Foretold of the Reign of Abraham* (1863).

[45] Herndon to Lamon, February 25, 1870, Lamon MSS.

finally Thomas Lincoln and Sarah Bush Lincoln, his second wife, had no children, which to Herndon proved the husband's impotence.[46] This was Herndon's entire stock of evidence on the subject. Its flimsiness is quite apparent. The allegation that Thomas Lincoln lost his manhood rested on the unsupported statement of Dennis Hanks, whom Herndon, in his more reasonable moments, repudiated. "What he says about anything must be taken with much allowance," Herndon correctly judged.[47] Even if Thomas Lincoln was so afflicted, there was nothing to place his misfortune in time; it was only a vague rumor. And as for Abraham Enlow, he was a beardless boy of fifteen at the time the future President was conceived — and in later years his nose was unabridged. In short, the tale of Lincoln's "illegitimacy" had no truth at all; it had not even plausibility.[48]

Had Herndon published his "evidences," he would have been revealed as the irrational and speculative man he was. But he did not. He suggested unmentionable things which it was "not necessary now and here to mention." [49] He begged those who attacked him to desist lest he be forced to reveal the sensational facts in his keeping. He whispered to his correspondents of a story too shocking ever to tell — and then he told it.

After relating this elaborate rigmarole to each of his friends, Herndon tried to hedge. He would conclude a long four-page letter detailing the evidences pointing toward Lincoln's illegitimacy with the admonition: "Here is the whole story as it has been told to me and I give you no opinion of fact nor inference. You must judge for yourself. It's a curious story and may all be true." [50] The debatable point in his mind was "the question of *castration*." If Thomas Lincoln lost his manhood before 1808, the birth of Abraham meant that Nancy Hanks Lincoln had "let a stray bull in the pasture." But if the elder Lincoln's (imagined) misfortune occurred later, Abraham was "the lawful child of *Thomas Lincoln* & Nancy Hanks and . . . she was a virtuous woman." "The presumption of law saves Abm's paternity," Herndon usually concluded, while admitting: "This is close shaving. . . ." [51]

Herndon mulled over the moot subject times without number. He did not gather fresh evidence on the alleged illegitimacy, nor did he

[46] Herndon summarized his case in a letter marked "Religiously private" to Weik, January 19, 1886, Herndon-Weik Coll.

[47] Herndon to Weik, May 6, 1885, *ibid.*

[48] The definitive work on this subject is W. E. Barton's *The Paternity of Abraham Lincoln.*

[49] Herndon to Editor of Indianapolis *Herald*, September 15, 1883, clipping in Lincoln National Life Foundation.

[50] Herndon to Weik, January 19, 1886, Herndon-Weik Coll.

[51] Herndon to Bartlett, September 20, 1887, Bartlett MSS.

criticize what testimony he had; he brooded and speculated. Half the time Herndon believed that Abraham Lincoln really was a bastard. The other half he saw himself as a crusader against those base knaves who dared insinuate that the President had been illegitimate. "I want . . . to make Lincoln appear — nay to be the lawful child and legitimate heir of Thomas & Nancy," he informed one surprised friend; then a little later he was relating this whole "terrible history" to another correspondent.[52] When he finally published his biography, Herndon neither affirmed nor denied Lincoln's legitimacy.[53]

This unsavory gossip has been repeated because it is a typical example of Herndon's mental processes during his latter years. He assumed unproved happenings; he then inferred that Lincoln knew about them; he guessed that the knowledge must have caused Lincoln's melancholy; and finally he concluded that it was this sadness which endeared Lincoln to the people. By combining intuitive biography and pseudo-psychoanalysis Herndon produced this his ultimate revelation of Lincoln. "I studied Lincoln critically for thirty odd years," he boasted, "and should know him well." [54]

[52] "Opinions of Men," Herndon monograph, September 6, 1887, Herndon-Weik Coll.; Herndon to James H. Wilson, October 1, 1889, copy, *ibid.*
[53] *Herndon's Lincoln,* I, 5–6.
[54] Herndon to Weik, November 21, 1885, Herndon-Weik Coll.

CHAPTER xx

Herndon's Memoirs of Lincoln

I

HERNDON had troubles. Through all his letters to Weik ran the monotonous refrain of poverty. "I have to struggle to-day for my tomorrow's bread." "Business is extremely dull here and every man is dunning every other, and those who have the dollar make it squeal before they let go of the wing." "Jesse, it's a bad thing to be poor aint it?" [1] As a persistent countermelody was the theme of illness. "I have been sick with . . . Neuralgia & pneumonia. . . ." "I am . . . sick as dog — with a terribly bad cold, which will surely be followed with a spell of neuralgia." "I am not well and have not been . . . don't do anything — can't." [2]

But for all his difficulties his enthusiasm for the Lincoln subject did not falter. In 1887, as twenty years earlier, he would let his potatoes grow up in cockleburs while he helped some stranger understand Lincoln. No one that knocked at this door was turned away. Truman Howe Bartlett, for example, a Vermont-born sculptor planning a bronze statuette of Lincoln, wrote to Herndon for help. Generously Herndon promised, "I . . . will assist you all I can . . . ," and he collected for Bartlett the pictures which best caught Lincoln's spirit. [3] But he reminded the sculptor that the frozen photographs did not give the animation and sparkle of Lincoln's face. "The moment Lincoln took his seat at the pho machine & looked down the barrel of it," Herndon remembered, "he became sad — rather serious, as all business with him was serious, life included." [4] In Herndon's mind there was not a single "no one pho [number one photograph] of Lincoln," [5] and he

[1] Herndon to Weik, January 9, 1887, January 18, 1886, and July 25, 1890, Herndon-Weik Coll.

[2] Herndon to Weik, March 25, 1886, and February 25, 1887, *ibid.;* Herndon to Weik, April 9, 1887, MS., Abraham Lincoln Book Shop.

[3] Herndon to Bartlett, June 8, 1887, Bartlett MSS.

[4] Herndon to Bartlett, February 27, 1891, *ibid.*

[5] Herndon to "Mr Barrett" [Herndon meant T. H. Bartlett], July 27, 1887, *ibid.*

tried to make up the deficiency by fresh verbal etchings of the man as he stilted Springfield's muddy streets. Though his letters must have cost hours of laborious thought, Herndon was modest about their value. "I am a weak brother," he confessed to Bartlett, "but will assist others with that weakness to the best of my heart and head." [6]

The more letters Herndon wrote, the more eager he became to push his long delayed Lincoln biography.[7] Weik was understandably hesitant about his partnership with the ailing and impoverished Herndon. Sometimes the younger man was discouraged; sometimes he wavered; sometimes he almost despaired. But Herndon never let him give up. "[Y]ou will succeed now or in the future," he predicted. "You deserve it, my boy." Subtly he flattered Weik with an untruth. "Sometimes I despair — you don't, & that's the difference between us. Dig on and I'll help. . . ." "[W]e will furnish the world with new & original & trustworthy facts — Characteristics &c. &c never before published of Lincoln. . . . You & I can do more in this line than any man or set of men, I think." [8]

"You must write," Herndon urged Weik, "& Ill give the facts." [9] As Weik learned the wealth of Herndon's material, he absorbed some of his collaborator's confidence. Soon both men were itching to get into print. In July 1886 Weik contributed a long Lincoln article to the Cincinnati *Commercial Gazette*, but he was bitterly disappointed when he was not paid for it.[10] Herndon sent an essay to the Chicago *Tribune*, but it was too long and was rejected.[11] An article proposed for the *Graphic* met with no better success.

Herndon and Weik had strong competition. The wartime secretaries of President Lincoln, John Hay and John G. Nicolay, were collaborating in an ambitious full-length biography, first serialized in the *Century Magazine* and later published as their ten-volume *Abraham Lincoln: A History*. Authorized by Robert Todd Lincoln, filio-pietistic in tone, and arch-Republican in politics, the Nicolay-Hay work was announced as the definitive life of Lincoln. Herndon had no ill will toward "the boys," as he usually referred to Hay and Nicolay, and he guessed that their work would be "a grand affair." Since his own book was intended to emphasize the "*individual — domestic — social — fo-*

---

[6] Herndon to Bartlett, August 7, 1887, *ibid.*
[7] For a vivid and at the same time scholarly account of the Herndon-Weik partnership see Benjamin P. Thomas, *Portrait for Posterity*, 132–164.
[8] Herndon to Weik, August 27 and September 23, 1886, Herndon-Weik Coll.
[9] Herndon to Weik, January 26, 1886, *ibid.*
[10] Herndon to Weik, July 30, 1886, *ibid.*; Cincinnati *Commercial Gazette*, July 11, 1886.
[11] Herndon to Weik, September 5, 1886, Herndon-Weik Coll.

rensic," Herndon thought there would be no rivalry between his informal biography and the stately Civil War panorama being painted by the secretary-biographers.[12] He cooperated with representatives of the *Century* and dug out rare old photographs for use in Nicolay and Hay's work. Even the *Century* editor, the snobbish Richard Watson Gilder, admitted that "Herndon, poor old fellow" had been extremely kind. Gilder sucked the orange and threw away the peel. When Herndon came up "smiling . . . with a proposition of an article on Lincoln," the *Century* editor conveniently forgot his earlier assistance.[13]

The announcement of the Nicolay-Hay biography made a splash in the publishing world. It is hard to realize the intense interest with which readers in the eighties and nineties followed protracted Civil War histories and memoirs and reminiscences. The Buel-Johnson "Battles and Leaders of the Civil War," which dragged through endless numbers of the *Century,* were avidly consumed. Ten years later Miss Ida M. Tarbell proved in a score of articles for *McClure's* that the Lincoln theme, though perhaps exhausting, had not been exhausted. But some publishers felt that Nicolay, Hay, and the *Century* had cornered the market on Lincoln biography. Mark Twain's firm, Charles L. Webster & Co., publisher's of Grant's *Memoirs* and many another historical best-seller, rejected the Herndon-Weik biography because the "Life of Lincoln, by General Hay and Mr. Nicolay, will give the public all that they wish to know of Lincoln, just at present." [14]

A Chicago house thought differently. The obscure Elder Publishing Company wanted to run Herndon's Lincoln memoirs in its magazine, *Literary Life.* "[W]e admit the risk we run in going into competition with the Century," the publisher told Herndon, "yet we feel we have in you as good a man as any of the Century writers and your articles will possibly make you famous like Byron in a day." [15]

Fame is about all Herndon would have won from the venture, for the canny publisher intended to pay nothing at all for the serial use of his manuscript and to give only ten per cent as royalties if and when his book was published.[16] Herndon was so eager to secure a publisher that he persistently misread Elder's letters. "It is a good chance," he thought, "& the Company's idea is a good one — namely a popular life

12 Herndon to Weik, September 23, 1886, *ibid.*
13 Gilder to Hay, August 18, 1886, Nicolay-Hay MSS.
14 Charles L. Webster & Co. to Weik, November 4, 188[6], Weik MSS.
15 Elder Publishing Company to Herndon, October 22, 1886, copy, *ibid.*
16 Elder Publishing Company to Herndon, October 4 and 13, 1886, copies, *ibid.*

— a cheap one of Lincoln." [17] Hastily he wrote to Weik, who talked things over with his mentor, Professor John Clark Ridpath. In late October 1886 Weik came over from Greencastle to consult with Herndon. At the Revere House in Springfield they talked grandly of their plans and "made [a] contract in duplicate in regard to writing book." [18] Herndon then informed Elder that he and Weik would supply the manuscript of a Lincoln biography for an advance payment of five thousand dollars.[19]

The publisher's tone became frigid. Herndon's demands were impossible, he was told. Weik's name could not appear in connection with the biography, and Herndon was unreasonable to expect any advance royalties. On second thought Elder concluded that all Herndon's materials had probably been published already in Lamon's biography and that his firm would be "unable to use [their biography] . . . under any circumstances." [20]

II

But Herndon and Weik were not discouraged. Their reverse was the cue to begin "going at things with a vim." Herndon's Lincoln Records, "once done up and numbered in good style," were now higgledy-piggledy and the task of rearranging his papers was now too much for the old lawyer. The whole collection was shipped by express to Greencastle, and for over a month Jesse spent his "spare time assorting Lincoln papers." [21]

As he arranged the documents, some notable gaps became apparent which Weik planned to fill by firsthand investigation of his own. Herndon had never collected data in Kentucky, and Weik's first research task was to gather what information he could from Lincoln's childhood contemporaries. In March 1887 Jesse Weik went to Lexington, Paris, and Elizabethtown and interviewed the few old settlers who had any memories of the young Lincoln. His gleanings were meager. About the best he could do was to find one old gentleman (M. M. Cassidy of Mt. Sterling, Kentucky) who furnished "his account of the traditions in his family going to show that his granduncle Abraham Enloe or Inlow

[17] Herndon to Weik, October 2, 1886, Herndon-Weik Coll.
[18] Weik Diary, October 17, 26, and 27, 1886.
[19] Herndon to Elder Publishing Company, October [26], 1886, copy, Weik MSS.
[20] A. T. P. Elder to Herndon, November 4, 1886, copy, *ibid.*
[21] Herndon to Weik, November 6 and 15, 1886, *ibid.;* Weik Diary, November 17–December 27, 1886.

was the real father of Abraham Lincoln." For the most part, people "knew so little of the Inlow Lincoln matter" as to make his trip unprofitable. But Weik returned home feeling that he had at least tried.[22]

Herndon was eager to begin work on his biography, but he still faced his old enemy poverty. By 1886 his finances were at a new low. For years Herndon had proudly clung to his amateur status; he would not capitalize on his friendship with Lincoln. He had willingly "assisted all of his biographers with facts and opinions" and he "did so freely and without charge to any one." In addition, he had "*given* yes GIVEN away hundreds of things — letters — speeches — &c. &c . . . to all persons who requested them — mere strangers and took no pay." [23]

Now he was forced to abandon that proud boast. Two hustling Springfield men, John M. Keys and S. B. Munson, were trying to get up a "Lincoln Memorial Collection" of letters, relics, and other souvenirs of Lincoln, which they planned to exhibit in the major cities of the country. Naturally they turned to Herndon for help, and reluctantly he parted with his remaining association items: a pair of Lincoln's gloves, the desk and table from the Lincoln & Herndon office, a leaf from Lincoln's boyhood copybook, and the like.[24] For his services in rounding up and vouching for "relics" Herndon received a trifling sum, but he was so poor that a check for fifteen dollars seemed "like heat & light in a cold dark cellar of a freezing night." [25] Keys and Munson even talked Herndon into promising to sell some documents from his Lincoln Record, but a pointed protest from Weik put a stop to this raffling off of the partners' literary capital.

When the Lincoln Memorial Collection opened on Market Street in Chicago, patronage proved disappointingly small, and the proprietors decided to hire Herndon to act as curator. In the winter of 1886–87 he spent two months in Chicago "pushing the collection along." At first he found his job great fun. "I . . . am as fat — hearty & jolly as a pig," he wrote Weik. "I am not run and kicked to death — have a little time to laugh & be merry." [26] He welcomed visitors "with entertaining reminiscences of his personal experiences with the greatest man who ever

[22] Weik Diary, March 21 and 22, 1887.

[23] Herndon to Charles Frederick Gunther, February 5, 1887, MS., Chicago Hist. Soc.

[24] For a list of the relics see *Catalogue of Articles Owned and Used by Abraham Lincoln. Now Owned by the Lincoln Memorial Collection of Chicago* (1887). Herndon's letters to Keys and Munson vouching for the authenticity of various items are in the Historical Society of Pennsylvania and in the Illinois State Historical Library.

[25] Herndon to S. B. Munson, April 28, 1887, MS., Ill. State Hist. Lib.

[26] Herndon to Weik, December 1, 1886, Herndon-Weik Coll.

lived," [27] and his work kept him "blabbing all the time." Along with his anecdotes Herndon managed to hint that he and Weik were about to prepare a true biography of Lincoln, no official, stilted history like Nicolay and Hay's articles. And, he happily confided to Weik, his visitors usually said: "If that be the Case Ill wait for your life You'll tell the truth." [28]

Chicago had grown up since the war. Herndon found it "a great place: It has vim — rush & get up — wealth & aristocracy." But for all its bustling efficiency Herndon thought the city cold and unsocial and he became homesick. In the dreary December evenings he sat alone in his cheap hotel room and scribbled long letters to Weik. "I am here and somewhat lonesome," he confessed, "and I will have to talk to you — make a companion of you." [29]

Herndon kept a watchful eye on the articles Nicolay and Hay were publishing in the *Century*. It seemed to him that the secretary-biographers had purposely suppressed some of the most material facts of Lincoln's life; in their articles they were glossing over "L's genealogy — paternity — the description of Nancy Hanks — old Thomas Lincoln — the Ann Rutledge story — L's religion — L's insanity — the facts of L's misery with Mary Todd — L's *back down* on the night that he & Mary Todd were to be married." How could they so slight "the story of Anne Rutledge — the finest story in Lincoln's life?" Hay and Nicolay were trying to please Robert Lincoln, Herndon was sure; they "handle things with silken gloves & 'a cammel hair pencil': they do not write with an iron pen." Their biography, he rightly judged, was of tedious length, with "too much little unimportant stuff in it." "I will bet you a chicken cock that Nicolay & Hay's book will tire out the public by its length and its unimportant trash." [30]

Soon Herndon was longing to be back at home. His employers urged him to remain, but he determined to return to Springfield on January 15, 1887, to *"buss the old woman and the babies."* Another motive was to get started on his Lincoln biography. The none-too-favorable critical reaction to the Nicolay-Hay articles renewed his faith that "the reading world wants *all* those little & big things, thought & done, while L was growing up — all those little things in youth that he did — incidents — idiocyncrisies [*sic*] — Characteristics . . . that will *let light into young L's life & Character* — little things that made L what he is." If Weik would collect information in Indiana and Kentucky, Hern-

---

[27] Chicago *Tribune*, December 24, 1886
[28] Herndon to Weik, December 5 and 13, 1886, Herndon-Weik Coll.
[29] Herndon to Weik, November 26 and December 9, 1886, *ibid.*
[30] Herndon to Weik, December 5, 1886, and January 2, 1887, *ibid.*

don would try to complete his records by interviewing once more the older generation of Menard County. Then they would be ready to write.[31]

When he went to Petersburg in March, Herndon found that "the People are drained — pumped dry," yet he hoped that "some good thunder storm and some rain will fill 'em up again — ie that is a close, critical and searching examination may wake up new ideas — stories — facts &c &c." But for all Herndon's thunder, the water level remained disappointingly low. The old-timers who had known Lincoln were mostly dead; their descendants knew only hearsay. When Herndon had first questioned New Salem survivors in 1865–66 he had collected sharply conflicting reminiscences on the Lincoln-Rutledge idyll; twenty years later gossip had worn away variant accounts and had left a "universal reputation . . . that Lincoln & Ann Rutledge were engaged to be married." [32]

Herndon thought it time to get some publicity for his proposed Lincoln biography. With Weik's help he drew up a notice to be inserted in the newspapers. The partners up to now had not selected a title for their work, for Herndon had counseled: "Do not let the title of the book bother you — write the book and in doing so the name will suggest itself naturally — instinctively." [33] Now Jesse proposed "Herndon's Memoirs of Lincoln," and Herndon enthusiastically approved. Their book, the Springfield *Daily News* announced in March 1887, was not intended to supersede any other Lincoln biography, but it would treat "the personal life of Lincoln individually — domestically — as lawyer — citizen — friend — politician, including his courtships with different women." [34]

The announcement was not well received. The New York *Sun* presumed that Herndon intended to exhibit "the martyr President . . . with less drapery than he was on Mr. Lamon's pedestal." "If Lamon's book raised terror in the souls of the squeamish; if it was handled like a bomb by the publishers, surreptitiously tinkered, and at last practically suppressed," the *Sun* conjectured, "what are we to anticipate for Herndon's?" [35] Herndon, too, predicted abuse. ". . . I am going to write the life of Lincoln as I saw him," he pledged, "honestly — truthfully — co[u]rageously — fearlessly cut whom it may." "This life," he

[31] Herndon to Weik, January 13, 1887, *ibid.*
[32] Interview of Herndon with Jasper Rutledge, Petersburg, March 9, 1887, *ibid.*
[33] Herndon to Weik, March 29, 1886, *ibid.*
[34] Herndon's draft of notice [March 5, 1887?] to be inserted in Springfield *Daily News, ibid.* Cf. the announcement in *Religio-Philosophical Journal*, XLII (March 26, 1887), 5.
[35] Undated clipping from New York *Sun*, Lincoln National Life Foundation.

ROBERT TODD LINCOLN

The President's oldest son, whom Herndon called "a d—d fool."

JOSIAH GILBERT HOLLAND

Herndon thought this Massachusetts author treated him "shabbily."

CHAUNCEY FORWARD BLACK

Lamon's "literary friend" and ghostwriter.

ISAAC NEWTON ARNOLD

According to Herndon, "a creadulus man without any critical ability at all."

MY FRIEND, MR. WEIK

Herndon praised his literary collaborator as "an honest man & a man of ability." This previously unpublished photograph is used through the courtesy of Miss Mary Hays Weik.

wrote, almost with satisfaction, "if it ever sees the light will cause a squirm." [36]

III

Herndon planned to join Weik in Greencastle, and there the partners would write their Lincoln biography. Back from his researches in Kentucky, Weik was sanguine; he hoped to finish off the whole business in short order. Herndon, for once, was despondent. He had no time for writing, because he had to "plant — hoe — grub — put up fences &c. &c." When the time came for him to go to Indiana, Herndon found it impossible to get off. He had no money at all, and he could not "leave [his] . . . family without bread & butter." "Possibly," he suggested, "I can pledge my Lincoln materials for some money — say $100." [37]

Eager to begin, Weik offered to advance that sum, taking a lien on the Lincoln Record as security. It took all of Weik's check to pay Herndon's most pressing debts, and he still did not have enough money for train fare. But now he knew the trick, and he wrote Weik what was to be the predecessor of a dozen letters of the kind: "Please send me next week without fail twenty five dollars & Ill compensate you in the future. I can't get to your place without it." Weik again obliged, and leaving his family "to rub through the best they Can," Herndon left home on August 1, 1887.[38] Twenty-two years after his partner's death he was ready to begin writing Lincoln's biography.

Greencastle was a sleepy little Hoosier town, huddled about the county courthouse. Louis Weik, Jesse's father, owned a store-bakery on the public square,[39] and the son made an oven-like room on the second floor his literary headquarters. The flat tin roof caught every ray of the August sun; the building was a bakery on the second floor as well as on the first. The summer of 1887 was a scorcher. "It's hot & dusty here," Herndon complained upon arrival, "hot as — well — well." [40] Despite the weather he and Weik set about their writing in grim earnest. Weik's diary recorded their progress. Day after day for over a month the entries ran: "Mr. Herndon and I spent almost all day in my room, warm as it was"; or "I spent almost the whole day in [the] room with Mr. Herndon writing." They worked manfully, sometimes until eleven o'clock at night. Weik's dry diary comment revealed how

[36] Herndon to H. C. Whitney, April 16, 1887, MS., Huntington Lib.; Herndon to Bartlett, August 22, 1887, Bartlett MSS.
[37] Herndon to Weik, June 2, 1887, Herndon-Weik Coll.
[38] Herndon to Weik, July 16 and 23, 1887, *ibid.*
[39] For information on the Weik family see Jesse W. Weik, *Weik's History of Putnam County, Indiana*, 704–705.
[40] Herndon to Whitney, August 11, 1887, MS., Ill. State Hist. Lib.

the writing went: "Spent the bulk of the day . . . in the office. Herndon at work on the philosophy of Lincoln and I, on the narrative of his life." [41]

For the first time in twenty years Herndon had literary leisure, and he threw himself into his writing with the enthusiasm of a man half his age. He dashed off draft chapters on a dozen subjects — Lincoln and Ann Rutledge, Lincoln's domestic life, Mary Todd, Lincoln's power over the people, Lincoln's (alleged) ingratitude, Lincoln the lawyer. In "Lincoln Individually" Herndon resurrected his 1865–66 "Analysis of the Character of Abraham Lincoln," intending this condensed version of his lectures as an appendix or supplementary chapter in the biography.[42] These monographs which he penned so rapidly were not finished literary products; they were but "footlights" for Weik's guidance. "I never read any of the notes over," Herndon explained, "and did not criticise them — nor care for them except as to matter — ideas — facts — &c. &c. I wished you [Weik] to use the matter — facts. . . ." [43]

Weik's task was to prune and arrange and synthesize Herndon's somewhat garrulous narrative. The junior partner's share in this literary collaboration has not received sufficient recognition. So far as can be determined from existing manuscripts, Herndon's rough drafts were extensively followed in only five of the twenty chapters in the completed Lincoln biography.[44] The other chapters were composed by Weik, using Herndon's monographs, his hundreds of letters, and the documents and interviews he had collected in his Lincoln Record. The content and interpretation in the Herndon-Weik biography was Herndon's; the composition, largely Weik's.[45]

Long hours of hard work made the book grow rapidly, but by the

[41] Weik Diary, August 3, 13, and 29, 1887.

[42] These Herndon monographs are in the Herndon-Weik Collection. Herndon revived his lectures at the suggestion of Henry C. Whitney. (Whitney to Herndon, July 4, 1887, Herndon-Weik Coll.) Since Herndon's manuscript lectures had been sold to Lamon in 1869, he expanded the extracts published in Carpenter's *Six Months at the White House* and in Oldroyd's *Lincoln Memorial: Album-Immortelles.*

[43] Herndon to Weik, September 20, 1888, Herndon-Weik Coll.

[44] These were Chapters VI (the Lincoln-Rutledge romance), IX (the Lincoln-Todd wedding), XI (Lincoln as lawyer), XIV (Lincoln's domestic difficulties), and XX (analysis of Lincoln's character). Sometimes Weik wove a few paragraphs from a Herndon monograph into the narrative — e.g., the description of Lincoln on the stump in Chapter XIII. Herndon's draft chapter on Mary Owens was hardly used at all in Chapter VII, and his comments on Lincoln's power over the people were omitted entirely.

[45] For a statement of Weik's share in the writing of *Herndon's Lincoln,* see the rejected preface to the biography [November 1888?], MS., Ill. State Hist. Lib. See below, pp. 327–8.

end of a month Herndon, unused to concentrated effort, was worn out. "There is hard thinking to be done in writing L's life," he found. "As I trail the man step by step like a dog trails a fox I find many new *spots* — many new *holes* — much to admire and much to regret. It nearly kills me in my old age to persist in my search." [46] By the first of September both Herndon and Weik were getting tired. When Jesse finished his section on Lincoln's inauguration, Herndon "felt as if we had so neared the end he could go home." [47] There was much work yet to be done, but a good beginning had been made. On September 5 Herndon took the train for Springfield. "I . . . am worn out — must take rest and recover," he reported, "am getting along admirably well in my book, *as I see it*." [48]

IV

Two tasks now remained: finishing the manuscript and finding a publisher. The central group of chapters had been left in semicomplete form, and Herndon trusted Weik to finish them. But neither the beginning nor the conclusion of the book had been agreed upon. At the suggestion of Professor Ridpath, Weik proposed to end the book with Lincoln's first inauguration. With surprisingly good judgment Herndon reversed his earlier stand and decided that it was indispensable to include "a *short* chapter on Ls civil policy and a *short* one on L[incoln's] war policy." The Herndon-Weik biography, he suggested, was not intended for the historical expert such as Dr. Ridpath but for the general public. It was necessary to explain to such readers "what all this hell was about." To write about Lincoln without discussing his presidency seemed to Herndon like giving "the play of Hamlet with Hamlet left out." As soon as he got home from Greencastle Herndon prepared an essay on the political background of the war, but not knowing Weik's plans and not wishing to write more until he and Weik could "understand one an other as to what things shall be said & how & when said," he dropped the matter. [49] When the book finally appeared, Weik's hasty and rather characterless sketch of the war years was tacked on.

The introductory chapter offered a more ticklish problem. As they drafted it in Greencastle, Herndon and Weik included an examination of the rumors that Lincoln had been illegitimate but concluded

[46] Herndon to Bartlett, August 22, 1887, Bartlett MSS.
[47] Weik Diary, September 1 and 3, 1887.
[48] Herndon to Bartlett, September 2, 1887, Bartlett MSS.
[49] Herndon to Weik, September 25 and October 22, 1887, Herndon-Weik Coll.

that Abraham was "the lawful child of Thos & Nancy Lincoln."[50] (Lacking the original manuscript one can only conjecture exactly what Herndon meant. He may have wished to say that Abraham actually was the son of Thomas — or that he was only "in law" his heir. Herndon's own belief in this matter shifted almost daily.) After Herndon returned home he made a special pilgrimage to ask the oracles of Springfield what course he should follow. Governor John M. Palmer neatly side-stepped. "This is too delicate a question," he told Herndon, "and I do not wish to give my advice on the matter. . . ." Herndon's former partner, Alfred Orendorff, urged him to "tell the whole story and clear up Lincoln's legitimacy." Republicans William Jayne and Shelby M. Cullom, both surprised that Herndon planned to show Lincoln as legitimate, advised "if you say anything about the matter you had better tell it out, giving all the facts." And wartime Governor Richard Oglesby replied: ". . . it would be better for your book to say nothing about it at all." So the oracles responded, and Herndon was not a whit the wiser.[51]

Weik, too, was much concerned about this matter. A veiled hint of Lincoln's illegitimacy had done much to ruin Lamon's book in 1872; neither Herndon nor Weik could afford a similar failure. In October 1887 Weik took sections of the manuscript to Chicago, seeking advice and hoping to find a publisher. He was welcomed by Herndon's old friend from circuit-riding days, Henry Clay Whitney, now a Chicago lawyer, cultivating impressive sideburns and an unsavory reputation as a divorce lawyer. For years Whitney had kept a desultory correspondence with Herndon, whom he regarded as the world's greatest authority on Lincoln. "No one certainly knew him except you," Whitney wrote Herndon, "and you knew him thoroughly." "A successful biographer must know his subject as Boswell knew Johnson or you knew Lincoln."[52] When Weik read the early chapters of "Herndon's Memoirs" aloud, Whitney seemed pleased.[53]

Another of Herndon's long-term friends gave Weik quite a different reception. Leonard Swett, too, had moved to Chicago, where he built up a legendary reputation by securing acquittals for nineteen out of twenty defendants in murder trials. Long hovering on the edge of political recognition, Swett had acquired the cynicism of the man of affairs. Shortly after Lincoln's death he had written for Herndon his detailed, realistic reminiscences of the President. In 1887 when Herndon

[50] Herndon to Weik, September 10, 1887, *ibid.*
[51] "Opinions of Men," Herndon's record of interviews, September 6, 1887, *ibid.*
[52] Whitney to Herndon, July 4 and August 27, 1887, *ibid.*
[53] Weik Diary, October 4, 1887.

requested permission to quote this letter, Swett first expurgated every statement even slightly critical of Lincoln. ". . . I have stricken out all allusion to Mr Lincoln's swearing, and reading the Bible," he told Herndon, "& the reason is that I am satisfied the public does not want to hear them[.] Lamon's book fell flat, every body connected with it lost money & the public have not yet forgiven him for writing it, because it stated things which the public did not want to hear of its hero. . . . If I should say Mr Lincoln ever swore & you were to publish it, the public would believe I lied about it." "It would damage your book," Swett predicted, almost clairvoyantly in view of what later happened to *Herndon's Lincoln*, "and if the book were otherwise acceptable, the next edition would leave out that fact in the publication." [54]

When Weik read him the early chapters of "Herndon's Memoirs," Swett emphatically objected to the section on Lincoln's paternity and urged expurgation. He convinced Weik, and Herndon, always receptive to advice from his friends, reluctantly agreed to abandon his truth-at-any-cost stand. Now (to use Whitman's phrase) "old, alone, sick, weak-down, melted-worn with sweat," he was too tired to fight.

I guess that we had better bow to the . . . omnipotence of public Opinion [he advised Weik] and bend to the inevitable with grace and as much dignity as we can reserve. . . . We need not, *nor must we lie.* Let us be true as far as we do go, but by all means let us with grace bow to the inevitable. If the people will not take the truth . . . let the crime rest on them and not on our heads. Talk to me of the progress of this age! Sugar Coat a lie and it goes down sweetly. . . . men vomit at the truth unless it is sweetened with the lie. Falsehood is worshipped and the truth crucified: it always has been so and always will be so. *I say bow down to the inevitable.* . . . the 1st Chap [concerning Lincoln's ancestry] will have to be changed — re-written — modified — gutted. "Make things straight & rosy." Success is what we want. We want no failures. [55]

[54] Swett to Herndon, August 30, 1887, Herndon-Weik Coll.
[55] Herndon to Weik, October 22, 1887, *ibid.*

CHAPTER *xxi*

The True Story of a Great Life

I

I AM as ignorant as a horse about the book business . . . ," Herndon sadly admitted.[1] Weik, for all his air of worldly wisdom, knew scarcely more. Before a word of their Lincoln biography had been written they had talked of picking among dozens of eager publishers; now with a manuscript almost completed, they found not one interested buyer. Mrs. Gertrude Garrison, a literary agent of New York City, for one hundred dollars paid in advance promised the would-be authors entree to the sacred offices of metropolitan publishers. Though Herndon grumbled that the lady was "avaricious and selfish in the extreme" to ask such a fee, he finally agreed to employ her; after all, it was Weik's money.[2] In July 1888 the final copy of the Herndon-Weik manuscript was shipped to New York, where Mrs. Garrison stood ready to perform her miracle.[3]

Reputable publishers would not touch the book. After all Herndon's urging, Weik refused to delete the passages on Lincoln's ancestry and childhood which were certain to offend. Instead, he accompanied the unexpurgated manuscript with a memorandum promising that "several anecdotes of a too realistic nature" were subject to modification if the prospective publisher preferred.[4] Even so, the Herndon-Weik biography was a bad risk. This portrait in undress was likely to offend thousands of Lincoln-worshiping Republicans. Lamon's Lincoln, containing almost identical materials, had been a costly failure; Herndon's would reach a market glutted by Nicolay and Hay's protracted articles.

Mrs. Garrison's assignment was no easy one. First of all, she tried to

[1] Herndon to Weik, August 31, 1888, Herndon-Weik Coll.
[2] Herndon to Weik, December 13, 1886, *ibid.*
[3] Weik Diary, July 30, 1888.
[4] "Things the Author of the Life of Lincoln wishes the publisher . . . to know," undated memorandum [August 1888?] in writing of Mrs. Garrison, Weik MSS.

polish up the manuscript a bit. It seemed to her that any biography of Lincoln should contain some account of the assassination — and it just happened that she had once written a narrative of Lincoln's murder which she would be happy to donate to Herndon and Weik. This contribution Herndon thought "eminently proper," and Weik gladly appended Mrs. Garrison's article to his manuscript.[5] It was at the agent's suggestion also that Weik entered "Herndon's Memoirs of Lincoln" at the copyright office.[6]

At publishers' offices Mrs. Garrison met sales resistance. After repeated rebuffs she turned to the third-rate New York and Chicago firm which had recently published her silly novelette, *The Wrong Man*. Belford, Clarke & Company was probably the most inefficient publishing house in the United States. Ever since its establishment in 1879 it had been known for its reckless business methods and its "attempt to conduct . . . business without regard to business principles, ignoring trade courtesy and justice to their customers, the jobbers and retail book-sellers."[7] Such small profits as it made were derived from shoddy, pirated editions of English works. Its original publications included only such classics as Selina Dolar's *Mes Amours: Poems, Passionate and Playful*, Celia Logan's *Her Strange Fate*, and Ella Wheeler Wilcox's *Poems of Passion*.

Belford, Clarke & Company was a poor chance, but the only one. At Mrs. Garrison's insistence the publishers' reader examined the Herndon-Weik manuscript. Enthusiastically he reported it a work "of unusual merit, and untold interest" and he urged that "the first chapters of the book, poetry and all [the "Chronicles of Reuben," etc.] should be left as they are." ". . . I predict," the anonymous reader forecast, "an immense sale for it, and liberal abuse by the critics."[8]

This was precisely the kind of report that appealed to the president of Belford, Clarke & Company. Abuse could not hurt his firm. "Mr. Belford said to me that he did not believe another publisher in the city [New York] would touch it because it *did* tell so many plain . . . truths," Mrs. Garrison wrote Weik, "but he rather talked as though he saw an advantage in that to a firm who had the courage to print it, as it was sure to make it much talked about." Making no effort to mislead Weik, Mrs. Garrison urged him to talk business with Belford, Clarke & Company. "As for their honesty," she frankly admitted, "I

[5] Mrs. Garrison to Weik, August 14, 1888, *ibid.;* Herndon to Weik, September 7, 1888, Herndon-Weik Coll.

[6] Mrs. Garrison to Weik, August 1, 1888, Weik MSS.; Copyright Entry No. 22607 (August 6, 1888), Copyright Office Records.

[7] *Publishers' Weekly*, XXXVI, 470, 478, 540, 637, 693.

[8] Memorandum signed L. McM. D., New York, July [*sic*] 25, 1888, Weik MSS.

know nothing against it; but have been led to believe that all publishers are *sharp* to say the least." [9] Armed with Herndon's power of attorney, Weik signed a contract for the publication of "Herndon's Life of Lincoln" in either two or three volumes. The publishers were to receive all the receipts from the sales of the first fifteen hundred copies of the work, and thereafter profits were to be divided equally between Belford, Clarke & Company and Weik.[10] Herndon, in great doubt and greater ignorance, ratified Weik's action.

Weik now set about giving the manuscript the final touches. On September 10, 1888, he took the train to Springfield, where he and Herndon spent two days re-reading and reviewing their book. On September 13 with a sigh of relief Jesse "Packed up remainder of MS. and sent [it] to New York." [11]

II

As the manuscript went off to the publishers, Herndon and Weik were jubilant. Then, like many another author, they discovered that their work was but beginning. There were dozens of little jobs yet to do. Herndon had to gather up photographs for illustrations. All over Springfield he trudged begging pictures of Sangamon County bar members. Some feared his book might become notorious; others hung back because their photographs showed the wrinkles of age; still other old-time lawyers were dead, and Herndon had to persuade forgetful descendants to rummage through attic trunks for faded daguerreotypes. Plodding the six weary miles home after a day of fruitless pleading Herndon groaned that his "old legs [were] . . . worn off and . . . 'sorter' stumpy and raw at the ends." [12]

Weik, too, had troubles. Once the contract was signed, Belford, Clarke & Company proved decidedly uncooperative. Deep in debt, pressed by creditors, facing complete collapse within a few hasty months, the publishers had no time to humor authors. Decisions were made and handed down to Herndon and Weik. The biography, it was ruled, would be issued in three boxed volumes, and though Herndon objected to the sets as unwieldy and expensive, his suggestions went unheard.[13] The very title of the biography seems to have been picked by the publisher. Rejecting "Reminiscences of Lincoln at Home,"

[9] Mrs. Garrison to Weik, August 1, 1888, *ibid.*
[10] Contract between Jesse W. Weik and Belford, Clarke & Company, August 10, 1888, *ibid.*
[11] Weik Diary, September 10–13, 1888.
[12] Herndon to Weik, November 3, 1888, Herndon-Weik Coll.
[13] Herndon to Weik, January 15, 1889, *ibid.*

The True Story of a Great Life

"Herndon's Life of Lincoln," and "Herndon's Memoirs of Lincoln," Belford, Clarke & Company made the happy choice of "Herndon's Lincoln: The True Story of a Great Life."

On a close second reading the publishers objected "to all Courtship — all New Salem &c" and without consulting either Herndon or Weik curtly expurgated long passages dealing with Lincoln's early life. Herndon was outraged. "Critics," he fumed, "are good judges of the mechanics of literature, but what do they know of the great heart of this human world of ours — Eh." [14] His irritation seems somewhat inconsistent, since the deleted paragraphs were precisely those which he had urged Weik to strike out before submitting the manuscript. "No one will get mad because we suppress Nancy Hanks illegitimacy or unchastity, if true," he had told Weik, "but thousands will go crazy — wrathy — furious — wild &c if we insert such a suggestion. Jesse, get on the safe side and be prudent." [15] After all, his main object now was for the "book to be a success." "Bear in mind that I am first for the *dimes* — second for the *dimes*   third for the *dimes* &c; & as to glory if it Comes let it Come." [16]

When Jesse did not "get on the safe side," his publishers objected to those very passages. Herndon now assumed the martyr's role, a part for which he needed no rehearsal. "I would," he confided to a friend, "tell all the truth — 'God's naked truth,' if the publishers would let me." But the business was out of his hands and the alterations were made. "We have, I suppose, to bend to the inevitable." [17]

Bookmaking was a process Herndon did not understand, and he found it involved tedious waiting and irritating delay. In October 1888 dribbles of proof began to reach him — page proof, on which verbal revisions might be made but, as he sadly learned, "fixed like the law of the Medes and persians cast ironed" when more substantial alterations were proposed.[18] In print his book looked cruelly different from what it had seemed in manuscript. Day by day Herndon waded through proof sheets, pointing out hundreds of corrections, suggestions, and alterations for Weik to make. As he read he thought of new anecdotes and ideas which he begged to insert. But a book in page proof cannot be materially altered without great expenditure of time and money, and his shabby publishers had neither to spare. When

[14] Herndon to Weik, October 25, 1888, *ibid.*
[15] Herndon to Weik, December 1, 1888, *ibid.*
[16] Herndon to Weik, July 5, 1889, *ibid.*
[17] Herndon to Joseph S. Fowler, October 30, 1888, Herndon Papers; Herndon to Weik, December 3, 1888, Herndon-Weik Coll.
[18] Herndon to Weik, January 4, 1889, *ibid.* Apparently neither Herndon nor Weik ever saw galley proof on their biography.

Herndon's Lincoln finally appeared, the sad author found that most of his suggestions had been disregarded. Errors had crept in, Herndon reported — "small things, I admit & yet they look bad *to me.*" [19]

III

A book is a brain child, and it is hard for two mothers to share the same baby. As long as their affairs progressed satisfactorily, Herndon and Weik got along pleasantly enough. When there was frustration and disappointment, each pointed an accusing finger at the other. Ailing and crotchety, Herndon grew more sensitive and high tempered with age. Weik was ambitious and rather aggressive, with no disposition to ignore his own merits. Inevitably there was friction.

Sometimes it seemed to Herndon that Weik had forgotten the senior partner in this literary enterprise. Particular passages dear to Herndon were deliberately omitted from the biography — his dithyrambic description of the New Salem pioneers, his analysis of the causes of the Civil War, his discussion of Lincoln's power over the people. Herndon found even more irritating Jesse's failure to consult with him on every detail, to write long, comforting letters, to speculate on the progress of the book and its prospects for success. "Jesse," he repeatedly complained, "you are a very clever good natured gentlemanly fellow, generally, but you are a d — d poor correspondent." [20]

Weik too had his moments of irritation. He retained a deep affection and a respect amounting almost to veneration for Herndon, but sometimes he did become tired of those begging letters. It seemed to Weik that he was bearing the whole load of the partnership. Again and again he received Herndon's pitiful requests for ten dollars, twenty dollars, fifty dollars, to help him over a hard shoal. Weik did his best, and by 1891 Herndon owed his partner $650.00. [21]

As recompense Weik thought he should be given Herndon's Lincoln Records. Herndon saw some justice in Weik's claim, but he refused to be rushed into making an outright gift. [22] "It has always been my purpose," he explained, "to give you the Lincoln records . . . under Conditions." "Jesse, After our book is out and when I hear a statement of

[19] Herndon to Weik, July 5, 1889, *ibid.*

[20] Herndon to Weik, June 24, 1890, *ibid.*

[21] Memorandum of Herndon-Weik finances [1897], Weik MSS.; Weik to W. B. Ralston, May 3, 1897, File 4118, office of the clerk of the Sangamon County Probate Court.

[22] Realizing that his Lincoln papers were the only legacy he could leave his children, Herndon earlier had hoped that on his death the collection might be sold to the Chicago Historical Society. Herndon's "A Statement — Memoranda," January 8, 1886, Herndon-Weik Coll.

your Case, accounts &c. I will do what is fair — honest — just between man & man[.] I think I am a reasonable creature and easy to deal with. I think you can risk my word on the question of justice — right — & Equity: So let the thing rest till the book . . . is out." [23]

Such an uneasy postponement of the issue was really satisfactory to neither partner, and the next time Herndon needed to borrow money, he felt obliged to propose something more specific. In September 1888 he offered to "give or sell" Weik the Lincoln Record if Jesse would pay him fifteen or twenty dollars each month until royalties on the biography began to pour in.[24] Later Herndon made a second suggestion. "I will sell you all my right, title, and interest in & to the whole of the Lincoln records," he proposed to Weik, "for One hundred dollars cash paid down, upon the condition that you & I . . . have free access to them if we wish to issue a second — third &c edition of our book." "I said once that I would do something for you and I do it in this proposition. Twentyfive years of toil for $100. is nothing." Herndon added a telltale postscript: "I greatly need the money or would not say cash down." [25] Even these terms seem not to have suited Weik, and no agreement was reached as to the ultimate disposal of the collection. After Herndon's death the manuscripts remained in Weik's possession. They were sold by Weik's heirs to an autograph dealer, and in 1941 the Herndon-Weik papers were purchased by the Library of Congress.

If Weik was dissatisfied with his financial returns from the biographical partnership, he was more aggressively displeased with his lack of recognition. The original Herndon-Weik contract has been lost, but it seems clear that the book was to be called "Herndon's Memoirs of Lincoln . . . Edited by Jesse W. Weik." [26] Herndon's early draft of the preface concluded: "I am especially grateful to my associate in this undertaking, Mr. Jesse W. Weik, of Greencastle, Indiana, whose industry in investigation of facts, and whose literary assistance and zeal deserve the commendation of every reader of this book." [27]

Understandably Weik considered this scant recognition for his very considerable share in preparing the Lincoln biography. His discontent was fed by his publisher, who urged that an explicit statement of the individual responsibility of the joint authors be included in the book.

[23] Herndon to Weik, August 13, 1888, *ibid.*
[24] Herndon to Weik, September 7, 1888, *ibid.*
[25] Herndon to Weik, June 7, 1889, MS. in collection of Mr. W. H. Townsend.
[26] Herndon to Weik, November 7, 1888, Herndon-Weik Coll.
[27] Typewritten preface (identified by Weik as "1st MSS"), September 1, 1887, Weik MSS.

A supplement to the preface was submitted for Herndon's consideration:

> In a work produced under joint authorship it is of the first importance that the part of each shall be clearly stated. Generally speaking the *materials* of these volumes were my [i.e., Herndon's] production. . . . But my col[l]aborator, Mr. Jesse W. Weik . . . has by his personal investigations greatly enlarged our common treasure of facts and information. He has been for several years indefatigable in exploring the course of Lincoln's life. . . . If by authorship is meant the *composition* of the following narrative . . . then the work belongs to Mr. Weik rather than to me. . . . The formal part of the composition considered as a whole is his, while the material elements of the same are my own.[28]

When Herndon received this extraordinary document, he hit the ceiling. ". . . I would be astonished at it," he complained, "if I had not ceased to be astonished at anything." "[I]t is not the truth — the whole truth," he bitterly protested. ". . . I shall never agree to it, nor have my name attached to it."

> . . . you make me stultify myself [he continued] and to that extent it is insulting, but as it comes from a friend I shall pass that over. I may not be familiar with the technical terms or words of . . . book making, but I know shugar [*sic*] from salt. . . . The great future will know how much you have done and you Can't be deprived of *that fame*. . . . You are entitled to Honor & Honor you will get for generations, but both of our names will be dropt in a century or two, probably sooner. You may subject to my approval put in . . . a paragraph in the preface . . . which shows that you are entitled to great Honor, but don't go into particulars — say in substance that our book is the joint product of Jesse W Weik & myself and that will be the truth. . . . Let the future if it is fool enough discuss what you did and what I did and the merits of each exactly in matter or composition &c. &c, but good Lord, Jesse let you and I quit such follies. In the title page of our book . . . it is said "Edited by Jesse W. Weik." That tells the story sufficiently for all practical purposes.

"What is said here," Herndon concluded, "is said in all kindness and in good spirit, but it is firmly said." [29]

The offending passage was not added to the preface, but Weik was still not satisfied. As he revised the manuscript, his own name began

---

[28] Rough draft of supplement to preface, in unidentified handwriting, undated (but c. November 7, 1888), MS., Ill. State Hist. Lib. This manuscript has been published in the Abraham Lincoln Association *Bulletin*, No. 53, where it is incorrectly stated to be in Herndon's writing.

[29] Herndon to Weik, November 7, 1888, Herndon-Weik Coll.

to appear more and more frequently. When Herndon received his copy of the published book in June 1889, he was astonished at the title page.[30]

HERNDON'S LINCOLN

THE TRUE STORY OF A GREAT LIFE

Etiam in minimis major.

THE HISTORY AND PERSONAL RECOLLECTIONS

OF

ABRAHAM LINCOLN

BY

WILLIAM H. HERNDON
For Twenty Years His Friend and Law
Partner

AND

JESSE WILLIAM WEIK, A. M.

VOL. I.

CHICAGO, NEW YORK, AND SAN FRANCISCO
BELFORD, CLARKE & COMPANY
Publishers

———

London, HENRY J. DRANE, Lovell's Court, Paternoster Row

[30] The distinguishing feature of the title page of this first edition of *Herndon's Lincoln* is the absence of the date of publication. The second edition, the text of which is identical with the first, has imprint Chicago: Belford-Clarke Co., 1890. For an authoritative statement on the editions of the Herndon biography see "Herndon's Lincoln: A Study," *Publishers' Weekly*, CXL, 2019–2021.

Lincoln's Herndon

As he read the book, Herndon was shocked to see how much credit Weik had assumed. ". . . I find your name," he bluntly protested, "scattered around — as author — aide — assistant &c. &c. You took a kind of shot gun idea of things." [31]

It would be easy to overemphasize these difficulties between Herndon and Weik. Both men were on edge. A trifle could cause a flare-up of anger, but in a moment the eruption would be deeply regretted. Despite occasional temper tantrums and flighty fits of irritation, Herndon and Weik kept up the warmest personal relations.[32] At Christmas time every year Jesse sent his partner a box, and the Herndons were so poor they thought Santa Claus lived in Greencastle.

> I recd . . . the box containing the "goodies" sent me [Herndon wrote a few days after Christmas]; and now let me thank you, in the name of the whole family. . . . I have been sick with a terribly bad cold, accompanied by a sharp spell of neuralgia. When my son went to the City [Springfield] on Monday morning I forgot to send for some sardines. I wanted some badly and when he brought home the box, lo and behold there, in the box, was what my nature craved, longed for so badly. I opened the Can of mackerel and, to use a slang expression — you bet I went for them in hungry earnestness. I thoroughly satisfied myself and feel better. The "babies," including my better half, jumped into things, the candies, plum pudding &c. &c, and enjoyed themselves "hugely" all Christmas, day and night. We had no turkey, no goose but the box . . . was many times better. What you sent me will last a week or more.[33]

A can of mackerel is a wonderful peacemaker.

IV

Time passed for Herndon with agonizing slowness. Eager for financial reward and for recognition of his services to Lincoln biography, he impatiently waited for his book to appear. The publishers were so slow; Weik was not an obliging correspondent; repeated delays seemed so unwarranted. All during the spring of 1889 people kept asking him when his biography would be out. Springfield was in a furor about it; in stuffy parlors it was the subject of excited whispering. The worst was joyfully anticipated. Milton Hay pontifically assured his visitors

[31] Herndon to Weik, June 22, 1889, Herndon-Weik Coll.

[32] "Herndon's occasional flighty fits of irritation, seen in some letters, were usually over before the letter left the Springfield post office. My father realized this and allowed for it, because he himself came of a flighty, irritable family. So the two got along beautifully. . . ." Mary Hays Weik (daughter of Jesse W. Weik) so wrote me, October 9, 1946.

[33] Herndon to Weik, December 29, 1888, Herndon-Weik Coll.

330

that whatever Herndon's book might contain, it would *"not* be reliable." [34]

Not until the middle of June did Herndon receive his copy of *Herndon's Lincoln*. His immediate, private reaction to the three little volumes bound in drab green was one of bitter disappointment. His corrections had been neglected; his suggestions had been ignored; Weik had broadcast his name through the book; there were a hundred mistakes. Now the book was in print, and the best he could do was to plan for an improved, corrected edition. "Jesse," Herndon begged, "let us make the book a perfect thing so far as truth is concerned and in every direction, if we can. . . . Blackstone devoted his whole life in perfecting his great work. Let us imitate his example — devote our after years in perfecting our book. Let us make it *the* life of Lincoln for some years to come." [35]

After the initial disappointment wore off, Herndon became better pleased with his product. "The book is not what it ought to be," he admitted, "but it is my idea of the life of Lincoln just now under all conditions." "[T]he picture drawn of Lincoln is correct to the letter and the spirit," he assured his correspondents. "I drew the picture of Mr. Lincoln as I saw and knew him. I told the naked God's truth, and Ill stand by it, let the consequences be what they may." [36]

His fortitude was soon in demand, for in early July his book was released. HERNDON'S LINCOLN, his publisher announced proudly, ONE OF THE GREAT HISTORICAL WORKS OF THIS CENTURY. Bound in half calf, the three boxed volumes sold for $9.00; in green cloth, for $4.50.[37] Belford, Clarke & Company sent advance copies to all the important newspapers, and during the early weeks of July most of them carried extended reviews. *Herndon's Lincoln* was welcomed with cheers and some pop bottles, but authors, publishers, reviewers, and readers agreed on one thing: it was an important book.

The principal impression one gets from the reviews of *Herndon's Lincoln* is that of relief — a kind of "Now it has all been told and still it wasn't so bad" attitude. A devastating demolition of Lincoln had been half-feared, half-expected; instead, the Herndon-Weik biography told of a quaint and human but indubitably great man. Herndon's book contained passages concerning Lincoln's personal life which

[34] Isaac N. Phillips to Daniel Fish, April 17, 1909, Fish MSS.

[35] Herndon to Weik, June 22, 1889, Herndon-Weik Coll.

[36] Herndon to "Mr. Foster" [the name should be Joseph S. Fowler], August 15, 1889, MS., Lib. of Cong.; letter of Herndon to unidentified correspondent, September 23, 1889, quoted in *A Catalogue of Lincolniana with an Essay on Lincoln Autographs by the Rev. Dr. William E. Barton* (Thomas F. Madigan, 1929), 56–57; Herndon to Bartlett, December 20, 1889, Bartlett MSS.

[37] Full-page advertisement on back cover of *Belford's Monthly,* July 1889.

many readers found objectionable, but his final verdict on his partner was far from unfavorable. Here was none of the cynicism of Lamon's work, none of its virulent anti-Republicanism; the sections of *Herndon's Lincoln* dealing with the secession crisis were written entirely from Weik's stalwartly Republican viewpoint. As a result, the Herndon portrait of Lincoln, while not in the idealized style of a Holland or a Hay, was nevertheless not unacceptable in the Republican galaxy of American saints. "The effect of this latest biography of the great war President can only be in the end to exalt his memory," reviewers were relieved to note.[38]

A handful of bouquets can be plucked from the newspaper notices. In Springfield itself the *Illinois State Register* declared: "There have been other lives of Lincoln written, but none that approaches this in the faithful portrayal of his real life, from his humble birth to his martyred death." [39] "[A]n important contribution to the ever-growing library of Lincoln literature," ruled the Philadelphia *Inquirer*.[40] "This life of Abraham Lincoln," according to the Portland (Maine) *Eastern Argus*, "casts all others into the shade. . . ." [41] "Mr. Herndon comes nearer giving the general reader an insight [in]to the real Lincoln than any one of the many writers who have made attempts in that direction," the Cincinnati *Enquirer* was positive.[42] And from Boston came the crowning tribute: "Herndon's 'Life of Lincoln' is a history worthy of a Macaulay." [43]

The hasty newspaper tributes were paralleled in the weeklies and the monthlies. The reviewer for the *Atlantic Monthly* found roughness and crudity in the work but gave it discriminating praise. "We think we are not mistaken in looking upon Herndon's Lincoln as a most timely and valuable contribution to a just understanding of that great man . . . ," was the final verdict. "It bears the marks of patient and painstaking labor in gathering all the facts regarding Lincoln's origin and early years. . . . [W]e do not see how any student of Lincoln's character . . . can avoid being strongly affected by this work." *Life*, which noticed only books considered of lasting interest, praised Herndon's biography as "a rugged picture, lacking the finish of expert work, but very interesting and suggestive." The *Literary World* was charmed by Herndon's "honesty and shrewdness." [44]

[38] *Literary World*, XX, 254.
[39] August 11, 1889.
[40] July 8, 1889.
[41] July 13, 1889.
[42] July 5, 1889.
[43] Boston *Commercial*, August 17, 1889.
[44] *Atlantic Mo.*, LXIV, 711–712; *Life*, XIV (July 25, 1889), 49; *Literary World*, XX, 253.

The True Story of a Great Life

Perhaps the most penetrating review was that of General Jacob D. Cox in the *Nation*, which had been strongly critical of Nicolay and Hay's eulogistic and partisan biography.

> Mr. Herndon's personal recollections of Lincoln [Cox believed] will doubtless remain the most authentic and trustworthy source of information concerning the great man in the period prior to his election to the Presidency. . . . Herndon's narrative gives, as nothing else is likely to give, the material from which we may form a true picture of the man from infancy to maturity. The sincerity and honesty of the biographer appear on every page. It is impossible to doubt that he has meant to tell us candidly what he knows about Lincoln. . . . The reader of these memoirs must not look for an adequate estimate of Lincoln's place in history, or for an authoritative judgment of his conduct of national affairs during the great civil war. He must expect, rather, to be helped to understand how Abraham Lincoln became the man he was. . . . We have much that is trivial, some things which are in bad taste, but we are made to feel, after all, that we are looking upon Lincoln's life as he actually lived it.[45]

There were other reviews, of course; every author expects them. There were rave reviews, venomous reviews, freak reviews, reviews which completely misunderstood what Herndon was saying. As always, there were the critics who chose this particular book as another pretext for spurring on a splintered hobbyhorse. With sectional smugness the Boston *Herald* complained that *Herndon's Lincoln* was written "in that peculiarly western spirit which revels in ugliness because it is ugly." This led to animadversions on the sorry state of things when "there is literally nothing which may not be openly printed, and which, being printed, will not be openly discussed in the country." Such literary degeneracy, this reviewer opined, was caused by the influx of immigrants with their "European coarseness." [46]

Some abuse was to be expected, and even Herndon, abnormally sensitive to criticism, was not greatly distressed when the Decatur (Illinois) *Republican* dismissed his work as "the vaporings of a silly old man" [47] or when the *Nebraska State Journal* termed it "a gross, and infamous slander from beginning to end," published with intent "to poison the minds of decent people against the dead President and martyr," "the work of a sneak and a villain." [48] "Whatever there may be of

[45] *Nation*, XLIX (August 29, 1889), 173–174. The review was unsigned, but Horace White identified the author in a letter to Weik, November 16, 1892, Herndon-Weik Coll.

[46] Boston *Herald*, July 8, 1889.

[47] July 15, 1889.

[48] Quoted in unidentified clipping, headed "From the New York Sun," Lincoln National Life Foundation.

fact in all this sad relation," carped the St. Paul *News*, "the objectionable, holier-than-thou air of the writer is repulsive to the last degree,
and a shudder creeps over the reader to realize that a 'friend' is thus
harshly revealing glimpses of a life that came to his knowledge as the
friend and law partner of twenty years and coolly makes merchandise
of the distorted tale." [49]

Such comments were more than counterbalanced by the dozens of
flattering and encouraging letters Herndon received. George William
Curtis, occupant of "The Easy Chair" in *Harper's Magazine,* considered the Herndon-Weik biography "a book of the greatest interest and
value" and strongly recommended it to his friends.[50] "Mr. Herndon,"
Senator Lyman Trumbull agreed, "has done more to picture Lincoln
as I knew him than any of the many others who have undertaken to
give histories of his life. . . ." [51] "It is not only the best of all the biographies of Lincoln that have been written," asserted Horace White, editor of the New York *Evening Post,* "but is in my judgment the best
American biography that has ever been written." [52]

When the returns were in, critical opinion was heavily on Herndon's
side. "The criticisms generally are favorable," he realized, "and yet
some of them are savage, but I guess I can stand it quite bravely." It
was especially pleasant to note that no reviewer called attention to a
single factual error in the biography. "[O]ur life of Lincoln," Herndon
crowed, "is born and will grow up to be a stout old man." [53]

V

Fed by praise, Herndon's optimism expanded prodigiously. And
Weik, hopeful for once, sailed for Europe on the strength of his anticipated royalties. The collaborators had happy dreams of prosperity
and success. Then disaster came. On September 14, 1889, more than
two months after *Herndon's Lincoln* was published, the Chicago *Evening Journal* launched a savage attack.

> An alleged biography of Abraham Lincoln by W. H. Herndon, of
> Springfield, Ill., has been recently . . . placed on the market [the
> *Journal* began, holding its nose]. It is an infamous book. It is one of the
> most infamous books ever written. . . . It vilely distorts the image of

[49] Undated clipping, Lincoln National Life Foundation.
[50] Martha McCook Curtis to Herndon, January 24, 1890, Weik MSS.
[51] Quoted in *Herndon's Lincoln. One of the Great Historical Works of this Century* (four-page 1890 folder advertising the biography).
[52] Horace White to Herndon, January 18, 1890, Herndon-Weik Coll.
[53] Herndon to Weik, November 4, 1889, *ibid.;* Herndon to Bartlett, October 5,
1889, Bartlett MSS.

an ideal statesman, patriot and martyr. . . . The author of this in-
describable book was a law partner and assumes to have been an intimate friend to Abraham Lincoln. . . . No man has ever before found
in his biographer so malevolent an enemy as Abraham Lincoln's "friend"
has proved to be to him. The book is the shame and disgrace of American literature. The obscenity of the work is surprising and shocking.
Anthony Comstock should give it his attention. It is not fit for family
reading. Its salacious narrative and implications . . . are simply out-
rageous. . . . In all its parts and aspects — if we are a judge, and we
think we are, of the proprieties of literature and of human life — we
declare that this book is so bad it could hardly have been worse.[54]

One week after the Chicago *Journal's* attack, Belford, Clarke & Company went into bankruptcy. No direct causal connection is to be implied, though one of the reasons for the firm's collapse was its publication of "erotic" books — such as *Herndon's Lincoln*. The failure was
not unexpected; anyone less optimistic than Herndon or less naïve
than Weik must have seen it coming. From the day his book was published, Herndon received dozens of letters complaining that no copies
of *Herndon's Lincoln* could be obtained in any of the book stores.
When Truman H. Bartlett in France tried to purchase a set of the biography, he was told by the booksellers that the President's son, Robert Todd Lincoln, then ambassador to Great Britain, had purchased
and destroyed every copy of the small English edition.[55] That story
was probably without foundation, for American readers encountered
the same problem: no copies on hand, no copies ordered.

Herndon liked to blame Robert Todd Lincoln, but the fault lay
squarely with his publishers. Belford, Clarke & Company had no standing in the publishing world — no agents, no list of authors, no outlets.
The firm was not equipped to distribute Herndon's book. By September 1889 its debts had mounted so enormously that it was forced into
bankruptcy by hungry creditors. The resulting legal squabbles — the
reorganization of the firm under the title "Belford Clarke Company,"
the pruning off of the New York offices from the Chicago headquarters, the scaling down of the firm's indebtedness by seventy-five per
cent [56] — are not a part of the Herndon story except as they affected

[54] Chicago *Evening Journal* quoted in *Illinois State Journal*, September 16,
1889, and in Cedar Rapids *Times*, October 26, 1889.
[55] Bartlett's letter quoted in Herndon to Weik, December 5, 1889, Herndon-
Weik Coll. There is no doubt that Robert Todd Lincoln found the Herndon-Weik
biography objectionable, but I have found no evidence to show that he tried to
suppress it, either in England or in America. The comparative rarity of the first edition of *Herndon's Lincoln* is best explained by the fact that only fifteen hundred
sets of the biography were printed in 1889.
[56] New York *Tribune*, September 24, 1889; *Publishers' Weekly*, XXXVI, 470,
478, 540, 568, 637.

the sale of his book. Though Herndon tried to keep his hopes high, the fact was that his publisher had failed at precisely the moment when promotion of *Herndon's Lincoln* might have brought returns. By the time the reorganized firm was convalescent, public interest had died and with it all chances for Herndon's financial success.

Hurriedly summoned from Europe, Weik did what he could in the emergency. In November 1889 a new contract with the Belford Clarke Company was signed, less favorable to the authors in royalty percentage than the original agreement.[57] In return the publishers smilingly promised an elaborate promotion campaign. A prospectus and broadsides, quoting extensively from the favorable reviews, were circulated, and apparently some effort was made to enter *Herndon's Lincoln* in the subscription book trade.[58]

As the advertising campaign got under way, Herndon and Weik at last learned why their Lincoln biography had been so difficult to procure. In the first edition only fifteen hundred sets of *Herndon's Lincoln* had been printed — precisely the number on which all profits were to go to the publishers. Up to January 1890, therefore, not a cent of royalty was due to the joint authors. It was shocking news to Herndon, whose expectations had been built up so high. "It seems to me that B C & Co have managed things badly from the beginning," Herndon grumbled, "but I suppose that financial troubles wilted them down flat." [59]

Now that their original, royalty-free stock was about exhausted, the publishers suddenly proposed to print a new edition of the biography, and Herndon and Weik were instructed to supply corrections and additional material at once. The demand came to Herndon "like a clap of lightning from a clear sky." ". . . I have no time to re-read & Correct," he complained to Weik. "You know my pecuniary Condition & [I] have to toil all the time in some way . . . to get my bread & butter. . . . It frets & annoys me so that I cannot read or think." [60] Weik's check for twenty-one dollars gave Herndon time to make a few sugges-

[57] Contract between Jesse W. Weik and Belford Clarke Company, November 30, 1889, Weik MSS.

[58] A four-page announcement of the book, quoting favorable reviews, was issued under the title *Herndon's Lincoln. One of the Great Historical Works of this Century.* . . . In the Lincoln National Life Foundation there has been preserved a small broadside, *The Life of the Great Emancipator! Herndon's Lincoln,* which concludes: "Agents Wanted. For Terms and Territory address, Belford-Clarke Co. . . ." The publishers claimed to have spent $3,000 in promoting *Herndon's Lincoln* during the first year of its publication. A. Belford to Weik, June 30, 1890, Weik MSS.

[59] Herndon to Weik, January 28 and February 5, 1890, Herndon-Weik Coll.

[60] Herndon to Weik, January 23, 1890, *ibid.*

tions, such as including in the revised edition an essay on "Lincoln's being Control[l]ed by events." [61] On the first of February Belford Clarke
informed him that there was no time to make any alterations at all.
A new printing of the biography appeared in the spring of 1890, identical in text with the original edition but bearing the publication date
on the title page.[62] To Herndon any move by the dilatory publishers
was good news. "I am glad to know that the 2d Edit of our book will
soon be out," he cheered, "& what is better to me is the money which I
hope will Come from the sale of it — the 2d Edit." [63]

Herndon could not stay despondent long. Already he was hoping for
a revised and expanded third edition. Edward L. Pierce, biographer
of Sumner, volunteered to contribute a section on Lincoln's 1848 visit
to New England, and Herndon welcomed his essay as a significant ad-
dendum to the biography.[64] From New York he received even more
valuable material. Reading Herndon's book revived Horace White's
memories of the pre-war days when he had reported the Lincoln-
Douglas debates for the Chicago *Tribune*. *Herndon's Lincoln* was
weak on the 1858 campaign, and White offered to furnish gratuitously
his recollections of those exciting times for a revised edition of the biography.[65] White's reminiscences made a substantial chapter, which
Herndon correctly termed "a fine — an eloquent contribution to the life
of Lincoln." [66]

V I

Herndon kept an anxious eye on sales of his biography. With all the
reviews, the laudatory letters, and the publishers' promised advertising
drive, it seemed that the books should be selling. Herndon's spirits,
once crushed to earth, easily rose again. "I never had a thought that
the book would in the end be a failure," he reassured Weik. "I, in other
words, always thought it would be a grand success in time, and so it
will be." [67]

---

[61] Herndon to Weik, January 28, 1890, *ibid.*

[62] See "Herndon's Lincoln: A Study," *Publishers' Weekly*, CXL, 2019–2021, for
significant comment by Ernest J. Wessen. A close check has failed to disclose any
changes (except on the title page) in the second edition. The few typographical
errors which occurred in the 1889 edition (e.g., Vol. I, pp. 23 and 59, and Vol. III,
pp. 484 and 488) were repeated in the 1890 reprinting.

[63] Herndon to Weik, February 8, 1890, Herndon-Weik Coll.

[64] Pierce to Herndon, December 23, 1889; Herndon to Weik, January 23, 1890,
ibid.

[65] White to Weik, February 6, 1890, *ibid.*

[66] Herndon to White, August 26, 1890, White MSS.

[67] Herndon to Weik, June 6, 1890, Herndon-Weik Coll.

Fifteen hundred sets of the second printing were issued, and, with his debts mounting, Herndon happily dreamed of royalties. In July 1890 Belford Clarke Company made the first report on sales. It was claimed that of the second printing 416 sets of *Herndon's Lincoln* had been distributed as review copies, on which the authors were due no return. The balance had been selling very slowly, the publishers explained, and the total amount due the authors was only about $110.00 — and all of Herndon's share was applied against his indebtedness to Weik.[68]

Herndon was in a white fury. Twice a week during the hot summer months he trudged six miles into Springfield, pushing his vegetable cart from door to door, "peddling . . . grapes — pears — apples — corn &c &c." [69] His one comforting thought had been of that royalty check which would end the pettiness of his exigent life. He felt that he had devoted his whole life to Lincoln biography. It seemed to him that he had sacrificed all — political preferment, legal career, personal happiness — for the cause of Truth in Biography. He knew he had suffered much, but always he had thought he would some day be repaid. Now this was his reward.

There was something radically wrong, he was positive. He suspected everybody — the publishers, Weik, that "Army of Editors" supposed to have received that preposterous number of review copies. The Belford Clarke report was surely a fraud. "You may stand & sanction all this," he heatedly wrote Weik, "but I shall not. I will hold some one responsible for the loss — wrong. . . ." Then burst out the suspicion that had been accumulating during the cold winter nights in his cabin, during sweaty hours in the potato patch, during dusty walks into Springfield. Jesse and the publishers were keeping him in the dark; Jesse had copyrighted the book and had signed the Belford Clarke contract in his own name; Jesse had refused to answer his urgent letters.

There has been from 1887 to this day [Herndon protested] a kind of mystery hanging & hovering over this whole book affair. You do not answer my letters nor the questions put to you in them. Human nature would teach you that your silence breeds suspicion. You should be prompt and Explicit in your business with me. . . . you are a d — d bad Correspondent. You ought to take it for granted that when I ask questions of you that those questions are interesting — important to me and rest on my mind, vexing me if not answered. Again I say that there was & is a perpetual mystery hanging over this book busi-

[68] A. Belford to Weik, June 30, 1890, Weik MSS.; Herndon to Weik, November 26, 1890, Herndon-Weik Coll.
[69] Herndon to Weik, August 19, 1890, Herndon-Weik Coll.

ness. Why were the Contracts . . . made in your *name alone* & not in the name of H & W? . . . Why did you not bounce the report sent me from B C Co? . . . I am determined not to be swindled. . . . A screw is loose somewhere and the thing to be done is to find it & put it in its place.[70]

So far as Weik was concerned, Herndon's charges were unfounded. When he calmed down, Herndon apologized: "I do not charge you with any wrong wilfully done, believe that you have done the best that you could. . . ."[71] But both Herndon and Weik were so inexperienced, so ignorant of the ways of the business world, so easily gulled. The blame, as Herndon finally realized, lay with his publishers. The third-rate, bankrupt house, without retail outlets, probably dishonest and certainly inefficient, had butchered Herndon's book. "[S]peaking of our book and its sale &c," Herndon groaned, "there never were as many blunders Committed in any book concern, since this old world began, as have been committed by B C Co." "Belford Clark[e] & C — Honest men — ! Business men! Good men!"[72]

VII

At this moment of utter despair Horace White appeared as Herndon's guardian angel. He cheered up the desponding authors, gave pointed, practical suggestions, and virtually took over the management of their affairs. First of all, he urged that the book be taken from the bungling hands of the Belford Clarke Company and entrusted to some reputable Eastern publisher. Before any established firm would touch it, *Herndon's Lincoln* would have to be revised, and a few paragraphs highly shocking to the Victorian mind would have to be expurgated. "I would advise," White strongly urged, "that the two or three passages . . . which suggest a taint in the legitimacy of L. be dropped out."[73]

Another portion of the Lincoln biography which delicate readers found frightfully offensive was the so-called "Chronicles of Reuben." This rough narrative, supposed to have been written by Lincoln in his youth, and intended to be in Biblical style, related the frontier practical joke of a double wedding at which (reputedly at Lincoln's instance) the brides were surreptitiously placed in the wrong beds.

[70] Herndon to Weik, July 6, 1890, *ibid.*
[71] Herndon to Weik, July 19, 1890, *ibid.*
[72] Herndon to Weik, October 5, 1890, *ibid.*; Herndon to Weik, March 11, 1891, MS. in collection of Mr. C. N. Owen.
[73] White to Weik, March 12, 1890, Herndon-Weik Coll.

Nearly every reviewer pointed to the "Chronicles" as uncouth, coarse, and vulgar. Like Herndon, the present-day reader finds it hard to understand why this not very amusing tale was considered so unspeakably revolting. "I admire the good tastes of life as well as any man or woman," Herndon bragged, "and Cannot be made to defend the nasty — obscene or vulgar under any Circumstances, but I *do* fail to see why the Episode causes a blush on any man's or woman's cheek. Some people are too nice for this material sphere — this muddy globe of ours." [74]

Still, pressed by White and Weik, he consented to "any reasonable corrections" in the third edition.[75] "I have no serious objections to mere *erasures* — mere innocent suppressions — a striking out of non essential things," he finally agreed, "but I do object to positive misstatements — lies." [76] Sadly he saw the offending paragraphs struck from his work. Twenty years earlier Herndon would have fought back; now, tired and old, he had learned to yield. In the mellowness of maturity it occurred to him that even he might not be infallible. "My motives were good in doing as I did," he explained to White. "I wished to throw light on the mysterious phases of Lincoln's wonderful life. I loved Lincoln & I loved the reading world. I thought the reading world wished the lights that I had and hence the facts told in the biography. . . . I may have erred in the head, but I think that my heart was in the right place." [77]

Through Horace White's influence, Charles Scribner's Sons became interested in the Lincoln biography, and, after the necessary expurgations were made, they agreed to republish it. Weik entered into protracted negotiations to purchase the plates of the book from the Belford Clarke Company and with a gift from White and an advance from the Scribners was able to free himself from his earlier contract. During the winter of 1890–91 plans were actively pushed for the new, third edition of *Herndon's Lincoln*.[78]

Too poor to help with buying the plates, too ill to correct the copy, Herndon's share in the undertaking was passive. Seventy-two years old, fragile as a sheet of yellowed paper, he was "sick pretty much all winter with the grippe." [79] His condition was not considered serious, but

[74] Herndon to Weik, March 7, 1890, *ibid.*
[75] Herndon to White, October 26, 1890, White MSS.
[76] Herndon to Weik, November 5, 1890, Herndon-Weik Coll.
[77] Herndon to White, October 26, 1890, White MSS.
[78] Weik to White, September 9, 1890, *ibid.;* Charles Scribner's Sons to White, October 16, 1890; Charles Scribner's Sons to Weik, October 20 and December 18, 1890, Weik MSS.
[79] Herndon to White, February 13, 1891, White MSS.

in March he was confined to his bed. Mrs. Herndon was more worried about her son than her husband. Willie Herndon, a fine boy of twenty-one, suffered from "an attack of catarral-fever which resulted in Pnumonia." His father too was uneasy about him. "I am afraid Willie will be taken from us," he told Anna Herndon.[80]

Early in the morning of March 18, 1891, Willie died. Though the news was carefully kept from his father, Herndon seemed to know that his son was gone. He suffered an abrupt relapse. Before noon Mrs. Herndon was hoarsely called to her husband's bed. "Anna," he whispered, "the summons has called. I am an overripe sheaf. I go and take the weak [meaning his son] with me and leave you the strong. All I ask is that you do not weep. Do not forget my first wife's children and tell them goodbye."[81]

Two days later, with a winter wind whipping about the hearse, the funeral procession plodded through muddy roads to Springfield's Oak Ridge Cemetery. A small group of old friends gathered for a moment on the slope opposite Lincoln's tomb. The preacher said simply: "We will leave his record with his Maker."[82] As the news of Herndon's death was wired over the land, newspapers paused to remember a man almost forgotten. One obituary Herndon would have liked best of all: "Gone to Meet Lincoln."[83]

A Supplementary Note

Herndon died believing that his book was to be republished by Scribner's. After all the negotiations were completed and the plates purchased from Belford Clarke, the Scribners quite suddenly informed Weik that "with sincere reluctance" they were going to drop the proposed publication.[84] Horace White explained this change of heart. Charles Scribner, head of the firm, had informed him that Robert Todd Lincoln bitterly objected to *Herndon's Lincoln*, that the Scribners "did not wish to be instrumental in putting out a book that was objectionable to the son of the subject of the book," and that "emendations to

[80] Mrs. Anna Herndon to Weik, April 9, 1891, Herndon-Weik Coll.

[81] This is the cherished family version of Herndon's last words as related to me by Mrs. Mollie Herndon Ralston, August 16, 1944. For a slightly different contemporary account see *Illinois State Journal*, March 19, 1891.

[82] Mrs. Minnie Brown to L. O. Renne, September 10, 1939, quoted in Renne, *Lincoln and the Land of the Sangamon*, 44.

[83] *Religio-Philosophical Journal*, I (new ser.), 691. For a sincere and moving tribute by an old friend see the obituary signed W[illiam] J[ayne] in *Illinois State Register*, March 20, 1891.

[84] Charles Scribner's Sons to Weik, October 1, 1891, Weik MSS.

the extent of making the book satisfactory to Mr. Robert Lincoln would spoil it or seriously impair its selling qualities." [85]

With White's assistance, Weik was able to secure a contract from D. Appleton & Company.[86] After minor expurgations were made (the footnotes concerning Lincoln's legitimacy and the "Chronicles" episode) and after new matter by Edward L. Pierce and Horace White was added, the Appleton two-volume edition of *Herndon's Lincoln* appeared in 1892. The book was never of any financial advantage to Herndon's heirs. By 1897 the half of the royalties accruing to the Herndon estate since publication in 1889 amounted to only $446.23 — $203.77 less than the sums Herndon owed Weik. In April 1897 Weik purchased Herndon's share of the copyright of the biography for one hundred dollars.[87]

[85] White to Weik, October 6, 1891, Herndon-Weik Coll.

[86] D. Appleton & Co. to Weik, November 10, 1891, Weik MSS.

[87] Memorandum of Herndon-Weik finances [1897], *ibid.;* Weik to W. B. Ralston (administrator of Herndon's estate), May 3, 1897, File 4118, office of the clerk of the Sangamon County Probate Court.

EPILOGUE

Herndon's Lincoln

I

HERNDON'S LINCOLN is the most controversial Lincoln biography ever written. Its appearance in 1889 elicited appeals to Anthony Comstock for suppression, shocked cries of indignation, a measure of discriminating praise, and not a little extravagant eulogy. Even today to mention Herndon divides Lincoln specialists into opposing and sometimes acrimonious factions. To some Herndon appears "a coarse, scandal-loving brute"; to others, "almost a fanatic in his devotion to the truth." His "life of Lincoln poisoned the source of Lincoln biography" — or it "contributed more than any other . . . to the factual knowledge of Lincoln's pre-presidential years." [1] In all the strident argument there has rarely been a dispassionate attempt to appraise Herndon's book by historical and literary standards. [2]

The original edition of *Herndon's Lincoln*, with 638 pages, bound in three ridiculous little volumes, has become a collector's item, but the contents have been absorbed into the stream of American folklore. It is usually safe to wager that any well-known anecdote about Lincoln derives from Herndon's writings. Poets, playwrights, biographers, and novelists have found in *Herndon's Lincoln* if not inspiration, at least local color. Winston Churchill, Carl Sandburg, Robert Sherwood, Edgar Lee Masters, and Vachel Lindsay have seen in the Herndon-Weik

[1] For these opinions, in the order quoted, see typed copy of an 1895 letter written by L. E. Chittenden, Lincoln National Life Foundation; Albert J. Beveridge to Weik, April 28, 1926, photostat, Hertz Coll.; Detroit *News*, June 11, 1931; *Saturday Review of Literature*, XVIII (February 12, 1938), 5.

[2] There are three notable exceptions to this statement. Mr. Paul M. Angle has made a penetrating and objective study of Herndon and his writings in the introduction to his edition of *Herndon's Life of Lincoln* and in *A Shelf of Lincoln Books*, 28–33. The chapters on Herndon in Dr. Benjamin P. Thomas's *Portrait for Posterity* are vigorously written, warmly human, and historically sound. In *Lincoln the President* Professor J. G. Randall has given an incisive analysis of Herndon's contributions to Lincoln biography.

biography a clue for interpreting Lincoln. So also have a host of lesser writers — Irving Bacheller, Denton J. Snider, Carrie D. Wright, and Mary Hartwell Catherwood, to name only a few. Herndon's portrait of Lincoln is unforgettable. As Paul M. Angle has remarked, "If this is not the real Lincoln, then it is a great work of artistic imagination." [3]

This picture of Lincoln is not unflattering. If he lacks the gushing hero worship of Holland, Herndon is even further removed from the debunking cynicism of Lamon. Contemporary reviewers correctly judged that Herndon's revelations about his partner were not "such as to diminish Lincoln's reputation." [4] The object of the biography was to make Lincoln stand out in contrast to his background. The structure of *Herndon's Lincoln* is revealed in one telling sentence of the preface:

> Many of our great men . . . have been self-made, rising . . . through struggles to the topmost round of the ladder; but Lincoln rose from a lower depth than any of them — from a stagnant, putrid pool, like the gas which, set on fire by its own energy and self-combustible nature, rises in jets, blazing, clear, and bright. [5]

Herndon's entire book was consciously designed to illustrate this contrast. [6] Basically the biography has the same pattern as the sentimental novel with its contrast between inauspiciously humble beginnings and invariably happy endings.

The "putrid pool," as Herndon conceived it, was the circumstances of Lincoln's birth and childhood. [7] A noisome mixture he presented: Thomas Lincoln, the father, "roving and shiftless," "careless, inert, and dull"; Nancy Hanks, his wife, "the illegitimate daughter of . . . a well-bred Virginia . . . planter," dragging out a life "beclouded by a spirit of sadness"; the "Illiterate and shiftless" Hanks-Sparrow family connections in Kentucky and Indiana; Nancy's cousin, "the irrepressible and cheerful waif, Dennis Hanks," who "came into the world through nature's back-door." There were hints that Abraham Lincoln himself made a similar surreptitious entrance — innuendo which *Herndon's Lincoln* related but did not refute.

The stages in Lincoln's rise to power from these lowly beginnings are familiar to every schoolboy, for Herndon's account of Lincoln has become an American tradition. In late 1816 Thomas Lincoln took his

---

[3] Angle, *A Shelf of Lincoln Books*, 32.
[4] New York *Tribune*, July 7, 1889.
[5] *Herndon's Lincoln*, I, ix.
[6] Herndon to Hart, December 28, 1866, Hart MSS.
[7] Many of Herndon's theories have been discarded or refuted by modern historical scholars. The present passage is to be understood as a summary of Herndon's thesis, not as a vindication of his veracity.

wife and family into southern Indiana, where, according to Herndon, they spent their first winter in a "half-faced" camp, entirely open on one side and having no floor, doors, nor windows. Nancy Hanks Lincoln died of "the milk-sick," and shortly afterward her husband presented to his orphaned children a stepmother, Sarah Bush Johnston, "industrious and thrifty, but gentle and affectionate." Those Indiana pioneer days, as described by Herndon, were rugged and unpleasant. Young Abe Lincoln split rails and husked corn; he attended schools by littles, less than twelve months in all; he rode miles to take corn to the gristmill and was once kicked senseless by his horse. Even as a boy he was a gaunt, awkward figure, tall and thin with excessively large hands and feet. And even as a youth he had acquired a reputation for wit of a rough sort, his literary effusions including scurrilous doggerel and an unpleasant parody on the Bible.

On reaching manhood and after two riverboat trips down the Mississippi, young Lincoln settled in New Salem, Illinois, where he successively served as clerk for Denton Offut, pilot of the *Talisman*, captain of militia in the Black Hawk War, owner of a grocery store that failed, deputy surveyor, and postmaster. He fell in love with Ann Rutledge, and then occurred, in Herndon's tale, "the saddest chapter in Mr. Lincoln's life." For when Ann died, Lincoln was almost deranged and "walked on that sharp and narrow line which divides sanity from insanity." "My heart," Lincoln is supposed to have said of Ann Rutledge's grave, "lies buried there." New Salem was also the locale of another romance — though romance hardly seems the appropriate term for an episode in which Lincoln was rejected by a lady whom he later unflatteringly described as "over-size," wanting teeth, and "weather-beaten" in appearance.

Lincoln entered politics, served in the state legislature, and achieved prominence in Whig circles in Illinois. After moving to Springfield, he was admitted to the bar and had as successive partners John Todd Stuart, Stephen T. Logan, and Herndon. Again he fell in love, this time with the "proud, but handsome and vivacious" Mary Todd. There followed, in Herndon's recital, a season of broken engagements, when Lincoln failed to appear on his appointed wedding day and was so mentally depressed that friends feared suicide. Later the affair was patched up, Lincoln and Mary married, and from that day, said Herndon, Mrs. Lincoln "led her husband a wild and merry dance."

So unpleasant was his home life that Lincoln began to take a more active interest in law and politics. In the former he soon became a leader of the state bar. Herndon considered his partner both "a very great and a very insignificant lawyer," but essentially a case lawyer. In politics a Whig, Lincoln served in Congress during the concluding months of the Mexican war. With the adoption of the Kansas-Nebraska act he re-entered politics, opposed Stephen A. Douglas, and in 1856 became prominent in the newly organized Republican party. Failing of election to the United States Senate in 1855, he was the obvious Republican candidate in 1858. In seven momentous debates he challenged Douglas and won, though the Little Giant, because of inequality in the legislative apportionment, retained his Senate seat.

Pausing a moment in his narrative of public events, Herndon turned again to Lincoln's domestic life and in a final fling at Mrs. Lincoln detailed the "bitter harvest of conjugal infelicity." And he could not resist one more opportunity to repeat his argument that Lincoln was not a Christian. Returning to politics, *Herndon's Lincoln* recounted the nominating conventions of 1860, Lincoln's selection as Republican standard-bearer, the campaign, the election, and the victory won. These were the steps by which Herndon traced his partner's ascent to that "topmost round of the ladder," the presidency. The remainder of the biography consisted of what Herndon correctly characterized as "a kind of one eye glimpse" of the Civil War years.[8] The final chapter was a condensation of Herndon's 1865 lectures on Lincoln.

II

Such, in brief, is the outline of *Herndon's Lincoln*. Ever since the first edition appeared the biography has perplexed students of Lincoln, particularly his admirers. The Herndon-Weik biography is so fundamental that it has to be considered in writing almost any book about Lincoln, yet every reader at times must have grave doubts as to its credibility.

Again and again the question has been asked: Is Herndon reliable? Unfortunately, like most important questions, it has no simple answer. Partly the fault is in the question. What does "reliable" mean? Every writer is subject to error; no book is perfect. Does reliability refer to intent or to practice? A biographer may make a willful distortion or he may be influenced by unconscious bias. There are mistakes of forgetful memory and those of faulty reporting. There are errors of inference from well established facts and those that spring from dependence on unreliable witnesses. And, of course, there are typographical blunders. What is a permissible margin of error? How many mistakes will be allowed the "reliable" author per page? Would ten typographical errors equal two faults of omission or one deliberate falsification?

The problem of subconscious bias in the Herndon-Weik biography is

<hr>

[8] Herndon to Bartlett, November 10, 1888, Bartlett MSS.

not one that will be discussed here; it cannot be solved by historical methods from the evidence now at hand. Sometimes it has been suggested that Herndon, disgruntled at Lincoln's failure to give him a rich federal appointment, undertook a "career of revenge" by maligning the memory of his dead partner.[9] If such was the case, it was a motivation of which Herndon himself was unaware. To attempt to psychoanalyze a man sixty years after his death by using a handful of manuscripts is a very dubious process indeed. A competent psychiatrist demands repeated interviews and prolonged personal contact before hazarding even a tentative diagnosis. Surely the historian should be at least as cautious in rendering his final verdict. It is those who most bitterly resent Herndon's amateur psychological interpretation of Lincoln who most frequently employ this same doubtful tool to measure Herndon himself.

There is not, to the present writer's knowledge, a single letter or other manuscript of Herndon's that reveals a desire or willingness to tell an untruth about Lincoln. Nowhere in his intimate letters to Jesse Weik did Herndon ever suggest the inclusion of a saying or anecdote which he knew to be false. Even his most improbable stories he vouched for as true and correct.[10] Herndon may have been in error, but he was not a liar. The honesty of his conscious purpose to tell the truth is revealed in everything he ever wrote. In an age before standards of historical criticism were highly developed such integrity was not common. At precisely the same time that Herndon and Weik were writing their biography, John G. Nicolay and John Hay, the President's former secretaries, were preparing their tedious ten-volume *Abraham Lincoln: A History.* "If I have anywhere called Tom Thumb undersized or insinuated that the onion is less sweet than the rose," wrote witty John Hay to his editor, "I am ready to draw my pen through it." "It is of the utmost moment," Hay informed his collaborator, "that we should *seem* fair to [General McClellan] . . . , while we are destroying him." [11]

One cannot find a parallel to these statements in the Herndon-Weik correspondence. It is true that after years of demanding an authentic Lincoln biography which would "suppress no truth & suggest no falsehood," [12] Herndon faltered. When his own book was in press, he favored omitting entirely the story of Nancy Hanks's alleged unchastity

---

[9] Robert Todd Lincoln to H. M. Alden, November 27, 1895, MS., Mass. Hist. Soc.; Isaac N. Phillips to J. R. B. Van Cleave, April 26, 1909, Lincoln Centennial Assoc. MSS.; Shelby M. Cullom, *Fifty Years of Public Service,* 44–45.

[10] Herndon to Weik, fragment of MS., c. 1888, Herndon-Weik Coll.

[11] Hay to R. W. Gilder, June 18, [1887], Hay MSS., Huntington Lib.; Tyler Dennett, *John Hay: From Poetry to Politics,* 139.

[12] Herndon to Lamon, March 15, 1870, Lamon MSS.

and for a later edition consented to "mere innocent suppressions." Even here, however, he vehemently objected "to positive misstatements — lies." [13] The suppressions and omissions so reluctantly agreed to were not intended to injure Lincoln; rather the reverse of that object was in view. Whatever else Herndon must account for, an intentional design to malign his dead partner is not among his sins.

III

But to tell the truth one must first be able to recognize that rare article. In order to describe an event accurately a biographer must have had firsthand opportunity of observation or he must use discriminatingly the testimony of representative and reliable witnesses. From tested evidences he must draw reasonable, logical inferences. Factual impeccability may sometimes be nullified by blunders of style or biographical approach.

In *Herndon's Lincoln* a surprisingly small proportion of the narrative is based on Herndon's own reminiscences. Though Herndon probably met Lincoln as early as 1832, they were certainly not intimate friends until 1837. Herndon saw Lincoln alive only once after 1861. These twenty-odd years comprise the only period during which Herndon's account of Abraham Lincoln can have authenticity as a primary historical source. Of the twenty chapters in the Herndon-Weik biography the first seven, concerning Lincoln's early history, and the three later chapters on the presidency, deal in large part with subjects beyond Herndon's personal competence.[14] Even within the limited period of his direct observation Herndon cannot always be regarded as a witness of the events he recorded. At no point is this more evident than in the chapter devoted to Lincoln's domestic life. The Herndons and the Lincolns did not move in the same social circles in Springfield. Even if the question of animus is disregarded (and there is no doubt that Herndon and Mary Lincoln cordially detested each other), Herndon's record of the Lincoln marriage is defective because he had no opportunity for personal observation.

At least half of *Herndon's Lincoln*, then, is not in any sense primary but is based exclusively on the testimony of other witnesses. Since the statements so carefully collected by Herndon are now available in the Herndon-Weik manuscripts in the Library of Congress, the present

[13] Herndon to Weik, December 1, 1888, and November 5, 1890, Herndon-Weik Coll.

[14] In pages this means that of the 611 pages (excluding appendix and index) of the original edition, 1–261 and 488–581 — or more than half the total — do not to any considerable extent record Herndon's own firsthand evidence.

usefulness of the biography to Lincoln students lies chiefly in the remaining sections drawn from Herndon's personal recollections. These pages might truly bear the title originally intended for the entire book, "Herndon's Memoirs of Lincoln." The problem of evaluating these passages, which include many very important statements of and about Lincoln, is complicated by the joint authorship of the biography. Herndon did not write the book; for many chapters he did not even make drafts to guide his literary collaborator; he was not satisfied with the result, for he thought that the biography contained "a hundred & one mistakes." [15] Even after a thorough study of the manuscript record one is not always certain whether the "I" speaking in *Herndon's Lincoln* is the abrupt voice of Herndon or the suaver tone of Weik.

A clear instance of this difficulty is the often repeated account of Herndon's first glimpse of Lincoln when the *Talisman* chugged up the Sangamon in 1832. As recorded in the printed biography, Herndon recalled the incident vividly, even after fifty-seven years: "It was my first sight of a steamboat, and also the first time I ever saw Mr. Lincoln. . . ." But from the manuscript record one learns that Herndon, after the biography had been set in type, was very uncertain. "Be sure," he warned Weik, "that Lincoln came all the way up to Bogue's Mill. It *seems* to me that he did and that, I at that time, saw Lincoln. . . . If L came up to Bogues Mill I saw Lincoln & if he did not then I did not see him. . . ." [16]

It is not to be inferred that Jesse Weik was improvising anecdotes or that he was ringing in imaginary incidents. He doubtless did the best he could under difficult conditions. The amount of material actually invented by Weik is negligible. The biography is Herndonian from cover to cover. But Weik was working with materials furnished — sometimes only orally, at that — by an aging partner, whose memory for dates, places, and facts was frequently shaky. On two of these counts Weik was able to give Herndon real assistance. He carefully, and on the whole accurately, attempted to fit the straggling Herndon recollections into a chronological framework. But his unfamiliarity with the Sangamon country occasionally led to blunders: James H. Matheny, an intimate friend of Lincoln and of Herndon for many decades, appears throughout *Herndon's Lincoln* as "Matheney"; Charles S. Zane, Herndon's own law partner, becomes "S. T. Zane."

Even in cases where the Herndon-Weik biography represents Herndon's own best recollection of events which he himself experienced, it

[15] Herndon to Weik, June 22, 1889, Herndon-Weik Coll.
[16] *Herndon's Lincoln*, I, 87; Herndon to Weik, November 10, 1888, Herndon-Weik Coll.

cannot invariably be accepted as correct. No man is able to reproduce from memory detailed conversations which occurred a half century earlier. "I cannot recollect everything exactly as it was in minutia," Herndon confessed at the age of sixty-nine, "though I can in substance — as well as I ever could. . . ." [17] There was in Herndon nothing of the humility which led one old-timer to conclude his reminiscences: "Please . . . make the necessary allowance for my Dotage." [18]

The narrator of belated rememberings almost invariably indulges in a kind of self-glorification; Herndon was no exception. A casual reader of the Lincoln biography may feel that its author exhibited himself in a modest and unassuming role. Herndon expressly stated: "I never wrote a line for him [Lincoln]; he never asked me to. I was never conscious of having exerted any influence over him." [19] A more careful perusal, however, points up the fact that at every crisis in Lincoln's career Herndon appears in the book as the guiding force. It was Herndon, according to the biography, who converted his partner to freesoilism, who saved him from the abolitionists in 1854, who "forged" his name and brought him into the Republican fold in 1856, who alone supported his house-divided doctrine, who urged the Cooper Union address in 1860, who pointed out to President Lincoln the need for an emancipation proclamation.

Most of these claims are simply nonsense. If one believes the enormous mass of recollection, reminiscence, and gossip published by friends of Lincoln in the postwar decades, he is likely to conclude that the President had neither mind nor will of his own. After 1865 there appeared a legion of claimants for the title of "*Mr. Lincoln's particular and confidential friend.*" It was, a Springfield editor remarked whimsically, something like the legal dispute over who was the original Dr. Jacob Townsend of Townsend's Sarsaparilla.[20] Self-glorification of this type is perfectly normal; it is expected. When other aging men make exaggerated claims, their statements are accepted at a heavy discount. But because of his undoubted intimacy with Lincoln, his angry and repeated protestations of telling the whole truth, and his air of seeming reticence, Herndon has generally escaped criticism on this score. "Herndon's Herndon," as this puffed-up figure of postwar reminiscence may be called, has been accepted at an inflationary value by most Lincoln biographers.

Even where *Herndon's Lincoln* gives authentic details, it may be so

[17] Herndon to Weik, February 9, 1887, *ibid.*
[18] Ira Haworth to J. R. B. Van Cleave, June 25, 1908, Lincoln Centennial Assoc. MSS.
[19] *Herndon's Lincoln,* III, 479.
[20] *Illinois State Journal,* March 25, 1872.

lacking in understanding of the historical background as to be misleading. After twenty years, the Civil War still appeared to Herndon as a struggle between Good and Evil. He seriously considered [21] inserting in the biography a passage describing Jefferson Davis's address to the Confederate congress in the words of Milton's Satan:

> He call'd so loud, that all the hollow deep
> Of Hell resounded. Princes, Potentates, [etc.] . . .
> Awake, arise, or be for ever fall'n.

In such a clear-cut conflict between black and white there could be no shading of differences. Douglas, who attempted compromise, exhibited to Herndon a "want of inflexibility and rectitude." [22] In politics Herndon was and remained a Lincoln man. Such bias is not surprising, but it does at times render Herndon's judgments suspect.

But after so much is said in the way of negative criticism, it must be emphasized that Herndon's own recollections, though occasionally biased, are on the whole remarkably accurate. The heart of the Herndon-Weik biography is its brief, vivid glimpses of Lincoln on the platform, in the law office, in the courts, walking Springfield's muddy streets. There are bits of description which have the precision of a Brady photograph: Lincoln bursting into uproarious guffaws at the recitation of Flora McFlimsey's perplexities over "Nothing to Wear"; the future President "stalking towards the market-house, basket on arm, his old gray shawl wrapped around his neck, his little boy Willie or Tad running along at his heels asking a thousand boyish questions"; the circuit lawyer sleeping in a short hotel bed with enormous feet and bare shins projecting over the footboard.

The best stories in the Herndon biography are based on personal observation. Such anecdotes, mostly written or narrated by Herndon in the first few years after Lincoln's death, can very generally be supported or paralleled by independent evidence. After allowance is made for self-glamorization due to belated recollection, for personal antagonisms (especially toward Mrs. Lincoln), and for the biographer's peculiar philosophical ideas (particularly in discussions of Lincoln's religion), with hardly an exception Herndon's accounts of events which he himself witnessed are reliable.

[21] Herndon to Weik, January 27, 1888, Herndon-Weik Coll.
[22] *Herndon's Lincoln*, II, 404.

I V

Fully half of *Herndon's Lincoln*, however, relates events which Herndon did not witness; frequently he was not acquainted with the persons involved. Herndon never visited Kentucky (though Weik did) and he never saw Thomas Lincoln. Nancy Hanks died before Herndon was born. As a boy he may have met Ann Rutledge, but he was only seventeen years old at the time of her death. Mary Owens he appears never to have seen. Herndon was not even rooming with Lincoln at the time of the imagined wedding supper which he described with such a wealth of detail. He was never well acquainted with Mrs. Lincoln and from personal observation knew almost nothing of the Lincolns' domestic affairs. As for his chapters on Lincoln's presidential years, perhaps the less said about them the better. The section of *Herndon's Lincoln* describing the assassination was written by a literary hack, Gertrude Garrison.

These portions of the Herndon-Weik biography can have at best only secondary validity. The Lincoln biographer has access to all of Herndon's sources and in addition to countless manuscript and printed records that Herndon never saw. It would be ungrateful for a modern student to deny credit to Herndon for the effort, time, and money spent in collecting his elaborate Lincoln Record, but it would be stupid to rely on Herndon's interpretation of that record now that the manuscripts themselves are available.

Though not markedly inferior to other biographies written during the same period, *Herndon's Lincoln* exhibits major weaknesses in historical technique. Herndon was not thorough in testing the reliability of his witnesses. In spite of his avowed intent "to narrate facts, avoiding . . . any expression of opinion, and leaving the reader to form his own conclusions," [23] Herndon was less a historian than a lawyer. He had a case to present and he bolstered it with all the evidence at hand. As an attorney Herndon was familiar with the problems of evaluating evidence, of discounting bias, and of allowing for distorted recollection. Sharply and often accurately he criticized the statements and motives of many who were writing and speaking on the Lincoln theme. Dennis Hanks, he warned Weik, was "a blow-exag[g]erator — not a wilful liar." Mentor Graham, who claimed to have taught Lincoln, was "cranky — flighty — at times nearly non co[m]pus mentis — but good & honest." Nicolay and Hay, he observed with penetration, were "afraid of Bob [Robert Todd Lincoln]; he gives them materials and they in their turn play *hush*." As for Isaac N. Arnold, Herndon's

[23] *Ibid.*, I, x.

comment has a devastating note of truth: "He was a creadulus [*sic*] man without any critical ability at all. . . ."[24]

To Herndon historical criticism was a weapon to foil enemies; it was not an instrument to measure the strength of friends. His sentimentalized version of Lincoln's alleged infatuation with Ann Rutledge furnishes a good example of Herndon's historical technique.[25] Chapter VI of the printed biography closely follows Herndon's original draft entitled "Miss Rutledge & Lincoln"; Weik's share in the final product consisted of assorted commas and semicolons. "I knew Miss Rutledge myself," Herndon began, but he did not pretend to base his narrative on his own recollections. Nor had Lincoln ever mentioned the subject to his partner. Herndon's tale was drawn from reminiscences of old settlers of Menard County with whom he was personally acquainted — as though friendship was an infallible guarantee of honesty or accuracy.

The shaky character of reminiscence is so well known that one hesitates to labor the point, yet this is a matter of historical method that is very frequently overlooked. Herndon did not begin collecting statements until 1865 — thirty years after Ann Rutledge's death. Menard County old settlers were flattered by his interest. He was putting the county on the map. "[W]e look to Mr. Herndon," wrote a Petersburg editor, "to unearth the history of New Salem and give to the world a reality stranger than fiction."[26] Strange it was, and also fiction. Old-timers dug back into their store of gossip to reproduce, verbatim, conversations held with Lincoln fully thirty years before (and in some cases fifty years before). It was a kind of local contest to see who could remember the most.

Scattered through the Herndon manuscripts are many statements pertaining to the Lincoln-Rutledge romance, no two agreeing in every particular. At least nineteen persons furnished testimony on the subject. Some of the witnesses or reporters varied widely in their comments. The "official" Rutledge family recollection supported the Herndon story in the main; John McNamar, Ann's fiancé, never heard of the affair; Isaac Cogdal reported to Herndon an 1860 conversation with Lincoln in which the President Elect spoke affectionately of Ann

[24] Herndon to Weik, May 6, 1885, Herndon-Weik Coll.; interview of Herndon with Mrs. Lizzie Bell [daughter of Graham], no date, *ibid.*; Herndon to Weik, January 22, 1887, *ibid.*; Herndon to Horace White, August 26, 1890, White MSS.

[25] For a detailed analysis of Herndon's testimony on the Lincoln-Rutledge romance see Randall, *Lincoln the President*, II, 321–342. After an exhaustive appraisal, a model of historical method, Professor Randall concludes that the story, if not "*dis*proved," at least remains "*un*proved." ". . . it does not belong," he adds, "in a recital of those Lincoln episodes which one presents as unquestioned reality."

[26] *Menard County Axis*, January 5, 1867.

and said: "I did honestly — & truly love the girl & think often — often of her now"; Uncle Jimmie Short, a very close friend of Lincoln's, "did not know of any engagement or tender passages between Mr L and Miss R." And there were many others who added conjectures, hearsay, and deductions.

From this assortment of reminiscence, Herndon picked his sources. Most of his data was secondhand; some of it was third- or fourthhand; much of it was simply "folk say." Very little of it was independent testimony. Even the detailed statement of Ann's brother, R. B. Rutledge, was made after consultation with other members of the Rutledge family and was "caroborated" by them [27] — which means that differences of recollection had been ironed out before Herndon was addressed. Some statements were reported indirectly through Herndon's father-in-law, G. U. Miles. More frequently Herndon himself jotted down memoranda of conversations, and his notes sometimes reflected his own views as much as those of the person interviewed. In using these confusing, contradictory, and ambiguous manuscripts, Herndon acted as a lawyer. He quoted the statements that supported his case and forgot or ignored the rest. His own witnesses were not subjected to critical cross-examination and those who disagreed were not allowed to take the stand. The result was an apparently overwhelming case; the factual accuracy of Herndon's Ann Rutledge story was seldom questioned during his lifetime. His version has been so widely circulated that the Lincoln-Rutledge romance belongs to American folklore. The story has become more important than the facts.

If Herndon sometimes depended upon unreliable witnesses, he even more frequently drew unwarranted inferences from the facts he accepted. By rights Herndon should have been a writer of romantic novels. A splendid conversationalist, he loved to embellish, to add those human touches which make a story live. The vitality of his imagination is attested by the enduring hold which — regardless of truth or falsity — his narrative has on the public mind.

One can take, for example, the startling case of the defaulting bridegroom. From Lincoln's letters, from correspondence of contemporaries, and from reminiscences of Springfield folk Herndon learned that Lincoln experienced a major emotional crisis during the winter of 1840–1841 and that, by mutual consent, his engagement to Mary Todd was broken during this spell of melancholia. Springfield gossips had been buzzing about the affair for a quarter of a century when Herndon began collecting his Lincoln records, and the tale had lost

[27] R. B. Rutledge to Herndon, November 21, 1866, Herndon-Weik Coll.

nothing in the telling. From Mary Lincoln's sister, Mrs. Ninian W. Edwards, Herndon coaxed an account of that "fatal 1st of January, 1841." "Mr. Lincoln loved Mary," believed Mrs. Edwards; "he went Crazy in my own opinion . . . because he wanted to marry and doubted his ability & capacity to please and support a wife. Lincoln & Mary were engaged — Every thing was ready & prepared for the marriage — even to the supper &c —. Mr L. failed to meet his Engagement — Cause insanity." [28] Forty-two years after the Lincoln-Todd rupture, Mrs. Edwards repeated her story, this time to Weik, declaring that "arrangements for wedding had been made — even cakes had been baked — but L. failed to appear." [29]

Most Lincoln experts now tend, with justice, to discount Mrs. Edwards's statements very heavily. Her evidence is fragmentary and indirect; it is a long-delayed reminiscence in direct contradiction to the recollections of others; there is a notable absence of contemporary support for her testimony. But even if one accepted Mrs. Edwards's memory as absolutely veracious, the only story that could justifiably be drawn from her facts would be that of a planned wedding and a broken engagement.

Around these two fragmentary facts Herndon was able to spin a magnificent cobweb of detail. He supplied a marriage license held in the hand of a waiting minister, a gorgeously draped room where the ceremony was to be performed, an assembly of Springfield's "cultured — the wealthy — the brilliant," a splendid wedding supper all prepared, an anxiously waiting "brides maid and the groomsman," and even the "bride, bedecked in veil and silken gown, and nervously toying with the flowers in her hair." [30] Mrs. Edwards's contribution had been "Every thing . . . prepared for the marriage" and "cakes . . . baked"; Herndon provided the rest.

Herndon's uninhibited production of picturesque detail was paralleled by his unrestrained speculation as to the thoughts and emotions of the participants. So far as anyone else could determine, if there really was a broken engagement on January 1, 1841, its principal result was the postponement of the Lincoln-Todd wedding. But Herndon was sure the defaulting bridegroom episode must have had profound effects upon the personalities of the two leading actors. His conclusions on this subject were not based on any evidence at all; they were

[28] Interview of Herndon with Mrs. Edwards, undated, *ibid.* This statement is dated in *Herndon's Lincoln* (II, 227) as January 10, 1866.
[29] Weik Diary, December 20, 1883.
[30] *Herndon's Lincoln*, II, 214; "Lincoln & Mary Todd," Herndon monograph, Herndon-Weik Coll.

the product of his somewhat amateurish study of psychology and of mulling over his "facts" to determine intuitively what "must have been" the consequences.

Lincoln, he concluded, carried a permanent mental scar from the episode. Recovering from his "derangement" after the (alleged) jilting, he must have repented of his deed and "*self sacrificed* himself rather than to be charged with dishonor" — i.e., he again proposed to Mary. Said Herndon: ". . . he knew he did not love her, but he had promised to marry her! The hideous thought came up like a nightmare." Faced with the alternative of "sacrificing his *honor* and sacrificing his *domestic peace:* he chose the latter — . . . and threw away domestic happiness." Driven into a union with a woman he could not love, Lincoln must have been "self & otherwise tortured for years — a worse punishment . . . than by burning at the stake." [31]

As for Mary, Herndon believed he could fathom her motives too. Once she might have loved Lincoln, but now "Love fled at the approach of revenge." If one assumes that his statements have any semantic content, Herndon seems to have held the theory that Mary wedded Lincoln and then made his home life — and her own as well! — miserable so that she could be revenged on her husband for his earlier blow to her pride. "Mrs. Lincoln," Herndon speculated, "acted out in her domestic relation the laws of human revenge." As a result, "Lincolns domestic life was a home hell on this globe." Neither husband nor wife, it seemed to Herndon, deserved all the blame for this state of things; both were in part to blame, for both "acted along the lines of human conduct, and both reaped the bitter harvest of conjugal infelicity." [32] (As one of Herndon's reviewers pointed out, it is "difficult to perceive how Lincoln and his wife could by any possibility have acted otherwise than 'along the lines of human conduct.'") [33]

From two rather shaky statements provided by Mrs. Edwards Herndon had conjectured an intimately detailed account of a missing bridegroom episode, and from that had proceeded to evolve a complicated theory to "explain" the personalities and domestic relations of the Lincoln family. With Herndon a few facts went a long way.

[31] Herndon to Hart, December 12, 1866, Hart MSS.; *Herndon's Lincoln,* II, 229; "Lincoln & Mary Todd," Herndon monograph, Herndon-Weik Coll.

[32] *Herndon's Lincoln,* II, 230; III, 424; Herndon to Weik, January 9, 15, 16, and 23, 1886, Herndon-Weik Coll.

[33] New York *Tribune,* July 7, 1889.

V

In Herndon's lifetime his biography was assailed chiefly because of the alleged impropriety of his revelations; today the attack is on the factual accuracy of his narrative. There are seven major counts on which *Herndon's Lincoln* has drawn sharp criticism, and it may be convenient to summarize the findings of recent Lincoln scholarship.

(1) The illegitimacy of Nancy Hanks. According to Herndon, Abraham Lincoln's mother was born out of wedlock. Supporting this contention are the absence of a marriage license for Lincoln's grandmother before her daughter's birth; recollections of Kentucky and Indiana old settlers with whom Herndon corresponded; Lincoln's own statement that his mother was "of the name of Hanks" — i.e., the maiden and not the married name of his grandmother; and Lincoln's positive revelation to Herndon that his mother was illegitimate. Against this theory it has been urged with some justice that Abraham Lincoln was not a competent witness since his knowledge of his ancestry was gained only by hearsay. An effort has been made to identify Lincoln's grandmother with one Lucy Shipley (making Nancy Hanks the legitimate daughter of a first marriage), but, though there is much to be said for this genealogy, a definite identification has not been established. The evidence is far from conclusive, and on this, as on other points, there is room for honest difference of opinion. There seems to be a slight preponderance of testimony favoring the Herndon theory of illegitimacy.[34]

(2) The legitimacy of Abraham Lincoln (suggested only by imputation in *Herndon's Lincoln*). If one disregards the cynical assumption that no child's legitimacy can be proved absolutely, the legend of Lincoln's bastardy is utterly groundless. Studies by William E. Barton, Louis A. Warren, J. G. de R. Hamilton, and others have demonstrated conclusively that the various suggested sires of Abraham were ineligible for that honor, because of age, distance, or even death. In the lives of Nancy and Thomas Lincoln there is nothing whatever to support the allegation of Abraham's illegitimacy.[35]

The final answer to this groundless insinuation has been found in the recently opened Robert Todd Lincoln Collection in the Library of Congress. In 1849 Thomas Lincoln became seriously ill, and his stepson, John D. Johnston, wrote an urgent note to Abraham Lincoln.

---

[34] Barton's *Lineage of Lincoln,* after elaborate analysis, accepts the illegitimacy of Nancy Hanks. Louis A. Warren in *Lincoln's Parentage and Childhood* and many other publications has put up a strong argument for the Shipley connection.

[35] Barton, *Paternity of Lincoln;* Warren, *Lincoln's Parentage and Childhood;* Hamilton, "The Many-Sired Lincoln," *Am. Mercury,* V, 129–135.

"Dear Brother," Johnston began in his illiterate scrawl, "I hast to inform you that father is yet a Live & that is all & he Craves to See you all the time & he wants you to Come if you ar able to git hure, for you are his only Child that is, of his own flush & blood & it is nothing more than natere for him to crave to see you. . . ."[36]

(3) Thomas Lincoln's shiftlessness. Herndon was sure that the President's father was lazy, worthless, and a ne'er-do-well. That portrait of Thomas Lincoln neither began nor ended with Herndon. It derived from a general misunderstanding of society in the Old South which pictured Southern whites as falling in two classes — plantation owners and poor white trash. Obviously Thomas Lincoln was not of the former; therefore, he must have been a poor white. Recent historians have demonstrated that the great majority of Southerners were not of either extreme but were sturdy yeoman farmers. Thomas Lincoln was one of these. He was a solid citizen, of good repute, reasonably industrious, not wealthy but certainly not impoverished, no mental giant, but a sound, substantial middle-class farmer. On this point Herndon's biography is definitely incorrect.[37]

(4) Lincoln's love for Ann Rutledge. There really was an Ann Rutledge; she was engaged to John McNamar (or McNeil as he then called himself); McNamar went East to visit his family; during his absence Lincoln became interested in Ann; the girl died; and Lincoln sincerely grieved at her death. Whether Lincoln and Ann were in love, whether they were engaged, whether she died because of worry over "the conflict of duties, love's promises, and womanly engagements," whether Lincoln's mind "walked out of itself along the uncolumned air" after her burial — these are conjectures on which Herndon's own witnesses differed sharply. His further inferences that Lincoln's entire life was shaped by this romance, that Ann's death caused Lincoln to throw himself into politics, and that Lincoln never loved another woman rest upon no particle of proof; they are examples of Herndon's historical intuition.[38]

(5) The defaulting bridegroom. The testimony Herndon collected added up at most to a planned wedding between Lincoln and Mary Todd in the winter of 1840 and to a broken engagement around January 1, 1841. The embellishments found in the Herndon biography — decorated rooms, expectant guests, bride nervously toying with the flowers in her hair, awaiting a groom who never appeared — are fic-

[36] John D. Johnston to Lincoln, May 25, 1849, Robert Todd Lincoln Coll.

[37] The best account of Thomas Lincoln is Louis A. Warren's *Lincoln's Parentage and Childhood*.

[38] For the definitive analysis of the Ann Rutledge evidence see Randall, *Lincoln the President*, II, 321–342.

tion. Herndon's original evidence, as recent investigators have demonstrated, was very shaky; his inferences from that evidence were improbable and unsupported by facts.[39]

(6) "Domestic hell" in the Lincoln home. After a careful and sympathetic study of the Lincoln marriage, Paul M. Angle has concluded that "no fair-minded student can disregard what Herndon wrote" on the subject.[40] Herndon's own testimony and the reminiscences he collected as to Mrs. Lincoln's temper and to occasional "flare-ups" in the Lincoln home are supported by indisputable contemporary evidence. Mary Lincoln for years suffered from a mental ailment and eventually went insane. But Herndon did not have the whole story. Lincoln's letters to his wife, records of the Lincolns' participation in Springfield social life, reminiscences of many pleasant happenings in the house on Eighth Street are an equally important part of the record. Herndon's portrait was distorted, but recent biographers, striving to correct his error, have sometimes erred in the opposite direction.

(7) Lincoln's religion. The furious bickering over Lincoln's religious views was mostly a matter of muddy thinking and inadequate definition of terms. For example, Herndon asserted that Lincoln *"was in short an infidel* — was a Universalist — was a Unitarian — a Theist" — four distinct propositions in the same sentence.[41] Herndon correctly observed that his partner never joined any Christian church. He was probably warranted in asserting that Lincoln disliked the fundamentalist theology prevalent in his day. But so anxious was Herndon to prevent his partner's becoming a Calvinistic demigod that he overstated his case. Not all the cloudy logic was on Herndon's side. If Lincoln was no village atheist, neither was he a plaster saint. His own statement, recently discovered, is the final word on the religion controversy:

> That I am not a member of any Christian Church [Lincoln wrote in 1846], is true; but I have never denied the truth of the Scriptures; and I have never spoken with intentional disrespect of religion in general, or of any denomination of Christians in particular. . . . I do not think I could myself, be brought to support a man for office, whom I knew to be an open enemy of, and scoffer at, religion. — Leaving the higher matter·of eternal consequences, between him and his Maker, I still do not think any man has the right thus to insult the feelings, and injure the morals, of the community in which he may live.[42]

[39] *Ibid.*, I, 51–57; Angle and Sandburg, *Mary Lincoln: Wife and Widow*, 174–185.
[40] Angle's ed. of *Herndon's Lincoln*, xliv.
[41] Herndon to Lamon, February 25, 1870, Lamon MSS.
[42] *Abraham Lincoln Quar.*, II, 4. See also Barton, *The Soul of Abraham Lincoln.*

VI

"There is no mystery in book writing, especially in biographies," Herndon advised a friend. "Simply gather up all the facts and fill yourself full of them — have some general idea of your plan — sit down at your desk and your pen will run along of itself nearly."[43] Portions of *Herndon's Lincoln* read as though they were this sort of automatic writing, but in reality his book was designed to illustrate an elaborately developed theory of biography.

"The purposes . . . of writing the biography of *a hero*," declared Herndon, are "to make him *fully known* to the reading world." To that end "all the facts of the hero should be told — the whole of his life should be stated, including the smallest facts — and including feelings — thoughts, determinations and deeds . . . it is the religious duty of the biographer to state *all the facts*. . . ."[44] Judging from his practice, Herndon meant that any reminiscence, idea, or inference which he or anyone else might make was suitable material for a biography. Everything was grist for his mill. He noted everything with an impartial lack of discrimination: Lincoln "had an evacuation . . . about once a weak [*sic*]" and "ate blue mass" pills for chronic constipation; he was "the Ideal man of America"; he had "a devilish passion" and "*when a mere boy*, [contracted] the syphilis"; he was "the loveliest & noblest man since the world began to spin"; "Mr Lincoln had a strong if not a terrible passion for women"; "he has not a blot on his character — . . . *no blot*"; his anecdotes were "the very vulgarist and nastiest that possibly Could be told"; he was "*the* good man — the noble man — the strong — true lovely man — the gentle & kind man — the noblest — loveliest character, on the whole, *since Christ*."[45]

The purpose of collecting this heterogeneous assortment of diverse opinion, Herndon asserted, was twofold. "Out of the great initimate [*sic*] deeps of humanity" he heard "the voice of the great future beseeching" him to give every detail of his hero's life. If he suppressed, omitted, or misrepresented one faculty, appetite, or passion, it would inevitably lead to a distorted portrait. As a biographer he could not be

[43] Herndon to Mrs. Leonard Swett, March 14, 1890, Swett MSS.

[44] Herndon to Weik, January 10, 1887, Herndon-Weik Coll.

[45] For these gems of thought, in the order given, see Herndon to Bartlett, August 16, 1887, Bartlett MSS.; Herndon to Weik, October 22, 1888, Herndon-Weik Coll.; Herndon to Weik, January 1891, *ibid.*; Herndon to Mrs. Wycoff, December 24, 1866, MS., Huntington Lib.; Herndon to J. H. Wilson, September 23, 1889, copy, Herndon-Weik Coll.; Herndon to Gov. John A. Andrew, December 29, 1866, Andrew MSS.; Herndon to Weik, January 10, 1886, Herndon-Weik Coll.; Herndon to Caroline H. Dall, November 30, 1866, Dall MSS.

"sure . . . that the special points that form the ideal character of 1865 will be the ideal points of a million years [later]." The voice of the future demanded: "Give us the materials out of which, we can form our own ideal." [46]

But Herndon had another reason for telling every fact. This was what might be termed his biographer-as-policeman approach. Sober, proper Isaac N. Arnold had objected to sensational revelations about Lincoln's personal life, and Herndon retorted:

> The Philosophy you would teach me amounts to this . . . — All vice — infamy — wrong — injustice — meanness & deviltry which a man does in this life; and which the actor & doer . . . has left to the silences — the graves . . . must not be snatched from the grave and held up to mankind as warning. . . . I say it is [our] . . . obligation high as heaven and as deep as hell . . . to drag such things & men to light and expose them to all mankind forever. . . . Mr Arnold, let us vow this — let men . . . understand, that they cannot live famously [i.e., in fame] —, after a life of vice & wrong, except *infamously*. Begin now.

"Lincoln," he hastened to add, was above reproach and "almost spotless thank God"; his biography should set the precedent and "let the world understand from this time that all things . . . shall be brought to clear clean broad light." [47] Herndon was choosing his simile carefully when he wrote: "Mrs. Lincoln . . . hates me on the same grounds that a thief hates a policeman." [48]

It was not even enough to present all the evidence that could be raked together. Lincoln was such "a profound mystery — an enigma — a sphinx — a riddle" [49] that one must have more than the facts in order to understand him, or rather the facts could offer only a clue. Just as the "naturalist will stumble over and pick up a small bone, and by his science . . . tell you the size of the bird — its color — its shape — whether acquatic [sic] or otherwise," "so the historian will stumble in his search for facts and pick up a little fact here and there — one fact from this person and one from that and by his skill he will write a tolerably good account of the large fact sought for." [50] This process of inference from fragmentary evidence Herndon knew to be difficult, yet he considered himself remarkably intuitive in such matters. Lincoln's more profound secrets had to be inferred from "his facts — acts

---

[46] *Abraham Lincoln Quar.*, I, 440–441.
[47] Herndon to Arnold, November 30, 1866, copy, Herndon-Weik Coll.
[48] Herndon to Hart, November 26, 1866, copy, *ibid*.
[49] Herndon to Bartlett, October 1887, Bartlett MSS.
[50] "Lincoln & Mary Todd," undated Herndon monograph, Herndon-Weik Coll.

— hints — face, *as well as what he did not do nor say* — however absurd this last expression may appear to be." [51] Absurd or not, Herndon
thought himself qualified. "I understood Lincoln," he boasted, "inside
and outside." [52]

Somewhat inconsistently with this idea of presenting all the facts,
Herndon also wrote on another theory, that of enlisting his reader's
sympathy on the side of his protagonist. Lincoln, was his owlish pronouncement, had been "for *fifty* years . . . rolled by God through a
fiery furnace heated white hot & blue clouded." His meaning — if he
had any — was that Lincoln was supposed to have been tortured by a
knowledge of his mother's illegitimacy, by sadness at the death of Ann
Rutledge, and by Mary Todd Lincoln's temper. Perhaps the state of
his bowels and the extended convolutions of his brain had something
to do with it too. These factors "broadened — widened and deepened"
Lincoln's "sympathy & love for man." They made him "more liberal —
more feeling — more sympathetic — more tolerant, more kind & tender
— more noble — more lovely — the noblest & loveliest character since
Christ." Should he be robbed of "his crown and cross"? Lincoln's mind
was nothing to marvel at; he could never stand as an intellectual giant
in a world that had produced a Burke, a Shakespeare, and a Webster.
But just as "Christ binds the worlds love & sympathies to him with
cords of invisible power . . . by their feelings & sympathies for his
suffering," Herndon asserted, "I want & intend to have this from all
good men and women in the world" for Lincoln.[53] As a part of this
program of enlisting sympathy he determined to reveal everything
that was unpleasant in Lincoln's early life. This was apparently the
sole reason for relating the alleged illegitimacy of Nancy Hanks in
Herndon's Lincoln.[54] The chief object of the biography was to trace
Lincoln from the "stagnant filthy pool" of his origins to his inauguration, "leaving him a grand figure standing up against the clear deep
blue sky of the future." [55]

Perhaps merely to state these theories is to reveal their inadequa-
cies. It is one thing to give all the facts and another to present those
necessary truths which will enlist the reader's sympathy. All the facts
are not in existence; a biographer must struggle along as well as he can
with the facts that are available, but he is supposed to use some judgment as to their significance and meaning. For example, a sizable
chapter could be written giving verifiable incidents of Herndon's

[51] Herndon to Lamon, March 6, 1870, Lamon MSS.
[52] Herndon to Horace White, December 4, 1890, Herndon-Weik Coll.
[53] Herndon to Mr. Hickman, December 6, 1866, copy, *ibid.*
[54] Herndon to Weik, December 1, 1888, *ibid.*
[55] Herndon to Weik, December 13, 1886, *ibid.*

drunkenness — and spicy reading it would make, to be sure — but so to do would be to exaggerate the importance of alcohol in Herndon's life. In actual practice Herndon's biographical theory amounted to revealing everything he could find about Lincoln that was disagreeable. Herndon was correct in noting the great gaps that exist in our knowledge of any man's life, and particularly of Lincoln's, but it is questionable whether a biographer should rely on his intuition to fill in the blanks. Perhaps a confession of ignorance is not the unforgivable biographical sin.

The real objection to the Herndon biography, from the point of view of method, is that it is incomplete; it is but the torso of a gigantic figure — or perhaps only the legs. Lincoln's importance in American history does not consist in his having had — or not having had, for that matter — an illegitimate mother, nor does it rest on his having been a henpecked husband. Surely Lincoln is significant because of the momentous events of his presidential years. Only in terms of the Civil War crisis does his earlier life have historical meaning; otherwise his biography is sheer antiquarianism. *Herndon's Lincoln,* for all practical purposes, stops with 1861. It is a statue without a head.

VII

"I . . . wrote," Herndon said, "in a gallop — with a whoop."[56] Some of the chapters of *Herndon's Lincoln* move with almost the speed of a fox hunt; in others, the dogs of rhetoric lose the scent and tree a coon. Reviewers noted that the biography lacked the finish of expert work.[57] "The book," patronized General Jacob D. Cox in the *Nation,* "is not such a one as a trained writer would have produced."[58] For this fact the present-day reader should be sincerely thankful.

Herndon's Lincoln appeared in a high-flown era when orotundity of phrase and grandiloquence of style were much admired. Scientific history was in its infancy in America, and biography had usually a filiopietistic emphasis. The customary form was the life-and-letters variety, in which the subject's career was portrayed in a remote and stylized fashion (one gets the unpleasant impression that in those days every little boy in America spent his play hours reading Plutarch), and his speeches and hygienically depersonalized letters were quoted at solemn length. On alternate pages the biographer was expected to exclaim: "What a noble example!" or "What a lesson for today!"

[56] Herndon to Lamon, March 23, 1870, Lamon MSS.
[57] *Life,* XIV, 49 (July 25, 1889).
[58] *Nation,* XLIX, 173 (August 29, 1889).

The Herndon-Weik biography is a refreshing contrast. Men bought the multivolumed Nicolay and Hay *Abraham Lincoln: A History* and, like Marquand's H. M. Pulham, Esq., waded into it from a sense of duty. They read *Herndon's Lincoln* because it was readable. Even today Herndon's is one of the half-dozen Lincoln books with a distinct literary flavor. The general reader has judged this matter more accurately than the literary critic, for there have been more editions of *Herndon's Lincoln* than of any other Lincoln biography.[59]

In no small measure the literary excellence of the biography is due to Herndon himself. He had a flair for words, a gift for the telling phrase. He was not witty, nor was he profound, but he did have the power of vigorous description. There is, for example, his familiar word portrait of Lincoln's face; this is Herndon at his best.

His forehead was narrow but high—his hair was dark, almost black and lay floating where his fingers put it or the winds left it, piled up and tossed about at random: his cheek bones were high, sharp and prominent: his eye brows heavy and prominent, his jaw[s] were long upcurved and massive, looked solid, heavy and strong: his nose was large, long and blunt, a little awry toward the right eye: his chin was long, sharp and upcurved: his eye brows cropped out like a huge jutting rock out of the brow of a hill: his face was long—narrow, sallow and cadaverous, flesh shrunk, shrivelled, wrinkled and dry, having on his face a few hairs here and there: his cheeks were leathery and saffron colored: his ears were large and ran out nearly at right angles from the sides of his head, caused by heavy hats . . . and partly by nature: his lower lip was thick and on the top very red, hanging undercurved or down curved . . . : his neck was neat and trim . . . : his head was well balanced on his shoulders his little gray eyes in the right place. There was the lone mole on his right cheek just a little above the right corner of his mouth and Adam's apple on his throat.[60]

Herndon's literary ideal was to "write plainly, using the Anglo-Saxon language as much as possible, tersely, directly, clearly — truthfully — with spirit — force and energy." [61] At his best he achieved a racy, colloquial style characterized by color and precision. Then his writing has a breezy pace. "I can see him now — in my mind distinct," he would begin, and off he would start on a description of Lincoln that conveys an inescapable impression of verisimilitude.[62] He wrote rapidly, leav-

[59] I have found twenty-five different editions, issues, and printings of the Herndon biography.

[60] "Lincoln Individually," Herndon monograph, Herndon-Weik Coll. With grammatical revision by Weik the passage appears in *Herndon's Lincoln*, III, 587.

[61] Herndon to Weik, February 9, 1887, Herndon-Weik Coll.

[62] Herndon to Bartlett, July 19, 1887, Bartlett MSS.

ing his page a mass of blots, deletions, and marginal insertions. With a quill in his hand Herndon was too "spontaneous — quick — off handed" to take pains with his language; [63] he would abbreviate, misspell, or even entirely omit important words. But with an instinctive idea of form and a groping desire for the *mot juste* he could occasionally turn out a telling sentence.

Herndon's very talent was his worst defect. In searching for the exact word, he would string out, separated by dashes, a chain of synonyms. When his prose strove too strenuously for precision it lost movement. Perhaps it was well to introduce Mary Todd as "young, dashing, handsome — wit[t]y — sarcastic — haughty — aristocratic, cultured and handsome." But on the very next page of his manuscript Herndon would again characterize her in almost identical terms: "of a short build — chunky — compact and about of the average height — and waid [?] . . . about 130 pounds . . . haughtily dignified — moved easily — . . . a fine conversationa[li]st — witty and sometimes terribly sarcastic . . . intelligent — quick — intuitive." [64] He was likely to greet with an equal fanfare of adjectives every other character in his biography from Nancy Hanks to John Wilkes Booth.

This tendency toward excessive wordiness was accentuated by Herndon's fondness for obscure pronouncements and cryptic remarks, hinting of profound subterranean caverns of knowledge. His essay on "Lincoln's Philosophy & Religion" began, not with Lincoln's religion, but with a stately disquisition: "One of the greatest — the very greatest discoveries of the human mind and the widest — deepest — and grandest revolutions which it has undergone is because of the discovery that matter and mind and all sublimated ultimate and more refined back lying substances, if any were and are governed by laws, general, universal and Eternal." This is only the beginning. On the following page one finds a typical Herndon marathon of a sentence:

This law was a mighty declaration of the future independence of the human mind, in time — a time in which it should be freed from error and superstition — divorced from them and married to truth and a true philosophy of this planet — a declaration that Nature — Providence, God, if the reader pleases, had and now has a purpose — an intent — a plan, and if the reader pleases a design and that that intent — purpose and plan are carried out by and through laws — , constant — , continuous — , regular, — uniform and harmonious rithmetical [?] modes of operation, called law.[65]

[63] Herndon to Lamon, February 25, 1870, Lamon MSS.
[64] "Lincoln & Mary Todd," undated Herndon monograph, Herndon-Weik Coll.
[65] "Lincoln's Philosophy & Religion," *ibid.*

VIII

Fortunately Jesse Weik's literary skill in large measure compensated for Herndon's weaknesses.[66] The younger man seems consciously to have subordinated his own literary style to match that of his associate. So skillfully did Weik interweave Herndon's notes, letters, and conversations into the fabric of the biography that his own writing is almost indistinguishable from that of Herndon. The casual reader of *Herndon's Lincoln* is unable to determine where Herndon's contribution ends and Weik's begins.

Weik relentlessly pruned Herndon's draft chapters. Sometimes the proprieties dictated his deletions. In reporting an 1862 conversation held with the President in Washington, Herndon had concluded with a clause likely to be misunderstood; Weik dropped it.

Herndon's draft [67]	*Weik's revision* [68]
. . . [Lincoln] made this remark to me one day I think at Washington — "If ever this free people, if this government is ever overthrown — utterly demoralized, it will come from this struggle and wiggle for office — a way to live without work, from which nature I am not free myself."	He made this remark to me one day in Washington: "If ever this free people — this Government — is utterly demoralized, it will come from this human struggle for office — a way to live without work."

Most of Weik's alterations were designed to eliminate Herndon's philosophical mysticism and his exuberant crop of adjectives. The result is a narrative less racy but more readable. Herndon's fondness for physical descriptions was ruthlessly curtailed. Weik had no patience with Herndon's cracker-box philosophizing. He "dislike[d] such stuff terribly" and was likely to become quite "huffy" if Herndon insisted on its inclusion. He refused to insert a long disquisition on "Lincoln's popularity & Power" which Herndon considered essential.[69] He entirely omitted long stretches of Herndon's draft chapters and sharply reduced the rest. Where he felt obliged to include such a passage, his revision was in the direction of concreteness.

[66] Angle, *A Shelf of Lincoln Books*, 31.
[67] "Lincoln Individually," undated Herndon monograph, Herndon-Weik Coll.
[68] *Herndon's Lincoln*, III, 604–605.
[69] Herndon to Weik, February 25, 1887, November 22 and December 22, 1888, Herndon-Weik Coll.

Herndon's Lincoln

Mr Lincoln was a purely practical minded man, having great practical sagacities and did not as a general rule ever speculate on unknowable things: he never read any thing on such subjects as first & final causes — Time & Space — Noumena or phenomena — experienced ideas or universal inherent & necessary ideas — the attributes of Being — psychology or metaphysics. These were to him trash. He discovered through Experience that his mind — the mind of all men had limitations attached or placed on it and hence he economized his forces & his time, by applying his powers & his time in the field of the practical. In this field he thought — wrought & acted.

By reason of his practical turn of mind Mr. Lincoln never speculated any more in the scientific and philosophical than he did in the financial world. He never undertook to fathom the intricacies of psychology and metaphysics. Investigation into first causes, abstruse mental phenomena, the science of being, he brushed aside as trash — mere scientific absurdities. He discovered through experience that his mind, like the minds of other men, had its limitations, and hence he economized his forces and his time by applying his powers in the field of the practical.

Both Herndon and Weik emphasized the familiar event, the vivid episode, the concrete detail. Both had a flair for the dramatic, even when describing everyday occurrences. Specialists in American literature are inclined — with no little justice for the most part — to ignore the literary aspects of historical writing, but *Herndon's Lincoln* merits attention as one of the precursors of the Western local-color school of fiction. It is not simply coincidental that Herndon, Mary Hartwell Catherwood, Edward Eggleston, and Joseph Kirkland were publishing at the same time, and that all presented a harsh, sometimes uncouth, picture of the Old Northwest. Though he believed Herndon had romanticized Lincoln's love interests, Joseph Kirkland, author of the pioneer realistic novel, *Zury: The Meanest Man in Spring County,* welcomed *Herndon's Lincoln* for its honest emphasis on the crudity of frontier life.[72] Now that Herndon's manuscripts are available to the historian, his life of Lincoln must more and more be evaluated as literature rather than as biography. Slowly its literary merit is gaining

[70] "Lincoln's Philosophy & Religion," Herndon monograph, *ibid.*
[71] *Herndon's Lincoln,* III, 435.
[72] Unidentified review, signed by Kirkland, in John Hay Scrapbooks.

recognition. *Herndon's Lincoln* is the one Lincoln biography quoted by Mark Van Doren in *An Autobiography of America*.[73]

IX

To appraise Herndon solely in terms of verified facts contributed to the Lincoln story is to miss his real significance. One of the most important things about Herndon is the errors that he spread. Whether or not scholarly critics approve, Herndon's lectures, letters, and books have largely shaped current beliefs and traditions about Abraham Lincoln's life. The folklore Lincoln is essentially Herndonian in origin.[74]

Lincoln is a living force in American democratic thought; he is "first among the folk heroes of the American people." [75] In a sense the Lincoln cult is an American religion, with its high priests in the form of Lincoln authorities and its worshipers in the thousands of fans who think, talk, and actually live Lincoln every day. His birthday is a national holiday. His birthplace in Kentucky, his memorial in Washington, and his tomb in Illinois are national shrines. His very name retains a magic power — witness its use in advertising everything from taxicabs to barbershops. To gauge the widespread interest in the Lincoln theme one has only to glance at the 3,958 titles listed in Jay Monaghan's *Lincoln Bibliography*. Since 1865 on an average fifty books have been published each year about the Martyr President. For no other American has there been such a constant searching of the auguries to learn "What Would He Do Were He Here Today?" [76] Herndon's prediction has proved correct. "Lincoln," he forecast in 1888, "will be in the great, no distant future the Ideal man of America, if not . . . of all the English speaking people and every incident of his life will be sought for — however apparently trifling — read with pleasure and treasured up in the memory of men." [77]

It was inevitable that around the central figure of this cult there should spring up a huge body of mythology in the form of traditions, reminiscences, and anecdotes. Quite naturally there have been attributed to Lincoln sayings and jokes and aphorisms which he ought to have uttered even if he did not. Word-of-mouth tradition keeps con-

[73] "William Herndon Remembers Abraham Lincoln," in Mark Van Doren, ed., *An Autobiography of America*, 343–352.

[74] I have treated this idea at some length in "The Folklore Lincoln," Ill. State Hist. Soc., *Jour.*, XL, 377–396. See also Louis A. Warren, "Herndon's Contribution to Lincoln Mythology," *Ind. Mag. of Hist.*, XLI, 221–44.

[75] R. H. Gabriel, *The Course of American Democratic Thought*, 413.

[76] Emanuel Hertz, *The Many-Sided Lincoln: What Would He Do Were He Here Today?*

[77] Herndon to Weik, October 22, 1888, Herndon-Weik Coll.

stantly supplying a new crop of Lincoln anecdotes, and such Lincoln apocrypha are disseminated all over the nation by newspapers, magazines, lectures, sermons, and — more recently — by movies and radios. Lincoln is still front-page news.[78]

The popular conception of Lincoln may be called the Lincoln of legend. It is not that all the stories in current circulation are false, but that their acceptance is conditioned by a religious attitude, not by the presence or absence of verifiable facts. This mythical Lincoln is a relatively sophisticated type of folk hero, halfway between a legendary King Arthur and the purely synthetic führer constructed to order by a propaganda machine. By some the Lincoln cult has been deliberately promoted in order to gain political prestige from the use of his name, yet it is because they are essentially a haphazard growth that the Lincoln legends reveal so much of the American character.

At the time of Lincoln's death there was no single pattern into which stories and anecdotes about him could fit. In the blurred memories of former slaves there was the shadowy outline of a preternaturally shrewd Lincoln, half Moses, half Yankee. "I think Abe Lincoln was next to the Lord," said one ex-slave. "He done all he could for the slaves; he set 'em free." Then the aged Negro went on to reminisce:

> 'Fore the election he [Lincoln] traveled all over the South, and he come to our house and slept in Old Mistress' bed. Didn't nobody know who he was. . . . he come to our house and he watched close. . . . When he got back up North he writ Old Master a letter and told him that he was going to have to free his slaves, that everybody was going to have to. . . . He also told him that he had visited at his house and if he doubted it to go in the room he slept in and look on the bedstead at the head and he'd see where he'd writ his name. Sure enough, there was his name: A. Lincoln.[79]

Gradually the Negro built up a more emotional image of Lincoln, a perfect man and, in a peculiarly individual way, a personal emancipator. In Negro houses all over the country one could find "many old pictures of Lincoln pasted on the walls of the sitting room over the mantelpiece." "They just had to have Lincoln near them," explains their chronicler, John E. Washington; "they loved him so." "His life to these humble people was a miracle, and his memory has become a benediction," Dr. Washington adds. "To the deeply emotional and re-

---

[78] As one example out of hundreds, a preposterous story of Lincoln's sneaking into Washington in 1861 wearing "eye-shields" and carrying "iron fighting knuckles" was featured as sober truth in both the Chicago *Sun* and the Chicago *Tribune* on November 27, 1946.

[79] B. A. Botkin, ed., *Lay My Burden Down: A Folk History of Slavery,* 16. Quoted with the permission of the University of Chicago Press.

ligious slave, Lincoln was an earthly incarnation of the Savior of mankind." [80]

At the other extreme were stories spread by Lincoln's political enemies, who could see the Sixteenth President only as "a man of coarse nature, a self-seeking politician, who craved high office . . . to satisfy his own burning desire for distinction." [81] He was, so a Southern canard went, of Negro ancestry, or his presumptive parents were immoral, shiftless poor white trash. Unscrupulous as a lawyer, he was unprincipled as a politician. He was a man of low morality, with a "passion for indecent stories"; his "inordinate love of the lascivious, of smut," it was whispered, was "something nearly akin to lunacy." [82] But today, as Avery Craven has said, "the unreconstructed are few and growing fewer," [83] and most present-day Southerners would join the distinguished Louisiana historian, Charles Gayarré in characterizing Lincoln as "humane and pure, kindly disposed toward the South." [84]

Naturally it was in the North that the Lincoln myth had its strongest growth. One stream of tradition, essentially literary and often of Eastern or New England sponsorship, presented a prettified Lincoln, a combination of Christ and George Washington. [85] The story as found in the biographies of Holland, Raymond, Victor, and their successors is the epic of the perfect man, born to do great things, pure in heart, noble in action, and constant in principle. His early life showed how man can rise above circumstances. Elected President, he directed a victorious war, emancipated the slaves, crushed a huge rebellion, and saved the Union. Yet he kept throughout his simple humanity; there is a widespread notion that the Civil War President did little but comfort bereaved mothers, pardon sleeping sentinels, and strike manacles off Negroes. During the agony of war he maintained a supreme Christian faith, for his was "eminently a Christian administration." At the moment of triumph, he was foully murdered, giving his life to expiate a nation's sins. [86] This was Lincoln, "President, savior of the republic, emancipator of a race, true Christian, true man." [87]

[80] John E. Washington, *They Knew Lincoln*, 15, 149.

[81] Mrs. E. A. Meriwether, *Facts and Falsehoods Concerning the War on the South, 1861–1865*, 90.

[82] Chauncey F. Black to Herndon, February 27, 1871, Herndon-Weik Coll.

[83] Craven, "Southern Attitudes toward Abraham Lincoln," *Papers in Illinois History, 1942*, 10.

[84] Quoted in Randall, *Lincoln and the South*, 158.

[85] The changing conceptions of Lincoln in American literature are ably presented by Roy P. Basler in *The Lincoln Legend*.

[86] For an exciting analysis of the folklore clustering around Lincoln's death, see Lloyd Lewis, *Myths after Lincoln*.

[87] Holland, *Life of Abraham Lincoln*, 544. Only Holland is quoted here, but these sentiments could be duplicated in a dozen other Lincoln biographies of the

X

One wonders how long the Lincoln legend would have persisted had this purified literary tradition prevailed. Washington has been made so noble that it is hard to think of him as a man, much less a boy; he is a Houdon bust or a Gilbert Stuart painting. The very perfection of Robert E. Lee is boring. Lincoln was saved from this sort of apotheosis by a strong Western stream of legend and folklore. This Lincoln of "folk say" was something of a Paul Bunyan, a Mike Fink, a Davy Crockett. He was not a perfect man, but he had divinely human imperfections. He fell into the traditional pattern of the American folk hero: "a plain, tough, practical fellow, equally good at a bargain or a fight, a star-performer on the job and a hell-raiser off it, and something of a salesman and a showman, with a flair for prodigious stories, jokes, and stunts and a general capacity for putting himself over." [88]

This Lincoln was the practical joker, the teller of tall and lusty tales. Stupendously strong, he was also marvelously lazy. A true romantic, he pined over the grave of Ann Rutledge, but he was enough of a Till Eulenspiegel to lampoon one woman who refused his hand and to jilt another who accepted. He would bravely face his enemies, but he cowered before his wife. He was shrewd, a manipulator of men, whose art concealed his artfulness. He was incredibly tall, prodigiously strong, and unbelievably homely. This Lincoln was a Westerner, and his long flapping arms were not the wings of an angel.

It is obvious that much of this Western Lincoln portrait derives from Herndon. He did not originate the pattern. The saga of "the Pioneer Boy, and how he became President" was popularized in a series of campaign biographies during Lincoln's lifetime. And of course the acceptance and diffusion of the legend was conditioned by the excitement of the times — by the emotional impact of devastating war, hard-won victory, and calamitous assassination. But from the very beginning Herndon conceived his biography of Lincoln as a study in Western character; he consciously planned it to illustrate the "original western and south-western pioneer — the type of . . . open, candid, sincere, energetic, spontaneous, trusting, tolerant, brave and generous man." [89] It was he who discovered or publicized most of the familiar

---

period. It is amusing to note how closely, after concessions are made to nineteenth-century morality and to American forms of government, this conception of Lincoln fits the pattern of the idealized hero of classical mythology. See Lord Raglan, *The Hero, A Study in Tradition, Myth, and Drama,* 179–180.

[88] Botkin, *A Treasury of American Folklore,* 2–3.

[89] Owen Clark to Herndon, October 22, 1866, copy, Lamon MSS.; *Abraham Lincoln. Miss Ann Rutledge.*

human incidents in the story. One has only to count the Herndonian episodes: the ancestry of Lincoln and of Nancy Hanks; the pioneer days in Indiana; Lincoln's disastrous infatuation for Ann Rutledge; the jilting of Mary Todd on that "fatal 1st of January, 1841"; the widely credited stories of Lincoln's marital troubles; anecdotes of the law office — authentic and otherwise; behind-the-scenes stories of Lincoln's political career. The Western Lincoln myth is basically Herndonian.

It is a mistake to consider these two main streams of tradition as representing respectively the "ideal" and the "real" Lincoln. Each was legendary in character. The conflict in Lincoln biography between the Holland-Hay-Tarbell school and the Herndon-Lamon-Weik contingent was not essentially a battle over factual differences; it was more like a religious war. One school portrayed a mythological patron saint; the other, an equally mythological frontier hero. Gradually the two conceptions began to blend. In the huge file of newspaper "reminiscences" collected in the Lincoln National Life Foundation one can trace the rather amusing process by which demigod and frontier hero became inextricably scrambled. Lincoln has become a composite ideal. "To the folk mind," as Dixon Wecter has noted, "his appeal is stronger than that of other heroes because on him converge so many dear traditions." [90] The accepted conception of Lincoln today is as "a folk-hero who to the common folk-virtues of shrewdness and kindness adds essential wit and eloquence and loftiness of soul." [91] In the final portrait one cannot fail to recognize Herndon's brush marks.

It is customary for historians to assault the air castles of contemporary mythology, to raze the imaginary structures by the use of the sharp tools of criticism, to purify the ground by a liberal sprinkling of holy water in the form of footnotes, and to erect a new and "authentic" edifice. Such an approach has its merits. But there is also room for investigation of another sort. Referring to the debunking of historical myths and legends, W. A. Dunning, in his presidential address before the American Historical Association, reminded his hearers that in many cases "influence on the sequence of human affairs has been exercised, not by what really happened, but by what men erroneously believed to have happened." In turning to history for guidance, Dunning observed, men have acted upon "the error that passes as history at the time, not from the truth that becomes known long after." He con-

[90] Wecter, *The Hero in America: A Chronicle of Hero Worship*, viii, 270.
[91] *Nation*, May 17, 1919, quoted in Gabriel, *Course of American Democratic Thought*, 410.

cluded by warning that "for very, very much history there is more importance in the ancient error than in the new-found truth." [92]

His admonition applies in the field of Lincoln biography. "The history of any public character," as J. Frank Dobie remarked, "involves not only the facts about him but what the public has taken to be the facts." [93] It is valuable to study the air castles as they stand, for they express a collective wish-fulfillment of the American people. This is no Freudian abstraction; it is simply that "heroes embody the qualities that we most admire or desire in ourselves." [94] Fully realizing their general inaccuracy and almost universal distortion, the historian can use these myths for an understanding of what plain Americans have wished their leaders to be. "If the folk aspiration is worthy, its dreams of great men will be worthy too." [95]

As it has gradually become standardized, the Lincoln legend is as American as the Mississippi River. Essentially national, it is not nationalistic. It reveals the people's faith in the democratic dogma that a poor boy can make good. It demonstrates the incurable romanticism of the American spirit. There is much in the myth that is unpleasant — Lincoln's cunning, his fondness for rabelaisian anecdote, his difficulties with his wife (one wonders why folklore has not provided Lincoln with a shrewish mother-in-law) — but such traits seem to be attributed to every true folk hero.[96] The fundamental qualities of the legendary Lincoln reveal the essential dignity and humanity of our nation's everyday thinking. Americans can be proud that to the central figure in their history their folklore has attributed all the decent qualities of civilized man: patience, tolerance, sympathy, kindliness, sagacity, and humor. For years Herndon battled those who would have made Lincoln "a myth in a hundred years after 1865." [97] Paradoxically, his own writings have been a chief source for Lincolns' legends. Thus Herndon stands, in the backward glance of history, myth-maker and truth-teller.

[92] "Truth in History," *Am. Hist. Rev.*, XIX, 220, 225, 229.
[93] Quoted in Botkin, *Treasury of American Folklore*, 1.
[94] *Ibid.*, 2.
[95] Wecter, *Hero in America*, viii.
[96] Robert Price, "Johnny Appleseed in American Folklore and Literature," *Johnny Appleseed, A Voice in the Wilderness*, 3.
[97] Herndon to Lamon, December 1, 1885, Lamon MSS.

Bibliography

THIS is the first book-length biography of Herndon. In its preparation I have tried to consult all printed and manuscript materials which might supply me information. Books and articles which contain at least a passing reference to Herndon are numerous, for virtually every discussion of Lincoln mentions his law partner-biographer. With a few outstanding exceptions, however, this material proved biased or inaccurate. For this reason my study of Herndon has been based almost exclusively on primary sources — newspapers, manuscripts, and Herndon's own writings. Original research has outlined a portrait of Herndon very different from that drawn by many Lincoln biographers, but unless it has been essential to my story I have not in the preceding pages attempted to point out specific mistakes of my predecessors. So to do would be both uncharitable and unfair, for many significant Herndon manuscripts have only recently become available to the historian.

This bibliography gives fuller details concerning materials cited in the foregoing pages and also attempts for the first time a complete listing of Herndon's published writings.

As every student knows, the indispensable guide to Lincoln literature is Jay Monaghan's monumental *Lincoln Bibliography, 1839–1939* (Springfield: Illinois State Historical Library, 1943). For location of newspapers cited in my footnotes, the reader is referred to Winifred Gregory's *American Newspapers, 1821–1936: A Union List of Files Available in the United States and Canada* (New York: The H. W. Wilson Company; 1937).

MANUSCRIPT COLLECTIONS

The purpose of this list is to indicate the location of collections of unpublished materials cited in the preceding pages. No effort has been made to include detached or scattered manuscript items, the location of which is given in the footnotes.

Bibliography

Abraham Lincoln Association Files, Springfield, Illinois.

John Albion Andrew MSS., Massachusetts Historical Society, Boston.

Isaac Newton Arnold MSS., Chicago Historical Society.

Truman Howe Bartlett MSS., Massachusetts Historical Society.

Albert Jeremiah Beveridge MSS., Illinois State Historical Library, Springfield.

Jeremiah Sullivan Black MSS., Library of Congress, Washington, D.C.

Henry Pelham Holmes Bromwell MSS., Library of Congress.

Orville Hickman Browning MSS., Illinois State Historical Library.

Clinton Levering Conkling MSS., Illinois State Historical Library.

James Cook Conkling MSS., Illinois State Historical Library.

John Jordan Crittenden MSS., Library of Congress.

Caroline Wells Healey Dall MSS., Massachusetts Historical Society.

David Davis MSS., transcripts in Illinois State Historical Library.

Stephen Arnold Douglas MSS., University of Chicago Library.

Henry Enoch Dummer MSS., Illinois State Historical Library.

Zebina Eastman MSS., Chicago Historical Society.

Elmer Ephraim Ellsworth MSS., Illinois State Historical Library.

Ralph Waldo Emerson MSS., Harvard University Library, Cambridge, Massachusetts.

Pascal Paoli Enos MSS., Illinois State Historical Library.

Jesse W. Fell MSS., transcripts in Illinois Historical Survey, University of Illinois, Urbana.

Daniel Fish MSS., Lincoln National Life Foundation, Fort Wayne, Indiana.

Edward Carey Gardiner Collection, Historical Society of Pennsylvania, Philadelphia.

William Lloyd Garrison MSS., Boston Public Library.

Joseph Gillespie Collection, Chicago Historical Society.

Horace Greeley MSS., New York Public Library.

Charles Henry Hart MSS., Henry E. Huntington Library, San Marino, California.

John Hay MSS., Henry E. Huntington Library.

John Hay Scrapbooks, Library of Congress.

William Henry Herndon Papers, Library of Congress.

William Henry Herndon-Theodore Parker MSS., University of Iowa Library, Iowa City.

William Henry Herndon-Jesse William Weik Collection, Library of Congress.

Emanuel Hertz Collection, University of Illinois Library.

Caroline Hanks Hitchcock MSS., transcripts in Lincoln National Life Foundation.

Josiah Gilbert Holland MSS., New York Public Library.

Illinois College. Records of the Proceedings of the Faculty, Illinois College Library, Jacksonville.

Illinois Election Returns, Illinois State Archives, Springfield.

Illinois Warrant Ledgers, Office of the Auditor of Public Accounts, Springfield.

Ward Hill Lamon MSS., Henry E. Huntington Library.

Robert Todd Lincoln Collection, Library of Congress.

Lincoln Centennial Association MSS., Illinois State Historical Library.

John Alexander McClernand MSS., Illinois State Historical Library.

Menard County Circuit Court. Dockets, Files, Lincoln File, and Records, Office of the Circuit Clerk, Petersburg, Illinois.

John G. Nicolay-John Hay MSS., Illinois State Historical Library.

John McAuley Palmer MSS., Illinois State Historical Library.

Charles H. Ray MSS., Henry E. Huntington Library.

Logan Uriah Reavis MSS., Chicago Historical Society.

Sangamon County Circuit Court. Dockets, Files, and Records, Office of the Circuit Clerk, Springfield. For a description of these materials see the Historical Records Survey, *Inventory of the County Archives of Illinois: No. 83. Sangamon County (Springfield).*

Sangamon County Deed Record, Recorder's Office, Springfield.

Sangamon County Poll Books, Illinois State Archives.

Sangamon County Records of Marriages, Office of the County Clerk, Springfield.

Springfield City Council Records, Office of the City Clerk, Springfield.

Stuart-Hay MSS., Illinois State Historical Library. Family papers of Stephen Trigg Logan, John Todd Stuart, and Milton Hay.

Charles Sumner MSS., Harvard University Library.

Leonard Swett MSS., Illinois State Historical Library.

Ida Minerva Tarbell MSS., Allegheny College Library, Meadville, Pennsylvania.

Lyman Trumbull Collection, Illinois State Historical Library.

Lyman Trumbull MSS., Library of Congress.

United States Census. The manuscript census records for Illinois (1830–1870) have been consulted in The National Archives.

United States Interior Department Records, The National Archives.

United States Treasury Department Records, The National Archives.

Joseph Wallace Scrapbooks, Illinois State Historical Library.

Elihu Benjamin Washburne MSS., Library of Congress.

Jesse William Weik Diary, 1873–1888. A transcript has been supplied through the courtesy of Miss Mary Hays Weik.

Bibliography

Jesse William Weik MSS., Illinois State Historical Library.
Horace White MSS. Miss Amelia White has kindly supplied copies of
all Herndon items among her father's papers.
Samuel Willard MSS., Illinois State Historical Library.
Richard Yates MSS., Illinois State Historical Library.

HERNDON'S PUBLISHED WRITINGS

This list does not include letters or speeches of Herndon published in
newspapers.

Herndon, William Henry: *Abraham Lincoln. Concluded. By W. H.
Herndon.* Undated broadside (1865–66), Henry E. Huntington Library. A condensation of Herndon's second Lincoln
lecture.

———: *Abraham Lincoln. Miss Ann Rutledge. New Salem. Pioneering,
and* THE *Poem.* Broadside, copyrighted 1866, of Herndon's
fourth Lincoln lecture, delivered in Springfield, November
16, 1866. It has twice been reprinted: (1) *Abraham Lincoln,
Miss Ann Rutledge, New Salem, Pioneering, and The Poem:
A Lecture Delivered in the Old Sangamon County Court
House, November, 1866* (Springfield, Illinois: H. E. Barker;
1910); and (2) *Lincoln and Ann Rutledge and the Pioneers
of New Salem: A Lecture* . . . , introduction by Harry Rose-
crans Burke (Herrin, Illinois: Trovillion Private Press; 1945).

———: "Abraham Lincoln's Religion." *The Index,* Vol. 1 (April 2, 1870),
pp. 5–6. Herndon's letter to Francis Ellingwood Abbot, February 18, 1870. Reprinted in part under the same title in *The
Iconoclast,* Vol. 1 (April 1870), p. 4, and in *The Truth Seeker,*
Vol. 38 (February 11, 1911), pp. 86–87.

———: "Abraham Lincoln's Religious Belief." *The Truth Seeker,* Vol. 10
(February 24, 1883), pp. 114–115.

———: *Address on Free Trade vs. Protection* . . . *at Springfield, Illinois, January 28, 1870.* A thirty-seven page pamphlet, without imprint, in the Harvard University Library.

———: "Analysis of the Character of Abraham Lincoln: A Lecture." *The
Abraham Lincoln Quarterly,* Vol. 1 (September 1941), pp.
343–383, and Vol. 1 (December 1941), pp. 403–441. Herndon's first two lectures on Lincoln, delivered in Springfield on
December 12 and 26, 1865, are here published in full for the

first time. Extensive extracts from the first lecture appeared earlier in Francis Bicknell Carpenter, *Six Months at the White House with Abraham Lincoln. The Story of a Picture* (New York: Hurd and Houghton; 1866), pp. 323–350, and in Osborn H. Oldroyd, ed., *The Lincoln Memorial: Album-Immortelles* . . . (New York: G. W. Carleton & Co.; 1882), pp. 526–550. The original manuscripts of the lectures are in the Henry E. Huntington Library.

——: *Brief Analysis of Lincoln's Character: A Letter to J. E. Remsburg, Oak Mills, Kansas, from W. H. Herndon, Springfield, Illinois, September 10, 1887.* Privately printed for H. E. Barker; 1917. The original manuscript of this letter is in the Lincoln collection of Mr. Alfred W. Stern of Chicago.

——: *A Card and a Correction.* Broadside in Herndon-Weik Collection, Library of Congress, dated November 9, 1882. This item has been reprinted as *A Card and A Correction: A Broadside on Lincoln's Religion* . . . (Privately printed for H. E. Barker; 1917).

——: "Facts Illustrative of Mr. Lincoln's Patriotism and Statesmanship." *The Abraham Lincoln Quarterly*, Vol. 3 (December 1944), pp. 178–203. Herndon's third Lincoln lecture, delivered in Springfield on January 23, 1866, is here published from the manuscript in the Henry E. Huntington Library.

——: "A Herndon Letter on Lincoln." *The Truth Seeker*, Vol. 43 (November 25, 1916), p. 757.

——: "Herndon on Lincoln." *The Magazine of History with Notes and Queries*, Vol. 46 (Extra No. 181), pp. 17–19.

—— and Jesse William Weik: *Herndon's Lincoln: The True Story of a Great Life. Etiam in Minimis Major. The History and Personal Recollections of Abraham Lincoln.* Chicago, New York, and San Francisco: Belford, Clarke & Company; [1889]. 3 vols. This is the original edition of the famous Herndon biography. See "Herndon's Lincoln: A Study," *Publishers' Weekly*, Vol. 140 (November 29, 1941), pp. 2019–2021. Brentano's in London issued an identical edition in 1889. In 1890 a second edition, without changes, appeared under the imprint Chicago: Belford-Clarke Co. A new issue under this same title, printed, it was claimed, from the original plates, appeared in 1921 (Springfield: The Herndon's Lincoln Publishing Company) and was reprinted in 1922.

In 1892 a two-volume edition appeared under the title *Abraham Lincoln: The True Story of a Great Life* (New

Bibliography

York: D. Appleton and Company). In this new edition certain offensive passages were omitted — the "Chronicles of Reuben" episode and an insinuation that Lincoln was illegitimate — an introduction by Horace White was added, and material by White and Edward L. Pierce was incorporated into the text. This two-volume edition has been frequently reprinted — in 1893, 1895, 1896, 1900, 1901, 1902, 1908, 1909, 1913, 1916, 1920, 1924, 1928 (in the Appleton Dollar Library), and 1930. In the British Museum there is listed an edition with imprint London: Sampson Low & Co.; 1892.

In 1930 a one-volume edition was issued: *Herndon's Life of Lincoln: The History and Personal Recollections of Abraham Lincoln as Originally Written by William H. Herndon and Jesse W. Weik with an Introduction and Notes by Paul M. Angle* (New York: Albert & Charles Boni). This was reprinted in 1936. A low-cost printing of this same edition was published six years later: *Herndon's Life of Lincoln: The History and Personal Recollections of Abraham Lincoln as Originally Written by William H. Herndon and Jesse W. Weik with Introduction and Notes by Paul M. Angle* (Cleveland and New York: The World Publishing Company; 1942) and was reprinted in 1943.

——: *The Hidden Lincoln: From the Letters and Papers of William H. Herndon,* edited by Emanuel Hertz. New York: The Viking Press; 1938. A sampling from the Herndon-Weik, Bartlett, Hart, and Lamon MSS. The editing — if it can be called that — is poor.

——: *A Letter from William H. Herndon to Isaac N. Arnold Relating to Abraham Lincoln, His Wife, and Their Life in Springfield.* Privately printed, 1937. The original letter, dated October 24, 1883, is in the Arnold MSS.

——: *Letter to John W. Keys, Concerning the Character of Abraham Lincoln.* Deerfield, Wisconsin: Easton Printing Service; [1898?]. The original letter, dated April 14, 1886, is in the Historical Society of Pennsylvania.

——: *Letters on Temperance . . . Originally Published in the "Illinois Journal."* Springfield: "Journal" Print, 1855.

——: *Lincoln and Douglas. The Peoria Debates and Lincoln's Power.* 1866 broadside, Illinois State Historical Library. This item has been republished as *Lincoln and Douglas: The Peoria Debates and Lincoln's Power. A Broadside Published 1866 by Wm. H. Herndon* (Privately printed for H. E. Barker, 1917) and in Byron Cloyd Bryner, *Abraham Lincoln in Peoria, Illinois* (Peoria: Edward J. Jacob, Printer; 1926), pp. 63–72.

——: "Lincoln as a Personality." *Christian Advocate,* Vol. 84 (February 4, 1909), pp. 164–165. Reprinting in part of a Herndon letter which originally appeared in the *Illinois State Register,* March 4, 1883.

——: *Lincoln's Personal Characteristics, By William H. Herndon: A Letter Written Jan. 15, 1874, To an Unknown Correspondent in New York City.* Los Angeles: Privately printed for H. E. Barker; 1933.

——: *Lincoln's Philosophy of Life, By William H. Herndon. A Letter Written to a Friend of Uncertain Identity, Under Date of February 18th, 1886.* Los Angeles: Privately printed for H. E. Barker, 1933. The original letter, addressed to Joseph Smith Fowler, is now in the Lincoln collection of Mr. Charles N. Owen of Chicago.

——: "Lincoln's Religion." *The Truth Seeker,* Vol. 10 (March 10, 1883), pp. 148–149.

——: *Lincoln's Religion.* Broadside supplement to the *Illinois State Register,* December 13, 1873. This item, together with the lecture by James A. Reed which provoked it, has twice been republished: (1) *The Religion of Abraham Lincoln: Being a Reprint of the Lecture of Rev. Jas. A. Reed in 1872, and the Answering Lecture of W. H. Herndon in 1873* (Privately printed for Judd Stewart, 1915); and (2) *Lincoln's Religion: The Text of Addresses Delivered by William H. Herndon and Rev. James A. Reed and a Letter by C.F.B.,* edited by Douglas Crawford McMurtrie (Chicago: Black Cat Press; 1936).

——: *Mrs. Lincoln's Denial, and What She Says.* Broadside dated January 12, 1874, Massachusetts Historical Society.

——: *Some Hints on the Mind: A Lecture.* Springfield; 1864.

——: "An Unpublished Letter from Lincoln's Law Partner. Lincoln on Education — His View of Woman's Rights. — An Early Reformer." *The Independent,* Vol. 47 (April 4, 1895), p. 431. Reprinted in William Hayes Ward, compiler, *Abraham Lincoln: Tributes from his Associates* . . . (New York: Thomas Y. Crowell & Company, 1895), and in *The Magazine of History with Notes and Queries,* Vol. 49 (Extra No. 195), pp. 16–19.

——: *W. H. Herndon on the Democratic Platform.* 1864 broadside, Illinois State Historical Library.

Bibliography

——: "William Herndon Remembers Abraham Lincoln." *An Autobiography of America*, edited by Mark Van Doren (New York: Albert & Charles Boni; 1929), pp. 343–352.

PRINTED SOURCES

Abraham Lincoln. Two-page folder, signed J. B. Barnhill, Agent, announcing Herndon's 1882 lecture on Lincoln. The only known copy is at Lincoln Memorial University, Harrogate, Tennessee.

Abraham Lincoln Association, *Bulletin*, Nos. 1–58 (1923–1939). Numbers issued prior to 1929 bear the title Lincoln Centennial Association, *Bulletin*.

Abraham Lincoln Association, Papers Delivered before the Members . . ., 1929–1939. Issued as *Lincoln Centennial Association Papers*, 1924–1928.

The Abraham Lincoln Quarterly. Published by The Abraham Lincoln Association, Springfield, Illinois, 1940–date.

"Abraham Lincoln's Religion: His Own Statement." *The Abraham Lincoln Quarterly*, Vol. 2 (March 1942), pp. 1–4.

Anderson Auction Company. *Library of the Late Major William H. Lambert of Philadelphia: Part I. Lincolniana. . . .* New York: Metropolitan Art Association; [1914].

Angle, Paul McClelland: "Abraham Lincoln: Circuit Lawyer." *Lincoln Centennial Association Papers, Delivered Before the Members . . . , 1928*, pp. 19–41.

——: *"Here I Have Lived": A History of Lincoln's Springfield, 1821–1865.* Springfield: The Abraham Lincoln Association; 1935.

——: *Lincoln, 1854–1861: Being the Day-by-Day Activities of Abraham Lincoln from January 1, 1854, to March 4, 1861.* Springfield: The Abraham Lincoln Association; 1933.

——: "Lincoln in the United States Court, 1855–1860: New Light on His Law Practice." Lincoln Centennial Association, *Bulletin*, No. 8 (September 1, 1927).

——, ed.: *New Letters and Papers of Lincoln.* Boston: Houghton Mifflin Company; 1930.

——: "The Peoria Truce." *Journal of the Illinois State Historical Society*, Vol. 21 (January 1929), pp. 500–505.

——: *A Shelf of Lincoln Books: A Critical, Selective Bibliography of Lincolniana.* New Brunswick, New Jersey: Rutgers University Press in cooperation with The Abraham Lincoln Association; 1946.

———: "Where Lincoln Practiced Law." *Lincoln Centennial Association, Papers Delivered Before the Members . . . , 1927*, pp. 17–43.

———. See also Sandburg, Carl.

Arnold, Isaac Newton: *The Life of Abraham Lincoln.* Chicago: Jansen, McClurg, & Company; 1885.

Bancroft, Frederic: *The Life of William H. Seward.* New York: Harper and Brothers; 1900. 2 vols.

Baringer, William Eldon: "The Birth of a Reputation." *The Abraham Lincoln Quarterly,* Vol. 4 (March 1947), pp. 217–242.

———: "Campaign Technique in Illinois — 1860." *Transactions of the Illinois State Historical Society for the Year 1932,* pp. 203–281.

———: *Lincoln's Rise to Power.* Boston: Little, Brown and Company; 1937.

Barker, Harry Ellsworth: "Unveiling of the William H. Herndon Monument at Oak Ridge Cemetery, Springfield, Ill., Thursday, May 30, 1918." *Journal of the Illinois State Historical Society,* Vol. 11 (July 1918), pp. 197–209.

Barton, William Eleazar: "The Lincoln of the Biographers." *Transactions of the Illinois State Historical Society for the Year 1929,* pp. 58–116.

———: *The Lineage of Lincoln.* Indianapolis: The Bobbs-Merrill Company; 1929.

———: *The Paternity of Abraham Lincoln. Was He the Son of Thomas Lincoln? An Essay on the Chastity of Nancy Hanks.* New York: George H. Doran Company; 1920.

———: *The Soul of Abraham Lincoln.* New York: George H. Doran Company; 1920.

Basler, Roy Prentice, ed.: *Abraham Lincoln: His Speeches and Writings.* Cleveland: The World Publishing Company; 1946.

———: *The Lincoln Legend: A Study in Changing Conceptions.* Boston: Houghton Mifflin Company; 1935.

Bergen, A.: "Abraham Lincoln as a Lawyer." *American Bar Association Journal,* Vol. 12 (June 1926), pp. 390–394.

Beveridge, Albert Jeremiah: *Abraham Lincoln, 1809–1858.* Boston: Houghton Mifflin Company; 1928. 2 vols.

Bledsoe, Albert Taylor: "*The Life of Abraham Lincoln . . .* By Ward H. Lamon." *Southern Review,* Vol. 13 (April 1873), pp. 328–368.

Boston City Council. *A Memorial of Abraham Lincoln, Late President of the United States.* Boston; 1865.

Bibliography

Botkin, Benjamin Albert, ed.: *Lay My Burden Down: A Folk History of Slavery*. Chicago: University of Chicago Press; 1945.

——: *A Treasury of American Folklore: Stories, Ballads and Traditions of the People*. New York: Crown Publishers; 1944.

Browne, Francis Fisher: *The Every-day Life of Abraham Lincoln. . . .* First edition. New York: N. D. Thompson Publishing Co.; 1886.

Carpenter, Francis Bicknell: *Six Months at the White House with Abraham Lincoln. The Story of a Picture*. New York: Hurd and Houghton; 1866. Also published as *The Inner Life of Abraham Lincoln*.

Carruthers, Olive, and Robert Gerald McMurtry: *Lincoln's Other Mary*. Chicago: Ziff-Davis Publishing Company; 1946.

Catalogue of Articles Owned and Used by Abraham Lincoln. Now Owned by the Lincoln Memorial Collection of Chicago. Chicago; 1887.

A *Catalogue of Lincolniana with an Essay on Lincoln Autographs by the Rev. Dr. William E. Barton*. New York: Thomas F. Madigan; 1929.

Catalogue of the Officers and Students of Illinois College: 1836–7. Jacksonville: E. T. & C. Goudy; 1837.

Charnwood, Godfrey Rathbone Benson: *Abraham Lincoln*. New York: Henry Holt and Company; 1917.

Cole, Arthur Charles: *The Era of the Civil War, 1848–1870 (Centennial History of Illinois, Vol. 3)*. Springfield: Illinois Centennial Commission; 1919.

——: "President Lincoln and the Illinois Radical Republicans." *The Mississippi Valley Historical Review*, Vol. 4 (March 1918), pp. 417–436.

Commager, Henry Steele: *Theodore Parker*. Boston: Little, Brown and Company; 1936.

Constitution, and By-Laws, and Rules of Order, of Springfield [Illinois] *Temple of Honor, No. 3*. Springfield: Book & Job Office Print; 1852.

Constitution, Regulations, and By-Laws of the Library Association of Springfield, Illinois. Springfield: Bailhache & Baker; 1858.

Converse, Henry A.: "The House of the House Divided." *Transactions of the Illinois State Historical Society for the Year 1924*, pp. 141–171.

Craven, Avery: "Southern Attitudes Toward Abraham Lincoln." *Papers in Illinois History and Transactions* [of the Illinois State Historical Society] *for the Year 1942*, pp. 1–18.

Printed Sources

Creighton, James A.: "The Life and Services of Alfred Orendorff." *Transactions of the Illinois State Historical Society for the Year 1910*, pp. 34–37.

Cullom, Shelby Moore: *Fifty Years of Public Service: Personal Recollections.* Chicago: A. C. McClurg & Co.; 1911.

Dall, Mrs. Caroline Wells Healey: "Pioneering." *The Atlantic Monthly,* Vol. 19 (April 1867), pp. 403–416.

——: *Woman's Rights Under the Law: In Three Lectures, Delivered in Boston, January, 1861.* Boston: Walker, Wise, and Company; 1862.

Dennett, Tyler: *John Hay: From Poetry to Politics.* New York: Dodd, Mead & Company; 1933.

Donald, David: "Billy, You're Too Rampant." *The Abraham Lincoln Quarterly,* Vol. 3 (December 1945), pp. 375–407.

——: "The Folklore Lincoln." *Journal of the Illinois State Historical Society,* Vol. 40 (December 1947), pp. 377–396.

Dunning, William Archibald: "Truth in History." *The American Historical Review,* Vol. 19 (January 1914), pp. 217–229.

East, Ernest Edward: "The 'Peoria Truce': Did Douglas Ask for Quarter?" *Journal of the Illinois State Historical Society,* Vol. 29 (April 1936), pp. 70–75.

Eastman, Zebina: *History of the Anti-Slavery Agitation, and the Growth of the Liberty and Republican Parties in the State of Illinois.* Undated pamphlet in Chicago Historical Society.

Edmonds, George. See Meriwether, Mrs. Elizabeth Avery.

Enos, Zimri: "Description of Springfield." *Transactions of the Illinois State Historical Society for the Year 1909*, pp. 190–208.

Evans, William Augustus: *Mrs. Abraham Lincoln: A Study of Her Personality and Her Influence on Lincoln.* New York: Alfred A. Knopf; 1932.

Gabriel, Ralph Henry: *The Course of American Democratic Thought: An Intellectual History Since 1815.* New York: The Ronald Press Company; 1940.

Hamilton, Joseph Gregoire de Roulhac: "The Many-Sired Lincoln." *The American Mercury,* Vol. 5 (June 1925), pp. 129–135.

Heinl, Frank J.: "Congregationalism in Jacksonville and Early Illinois." *Journal of the Illinois State Historical Society,* Vol. 27 (January 1935), pp. 441–462.

Herndon, John Goodwin: *The Herndon Family of Virginia.* . . . Philadelphia: Privately printed by the Engineers Publishing Company; 1947.

——: "Six Herndon Immigrants to Colonial America." *William and*

Mary College Quarterly Historical Magazine, Vol. 23, new series (July 1943), pp. 331–335.

Herndon, John W.: "A Genealogy of the Herndon Family." *The Virginia Magazine of History and Biography*, Vol. 9 (January 1902), pp. 318–322. Continuations in succeeding numbers.

"Herndon's Lincoln: A Study." *The Publishers' Weekly*, Vol. 140 (November 29, 1941), pp. 2019–2021.

Herndon's Lincoln. One of the Great Historical Works of This Century. The Life of Abraham Lincoln, President of the United States. . . . Chicago: Belford-Clarke Co., Publishers; [1890?]. Four-page folder announcing Herndon's book and giving two pages of press notices.

"Herndon's Preface to His Life of Lincoln." Abraham Lincoln Association, *Bulletin*, No. 53 (September 1938), pp. 6–7. Publication of a manuscript incorrectly attributed to Herndon.

Hertz, Emanuel: *Abraham Lincoln: A New Portrait*. New York: Horace Liveright, Inc.; 1931. 2 vols.

——: *The Hidden Lincoln: From the Letters and Papers of William H. Herndon*. New York: The Viking Press; 1938.

——: *The Many-Sided Lincoln: What Would He Do Were He Here Today?* 1926.

Hill, Frederick Trevor: *Lincoln the Lawyer*. New York: The Century Co., 1906.

History of Sangamon County, Illinois. . . . Chicago: Inter-State Publishing Company; 1881.

Holland, Josiah Gilbert; *The Life of Abraham Lincoln*. Springfield, Massachusetts: Gurdon Bill; 1866.

House, Albert V., Jr.: "The Genesis of the Lincoln Religious Controversy." *Proceedings of the Middle States Association of History and Social Science Teachers*, Vol. 36 (1938), pp. 44–54.

——: "The Trials of a Ghost-Writer of Lincoln Biography: Chauncey F. Black's Authorship of Lamon's Lincoln." *Journal of the Illinois State Historical Society*, Vol. 31 (September 1938), pp. 262–296.

Irwin, Benjamin F.: *Lincoln's Religious Belief: Original Reminiscence and Research.* . . . Springfield: Privately printed for H. E. Barker; 1919.

Jayne, William: *Personal Reminiscences of the Martyred President, Abraham Lincoln.* . . . Chicago: Grand Army Hall and Memorial Association; 1908.

Johnny Appleseed, A Voice in the Wilderness: The Story of the Pio-

Printed Sources

neer John Chapman. Paterson, New Jersey: Swedenborg Press; 1945.

Krout, John Allen: *The Origins of Prohibition.* New York: Alfred A. Knopf; 1925.

Lamon, Ward Hill: *The Life of Abraham Lincoln from His Birth to His Inauguration as President.* Boston: James R. Osgood and Company; 1872.

Laws of Illinois College in Jacksonville, Illinois, Enacted by the Trustees. Jacksonville: E. T. & C. Goudy; 1837.

Lewis, Lloyd: *Myths After Lincoln.* New York: Harcourt, Brace and Company; 1929.

Lewis, Myrtle M.: "Herndon and Allied Families." *Americana,* Vol. 31 (October 1937), pp. 639–648.

Lincoln Herald. Published by the Lincoln Memorial University, Harrogate, Tennessee, 1938–date.

Lincoln Lore. The bulletin of the Lincoln National Life Foundation, Fort Wayne, Indiana, published 1929–date.

Ludlum, Robert Phillips: "Joshua Giddings, Radical." *The Mississippi Valley Historical Review,* Vol. 23 (June 1936), pp. 49–60.

Luthin, Reinhard H.: "Abraham Lincoln and the Tariff." *The American Historical Review,* Vol. 49 (July 1944), pp. 609–629.

——: *The First Lincoln Campaign.* Cambridge, Massachusetts: Harvard University Press; 1944.

McCormack, Thomas Joseph, ed.: *Memoirs of Gustave Koerner, 1809–1896.* Cedar Rapids, Iowa: The Torch Press; 1909. 2 vols.

McMurtrie, Douglas Crawford, ed.: *Lincoln's Religion: The Text of Addresses Delivered by William H. Herndon and Rev. James A. Reed and a Letter by C.F.B.* Chicago: The Black Cat Press; 1936.

McMurtry, Robert Gerald. See Carruthers, Olive.

Malin, James Claude: *John Brown and the Legend of Fifty-Six (Memoirs of the American Philosophical Society,* Vol. 17). Philadelphia: The American Philosophical Society; 1942.

Masters, Edgar Lee: *The Sangamon (The Rivers of America Series).* New York: Farrar & Rinehart, Incorporated; 1942.

Meriwether, Mrs. Elizabeth Avery: *Facts and Falsehoods Concerning the War on the South, 1861–1865.* Memphis: A. R. Taylor & Co.; 1904. Published under the pseudonym "George Edmonds."

Milton, George Fort: *The Eve of Conflict: Stephen A. Douglas and the Needless War.* Boston: Houghton Mifflin Company; 1934.

Bibliography

Monaghan, Jay: "New Light on the Lincoln-Rutledge Romance." *The Abraham Lincoln Quarterly*, Vol. 3 (September 1944), pp. 138–145.

Nevins, Allan: *Ordeal of the Union*. New York: Charles Scribner's Sons, 1947. 2 vols.

Newton, Joseph Fort: *Lincoln and Herndon*. Cedar Rapids, Iowa: The Torch Press; 1910.

Nicolay, John George, and John Hay: *Abraham Lincoln: A History*. New York: The Century Co.; 1890. 10 vols.

—— and ——, eds.: *Complete Works of Abraham Lincoln*. New York: The Tandy-Thomas Company; 1905. 12 vols.

Obsequies of Abraham Lincoln in Union Square, New York, April 25, 1865. New York: Printed for the Citizens' Committee; 1865.

Oldroyd, Osborn Hamiline, ed.: *The Lincoln Memorial: Album-Immortelles. Original Life Pictures, With Autographs, From the Hands and Hearts of Eminent Americans and Europeans.* . . . New York: G. W. Carleton & Co.; 1882.

Onstot, Thompson Gains: *Pioneers of Menard and Mason Counties . . . Including Personal Reminiscences of Abraham Lincoln.* . . . Forest City, Illinois: T. G. Onstot; 1902.

Parker, Theodore: *The Effect of Slavery on the American People. A Sermon Preached at the Music Hall, Boston, on Sunday, July 4, 1858*. Boston: W. L. Kent & Company; 1858.

——: *Theodore Parker's Experience as a Minister, with Some Account of His Early Life, and Education.* . . . Boston: Rufus Leighton, Jr.; 1859.

——: *The Collected Works of Theodore Parker* . . . , ed. by Frances Power Cobbe. London: Trübner & Co.; 1863–1871. 14 vols.

Peck, John Mason: *A Gazeteer of Illinois, In Three Parts.* . . . Philadelphia: Gregg & Elliot; 1837.

Peckham, Harry Houston: *Josiah Gilbert Holland in Relation to His Times*. Philadelphia: University of Pennsylvania Press; 1940.

Plunkett, Mrs. Hariette Merrick Hodge: *Josiah Gilbert Holland*. New York: Charles Scribner's Sons; 1894.

Power, John Carroll: *History of the Early Settlers of Sangamon County, Illinois*. Springfield: Edwin A. Wilson & Co.; 1876.

Pratt, Harry Edward, ed.: *Concerning Mr. Lincoln: In which Abraham Lincoln Is Pictured as he Appeared to Letter Writers of his Time*. Springfield: The Abraham Lincoln Association; 1944.

——: *Lincoln, 1809–1839: Being the Day-by-Day Activities of Abraham Lincoln from February 12, 1809, to December 31, 1839*. Springfield: The Abraham Lincoln Association; 1941.

Printed Sources

——: *Lincoln, 1840–1846: Being the Day-by-Day Activities of Abraham Lincoln from January 1, 1840, to December 31, 1846.* Springfield: The Abraham Lincoln Association; 1939.

——: "Lincoln Pilots the Talisman." *The Abraham Lincoln Quarterly,* Vol. 2 (September 1943), pp. 319–329.

——: "Lincoln's [Illinois] Supreme Court Cases." *Illinois Bar Journal,* Vol. 32 (September 1943), pp. 23–35.

——: *The Personal Finances of Abraham Lincoln.* Springfield: The Abraham Lincoln Association; 1943.

Raglan, Fitz Roy Richard Somerset: *The Hero: A Study in Tradition, Myth, and Drama.* New York: Oxford University Press; 1937.

Rammelkamp, Charles Henry: *Illinois College: A Centennial History, 1829–1929.* New Haven: Published for Illinois College by the Yale University Press; 1928.

Randall, James Garfield: *The Civil War and Reconstruction.* Boston: D. C. Heath and Company; 1937.

——: "Has the Lincoln Theme Been Exhausted?" *The American Historical Review,* Vol. 41 (January 1936), pp. 270–294.

——: *Lincoln and the South.* Baton Rouge: Louisiana State University Press; 1946.

——: *Lincoln the Liberal Statesman.* New York: Dodd, Mead & Company; 1947.

——: *Lincoln the President: Springfield to Gettysburg.* New York: Dodd, Mead & Company; 1945. 2 vols.

——: "The Unpopular Mr. Lincoln." *The Abraham Lincoln Quarterly,* Vol. 2 (June 1943), pp. 255–280.

Rankin, Henry Bascom: *Intimate Character Sketches of Abraham Lincoln.* Philadelphia: J. B. Lippincott Company; 1924.

——: *Personal Recollections of Abraham Lincoln.* New York: The Knickerbocker Press; 1916.

Reed, James A.: "The Later Life and Religious Sentiments of Abraham Lincoln." *Scribner's Monthly,* Vol. 6 (July 1873), pp. 333–343.

The Religion of Abraham Lincoln: Being a Reprint of the Lecture of Rev. Jas. A. Reed in 1872, and the Answering Lecture of W. H. Herndon in 1873. Privately printed for Judd Stewart; 1915.

Remsburg, John E.: *Six Historic Americans: Paine, Jefferson, Washington, Franklin, Lincoln, Grant, The Fathers and Saviors of Our Republic, Freethinkers.* New York: The Truth Seeker Company; [1906?].

Renne, Louis Obed: *Lincoln and the Land of the Sangamon.* Boston: Chapman & Grimes; 1945.

Bibliography

Richards, John Thomas: *Abraham Lincoln: The Lawyer-Statesman.* Boston: Houghton Mifflin Company; 1916.

Ross, Harvey Lee: *The Early Pioneers and Pioneer Events of the State of Illinois, Including Personal Recollections . . . of Abraham Lincoln, Andrew Jackson, and Peter Cartwright. . . .* Chicago: Eastman Brothers; 1899.

Sandburg, Carl: *Abraham Lincoln: The Prairie Years.* New York: Harcourt, Brace & Company; 1926. 2 vols.

———: *Abraham Lincoln: The War Years.* New York: Harcourt, Brace & Company; 1939. 4 vols.

———: *The American Songbag.* New York: Harcourt, Brace & Company; 1927.

——— and Paul McClelland Angle: *Mary Lincoln: Wife and Widow.* New York: Harcourt, Brace and Company; 1932.

Saunders, Horace: "Abraham Lincoln's Partner, Billy Herndon." [Chicago] *Lincoln Group Papers . . . , Second Series,* pp. 145–158.

Selby, Paul: "The Editorial Convention, February 22, 1856." *Transactions of the McLean County* [Illinois] *Historical Society,* Vol. 3 (1900), pp. 30–43.

———: "Republican State Convention, Springfield, Ill., Oct. 4–5, 1854." *Transactions of the McLean County Historical Society,* Vol. 3 (1900), pp. 43–47.

Sumner, Charles: *The Works of Charles Sumner.* Boston: Lee and Shepard; 1875–1883. 15 vols.

Thomas, Benjamin Platt: *Lincoln, 1847–1853: Being the Day-by-Day Activities of Abraham Lincoln from January 1, 1847, to December 31, 1853.* Springfield: The Abraham Lincoln Association; 1936.

———: "Lincoln and the Courts, 1854–1861." *Abraham Lincoln Association Papers, Delivered Before the Members . . . , 1933,* pp. 47–103.

———: *Portrait for Posterity: Lincoln and His Biographers.* New Brunswick, New Jersey: Rutgers University Press; 1947.

Townsend, George Alfred: *The Real Life of Abraham Lincoln. A Talk with Mr. Herndon, His Late Law Partner.* New York: Bible House; 1867.

Townsend, William Henry: *Lincoln and His Wife's Home Town.* Indianapolis: The Bobbs-Merrill Company; 1929.

———: *Lincoln and Liquor.* New York: The Press of the Pioneers, Inc.; 1934.

Printed Sources

——: *Lincoln the Litigant.* Boston: Houghton Mifflin Company; 1925.

——: "Lincoln's Law Books." *American Bar Association Journal,* Vol. 15 (March 1929), pp. 125–126.

Tracy, Gilbert Avery: *Uncollected Letters of Abraham Lincoln.* Boston: Houghton Mifflin Company; 1917.

Tyler, Mrs. Alice Felt: *Freedom's Ferment: Phases of American Social History to 1860.* Minneapolis: The University of Minnesota Press; 1944.

The Valuable Collection of Autographs and Historical Papers Collected by The Hon. Jas. T. Mitchell of the Supreme Court of Penna. Also the Entire Lincoln Memorial Collection. . . . Philadelphia; 1894.

Van Doren, Mark, ed.: *An Autobiography of America.* New York: Albert & Charles Boni; 1929.

The War of the Rebellion: A Compilation of the Official Records of the Union and Confederate Armies. Washington: Government Printing Office; 1880–1901. 70 "volumes"; 128 books.

Warren, Louis Austin: "Herndon's Contribution to Lincoln Mythology." *Indiana Magazine of History,* Vol. 41 (September 1945), pp. 221–244.

——: *Lincoln's Parentage & Childhood: A History of the Kentucky Lincolns Supported by Documentary Evidence.* New York: The Century Co.; 1926.

Warren, Sidney: *American Freethought, 1860–1914.* New York; 1943.

Washington, John E.: *They Knew Lincoln.* New York: E. P. Dutton & Co., Inc.; 1942.

Wecter, Dixon: *The Hero in America: A Chronicle of Hero-Worship.* New York: C. Scribner's Sons; 1941.

Weik, Jesse William: *The Real Lincoln: A Portrait.* Boston: Houghton Mifflin Company; 1922.

——: *Weik's History of Putnam County, Indiana.* Indianapolis: F. B. Bowen & Company; 1910.

White, Horace: *Abraham Lincoln in 1854: An Address Delivered Before the Illinois State Historical Society. . . .* 1908.

[White, Richard Grant]: *Book of the Prophet Stephen, Son of Douglas. Wherein Marvellous Things are Foretold of the Reign of Abraham.* New York: Feeks & Bancker; 1863. Scurrilous anti-Lincoln propaganda.

Whitney, Henry Clay: *Life on the Circuit with Lincoln,* ed. by Paul McClelland Angle. Caldwell, Idaho: The Caxton Printers, Ltd.; 1940.

Bibliography

——: *Lincoln the Citizen: February 12, 1809, to March 4, 1861* (Marion Mills Miller, ed., *Life and Works of Abraham Lincoln*, Vol. 1). New York: Lincoln Centenary Association; 1907.

Wish, Harvey: *George Fitzhugh: Propagandist of the Old South.* Baton Rouge: Louisiana State University Press; 1943.

Woldman, Albert A.: *Lawyer Lincoln.* Boston: Houghton Mifflin Company; 1936.

Zane, Charles S.: "Lincoln as I Knew Him." *Journal of the Illinois State Historical Society,* Vol. 14 (April 1921), pp. 74–84.

INDEX

Abbot, Francis E., editor: Herndon's letter to, on Lincoln's religion, 257, 271, 290; freethinker, 289, 290

Abell, Elizabeth (Mrs. Bennett Abell), 184, 187

Abolitionists: hated by Archer Herndon, 11, 13; supported by Illinois College, 11; Herndon and, 73–4 and *n*, 79 and *n*; crusading respected but deplored, 101–2; *see also* Radical Republicans

Abraham Lincoln Association, the, photostats of Lincoln legal papers, 35*n*

Allen, W. J., Illinois congressman, 158

Alton, Ill., Herndon speaks at, 95

American party, *see* Know-Nothing party

Andrew, John A., on Herndon's Ann Rutledge lecture, 231

Angle, Paul M., cited, 87, 91*n*, 119*n*, 243*n*, 359 and *n*; on *Herndon's Lincoln*, 344; *see also* Sandburg, Carl

Appleton, D., & Co., edition of *Herndon's Lincoln*, 342

Arnold, Isaac N.: approves Herndon's first two Lincoln lectures, 205; characterized, 239; and Herndon's Ann Rutledge lecture, 239–41; assisted by Herndon, 294–5; characterized by Herndon, 352–3; and Herndon, on biographer-as-policeman, 361

Ashmun resolutions, favored by Lincoln, 27

Athens, Ill., 43; Herndon speaks at, 95

Atlanta, Ill., Herndon speaks at, 84–5

Atlantic Monthly: read by Herndon,

Atlantic Monthly (continued) 54; publishes Dall article, 234–5; review of *Herndon's Lincoln*, 332

Bacheller, Irving, and *Herndon's Lincoln*, 343–4

Baker, Edward D., 21

Bale, Hardin: gossips to Herndon, 185–6; on Lincoln's religion, 214

Baltimore, convention of 1860, 137

Baltimore plot, report of, secured by Herndon, 173–4

Banks, Nathaniel P., 115

Barnhill, John B., Herndon's lecture agent, 293–4

Barrett, Joseph H., Lincoln biography studied by Herndon, 171

Barrett, Oliver R., Lincoln collection, 37 and *n*

Bartlett, Truman Howe, sculptor: aided by Herndon, 310–11; and scarcity of first edition of *Herndon's Lincoln*, 335

Barton, William E.: cited, 176*n*, 256*n*, 265*n*, 308*n*, 357 and *n*; and Herndon's files, 193

Basler, Roy P., cited, 370*n*

Bateman, Newton, Illinois superintendent of education, and debate over Lincoln's religion, 213–17

Beecher, Edward: influences Herndon, 10; and Lovejoy incident, 11–13

Beecher, Henry Ward: Herndon on, 54; lectures in Springfield, 61

Belford, Clarke & Co.: characterized, 323; arrangements with Herndon and Weik, 323–4; lack of co-operation, 324–6; inefficiency, 335; failure and reorganization, 335–6

Index

Index

Index

Index

Index

Index

Index

Index

Index

Index

Ridpath, John Clark (*continued*) sor and author: mentor of Weik, 297, 313; advice on *Herndon's Lincoln*, 319

Rochester, Ill., canvassed by Herndon, 138–9

Rochester *Express*, on Herndon as Lincoln biographer, 235 and *n*

Rock Island bridge case, 48

Rosette, John: member of Sangamon bar, 40; in Logan County fugitive slave case, 106–7

Rutledge, Ann: legend given undue emphasis by Herndon, 185–7; grave visited by Herndon, 218–21; story, as told by Herndon, 223–4, 228–9, 353–4, 358

Rutledge, R. B.: praises Herndon's Ann Rutledge lecture, 231; and Herndon's Lincoln-Rutledge story, 354

St. Paul *News*, on *Herndon's Lincoln*, 333–4

Sandburg, Carl: cited, 179*n;* and *Herndon's Lincoln*, 343–4

Sandburg, Carl and Angle, Paul, 228*n*, 359*n*

Sangamo Journal (Springfield), files studied by Herndon, 171

Sangamo Monitor, supports Herndon, 279–80

Sangamon County: anti-Nebraska convention, Herndon's story of, 86–8; Herndon campaigns in, 95–7; canvassed by Herndon in 1860, 138–43; carried by Douglas (1860), 142; antiwar feeling, 158–60; *see also* Springfield

Sangamon County Circuit Court: Lincoln & Herndon practice in, 23, 44 and *n*, 45; files cited, 39; members of bar characterized by Herndon, 40; Herndon & Zane practice in, 157–8, 246; Herndon's practice in, 292

Saunders, Horace, cited, 130*n*

Schools, public, supported by Herndon, 68–9

Scott, Winfield, 148

Scribner's, Charles, Sons, publishers, and *Herndon's Lincoln*, 340–2

Selby, Paul, cited, on Illinois Republican organization meeting, 77*n;* calls convention of editors, 83

Seward, William H.: and Douglas, 109; visited by Herndon, 114–15; relations with Herndon after 1858, 132

Sherman, W. T., Savannah and Carolina campaign, 163–4

Sherwood, Robert, and *Herndon's Lincoln*, 343–4

Shipley, Lucy, and legitimacy of Nancy Hanks, 357 and *n*

Short, James, 184; at New Salem, 218; and Herndon's Lincoln-Rutledge story, 354

Slavery: as issue at Illinois College, 10–13; Herndon's viewpoint on, 25, 99–104 *passim*, 139, 260; as issue in campaign of 1856, 93–7; and Dred Scott case, 100–2; reasons for Herndon's stand analyzed, 102–4

Slaves, apotheosis of Lincoln, 369–70

Smith, Caleb Blood, Secretary of Interior, 152

Smith, George Washington, visit to Herndon, 286–7

Smith, James, and Herndon's Ann Rutledge story, 236–8

Snider, Denton J., and *Herndon's Lincoln*, 343–4

Spears, George: quoted, 168; tells Herndon of difficulties in securing data, 174; and Herndon's Ann Rutledge lecture, 231

Speed, Joshua F.: employs Herndon, 14–15; on Lincoln's religion, 214

Spencer, Herbert: read by Herndon, 54; influence on Herndon's thinking, 59 and *n*

Spring Creek, Ill., Herndon speaks at, 95

Springer, John G., copies Herndon's Lincoln file, 192

Springfield, Ill., visited by "Gath,"

Index

Index

Other DACAPO titles of interest